The Legacy of Conquest

John and Joy Kasson

The Legacy of Conquest

The Unbroken Past of the American West

Patricia Nelson Limerick

W · W · NORTON & COMPANY · *NEW YORK* · *LONDON*

Printed in the United States of America.

The text and the display type of this book are composed in Baskerville. Composition and manufacturing are by The Maple-Vail Book Manufacturing Group. Book design is by Marjorie J. Flock.

First published as a Norton paperback 1988.

Library of Congress Cataloging-in-Publication Data
Limerick, Patricia Nelson, 1951–
    The legacy of conquest.

    Bibliography: p
    Includes index.
    1. West (U.S.)—History.   2. West (U.S.)—Historiography.
I. Title.
F591.L56   1987   978   86-23883

ISBN 0-393-30497-3

W. W. Norton & Company, Inc., 500 Fifth Avenue, New York, NY 10110
W. W. Norton & Company Ltd., 10 Coptic Street, London WC1A 1PU

        8 9 0

To Jeff Limerick, and to our utterly Western nephews and niece,
Jay, Michael, and Francine

Contents

Acknowledgments

I GOT THE IDEA FOR this book on June 30, 1981, at a conference in Idaho called "The American West: Colonies in Revolt." During that first day of the conference, government and business officials complained about the current problems of the West, and the prevalent presumption seemed to be that these problems were quite recent in origin and bore little relation to the distant frontier West. I am grateful to Jeanette Germain for initiating the process that brought me to Idaho and to William K. Everson, William Goetzmann, Peter Hassrick, Bruce Jackson, Bud Johns, Annick Smith, and, especially, Alvin Josephy, Richard Hart, and Bob Waite for organizing the event. Those Sun Valley conferences were one of the best things going in Western affairs; I deeply regret their disappearance.

At that conference, after listening to the first day's speakers, I said in my own speech that the West needed someone comparable to C. Vann Woodward to write *The Burden of Western History*. The fact is that there is no one comparable to C. Vann Woodward. But Woodward's example and his encouragement early in the project made the difference between a vision that might have vanished and one that stayed and brought forth at least limited results.

My adviser, Howard Roberts Lamar, not only read the man-

uscript but made it possible. When I left California for graduate
school at Yale, I had no particular interest in the history of my
home region. It was about the luckiest thing that ever happened
to me: to have Howard Lamar show me what I had missed in my
first twenty-one years in the West. As an adviser, Lamar is nearly
unrivaled in academic circles for his kindness, good humor, and
enthusiasm for widely varying approaches to history. The sound
parts of this book are a tribute to his guidance; any tenuous sections are a credit to his tolerance.

Harvard University and the Charles Warren Center gave me
a full year of leave in 1983–84. That year gave me not only
essential working time but working and thinking conditions as
close to heaven as I expect to get. Any time I wanted to test an
idea, I had only to step outside my office to see who was around.
With Bernard Bailyn, Barbara DeWolfe, Pat Denault, Jon Roberts, Drew McCoy, Don Bellomy, Alan Brinkley, and Helena Wall
at hand, the intellectual equivalent of a brisk physical workout
was always available. That none of these people found enormous significance in the American West only added to the value
of their company, reminding me of what I most hope for in the
way of reader response: not agreement, but spirited discussion.

In 1981, James Thomson, Jr., introduced me to his Nieman
program at Harvard and transformed a minor interest in journalism and current events into a passion. I am grateful as well to
John Seigenthaler and Sid Hurlburt of *USA Today* for allowing
me to move from consumer to occasional producer in journalistic matters, for reacquainting me with brevity, and for providing
the income supplement that allowed me to stay a jump ahead of
library acquisitions.

From the start of this project, Ed Barber and Steve Forman
of Norton have been committed and responsive editors. Ed
Barber's significance escalated in July of 1984, when I moved
to Boulder and we agreed it was time for him to put the pressure on, if this book was to be finished in our lifetimes. He is, the
next two years proved, unrelentingly a man of his word. Relieved
of the obligation to remind me of deadlines, Steve Forman
was an ideal coach, kind and critical without contradiction. I am

grateful, as well, to Otto Sonntag for his scrupulous attention to the manuscript.

Alfonso Ortiz, John Echohawk, Roger Echo-hawk, Karen Easton, and George Phillips helped me by reading chapter 6; Bill Taylor, S. L. Cline, and George Sanchez, by reading chapter 7. Chris Miller, Helena Wall, and Alan Brinkley counseled me on various parts of the text. Peter Decker, Richard White, William Cronon, and Jim O'Brien read nearly the whole manuscript and responded with comments in many ways more interesting than the text they read. Near the end of the project, Ruth Friedman stepped in as proofreader and general manuscript reviewer; her sharpness of eye and vigor of mind came at exactly the right time, when these properties in the author were a bit worn down.

Over the years, I have had the help of a number of talented undergraduates: Yvette Huginnie, Joe Bowen, Paul Fisher, Allison Brown, Gail Bash Butler, Eve Baldwin, Jim Baker, Richard DiNucci, Ann Skartvedt, Dayna Bateman, and Tom Patterson. These people were not only fine research assistants but also great conversationalists and promising scholars (and lawyers, novelists, and banjo players) in their own right.

The Department of History of the University of Colorado at Boulder has a great office staff. Pat Murphy, Sandy Marsh, Veta Hartman, and Rosella Chavez helped ride herd on the manuscript and were my pals during an unsettling two years of falling behind deadlines in a new location. Pat Murphy was nothing short of heroic in her mastery of high technology that still frightens me, in her capacity to follow tangled instructions to add, delete, or transfer, and in her unbroken good humor and enthusiasm for the project. If I had written the words as well as she managed them, this would be an extraordinary book.

For help in finding illustrations, I am indebted to Eleanor Gehres, Augie Mastrogiuseppi, and Kathey Swan of the Western History Collection, Denver Public Library, Jim Lavender-Teliha and Eric Paddock of the Colorado Historical Society, and Stephanie Edwards of the Oregon Historical Society.

Some readers may see my point of view as the product of a

1960s sensibility, formed in the years of student protest. That presumption targets the wrong decade. I have had the happy intergenerational experience of being in complete political agreement with my parents. My sensibility is thus shaped by the 1930s as well as the 1960s; I suspect my point of view is closer to Eleanor Roosevelt's than to Angela Davis's. My parents provided not only the political perspective of this book but also much of the method. As masters of the anecdote drawn from real life, Grant and Patricia Nelson gave me early training both in story selecting and in storytelling; anyone who cares to see how far the apprentice falls short has only to attend an anecdote session with the masters. I would like, also, to take this occasion to acknowledge my good luck in teachers. In high school and college, Lewis Robinson, Robert Bowser, Mike Rose, Laurence Veysey, Michael Cowan, John Dizikes, Jasper Rose, and Page Smith led me to history and to writing; this book is in many ways the outcome of their teaching.

Working on this book has been consuming. I owe a number of apologies to people—especially correspondents—who found me divided in attention over the last few years. My colleagues Fred Anderson, Virginia Anderson, Steve Epstein, Jack Main, and Gloria Main went beyond tolerating the obsession, to accepting and even encouraging it, and thus helped keep me sane.

Though offered the role of quietly self-sacrificing spouse, Jeff Limerick preferred to exercise his customary rights of free speech. Heaven knows, he can talk about history a lot better than I can talk about architecture, and with many hours of conversation about Western affairs, he more than earned his place on the dedication page.

By the nature of this book, I am most in debt to people I have never met—to historians and journalists whose words I have followed closely, but whose faces I have never seen. In the tradition of Western resource exploitation, I have profited greatly from the labor of others. "Thank you" is a mild and inadequate expression for the hard work that produced the material I rely on here.

Life in Boulder, Colorado, at the foot of the Flatirons, reminds you daily that the West is *here* and not "out there." Meanwhile, the interesting weather that blows over those mountains reminds you that the "conquest of nature" remains a bit incomplete. Although I am in no conventional sense an outdoorsperson, I appreciate the reminders.

Boulder, Colorado
November 24, 1986

The Legacy of Conquest

Introduction
Closing the Frontier and Opening Western History

Each age writes the history of the past anew with reference to the conditions uppermost in its own time. . . .
The aim of history, then, is to know the elements of the present by under-standing what came into the present from the past. For the present is simply the developing past, the past the undeveloped present. . . . The antiquarian strives to bring back the past for the sake of the past; the historian strives to show the present to itself by revealing its origin from the past. The goal of the antiquarian is the dead past; the goal of the historian is the living present.[1]
—Frederick Jackson Turner, 1891

IN 1883 NANNIE ALDERSON married, left her home in Virginia, and traveled to her new life on a ranch in Montana. Reminiscing about those years, Mrs. Alderson noted a particular feature of Montana cuisine and landscape. "Everyone in the country lived out of cans," she said, "and you would see a great

---

Miners at dinner. The men themselves might move on, but the evidence of their presence would remain. *Courtesy Colorado Historical Society*

heap of them outside every little shack."[2]

Hollywood did not commemorate those heaps in Western movies, and yet, by the common wisdom of archaeologists, trash heaps say a great deal about their creators. Living out of cans, the Montana ranchers were typical Westerners, celebrating independence while relying on a vital connection to the outside world. More important, the cans represented continuity, simply by staying in place. The garbage collector never came. And the evidence of last week's—last year's—meals stayed in sight.

When Western historians yielded to a preoccupation with the frontier and its supposed end, past and present fell apart, divided by the watershed of 1890. But Western reality followed other patterns. Matter, issues, memories, and dilemmas were all conserved. In the mountains of Colorado, miners dug shafts, worked mines, and then gave them up. The miners left; their works remain. One walks with some caution in these historic regions; land that appears solid may be honeycombed, and one would not like to plunge unexpectedly into the legacy of Western history.

The conquest of Western America shapes the present as dramatically—and sometimes as perilously—as the old mines shape the mountainsides. To live with that legacy, contemporary Americans ought to be well informed and well warned about the connections between past and present. But here the peculiar status of Western American history has posed an obstacle to understanding. Americans are left to stumble over—and sometimes into—those connections, caught off guard by the continued vitality of issues widely believed to be dead.

Like slavery, conquest tested the ideals of the United States. Conquest deeply affected both the conqueror and the conquered, just as slavery shaped slaveholder and slave. Both historical experiences left deep imprints on particular regions and on the nation at large. The legacy of slavery and the legacy of conquest endure, shaping events in our own time.

Here, however, we reach a principal difference: to most twentieth-century Americans, the legacy of slavery was serious business, while the legacy of conquest was not. Southern historians successfully fought through the aura of moonlight and magnolias, and established slavery, emancipation, and black/white relations as major issues in American history. The Civil War, Reconstruction, the migration of Southern blacks into other regions, and the civil rights movement all guaranteed that the nation would recognize the significance of slavery and the South.

Conquest took another route into national memory. In the popular imagination, the reality of conquest dissolved into stereotypes of noble savages and noble pioneers struggling quaintly in the wilderness. These adventures seemed to have no bearing on the complex realities of twentieth-century America. In Western paintings, novels, movies, and television shows, those stereotypes were valued precisely because they offered an escape from modern troubles. The subject of slavery was the domain of serious scholars and the occasion for sober national reflection; the subject of conquest was the domain of mass entertainment and the occasion for lighthearted national escapism. An element of regret for "what we did to the Indians" had entered the picture, but the dominant feature of conquest remained "adventure." Children happily played "cowboys and Indians" but stopped short of "masters and slaves."

When the history of conquest lost solidity, the history of an entire region suffered the same loss. Just as black/white relations and slavery were particularly associated with the South, so conquest was particularly associated with the West. Of course, the entire New World had been conquered; the West was hardly unique in this regard. But if the American West was mentioned to an American—or, perhaps even more, to a European—frontier wars and pioneering came immediately to mind. For various reasons, the West acquired an identity as the focal point of conquest. In that character, the West enjoyed its few moments of celebrity in mainstream American history as the necessary stage setting for the last big sweep of national expansionism. But when conquest reached the Pacific and filled in the areas in between, attention returned eastward. Historical significance had been a tourist—visiting the West for the peak of adventure and heading home when the action slowed down.

Professional historians of the American West thus became a people locked in an identity crisis, given to brooding about their

place in the profession. Reasons for brooding appeared in a variety
of forms: the failure of universities to replace older Western historians when they retired; the reluctance of East Coast publish-
ers and reviewers to pay attention to Western history; the
occasional remarks revealing that well-established American historians did not have much respect for the field. In 1984, at a
conference on American Indian history, I sat in the audience
and heard one colonial historian confirm the Western historians'
worst fears:

Yet how important is the "West" (minus California and urban population clusters in the Pacific Northwest) in the twentieth century or even
in the nineteenth century? . . . For, in our role as scholars, we must
recognize that the subject of westward expansion itself no longer engages
the attention of many, perhaps most, historians of the United States.
Surveys of college and university curricula indicate a steady decline in
courses dealing with "history of the west"; significant numbers of graduate students no longer write dissertations on this subject; and few of
the leading members of our profession have achieved their scholarly
reputations in this field.[3]

What had happened to Western history?

Paradoxically, the problem stemmed from the excess of respect
given to the ideas of the field's founder, Frederick Jackson Turner,
ideas presented in Turner's famous 1893 address, "The Significance of the Frontier in American History." Turner was a scholar
with intellectual courage, an innovative spirit, and a forceful
writing style. But respect for the individual flowed over into
excessive deference to the individual's ideas. To many American
historians, the Turner thesis *was* Western history. If something
had gone wrong with the thesis, something had gone wrong with
Western history.

The center of American history, Turner had argued, was
actually to be found at its edges. As the American people proceeded westward, "the frontier [was] the outer edge of the wave—
the meeting point between savagery and civilization" and "the
line of most effective and rapid Americanization." The struggle
with the wilderness turned Europeans into Americans, a process
Turner made the central story of American history: "The exis-

tence of an area of free land, its continuous recession, and the advance of American settlement westward, explain American development." But American development came to an unsettling close when the 1890 census revealed that no vast tracts of land remained for American conquest. "And now," Turner noted at the conclusion of his essay, "four centuries from the discovery of America, at the end of a hundred years of life under the Constitution, the frontier has gone, and with its going has closed the first period of American history."[4]

Turner, in 1893, seemed to have the field of Western American history fully corralled, unified under the concept "frontier." Exploration, fur trade, overland travel, farming, mining, town founding, merchandising, grazing, logging—the diverse activities in the nineteenth-century West were all supposed to fit into the category. In fact, the apparently unifying concept of the frontier had arbitrary limits that excluded more than they contained. Turner was, to put it mildly, ethnocentric and nationalistic. English-speaking white men were the stars of his story; Indians, Hispanics, French Canadians, and Asians were at best supporting actors and at worst invisible. Nearly as invisible were women, of all ethnicities. Turner was also primarily concerned with agrarian settlement and folk democracy in the comparatively well watered Midwest. Deserts, mountains, mines, towns, cities, railroads, territorial government, and the institutions of commerce and finance never found much of a home in his model.

Like many historians, Turner was interpreting the past in light of recent events. This presentism had great benefits and also great risks. History was bound to go on. Any definitive statement on the meaning of the West offered in 1893 would soon show its age. On this count, many of Turner's protégés did him a disservice. Their respect for him left the 1893 thesis set in stone. Turner himself moved on. In his later essays and his courses, he kept adding "more history" as it accumulated, noting, for instance, the Western oil boom that occurred after 1890 and yet showed many frontier-like characteristics. But while Turner moved on, the Turner thesis kept its 1893 form. By definition, the twentieth-century West fell outside the 1893 model. The frontier thesis, Howard Lamar wrote in 1968, "implied that a discontinuity

existed between America's rural past and its urban-industrial
present." Stressing discontinuity and the end of "the first period
of American history," the thesis was by its own admission, Lamar
pointed out, "useless as a guide for the present and future."[5]

The rigidity of the Turner Thesis left it particularly vulnerable to a great expansion of scholarship, accelerating in the 1960s
and afterward. Individual historians simply set aside the Thesis
and studied particular Western places, people, and events. The
diversity and complexity those studies revealed, especially in the
history of the West's "minorities" (some of whom were, in earlier
phases, majorities), represented an intellectual revolution. Few
of the findings fit the Turnerian conceptual model. Thus, a central irony: the very vitality of Western research, by exploding
the model, made mainstream historians declare that the field
was dead.

Teachers often encountered the problem in the classroom.
If they tried to keep up with the field, read new books and articles, and synthesize those findings for the students, they had no
clear way to organize the course. The old Turnerian model of
Anglo-Americans purposefully moving westward provided no
help. The new Indian history alone rendered old course outlines
untenable; the recognition of tribal diversity and of the active
role Indians played in shaping history made for a much richer
story, but also for one without a simple chronological shape. The
breakdown of the old organizing idea fostered chaos; the corral
built to contain Western history had been knocked apart.

Conceptual change in Western history occurred slowly: the
Turner corral served a variety of functions. Since Turner had
given the American frontier national significance, abandoning
him threatened the West's place in the mainstream of American
history. The Turner concept also was tidy. In identifying an 1890
watershed, Turner labored to create what colonial historians and
Southern historians got without effort. The American Revolution periodized colonial history. The Civil War and emancipation periodized Southern history. Both events provided writers
of history with graceful ways to begin and end. Historians proceed with a safe conviction that 1776 and 1865 were real
watersheds.

Western historians had good reason to envy that windfall. The fact remained: the West never went to war for its independence. There is, of course, plenty of revolutionary rhetoric: complaints of exploitation and colonialism; comparisons of the Department of the Interior to the ministers of George III; laments over autonomy lost to meddling bureaucrats—but no confederation of Western states, no war for independence, and thus no watershed comparable to the Revolution or the Civil War.

Left without a major turning point, Western historians had to create one. The opening and closing of the frontier were set up like flags marking the start and finish of a racecourse, to give the West its significant chronology.

There was no conceptual problem in getting the frontier opened—with the arrival of white people in territory new to them or with the discovery of unexploited resources. The problem came at the other end. There is simply no definition of "the closing of the frontier" that is anything but arbitrary and riddled with exceptions and qualifications.

What did Turner and the director of the census mean by the "end of the frontier"? "Population in the West," Harold Simonson wrote, "had reached the figure of at least two persons per square mile, the basis for calling an area settled."[6] This is an odd definition. If population density is the measure of a frontier condition, then the existence of a city, a town, or even a small mining camp closes the frontier for that site. One could easily argue the opposite—that a sudden concentration of population marks the opening stage and that a population lowered through, for instance, the departure of people from a used-up mining region marks the end of the frontier and its opportunities. Hinging his definition on population density, Turner referred to the fact that most of the frontier had been transformed into individually owned property; and yet in the Far West of 1890 one-half of the land remained federal property.

On a solely agrarian frontier, Turner's definition might make some sense. One could say that when every arable acre was privately owned, if not yet in cultivation, the frontier had closed. In mining or grazing, though, use was never dependent on conventional ownership. Mineral claims on federal lands tended to be transitory, subsurface rights often being detached from surface ownership. Similarly, nerve, enterprise, and finally leasing—not ownership—determined grazing rights on the public domain.

Regardless of the percentage of land in private ownership, opportunity in the discovery and development of natural resources reached no clear terminus. If the frontier ended in 1890, what was going on when prospectors and miners rushed to the southern Nevada mining discoveries—in 1900? What of the expansion of irrigated farming following the passage of the Newlands Reclamation Act—in 1902? How does one dismiss the 1901 Spindletop gusher and the boom in Western oil, irregular but persistent through the century? How can one discount the uranium rushes of the late 1940s and 1950s? Are Geiger counters and airplanes less frontier-like than picks and shovels?

The effort to exclude twentieth-century events from the category "frontier" immersed the Western historian in conceptual fog. Hinging the admissions requirement on simple technology seemed arbitrary. Frontiers involve mules, horses, and oxen but not jeeps; pickaxes and pans but not air drills and draglines; provisions in sacks and tins but not in freeze-dried packets; horse-drawn plows but not mechanized combines with air-conditioned drivers' modules; bows and arrows but certainly not nuclear tests in Nevada; amateurs but not engineers. This is at base a judgment of sentiment and nostalgia—in favor of tools controllable by one person, and supposedly closer to nature, and against the intrusion of modern machinery. The distinction says a great deal about the emotions of historians but little about Western history.

A frequent, less sentimental strategy for frontier definition involves a focus on symbolic events. This is an intellectually stimulating exercise, but it serves only to accent the intractable diversity of Western events. For this exercise, one selects first a defining characteristic of the frontier and then an associated event. If contiguous territorial acquisition is the key process, 1848 and the acquisition of Oregon and the Mexican territories (or, alternatively, the Gadsden Purchase in 1854) mark the end of the frontier. If individual opportunity is preeminent, the Comstock Lode in the 1860s stands out, signaling the consolidation of industrial underground mining and the shift in aspiration from windfalls to wages. If the workability of the West as a refuge for distinctive societies is deemed essential, the 1890 Mormon concession on polygamy signals the closing. If unrestricted use of the public domain is crucial, the frontier ended in 1934, with the Taylor Grazing Act and the leasing of grazing rights on the public lands. If political dependence in the form of territorial organization is the representative factor, the frontier ended in 1912, with the admission of New Mexico and Arizona to statehood—or, if one includes the noncontiguous territory, in 1959, with the admission of Alaska.

My own preferred entry in the "closing" competition is the popularization of tourism and the quaintness of the folk. When Indian war dances became tourist spectacles, when the formerly scorned customs of the Chinese drew tourists to Chinatown, when former out-groups found that characteristics that had once earned them disapproval could now earn them a living, when fearful, life-threatening deserts became charming patterns of color and light, the war was over and the frontier could be considered closed, even museumized. My nomination has a problem too—it does not come with clear divisions in time. Let the car break down in the desert, or let the Indians file a lawsuit to reassert an old land claim, and the quaint appeal of nature and native can abruptly vanish. The frontier is suddenly reopened.

Frontier, then, is an unsubtle concept in a subtle world. Even so, the idea of the frontier is obviously worth studying as a historical artifact. The idea played an enormous role in national behavior, but so did the ideas of savagery and civilization, concepts that are currently not well respected as analytic terms. I certainly do not discount the power of the concept "frontier" in American history. My point is that the historian is obligated to understand how people saw their own times, but not obligated to adopt their terminology and point of view. That one may study how Westerners depended on the Colt repeating revolver is not an argument for using a gun in professional debate.

If we give up a preoccupation with the frontier and look instead at the continuous sweep of Western American history, new organizing ideas await our attention, but no simple, unitary model. Turner's frontier rested on a single point of view; it required that the observer stand in the East and look to the West. Now, like many scholars in other fields, Western historians have had to learn to live with relativism.

A deemphasis of the frontier opens the door to a different kind of intellectual stability. Turner's frontier was a process, not a place. When "civilization" had conquered "savagery" at any one location, the process—and the historian's attention—moved on. In rethinking Western history, we gain the freedom to think of the West as a place—as many complicated environments occupied by natives who considered their homelands to be the center, not the edge.

In choosing to stress place more than process, we cannot fix exact boundaries for the region, any more than we can draw precise lines around "the South," "the Midwest," or that most elusive of regions "the East." Allowing for a certain shifting of borders, the West in this book will generally mean the present-day states of California, Oregon, Washington, Idaho, Utah, Nevada, Arizona, New Mexico, Colorado, Kansas, Nebraska, Oklahoma, Texas, Montana, Wyoming, North Dakota, and South Dakota and, more changeably, Iowa, Missouri, Arkansas, and Louisiana. (Many patterns explored here apply also to Alaska, but limits of space and time have prohibited its full inclusion.) This certainly makes for a complicated package, but the West as place has a compensatory, down-to-earth clarity that the migratory, abstract frontier could never have.

Reorganized, the history of the West is a study of a place undergoing conquest and never fully escaping its consequences. In these terms, it has distinctive features as well as features it shares with the histories of other parts of the nation and the planet. Under the Turner thesis, Western history stood alone. An exciting trend in modern scholarship leads toward comparative history—toward Western American history as one chapter in the global story of Europe's expansion. Studies in "comparative conquests" promise to help knit the fragmented history of the planet back together. Western American history can be a prime contributor to that endeavor.

Deemphasize the frontier and its supposed end, conceive of the West as a place and not a process, and Western American history has a new look. First, the American West was an important meeting ground, the point where Indian America, Latin America, Anglo-America, Afro-America, and Asia intersected. In race relations, the West could make the turn-of-the-century Northeastern urban confrontation between European immigrants and American nativists look like a family reunion. Similarly, in the diversity of languages, religions, and cultures, it surpassed the South.

Second, the workings of conquest tied these diverse groups into the same story. Happily or not, minorities and majorities occupied a common ground. Conquest basically involved the drawing of lines on a map, the definition and allocation of ownership (personal, tribal, corporate, state, federal, and international), and the evolution of land from matter to property. The process had two stages: the initial drawing of the lines (which we have usually called the frontier stage) and the subsequent giving of meaning and power to, those lines, which is still under way. Race relations parallel the distribution of property, the application of labor and capital to make the property productive, and the allocation of profit. Western history has been an ongoing competition for legitimacy—for the right to claim for oneself and sometimes for one's group the status of legitimate beneficiary of Western resources. This intersection of ethnic diversity with property allocation unifies Western history.

The contest for property and profit has been accompanied by a contest for cultural dominance. Conquest also involved a struggle over languages, cultures, and religions; the pursuit of legitimacy in property overlapped with the pursuit of legitimacy in way of life and point of view. In a variety of matters, but especially in the unsettled questions of Indian assimilation and in the disputes over bilingualism and immigration in the still semi-Hispanic Southwest, this contest for cultural dominance remains a primary unresolved issue of conquest. Reconceived as a running story, a fragmented and discontinuous past becomes whole again.

With its continuity restored, Western American history carries considerable significance for American history as a whole. Conquest forms the historical bedrock of the whole nation, and

Wagon train with railroad. *Southern Pacific photo, courtesy Denver Public Library, Western History Department*

the American West is a preeminent case study in conquest and its consequences. Conquest was a literal, territorial form of economic growth. Westward expansion was the most concrete, down-to-earth demonstration of the economic habit on which the entire nation became dependent. If it is difficult for Americans to imagine that an economy might be stable and also healthy, many of the forces that fostered that attitude can be traced to the Western side of American history. Cultural pluralism and responses to race form primary issues in American social relations, and the American West—with its diversity of Indian tribes, Hispanics, Euro-Americans of every variety, and blacks—was a crucial case study in American race relations. The involvement of the federal government in the economy and the resulting dependence, resentment, and deficit have become major issues in American history and in contemporary politics, and the American West was the arena in which an expanded role for the federal government first took hold. Cycles of prosperity and recession have long characterized the American economy, and in that long-running game of crack-the-whip, the West has been at the far end of the whip, providing the prime example of the boom/bust instability of capitalism. The encounter of innocence with complexity is a recurrent theme in American culture, and Western history may well be the most dramatic and sustained case of high expectations and naïveté meeting a frustrating and intractable reality. Many American people have held to a strong faith that humans can master the world—of nature and of humans —around them, and Western America put that faith to one of its most revealing tests. A belief in progress has been a driving force in the modern world; as a depository of enormous hopes for

Horses with automobiles: Ute Indians and spectators at reburial of Chief Ouray, 1925. *Courtesy Colorado Historical Society*

progress, the American West may well be the best place in which to observe the complex and contradictory outcome of that faith.

Beyond its national role, Western America has its own regional significance. Remoteness from both New York and Washington, D.C.; the presence of most of the nation's Indian reservations; proximity to Mexico; ports opening to the Pacific Basin and Asia; dependence on natural-resource extraction; the undergoing of conquest at a time when the American nation was both fully formed and fully self-conscious; the association of the region with a potent and persistent variety of nationalistic myth; the aridity of many areas: all these factors give Western America its own, intrinsic historical significance.

In this book, I have undertaken to pull the pieces together, to combine two or three decades of thriving scholarship with a decade of thriving journalism in Western American subjects. Much of the most interesting work in Western history has been done by individuals who consider themselves first and foremost urban, social, business, labor, Chicano, Indian, or environmental historians—not Western historians. Work in these specialties has prospered, but efforts at a regional synthesis have lagged behind. In the same way, journalists and historians often labor in separate spheres, unaware of the themes that unite their work. Their findings fit together to form a revived version of Western history, and this book is therefore an interpretation and a synthesis, not a monograph and not a survey or summary.

This book has taught me why historians might flee the challenge of synthesis. The genre breeds two alternating fears: that one is only echoing platitudes, and that one has gone out on a limb. The second fear has at least a kind of exhilaration; I am sometimes fully convinced that life out on a limb is the only life worth living. Everything I have written here, I believe. But because the field is vital and changing, I anticipate new developments every week; if Western history continues to thrive, I will look back at certain passages and shudder at my shortsightedness.

Despite those moments of exhilaration and because this book, by definition, relies on secondary sources, I am saying some familiar things. Earl Pomeroy has long stressed continuity in Western history and downplayed the frontier. In an essay published in 1959, John Caughey carefully explored the distinction between the West as frontier and the West as place or region. My own adviser, Howard Lamar, has long studied the twentieth-century West.[7] Why repeat their arguments? Because the message has not gotten through. The public holds to the idea of a great discontinuity between the frontier and the Western present. Even in universities, the old perceptions of Western history seem to thrive. Young scholars, hired to teach Western American history, learn that their departments expect their courses to end in 1890. My own courses in Western history at the University of Colorado carry the title "The Early American Frontier" and "The Later American Frontier," while I postpone the labor of going to the committee on courses to explain how the field has changed and why a new title is in order. Others, then, have said much of what I say in this book; nonetheless, the importance of the message and a widespread reluctance to receive it justify the deployment of many messengers.

Just as Turner did, I take my cues from the present. I am thus sure to be overtaken by unplanned obsolescence. A presentist view seems to me, as it did to Turner, worth the risk. In the second half of the twentieth century, every major issue from "frontier" history reappeared in the courts or in Congress. Struggles over Indian resources and tribal autonomy; troubled relations with Mexico; controversy over the origins of Mormonism; conflicts over water allocation; another farm crisis; a drastic swing downward in the boom/bust cycles of oil, copper, and timber; continued heavy migration to some parts of the West, with all the familiar problems of adjusting to growth and sorting out power between natives and newcomers; disputes over the use of the public lands; a determined retreat on federal spending in the West: all these issues were back on the streets and looking for trouble. Historians of the future will find meanings in these events beyond my imagination, but I firmly believe they will find the 1980s to be a key period in Western American history. If the federal government implements the Reagan policy of reversing the historical pattern of using federal money to stabilize Western economies, historians will see the 1980s as a watershed decade.

In countless ways, events in the 1980s suggest a need to reevaluate Western history. Consider the case study offered by Louis L'Amour, author of "88 books about life on the American frontier" (as of March 1984). L'Amour is the mid-twentieth century's successor to Zane Grey, a writer still intoxicated with the independence, nobility, grandeur, and adventure of the frontier. He remains true to the plot formula of tough men in the tough land. "A century ago," L'Amour wrote in a commentary in 1984, "the Western plains were overrun by buffalo, and many a tear has been shed over their passing, but where they grazed we now raise grain to feed a large part of the world. . . ." This process of progress through conquest reached no terminus: "We are a people born to the frontier, and it has not passed away. Our move into space has opened the greatest frontier of all, the frontier that has no end."[8]

But only a year later, in 1985, circumstances disclosed a different Louis L'Amour. "Louis L'Amour's Real Life Showdown," the headline in the *Denver Post* read, "Western Author, Colorado Ute Duel over Proposed Power-Line." L'Amour's idyllic ranch in southwest Colorado faced the threat of "a 345,000-volt power line," which would frame his view of the mountains "with cables and towering support poles" and which might also trigger "health problems, ranging from headaches and fatigue to birth defects and cancer." L'Amour fought back with the conventional Western American weapon—the lawsuit—not the six-gun.[9]

If L'Amour recognized the irony in his situation, he did not share it with reporters. The processes of Western development do run continuously from past to present, from mining, cattle raising, and farming on to hydroelectric power and even into space. The power line is a logical outcome of the process of development L'Amour's novels celebrate. But in this particular case, the author was facing the costs of development, of conquest, and not simply cheering for the benefits. "People never worry about these things until it's too late," L'Amour said of the power line in 1985. Eight-eight books later, he was at last hot on the trail of the meanings of Western history.

Part 1

The Conquerors

One

Empire of Innocence

WHEN ACADEMIC TERRITORIES were parceled out in the early twentieth century, anthropology got the tellers of tales and history got the keepers of written records. As anthropology and history diverged, human differences that hinged on literacy assumed an undeserved significance. Working with oral, preindustrial, prestate societies, anthropologists acknowledged the power of culture and of a received worldview; they knew that the folk conception of the world was not narrowly tied to proof and evidence. But with the disciplinary boundary overdrawn, it was easy for historians to assume that literacy, the modern state, and the commercial world had produced a different sort of creature entirely—humans less inclined to put myth over reality, more inclined to measure their beliefs by the standard of accuracy and practicality.

When anthropology and history moved closer together, so did their subjects of inquiry. Tribal people or nationalists, tellers of stories or keepers of account books, humans live in a world in which mental reality does not have to submit to narrow tests of accuracy.

To analyze how white Americans thought about the West, it helps to think anthropologically. One lesson of anthropology is the extraordinary power of cultural persistence; with American

Indians, for instance, beliefs and values will persist even when
the supporting economic and political structures have vanished.
What holds for Indians holds as well for white Americans; the
values they attached to westward expansion persist, in cheerful
defiance of contrary evidence.

Among those persistent values, few have more power than
the idea of innocence. The dominant motive for moving West
was improvement and opportunity, not injury to others. Few white
Americans went West intending to ruin the natives and despoil
the continent. Even when they were trespassers, westering
Americans were hardly, in their own eyes, criminals; rather, they
were pioneers. The ends abundantly justified the means; personal interest in the acquisition of property coincided with national
interest in the acquisition of territory, and those interests overlapped in turn with the mission to extend the domain of Christian civilization. Innocence of intention placed the course of events
in a bright and positive light; only over time would the shadows
compete for our attention.

One might expect John Wesley Hardin, the Texan mass murderer and outlaw, to forswear the role of innocent. But this is an
assumption to be made with caution in Western history. Hardin
was, after all, of innocent stock, the son of a preacher who named
his son John Wesley, after the founder of Methodism. "In prison,"
a recent editor of Hardin's autobiography notes, "Hardin read
the Bible and many books on theology. There he was appointed
superintendent of the Sunday schools." If one read Hardin's
autobiography with no knowledge of the author's later career,
one might mistake the tone for that of a model citizen and pillar
of the community. "Our parents taught us from infancy to be
honest, truthful and brave," he said, going on to provide further
evidence of his good character: "I always tried to excel in my
studies, and generally stood at the head," and if that was not
enough, "I was always a very child of nature, and her ways and
moods were my study."[1]

To be sure, Hardin fought a lot, but this was consonant with
parental instructions that honor and the willingness to defend
that honor came in the same package. When he was fifteen, he
shot and killed a black man. This was to Hardin's mind not a loss

of innocence, but a defense of it. The Negro, he said, had tried to bully him; the year was 1868, and Texas was at the mercy of postwar Reconstruction, bullied by "Yankee soldiers," "carpet-baggers and bureau-agents," blacks, and "renegades"—all of them "inveterate enemies of the South." And so, Hardin said, "unwillingly, I became a fugitive, not from justice be it known, but from the injustice and misrule of the people who had subjugated the South." Hardin did go on to kill twenty or more men, but he appears never to have wavered from his chosen role: the gunfighter as Western injured innocent, with a strong Southern accent.[2]

The idea of the innocent victim retains extraordinary power, and no situation made a stronger symbolic statement of this than that of the white woman murdered by Indians. Here was surely a clear case of victimization, villainy, and betrayed innocence. But few deaths of this kind occurred in American history with such purity; they were instead embedded in the complex dynamics of race relations, in which neither concept—villain or victim—did much to illuminate history.

Narcissa Prentiss Whitman made a very unlikely villain. Deeply moved by the thought of Western Indians living without knowledge of Christianity, Narcissa Prentiss wrote her mission board in 1835, "I now offer myself to the American Board to be employed in their service among the heathen. . . ."[3] In 1836, she left her home in New York to rescue the Indians in Oregon. An unattached female could hardly be a missionary, and before her departure Narcissa Prentiss hastily married another Oregon volunteer, Marcus Whitman. The Whitmans and Henry and Eliza Spalding set off to cross the country. Pioneers on the overland trail, they faced stiff challenges from nature and some from human nature. The fur trappers and traders with whom they traveled resented the delays and sermons that came with missionary companionship. The missionaries themselves presented less than a united front. They had the strong, contentious personalities of self-appointed agents of God. They also had a history; Henry Spalding had courted Narcissa, and lost. Anyone who thinks of the nineteenth-century West as a land of fresh starts and new beginnings might think of Henry Spalding and

Narcissa Whitman and the memories they took with them to
Oregon.

Arrived in the Oregon country, the missionaries—like sales-
men dividing up markets—divided up tribes and locations. The
Whitmans set to work on the Cayuse Indians. Narcissa Whitman's life in Oregon provides little support for the image of life
in the West as free, adventurous, and romantic. Most of the time,
she labored. She had one child of her own; she adopted many
others—mixed-blood children of fur trappers, and orphans from
the overland trail. "My health has been so poor," she wrote her
sister in 1846, "and my family has increased so rapidly, that it
has been impossible. You will be astonished to know that we have
eleven children in our family, and not one of them our own by
birth, but so it is. Seven orphans were brought to our door in
Oct., 1844, whose parents both died on the way to this country.
Destitute and friendless, there was no other alternative—we must
take them in or they must perish."[4]

Depending on one's point of view, the Whitman mission had
a lucky or an unlucky location—along the Oregon Trail, where
exhausted travelers arrived desperate for food, rest, and help.
Narcissa Whitman's small home served as kitchen, dining hall,
dormitory, and church building, while she longed for privacy
and rest. She often cooked three meals a day for twenty people.
For five years, she had no stove and cooked in an open fireplace.

In the midst of crowds, she was lonely, writing nostalgic letters to friends and family in the East who seemed to answer
infrequently; she went as long as two years without a letter from
home. Separated by distance and sometimes by quarrels, Narcissa and the other missionary wives in Oregon tried for a time
to organize a nineteenth-century version of a woman's support
group; at a certain hour every day, they would pause in their
work, think of each other, and pray for the strength to be proper
mothers to their children in the wilderness.

Direct tragedy added to loneliness, overwork, and frustration. The Whitmans' only child, two years old, drowned while
playing alone near a stream. Providence was testing Narcissa
Whitman's faith in every imaginable way.

Then, in November of 1847, after eleven years with the missionaries among them, when the white or mixed-blood mission population had grown to twenty men, ten women, and forty-four children, the Cayuse Indians rose in rebellion and killed fourteen people—including Marcus and Narcissa Whitman.

Was Narcissa Whitman an innocent victim of brutality and ingratitude? What possessed the Cayuses?

One skill essential to the writing of Western American history is a capacity to deal with multiple points of view. It is as if one were a lawyer at a trial designed on the principle of the Mad Hatter's tea party—as soon as one begins to understand and empathize with the plaintiff's case, it is time to move over and empathize with the defendant. Seldom are there only two parties or only two points of view. Taking into account division within groups—intertribal conflict and factions within tribes and, in Oregon, settlers against missionaries, Protestants against Catholics, British Hudson's Bay Company traders against Americans —it is taxing simply to keep track of the points of view.

Why did the Cayuses kill the Whitmans? The chain of events bringing the Whitmans to the Northwest was an odd and arbitrary one. In a recent book, the historian Christopher Miller explains that the Whitman mission was hardly the first crisis to hit the Columbia Plateau and its natives. A "three hundred year cold spell," a "result of the Little Ice Age," had shaken the environment, apparently reducing food sources. Moreover, the effects of European presence in North America began reaching the plateau even before the Europeans themselves arrived. The "conjunction of sickness, with the coming of horses, guns, climatic deterioration and near constant war" added up to an "eighteenth-century crisis." Punctuated by a disturbing and perplexing ash fall from a volcanic explosion, the changes brought many of the Plateau Indians to the conviction that the world was in trouble. They were thus receptive to a new set of prophecies from religious leaders. A central element of this new worldview came in the reported words of the man known as the Spokan Prophet, words spoken around 1790: "Soon there will come from the rising sun a different kind of man from any you have yet seen, who will bring with them a book and will teach you everything, after that the world will fall to pieces," opening the way to a restored and better world. Groups of Indians therefore began to welcome whites, since learning from these newcomers was to be an essential stage in the route to a new future.[5]

In 1831, a small party of Nez Percé and Flathead Indians journeyed to St. Louis, Missouri. For years, Western historians said that these Indians had heard of Jesuits through contacts with fur traders and had come to ask for their own "Black Robes." That confident claim aside, Christopher Miller has recently written that it is still a "mystery how it all came to pass." Nonetheless, he argues persuasively that the Northwest Indians went to St. Louis pursuing religious fulfillment according to the plateau millennial tradition; it was their unlikely fate to be misunderstood by the equally millennial Christians who heard the story of the visit. A Protestant man named William Walker wrote a letter about the meetings in St. Louis, and the letter was circulated in church newspapers and read at church meetings, leaving the impression that the Indians of Oregon were begging for Christianity.[6]

And so, in this chain of circumstances "so bizarre as to seem providential," in Miller's words, the Cayuses got the Whitmans, who had responded to the furor provoked by the letter. Irritations began to pile up. The Whitmans set out to transform the Cayuses from hunters, fishers, and gatherers to farmers, from heathens to Presbyterians. As the place became a way station for the Oregon Trail, the mission began to look like an agency for the service of white people. This was not, in fact, too far from the founder's view of his organization. "It does not concern me so much what is to become of any particular set of Indians," Marcus Whitman wrote his parents, "as to give them the offer of salvation through the gospel and the opportunity of civilization. . . . I have no doubt our greatest work is to be to aid the white settlement of this country and help to found its religious institutions."[7]

The Cayuses began to suffer from white people's diseases, to which they had no immunity. Finally, in 1847, they were devastated by measles. While the white people at the mission seldom died from measles, the Indians noticed that an infected Cayuse nearly always died. It was an Indian conviction that disease was "the result of either malevolence or spiritual transgression"; either way, the evidence pointed at the missionaries. When the Cayuses finally turned on the Whitmans, they were giving up "the shared prophetic vision" that these newcomers would teach a lesson essential to reshaping the world.[8] The Cayuses were, in other words, acting in and responding to currents of history of which Narcissa Whitman was not a primary determinant.

Descending on the Cayuses, determined to bring light to the "benighted ones" living in "the thick darkness of heathenism," Narcissa Whitman was an intolerant invader. If she was not a villain, neither was she an innocent victim. Her story is melancholy but on the whole predictable, one of many similar stories in Western history that trigger an interventionist's urge. "Watch out, Narcissa," one finds oneself thinking, 140 years too late, "you think you are doing good works, but you are getting yourself—and others—into deep trouble." Given the inability of Cayuses to understand Presbyterians, and the inability of Presbyterians to understand Cayuses, the trouble could only escalate. Narcissa Whitman would not have imagined that there was anything to understand; where the Cayuses had religion, social networks, a thriving trade in horses, and a full culture, Whitman would have seen vacancy or, worse, heathenism.

Narcissa Whitman knew she was volunteering for risk; her willingness to take on those risks is, however, easier to understand because it was based on religion. Irrational faith is its own explanation; one can analyze its components, but the fact remains that extraordinary faith leads to extraordinary action. The mystery is not that Narcissa Whitman risked all for the demands of the deity but that so many others risked all for the demands of the profit motive.

II

Missionaries may be an extreme case, but the pattern they represent had parallels in other Western occupations. Whether the target resource was gold, farmland, or Indian souls, white Americans went West convinced that their purposes were as commonplace as they were innocent. The pursuit of improved fortunes, the acquisition of property, even the desire for adven-

ture seemed so self-evident that they needed neither explanation nor justification.

If the motives were innocent, episodes of frustration and
defeat seemed inexplicable, undeserved, and arbitrary. Squatters defied the boundaries of Indian territory and then were
aggrieved to find themselves harassed and attacked by Indians.
Similarly, prospectors and miners went where the minerals were,
regardless of Indian territorial claims, only to be outraged by
threats to their lives and supply lines. Preemptors who traveled
ahead of government surveys later complained of insecure land
titles. After the Civil War, farmers expanded onto the Great Plains,
past the line of semiaridity, and then felt betrayed when the rains
proved inadequate.

Western emigrants understood not just that they were taking
risks but also that risks led to rewards. When nature or natives
interrupted the progression from risk to reward, the Westerner
felt aggrieved. Most telling were the incidents in which a rush of
individuals—each pursuing a claim to a limited resource—produced their own collective frustration. In resource rushes, people hoping for exclusive opportunity often arrived to find a crowd
already in place, blanketing the region with prior claims, constricting individual opportunity, and producing all the problems
of food supply, housing, sanitation, and social order that one
would expect in a growing city, but not in a wilderness.

If one pursues a valuable item and finds a crowd already
assembled, one's complicity in the situation is obvious. The crowd
has, after all, resulted from a number of individual choices very
much like one's own. But frustration cuts off reflection on this
irony; in resource rushes in which the sum of the participants'
activities created the dilemma, each individual could still feel
himself the innocent victim of constricting opportunity.

Contrary to all of the West's associations with self-reliance
and individual responsibility, misfortune has usually caused white
Westerners to cast themselves in the role of the innocent victim.
One large group was composed of those who felt injured at the
hands of nature. They had trusted nature, and when nature
behaved according to its own rules and not theirs, they felt
betrayed. The basic plot played itself out with a thousand variations.

Miners resented the wasted effort of excavating sites that had looked promising and proved barren. Cattlemen overgrazed the grasslands and then resented nature's failure to rebound. Farmers on the Southern Plains used mechanized agriculture to break up the land and weaken the ground cover, then unhappily watched the crop of dust they harvested. City dwellers accumulated automobiles, gas stations, and freeways, and then cursed the inversion patterns and enclosing mountains that kept the automobile effluvia before their eyes and noses. Homeowners purchased houses on steep slopes and in precarious canyons, then felt betrayed when the earth's surface continued to do what it has done for millennia: move around from time to time. And, in one of the most widespread and serious versions, people moved to arid and semiarid regions, secure in the faith that water would somehow be made available, then found the prospect of water scarcity both surprising and unfair.

In many ways, the most telling case studies concern plants. When, in the 1850s, white farmers arrived in Island County, Washington, they had a clear sense of their intentions: "to get the land subdued and the wilde nature out of it," as one of them put it. They would uproot the useless native plants and replace them with valuable crops, transforming wilderness to garden. On one count, nature did not cooperate—certain new plants, including corn, tomatoes, and wheat, could not adapt to the local climate and soil. On another count, nature proved all too cooperative. Among the plants introduced by white farmers, weeds frequently did better than crops. "Weeds," Richard White notes, "are an inevitable result of any human attempt to restrict large areas of land to a single plant." Laboring to introduce valued plants, the farmer came up against "his almost total inability to prevent the entry of unwanted invaders." Mixed with crop seeds, exotic plants like the Canadian thistle prospered in the plowed fields prepared for them, and then moved into the pastures cleared by overgrazing. The thistle was of no interest to sheep: "once it had replaced domesticated grasses the land became incapable of supporting livestock."[9]

A similar development took place between the Rockies and the Sierras and Cascades. There, as well, "species foreign to the region, brought accidentally by the settlers, came to occupy these sites to the virtual exclusion of the native colonizers." With the introduction of wheat, "entry via adulterated seed lots of the weeds of wheat ... was inevitable." One particular species—cheatgrass—took over vast territories, displacing the native bunch grasses and plaguing farmers in their wheatfields. There is no more effective way to feel authentically victimized than to plant a crop and then to see it besieged by weeds. Farmers thus had their own, complicated position as injured innocents, plagued by a pattern in nature that their own actions had created.[10]

Yet another category of injured innocents were those who had believed and acted upon the promises of promoters and boomers. Prospective miners were particularly susceptible to reading reports of the gold strikes, leaping into action, and then cursing the distortions and exaggerations that had misled them into risking so much for so little reward. The pattern was common because resource rushes created a mood of such fevered optimism that trust came easily; people wanted so much to believe that their normal skepticism dropped away.

The authenticity of the sense of victimization was unquestionable. Still, there was never any indication that repeated episodes of victimization would reduce the pool of volunteers. Bedrock factors kept promoters and boomers supplied with believers: there *were* resources in the West, and the reports might be true; furthermore, the physical fact of Western distances meant, first, that decision making would have to rely on a chain of information stretched thin by the expanse of the continent and, second, that the truth of the reports and promises could not be tested without a substantial investment of time and money simply in getting to the site. One might well consume one's nest egg merely in reaching the place of expected reward.

Blaming nature or blaming human beings, those looking for a scapegoat had a third, increasingly popular target: the federal government. Since it was the government's responsibility to control the Indians and, in a number of ways increasing into the twentieth century, to control nature, Westerners found it easy to shift the direction of their resentment. Attacked by Indians or threatened by nature, aggrieved Westerners took to pointing accusingly at the federal government. In effect, Westerners centralized their resentments much more efficiently than the federal government centralized its powers.

Oregon's situation was a classic example of this transition. The earliest settlers were rewarded with Congress's Oregon Donation Act of 1850. Settlers arriving by a certain year were entitled to a generous land grant. This act had the considerable disadvantage of encouraging white settlement without benefit of treaties and land cessions from Oregon Indians. The Donation Act thus invited American settlers to spread into territory that had not been cleared for their occupation. It was an offer that clearly infringed on the rights of the Indians and that caused the government to stretch its powers thin. After the California gold rush, when prospectors spread north into the Oregon interior, a multifront Indian war began. Surely, the white miners and settlers said, it is now the obligation of the federal government to protect us and our property.[11]

At this point, a quirk of historical casting brought an unusual man named General John Wool into the picture. As the head of the Army's Pacific Division, General Wool was charged with cleaning up the mess that Oregon development had created. He was to control the Indians, protect the settlers, and end the wars. Here Wool's unusual character emerged: assessing this situation, he decided—and said bluntly—that the wars were the results of settler intrusion; he went so far as to propose a moratorium on further settlement in the Oregon interior, a proposal that outraged the sensitive settlers. Wool's personality did not make this difference of opinion more amicable. He was, in fact, something of a prig; in pictures, the symmetrical and carefully waxed curls at his temples suggest that he and the Oregon pioneers might have been at odds without the troubles of Indian policy.[12]

Denounced by both the Oregon and the Washington legislatures, Wool's blunt approach did not result in a new direction in Indian affairs. The wars were prosecuted to their conclusions; the Indians, compelled to yield territory. But the Oregon settlers in 1857 knew what they thought of Wool. He was a supposed agent of the federal government, an agent turned inexplicably into a friend of the Indians and an enemy of the Americans.

It was not the first or the last time that white Americans would suspect the federal government and Indians of being in an unholy alliance. To the degree that the federal government fulfilled its treaty and statutory obligations to protect the Indians and their land, it would then appear to be not only soft on Indians but even in active opposition to its own citizens.

One other elemental pattern of their thought allowed Westerners to slide smoothly from blaming Indians to blaming the federal government. The idea of captivity organized much of Western sentiment. Actual white men, women, and children were at times taken captive by Indians, and narratives of those captivities were, from colonial times on, a popular form of literature. It was an easy transition of thought to move from the idea of humans held in an unjust and resented captivity to the idea of land and natural resources held in Indian captivity—in fact, a kind of monopoly in which very few Indians kept immense resources to themselves, refusing to let the large numbers of willing and eager white Americans make what they could of those resources. Land and natural resources, to the Anglo-American mind, were meant for development; when the Indians held control, the excluded whites took up the familiar role of injured innocents. The West, in the most common figure of speech, had to be "opened"—a metaphor based on the assumption that the virgin West was "closed," locked up, held captive by Indians.

As the federal government took over Indian territory, either as an addition to the public domain or as reservations under the government's guardianship, white Westerners kept the same sense of themselves as frustrated innocents, shut out by monopoly, but they shifted the blame. Released from Indian captivity, many Western resources, it seemed to white Americans, had merely moved into a federal captivity.

In 1979, the Nevada state legislature, without any constitutional authority, passed a law seizing from the federal government 49 million acres from the public domain within the state. This empty but symbolic act was the first scene in the media event known as the Sagebrush Rebellion, in which Western businessmen lamented their victimization at the hands of the federal government and pleaded for the release of the public domain from its federal captivity. Ceded to the states, the land that once belonged to all the people of the United States would at last be at the disposal of those whom the Sagebrush Rebels considered to be the *right* people—namely, themselves.[13]

Like many rebellions, this one foundered with success: the election of Ronald Reagan in 1980 and the appointment of James Watt as secretary of the interior meant that the much-hated federal government was now in the hands of two Sagebrush Rebels. It was not at all clear what the proper rebel response to the situation should be. In any case, the rebel claim to victimization had lost whatever validity it had ever had.

Reciting the catalog of their injuries, sufferings, and deprivations at the hands of federal officials, the rebels at least convinced Western historians of the relevance of their expertise. It was a most familiar song; the Western historian could recognize every note. Decades of expansion left this motif of victimization entrenched in Western thinking. It was second nature to see misfortune as the doings of an outside force, preying on innocence and vulnerability, refusing to play by the rules of fairness. By assigning responsibility elsewhere, one eliminated the need to consider one's own participation in courting misfortune. There was something odd and amusing about late-twentieth-century businessmen adopting for themselves the role that might have suited Narcissa Whitman—that of the martyred innocents, trying to go about their business in the face of cruel and arbitrary opposition.

Even if the Sagebrush Rebels had to back off for a time, that did not mean idleness for the innocent's role. In 1982, Governor Richard Lamm of Colorado and his coauthor, Michael McCarthy, published a book defending the West—"a vulnerable land"—from the assault of development. "A new Manifest Destiny," they said, "has overtaken America. The economic imperative has forever changed the spiritual refuge that was the West." The notion of a time in Western history when "the economic imperative" had not been a dominant factor was a quaint and wishful thought, but more important, Lamm and McCarthy thought, some Westerners now "refused" to submit to this change. "They—we—are the new Indians," Lamm and McCarthy concluded. "And they—we—will not be herded to the new reservations."[14]

In this breakthrough in the strategy of injured innocence,
Lamm and McCarthy chose the most historically qualified innocent victims—the Indians facing invasion, fighting to defend their
homelands—and appropriated their identity for the majority
whites who had moved to the West for the good life, for open
space and freedom of movement, and who were beginning to
find their desires frustrated. Reborn as the "new Indians," Lamm's
constituency had traveled an extraordinary, circular route. Yesterday's villains were now to be taken as today's victims; they
were now the invaded, no longer the invaders. In keeping with
this change, the *old* Indians received little attention in the book;
as capacious as the category "injured innocent" had proven itself
to be, the line had to be drawn somewhere.

Occasionally, continuities in American history almost bowl
one over. What does Colorado's utterly twentieth-century governor have in common with the East Coast's colonial elite in the
eighteenth century? "Having practically destroyed the aborigi-
nal population and enslaved the Africans," one colonial historian has said, "the white inhabitants of English America began
to conceive of themselves as the victims, not the agents, of Old
World colonialism." "The victims, not the agents"—the changes
and differences are enormous, but for a moment, if one looks
from Revolutionary leaders, who held black slaves as well as the
conviction that they were themselves enslaved by Great Britain,
to Governor Richard Lamm, proclaiming himself and his people
to be the new Indians, American history appears to be composed
of one, continuous fabric, a fabric in which the figure of the
innocent victim is the dominant motif.[15]

III

Of all the possible candidates, the long-suffering white female
pioneer seemed to be the closest thing to an authentic innocent
victim. Torn from family and civilization, overworked and lonely,
disoriented by an unfamiliar landscape, frontierswomen could
seem to be tragic martyrs to their husbands' willfull ambitions.

But what relation did these sufferers bear to the actual white
women in the West? Did their experiences genuinely support
the image? Where in Western history did women fit? By the 1970s,

it was commonly recognized that Turner-style history simply left women out. How, then, to address the oversight? Was it the sort of error that one could easily correct—revise the shopping list, retrace one's steps, put the forgotten item in the grocery cart, and then proceed with one's usual routine? Or was the inclusion of women a more consequential process of revision that would make it impossible to resume old habits and routines?

We can best answer the question by considering the Western women apparently at the opposite end of the spectrum from Narcissa Whitman—the women who came West not to uplift men but to cater to their baser needs. The prostitute was as much a creature of Western stereotype as the martyred missionary, and in many ways a more appealing one. But while the colorful dance hall girl held sway in the movies, Western historians either looked discreetly away from this service industry or stayed within the stereotypes of a colorful if naughty subject.

When professional scholars finally took up the subject, their investigations disclosed the grim lives led by the majority of Western prostitutes. With few jobs open to women, prostitution provided a route to income, though it seldom led past subsistence. A few well-rewarded mistresses of rich men and a few madams skilled in a complicated kind of management may have prospered, but most prostitutes did well to keep revenue a fraction ahead of overhead costs—rent, clothing, food, payoffs to law officers. A woman might work independently, renting her own quarters and conducting her own solicitation, or she might try for security (shelter, food, and a degree of protection from violence) by working in a brothel. At the bottom ranks, even those unappealing alternatives disappeared; vagrant women at the farthest margins of society, or Chinese women controlled as virtual slaves, had little choice open to them. Western prostitution was, in other words, a very stratified operation: the adventuress of doubtful morality and the respectable married woman, though in different spheres, were both far removed from the down-and-out cribworker, without even a brothel to call home.

When prostitutes tried to find stability in marriage, they found their partners in an unpromising pool of saloon owners, pimps, and criminals, men who were often violent and who were nei-

ther inclined nor able to rescue their spouses from their rough
lives. When prostitutes bore children, as they often did, their
occupation made child care an extraordinary challenge and the
children stood scant chance of rising to reputability. Many
daughters of prostitutes followed their mothers into the business. Many factors—the sense of entrapment, the recognition
that age was sure to reduce a woman's marketability, financial
troubles—drove prostitutes to suicide. "Suicide," the historian
Ann Butler has noted, "emerged as the most commonly employed
means to retire from prostitution."[16] Excluded from much of
society, prostitutes could not even expect to find comradeship
with their colleagues; the intrinsic competition of the business
put them at odds, and this rivalry, often unleashed by alcohol,
led to frequent quarrels and even physical fights.

A study of Western prostitution leaves certain general lessons for Western history at large. First and foremost, one learns
that the creature known as "the pioneer woman" is a generic
concept imposed on a diverse reality. White, black, Hispanic,
Chinese, and Indian women composed the work force of prostitution, scattered across a wide range of incomes. Moreover,
anyone inclined to project a sentimentalized hope for women's
essential solidarity into the past need only consider the case of
Julia Bulette, a prostitute murdered in Virginia City in 1867.
John Milleain was convicted of her murder after items stolen
from Bulette were found in his possession. But he had murdered a prostitute, and this engaged the sympathy and support
of some of the town's respectable ladies. "Respectable women,"
Marion S. Goldman has reported, "circulated a petition to the
governor to commute Milleain's sentence from death to life
imprisonment, visited him in jail, and made sure that he drank
wine and ate omelettes during the days following his conviction." Just before his execution, Milleain offered his gratitude:
"I also thank the ladies of Virginia who came to see me in my
cell and brought with them consolation that only they could find
for the circumstances."[17]

This curious sympathy pointed to the larger pattern: the ele-
vation of respectable women rested on the downgrading of the
disreputable. Fallen women could initiate young men into sexual

activity and thus allow respectable young women to avoid the fall. Prostitutes offered men an outlet that enabled wives to hold on to the role of pure creatures set above human biological compulsions. Most of all, prostitution was an unending reminder of the advantages of conventional female domestic roles. The benefits of marriage never appeared more attractive than in contrast to the grim and unprotected struggle for subsistence of the prostitute. Accordingly, few Western communities tried to eliminate prostitution; instead, they tried to regulate and contain it. In towns dependent on mining, cattle, or military posts, with a substantial population of male workers, prostitution was essential to the town's prosperity. The whole exercise of regulating prostitution, beyond the economic benefits, "emphasiz[ed] the respectable community's behavioral boundaries, and heighten[ed] solidarity among respectable women."[18]

Second, the history of prostitutes also serves to break up an apparently purposeful monolith: white society under the compulsions of Manifest Destiny. If women were victims of oppression, who were their oppressors? In a mining town like Nevada City, the prostitute's most frequent patrons were wageworkers, miners who risked their lives daily in hard underground labor. The miners, as Marion Goldman has suggested, were themselves "treated like objects rather than individuals" and were thus conditioned to "think of themselves and others that way."[19] The economic elite of the towns often owned the real estate in which prostitution took place; vice districts were among the more rewarding Western investment opportunities. And the official representatives of the law took their cut of the enterprise, in regular payoffs to prevent arbitrary arrests. In the broad sweep of Western history, it may look as if a united social unit called "white people" swept Indians off their lands; that group, as the history of prostitution shows, was not a monolith at all but a complex swirl of people as adept at preying on each other as at preying on Indians.

Third, the history of prostitution restores the participants of Western history to a gritty, recognizably physical reality. Testifying as a witness in a Nevada case in 1878, Belle West was asked to identify her occupation. "I go to bed with men for money," she said.[20] A century later, Belle West's frankness will not let us take refuge in sentimental and nostalgic images of the Western past. Acknowledge the human reality of Western prostitutes, and you have taken a major step toward removing Western history from the domain of myth and symbol and restoring it to actuality. Exclude women from Western history, and unreality sets in. Restore them, and the Western drama gains a fully human cast of characters—males and females whose urges, needs, failings, and conflicts we can recognize and even share.

It appears to be an insult and a disservice to place the murdered Narcissa Whitman and the murdered Julia Bulette in the same chapter. But women who in their own times would have fled each other's company turn out to teach similar historical lessons. It is the odd obligation of the historian to reunite women who would have refused to occupy the same room. Examine the actual experiences of white women in the West, at any level of respectability, and the stereotypes are left in tatters.

Consider Mrs. Amelia Stewart Knight. In 1853, she, her husband, and seven children went overland to Oregon and met the usual hazards—a grueling struggle through the muddy Midwestern prairies, difficult river crossings, dangerous alkali water, failing livestock. Mrs. Knight did occasionally record a bout of poor health, but frailty did not afflict women to the exclusion of men. "Still in camp," she wrote one day early in the journey, "husband and myself being sick. . . ."[21]

Supervising seven children elicited few complaints from Mrs. Knight. One simply has to imagine what some of her terse entries meant in practice: "Sunday, May 1st Still fine weather; wash and scrub all the children." The older children evidently helped out in caring for the younger ones; even with the best management, though, misadventures took place. The youngest child, Chatfield, seemed most ill-fated: "Chat has been sick all day with fever, partly caused by mosquitoe bites. . . . Here Chat fell out of the wagon but did not get hurt much. . . . [and then just five days later] Here Chat had a very narrow escape from being run over. Just as we were all getting ready to start, Chatfield the rascal, came around the forward wheel to get into the wagon and at that moment the cattle started and he fell under the wagon. Somehow he kept from under the wheels and escaped with only

a good or I should say, a bad scare. I never was so much fright-
ened in my life."[22]

In the days just before they left the trail and headed for the
Columbia River, a trying road through forests forced Mrs. Knight
and the children to walk. "I was obliged to take care of myself
and little ones as best I could," she wrote, and they spent their
days "winding around the fallen timber and brush, climbing over
logs creeping under fallen timber, sometimes lifting and carrying Chat."[23]

And then, near the end of the journey, Mrs. Knight had her
eighth child. She had throughout this trip been in the later stages
of pregnancy, and, in that final phase of walking, she had been
at full term.

In endurance and stamina, Mrs. Knight was clearly the equal—
if not the better—of the Kit Carsons and the Jedediah Smiths.
The tone of her diary suggests few complaints and no self-glor-
ification. It seems illogical to feel sorry for her, when she appears
not to have felt sorry for herself.

The developing pictures of Western women's history suggest
that Mrs. Knight, while perhaps braver than most women (and
men), was no anomaly. Far from revealing weak creatures held
captive to stronger wills, new studies show female Western settlers as full and vigorous participants in history. A recent close
study of homesteading in northeastern Colorado demonstrates
that single women took advantage of the spinster's and widow's
right to claim land under the Homestead Act. In two counties,
claim entries by women were 12 percent of the whole and, later
in the process, as high as 18 percent. Many wives, though not
entitled to claims of their own, nonetheless acted as genuine
partners in the homestead, contributing equal labor and taking
part in decisions.[24] While individuals may have conformed to the
image of the passive, suffering female pioneer, the majority were
too busy for such self-dramatization. Cooking, cleaning, washing, caring for children, planting gardens—any number of activities took priority over brooding.

One measure of independence and freedom in Western male
settlers was the capacity to scorn others—to see oneself as being
a superior sort of creature, placed above others. On that and
many other counts, white women were active self-determiners.

Downgrading Indians, Hispanics, Mormons, immoral men, or fallen women, many white women made it clear that the disorientation of migration had not stolen their confident ability to sort and rank humanity from best to worst.

In the record of their words and actions, the women of Western history have made a clear statement that they do not deserve or need special handling by historians. There is no more point in downgrading them as vulnerable victims than in elevating them as saintly civilizers. The same woman could be both inspirational in her loyalty to her family's welfare and disheartening in her hatred of Indians. Those two attributes were not contradictory; they were two sides to the same coin. We cannot emphasize one side at the expense of the other, without fracturing a whole, living person into disconnected abstractions.

Our inability to categorize the murdered Narcissa Whitman, or the murdered Julia Bulette, teaches us a vital lesson about Western history. Prostitutes were not consistently and exclusively sinners, nor were wives and mothers consistently and exclusively saints. Male or female, white Westerners were both sinned against and sinning. One person's reward often meant another person's loss; white opportunity meant Indian dispossession. Real Westerners, contrary to the old divisions between good guys and bad guys, combined the roles of victim and villain.

Acknowledging the moral complexity of Western history does not require us to surrender the mythic power traditionally associated with the region's story. On the contrary, moral complexity provides the base for parables and tales of greater and deeper meaning. Myths resting on tragedy and on unforeseen consequences, the ancient Greeks certainly knew, have far more power than stories of simple triumphs and victories. In movies and novels, as well as in histories, the stories of men and women who both entered and created a moral wilderness have begun to replace the simple contests of savagery and civilization, cowboys and Indians, white hats and black hats. By questioning the Westerner's traditional stance as innocent victim, we do not debunk Western history but enrich it.

Two

Property Values

IF HOLLYWOOD wanted to capture the emotional center of Western history, its movies would be about real estate. John Wayne would have been neither a gunfighter nor a sheriff, but a surveyor, speculator, or claims lawyer. The showdowns would occur in the land office or the courtroom; weapons would be deeds and lawsuits, not six-guns. Moviemakers would have to find some cinematic way in which proliferating lines on a map could keep the audience rapt.

Western history is a story structured by the drawing of lines and the marking of borders. From macrocosm to microcosm, from imperial struggles for territory to the parceling out of townsite claims, Western American history was an effort first to draw lines dividing the West into manageable units of property and then to persuade people to treat those lines with respect.

White Americans saw the acquisition of property as a cultural imperative, manifestly the right way to go about things. There was one appropriate way to treat land—divide it, distribute it, register it. This relationship to physical matter seems to us so commonplace that we must struggle to avoid taking it for granted, to grasp instead the vastness of the continent and the enormous project of measuring, allocating, and record keeping involved in turning the open expanses of North America into

transferable parcels of real estate. Like the settlers themselves, we steadfastly believe in the social fiction that lines on a map and signatures on a deed legitimately divide the earth. Of all the persistent qualities in American history, the values attached to property retain the most power.

As usual, Mark Twain had an infallible instinct for the irony hidden in a widespread social fiction. In *Roughing It,* he told the story of a hoax perpetrated by the locals in Nevada on an appointed U.S. attorney. A landslide, the practical jokers claimed, had thrown local property arrangements into disorder; Tom Morgan's cabin and ranch slid down a hill and landed on top of Dick Hyde's farm. Morgan then claimed ownership of both lay-

The key force of Western settlement: land rush at Hollister, Idaho. *Courtesy Denver Public Library, Western History Department*

ers of the now consolidated property. With the U.S. attorney persuaded to defend Hyde's right to his buried farm, the case went to arbitration. Hyde had lost his ranch "by the visitation of God," the verdict came in, though Hyde retained the right to dig his ranch out from under the intruding thirty-five feet of Morgan's property. The duped U.S. attorney went appropriately wild.[1]

True to form, Twain selected the story that stretched an already absurd situation. One has to feel a certain sympathy for the U.S. attorney; people in the West had made many peculiar claims in this matter of property. A reliable line on credulity was not easy to draw. The recognition of legitimacy in property was

visibly a social fiction, supported by the majority's willing sus-
pension of disbelief. The inability of Twain's lawyer to recognize
fabrication was, if anything, a measure of his adaptation to the
West.

If the actual workings of property could mystify the unini-
tiated, the ideal could not have been clearer. The founders of
the American Republic had Europe to warn them of what happened to a society when population moved out of balance with
the land supply. It was a common assumption that societies followed an inevitable sequence of development, from hunting and
gathering to herding, agriculture, and, finally, manufacturing.
To the planners of the American Republic, the third stage was
the happiest. Independent and hardworking farmers provided
the ideal citizenry, at once anchored and supported by their
property. If America went past the third stage and into the fourth,
the nation would face many of the same problems that plagued
Europe—a small elite addicted to luxury, and a large population, perhaps a majority, of landless, dependent people whose
very existence could ruin the prospects for a healthy republic.

America's hope thus lay in westward expansion—in the
extended opportunities for the growing population to acquire
property and for the nation to remain at the happy and virtuous
stage of agriculture. In America, Thomas Jefferson said, "we
have an immensity of land courting the industry of the husband-
man. . . . Those who labor in the earth are the chosen people of
God, if ever He had a chosen people, whose breasts He has made
His peculiar deposit for substantial and genuine virtue." Jeffersonian thinkers thus evolved "a vision of expansion across space—
the American continent—as a necessary alternative to the development through time," Drew McCoy has explained, "that was
generally thought to bring both political corruption and social
decay." The success of the American experiment rested on the
property-holding success of many individuals. "Power always
follows property," John Adams said bluntly; property, widely
distributed among the people, would hold the line against pernicious concentrations of power.[2]

When the various seaboard states ceded their western lands,
the public domain provided the opportunity to put the ideal of

property into practice. The difficulty inherent in that project could be seen in the declining career of Elijah Hayward.

Appointed Andrew Jackson's land commissioner in 1830, Elijah Hayward got off to a good start. Hayward was, the historian Malcolm Rohrbough has written, "determined to create order and uniformity" in the General Land Office, a bureau under the secretary of the treasury charged with surveying, selling, and registering the public lands. Never a model of efficiency, the Land Office had fallen further and further behind in its duties. Charged with confirming land patents sent in from the district offices, the Washington office also had to oversee the record keeping of the many purchases on credit. It was also an information bureau, serving citizens interested in acquiring land. Its duties proliferated, but its staff did not. On behalf of their constituents, congressmen complained of the slowness with which the office worked; on their own behalf, congressmen made many of the requests for information that ate up the clerks' time; and for the sake of economy and retrenchment, congressmen refused to increase the office's appropriations.[3]

In 1832, Elijah Hayward had seventeen clerks to help him fight his way through the "forty thousand patents a year" he needed to issue "simply to meet the annual sales." Moreover, each of those land patents was to carry a presidential signature. Starting in December 1831 and continuing into June, "Andrew Jackson signed more than 10,000 patents. Yet when he paused for a rest, he was still 10,590 behind and losing ground." In 1833, Congress finally authorized an official patent signer; Jackson was relieved of his burdens, but Hayward continued to carry his. Understaffed and much criticized, Hayward struggled to supervise his often erratic field officers. The surveyor general in Florida was "always either ill or on leave to recover from periodic bouts of illness. Absent from his office for nine months from July 1831 to April 1832, he was so weakened on his return that he did nothing for the rest of the year." The director of operations in the active territories of Arkansas, Missouri, and Illinois "grew more and more pessimistic over the enormous backlog in his office. Eventually he refused to answer his mail. . . ."[4]

In a response that makes history seem predictable, Land

Commissioner Hayward took to drink. He "began to absent himself from the office for long periods, ostensibly because of illness." Andrew Jackson "ordered Hayward 'that he *must* desist entirely from taking *any spirits;* unless it was a table wine.' " The warning did not take. Hayward remained frequently incapacitated.[5]

Hayward resigned in 1835, and his successor had better luck. "Belatedly recognizing the volume of the land business and its complexity," Congress increased the staff of clerks from seventeen to eighty-eight. Moreover, reflecting national hard times, sales began to fall off. Nonetheless, at best the Land Office could stay narrowly ahead of its obligations, and every following land commissioner would have many moments when he would be tempted to raise a glass to the memory of Elijah Hayward.[6]

The temptation to drink aside, the business of land distribution entailed a whole range of complications not envisioned in the Jeffersonian ideal. Only in the imagination could virgin lands move smoothly into the hands of new owners, transforming wilderness to farmland, idle men to productive citizens. The "virgin lands" were not vacant, but occupied. Redistributing those lands to the benefit of white farmers required the removal of Indian territorial claims and of the Indians themselves—a process that was never simple. Indian residents were not the only complication; once the United States acquired land that had been in the possession of France or Spain, prior land claims under the laws of other empires added to the legal wilderness.

Then there was the problem of staffing the Land Office. There was no shortage of applicants for the positions of surveyors or agents, and that was the problem. Land Office employment promised a chance at inside information, prime positioning for investment in real estate. From the earliest years of the Land Office, its officials were widely involved in the buying and selling of land. In line with the Jeffersonian vision, the Land Office would have been staffed by high-minded officials; in fact, Malcolm Rohrbough has found, "the politicians who increasingly administered the public domain did not do so out of a feeling of service but to make a profit."[7]

Even with more dedicated public servants to administer it,

land law bore little resemblance to the simple Jeffersonian ideal. From 1789 to 1834, Congress passed a total of 375 land laws—laws adjusting the size of lots for sale, shifting the price per acre, altering the requirement for cash payments or adding the option of credit, and granting rights of preemption in specific regions. A great burden fell on the Land Office simply to keep up with those laws, while congressional parsimony guaranteed under-staffing and inefficiency. At one point, the Land Office commis-sioner did not have money to provide his field officers with copies of the federal land laws. Into the last half of the nineteenth cen-tury, variations in land law—the Homestead Act and its varia-tions, the Timber Culture Act, the Desert Land Law—kept matters as complex as ever.[8]

Whatever laws Congress passed, land distribution could never keep up with settlement. Orderly surveys were to precede sales; once a district had been divided and platted, a competitive auc-tion could be held. But surveying was often slow and inefficient, and impatient settlers pushed ahead of the surveys. Coping with these squatters caused headaches for federal officials. Using the U.S. Army to remove citizens by force was never an attractive political option, and presidential proclamations against intrud-ers in the public lands or on Indian reserves were exercises in futility. Without reliable forces to back it up, federal authority suffered from an ongoing shortage of respect. "The settlers of the West," Malcolm Rohrbough has remarked, "took the view that the land was there to be taken, and that the rules and reg-ulations of the government did not change their natural rights as citizens." Surely the most disheartening outcome for those who had shared Jefferson's hopes was the clear evidence that "all men were far from equal" in the competition for land. "The advantage," Rohrbough has said, "always accrued to the wealthy man of influence, regardless of what the law said."[9] Not even the Homestead Act, at last rewarding committed labor with free land, could reverse this pattern.

The Homestead Act, Paul Wallace Gates has shown, "did not end the auction system or cash sales." Moreover, "speculation and land monopolization continued after its adoption as widely perhaps as before, and within as well as without the law." The same problem of inefficient and sometimes corrupt administration persisted; the use of "dummy entrymen" permitted speculators, or mining, timber, or cattle companies to acquire land under falsified claims. In a variety of ways—huge grants to subsidize railroad construction, grants to states, the distribution of land warrants to veterans, the sale of tracts made available by further reductions of Indian reservations—much desirable land was taken from the reach of homesteaders. Moreover, much of the land made available to them was beyond the line of semi-aridity, in regions where the 160-acre farm and the methods of conventional farming could produce little except frustration. The Homestead Act had its successes, but it remained a tribute to the high ideal of the yeoman farmer, lodged "in an incongruous land system."[10]

II

Disrespect for federal authority did not lead to disrespect for property; on this count, the West was not so wild. Respect for property—other people's as well as one's own—evolved from a dizzying combination of consensus and conflict, agreement and competition. There was widespread agreement on what constituted a desirable resource, and yet that very agreement led to competition to secure exclusive control of the resource. In the other direction, the individualistic desire for exclusive, secure property meant that one's personal interests were best served by an agreement to respect other people's property, in return for their cooperation in protecting and defending one's possessions.

The historian Charles Howard Shinn saw these matters in different terms. A journalist in California who had spent time with the old-timers in the goldfields, Shinn went on to write a dissertation at Johns Hopkins. Shinn found the popular Johns Hopkins "germ theory," by which American institutions were shown to sprout from Anglo-Saxon and Germanic seeds, at work in the behavior of the mining camps. Strangers suddenly thrown together, in danger of disorder from the unregulated scramble for gold, groups of miners called meetings and wrote mining codes, providing rules for the making of claims and exclusive rights to the development of particular sites. This was self-reg-

ulation, performed in the absence of any federal statutes governing mining claims, and to Shinn it was happy proof of an
inherent Anglo-Saxon and Teutonic instinct for order.[11]

Shinn notwithstanding, this agreement was by no means
automatic or universal; Western history abounds with conflict,
armed or otherwise, over property. But such conflict was clearly
not in the interests of the dominant goal, the developing and
marketing of available resources. Instances of violent conflict set
up an atmosphere that could only be discouraging to investment
and serious commercial activity. To entrepreneurs delicately
conscious of the connection between favorable publicity and
prosperity, threats to property called for concerned citizens to
unite in defense of orderly procedure.

Fortunately, American society came equipped with an institutional framework that combined competitive struggle with
orderly procedure. Especially in matters of property, law took
the primal contest of ownership—the basic, reciprocal dialogue
consisting of "Mine, not Yours"—and channeled it into the
ritualized, rhetorical combat of the courtroom, providing at the
same time the happiest career opportunities for men like William Morris Stewart, portrayed in a recent biography by Russell
Elliott.

Born in 1825 in western New York, William Stewart was from
early childhood a model of the Jacksonian "expectant capitalist."
Like John Wesley Hardin, Stewart in his autobiography claimed
to have been the beneficiary of the finest parental model. "My
mother had great strength of character," he said, "and her life
was pure and honest. She loved truth and justice and never told
a falsehood." More central to his future career, Stewart's memory of childhood showed a curious precision in monetary matters. Writing in his eighties, Stewart recalled his first income:
$1.80 earned at age nine in coon hunting; $1.20 expended for
shoes and $0.20 for gingerbread and root beer, and $0.40 given
to his hardworking mother. The next coon season netted him
$4.35 and brought a similar accounting of its disbursement.
Stewart's most significant memories of childhood came in the
standardized measurements of dollars and cents.[12]

Stewart left home at age fourteen; he worked so hard that

he was able to enter Yale University. As opportunities went, however, educational opportunity ranked second to gold rush opportunity. Stewart left New Haven in 1849, before graduation, and headed for California.

Early exposure to hard physical labor made Stewart a quick learner of a basic gold rush lesson: in the mining districts, there were far more appealing ways to make money than by mining. A year or two of direct mining work convinced him of the appeal of the law. He was hardly the first, and certainly not the only, man to recognize that greater rewards lay in mining the miners, especially in profiting from their disputes and conflicts over claims and property.

When the Comstock Lode mines opened, in 1859, Stewart was an early and eager arrival in Nevada. Experience and enterprise soon launched him into a commanding position on the Comstock Lode. Representing the major mining companies, Stewart proved himself as a vigorous trial lawyer. It was natural that a man of his talents would turn to politics.

Elected to the Senate, Stewart remained an utterly adapted creature of a world in which politics, property, and profit played a happy game of leapfrog. Outside the Senate, Stewart worked for the Southern Pacific Railroad, a dominant power in Nevada and California. Once in the Senate, he did not let old ties wither. He looked out for the railroad's interests and received an appropriate compensation. The railroad's Collis Huntington wrote his partner on the matter of appreciating Stewart: "Stewart leaves here this week for California and you must see him and let him into some good things in and about San Francisco and Oakland. He has always stood by us. He is peculiar, but thoroughly honest, and will bear no dictation, but I know he must live, and we must fix it so that he can make one or two hundred thousand dollars. It is to our interest and I think his right."[13]

Senator Stewart may have received special favors from the railroad, but that did not mean that he had lost his principles or, more to the point, his appearance of principles. One supporter, Russell Elliott has reported, "sent him $100 for doing a favor" and received Stewart's reply along with the returned money: " 'I am surprised that you should send the money to me and regret that you supposed I would accept it.' " Stewart, in other words, put a high price on his integrity—a price railroads and mining companies, but not average citizens, could meet.[14]

As a Westerner capitalizing on the opportunities offered by conflict over property and politics, Stewart was a significant figure in his own right; more important, his legislative activities had a permanent impact on the use of mineral resources. In the Senate, Stewart addressed the absence of a federal mining law. At the time of the gold rush, for all its proliferating land laws, the federal government was silent on the procedure for establishing mining claims. Even more significant, the federal government exacted no revenue from the returns of precious metal mining. The Spanish king might have taken the royal fifth from the empire's gold and silver, but Uncle Sam, steward for the American people, took nothing. For seventeen years, the United States had an active mining frontier in the Far West, and no federal mining law.

William Stewart, always sensitive to opportunity, filled the void with the 1866 Mining Law. Did this law give the federal government a strong role of leadership in matters of mining property? On the contrary, it essentially ratified local procedures, the improvisations Charles Howard Shinn had celebrated. "The mineral lands of the public domain, both surveyed and unsurveyed, are hereby declared to be free and open to exploration and occupation by all citizens of the United States," the law declared, ". . . subject also to the local customs or rules of miners in the several mining districts. . . ." Slightly revised in 1872, the mining law remained on the books, despite various campaigns to modernize it. If Stewart's law represented the preference of the frontier for minimal federal involvement, its persistence was another argument for continuity in Western history. Serving the mining companies and the railroads, the man who remembered his youth in precise terms of income and expenditures remained true to his origins. Far from being the last of his breed, a rare and forgotten species of the frontier, Stewart was the man and the prototype for the future. Called by his biographer "a servant of power," Stewart was also a dedicated servant of property. They were, in fact, largely identical.[15]

III

For the large mining companies, the 1866/1872 Mining Law had the principal charm of validating the procedures that had worked to their advantage. In mining as in other matters, local improvisations, federal land laws, and judicial authority gradually converged on one principle for selecting among conflicting claims. Prior appropriation, the principle of "first in time, first in right," developed many applications. The preemption laws gave squatters the first chance at land on the basis of an early arrival. The Homestead Act gave the first claimant the right to file on a tract. Miners awarded legitimacy to claims based on primacy of arrival. Miners also agreed to allocate water on the basis of prior appropriation, and the miners' precedent was carried into water allocation for irrigation and domestic use. Such disparate resources as wildlife and oil came to be awarded by a similar principle of priority, the rule of capture. In the early phases of the cattle business, mavericks—wild unbranded cattle—became the property of the first claimant; similarly, a principle of "priority use of the range" allowed the first arrival to claim the local water supply and to hold the adjoining land.

In the complexity of American resource law, no one principle was applied with consistency, but "first in time, first in right," had a widespread influence. While prior appropriation sorted out innumerable property disputes, it did so by giving an almost mystical weight to the idea of getting there first. There are any number of standards by which human beings can allocate rights and opportunities—merit, need, and intention are commonly employed standards. By contrast, first arrival gave a great deal of power to the accidents of history and to luck. Moreover, it made the distinction between legitimate acquisition and theft a fine one. In both cases, the act was similar—one simply appropriated something for one's own use—but, by a sometimes subtle difference of timing, one act was honored and protected by law, and the other was punished.

The articulate and shrewd cowboy Charlie Siringo, author of *A Texas Cowboy; or, Fifteen Years on the Hurricane Deck of a Spanish Pony*, made the same point when he reflected on his chances of making a fortune. "In trying to solve the question," he said, "my mind darted back a few years, when, if I had taken time by the forelock, I might have now been wallowing in wealth with the rest of the big cattle kings—or to use a more appropriate name, cattle thieves. But alas! thought I, the days of honorable cattle stealing is past. . . ." A great deal of Western property right rested on this narrow margin of timing. Legitimacy came "by taking time by the forelock," and even though the passage of years might give those property rights an aura of venerability, they nonetheless rested on a principle still much in vogue in playground disputes: "It's mine; I got here first."[16]

One of the prime satisfactions of getting there first was the chance to profit from the subsequent rise in property values. To take up a piece of undifferentiated land, assign it boundaries, and then watch it acquire value was one of the most exhilarating experiences available in the Western economy. This addictive and pleasurable experience came to be known as speculation; prosaic and monetary as it was, speculation still fit in the category "adventure," involving equal doses of risk, unpredictability, and imagined reward.

Like so many activities in the American West, speculation could shift meaning when viewed from different angles. To the beneficiary, accumulating profit, it was just another legitimate reward for getting there first—for having the nerve, the enterprise, and the instinct to acquire title at the right time. To those who came later and faced the higher prices, speculation was an economic activity bordering on criminality and playing on unfair advantage; speculative profits were an unearned increment by which selfish individuals took advantage of the innocent and hardworking, whose labors constituted the real improvement of the country.

To this day, the widespread existence of speculation is a fact seldom acknowledged neutrally. References to speculation commonly carry an association of physical or mental disease, as in "speculative fever," "speculative frenzy," or "speculative mania." Faced with the reality of speculation, historians can still react with an emotion suggestive of a Baptist who, in the course of compiling a history of church socials, discovers that a good many in the congregation have been drinking from a spiked punch bowl. Speculation is extremely disillusioning *if* you are trying to hold on to the illusion that agriculture and commerce are significantly different ways of life, one representing nature and virtue and the other artifice and temptation to vice.

In truth, agriculture was not a refuge from or an alternative to commerce. Rather, the two were often intertwined.[17] The acquisition of land, the purchase of equipment, the marketing of the farm's surplus—many of the essential transactions of farming put the farmer in closer relation to the market than to nature. And even a farmer dedicated to his occupation might hope that over time his property value might increase. This was not a sign of acquisitive depravity concealed beneath a veil of pastoral simplicity; it was simply more evidence for the truism that gambling with the future drove Western enterprise. Contemporaries and even historians might draw a clear line between speculation and responsible property holding, but the difference more often came in shades of gray rather than black and white.

Speculation carried a distinguished pedigree; it was not invented in the nineteenth century trans-Mississippi West. In a carefully detailed study, Charles Grant found speculation rampant in the western Connecticut frontier in the 1730s. The conventional version of frontier speculation suggested that humble frontiersmen were at the mercy of a manipulative Eastern financial elite; in fact, Grant found that in the town of Kent the settlers themselves were the most vigorous speculators, buying and selling local lots with the fervor of stockbrokers. "Virtually all Kent settlers," Grant remarked, ". . . speculated actively once they had arrived in Kent." A comparative few settled contentedly into subsistence farming; otherwise, Grant noted, "one is impressed with [the settlers'] almost frantic pursuit of a wide variety of schemes or projects." Grant was also struck by "a curious moral attitude, a combination of self-righteousness and a propensity for cunning deceit." Two of the town's leading men, Joseph Fuller and Joshua Lassell, filed petitions with the Connecticut General Assembly, repeatedly requesting a grant of property adjoining the town. The petitions had a humble and pleading tone: "The said Joshua Lassell, having only a farm fit for grazing and little or no plowland, thought proper to look out for some land suitable for the plow. He learned that the tract aforesaid was suitable for the purpose." "When he was writing these words," Grant's search through property records disclosed, "Lassell was the largest landowner in Kent and the town's most active speculator. He bought and sold more 'plowland' in a single year than a dozen men could use." The colonial historian Bernard Bailyn has recently confirmed Grant's findings and extended them back to the seventeenth century:

Land speculation—the acquisition of land not for its use but for its resale value as a commodity in a rising market—was no special activity of absentee capitalists in the colonial period, and the western settlements were no agrarian preserves unsullied by commerce. Speculative commercial operations had been part and parcel of the settling of the earliest North American villages—of the founding of the very first Puritan New England towns, as well as those that followed in the eighteenth century.[18]

The precedents were well set early in the colonial era, both for the mechanisms of speculation and for the speculator's strategic assumption of the role of "innocent victim" on appropriate occasions. Why, then, was so much energy spent in lamenting and denouncing speculation? It stripped the social fiction of property of all its softer, justifying touches. Speculation revealed ownership to be a purely conceptual act. To the speculator, profit bore no relation to actual physical labor and derived instead from a manipulation of the legal principles set up to convey and protect property. A farmer, fully employed on his farm, supporting his family by its products, was a property owner full of good intention and willingness to labor. But to the absentee owner, holding land in anticipation of rising values, ownership was only an idea, not a physical fact. Property could never look more arbitrary or more distant from the ideal of the farmer-citizen made secure and independent by his land.

Few mechanisms could regulate speculation in its wild phases. As in so many matters, despite its centrality in land disposition, the federal government did little to moderate speculation. How was it that the government could be so important and so ineffective in directing the course of American landed property?

There are many ways to explain the confusion and complexity that characterized the federal land business. Perhaps none of them is necessary. Because much of the nation was initially in the public domain, the distribution and control of that property would have broken down the management techniques of the most modern multinational corporation. It is easy to explain the General Land Office's failures—the nonexistence of computers and telephones is almost an answer in itself.

With the public domain to administer, the federal government found itself in an anomalous position. It possessed a national resource but not a rationale for the management and use of that resource. With the public lands officially the property of "the people," the United States began with a giant nationalized holding that would have made perfect sense if the country had been socialistic. Viewed from outside, the situation looked like socialism; viewed from inside, it certainly was not socialism. What was it instead?

The United States took on the management of a vast nationalized resource, equipped only with an ideal of individual property owning. The system would be one in which the federal government served as the intermediary in making the people's resources available to the people who could use them; that was the Westerner's usual hope. But it was difficult to see what, if any, meaning that left for the idea that lands belong to the people at large, to the nation in general. Certainly, revenues from land sales and leases added to the national treasury, but even the use of public lands for national revenue was an inconsistent and irregular practice.

The conservation movement gave new meaning to the idea of the people's ownership. For nearly a century before, the system's goal was disposal; federal ownership was a temporary expedient on the way to private property. National forests, national parks, and public lands made available for grazing leases reoriented federal ownership from disposal to permanent land management—in the people's interests. The perplexity remained: Which people? Which interest? But the large percentage of land still in federal control made one lesson clear: the massive federal role in Western land and resource matters would not be a temporary, transitional "frontier" phenomenon.

With this perplexity in mind, one reads the words of earlier historians with something close to wonder. "So long as free land exists," Frederick Jackson Turner wrote, "the opportunity for a competency exists, and economic power secures political power." Turner and others of his persuasion echoed the faith of Benjamin Franklin, Thomas Jefferson, and John Adams, but the complex and confusing events of the intervening century did not alter that faith. That version of Western history—hinged on a simple model of "the existence of an area of free land" and "its continuous recession"—appears to describe the history of another, much simpler country.[19]

The events of Western history represent, not a simple process of territorial expansion, but an array of efforts to wrap the concept of property around unwieldy objects. Agricultural development on plains and prairies made this process deceptively simple. Surveys followed the unrelenting symmetry of the grid, and ownership was registered on clearly marked plats and deeds. But for different terrain or different resources, the concept of property began to show symptoms of stress.

Those different categories of prospective property made it necessary to adapt the concept of property to situations of impermanence and changeability. Consider the range of resources that the concept "property" would be asked to embrace:

Animal pelts and hides. Who owned the beaver in its prepelt state? Who owned the buffalo in possession of its hide? Who owned wildlife, and how did one go about staking a claim to a mobile, inherently uncontrollable animal population?

Valuable minerals. Here the goal was not necessarily permanent title. Who would want to retain ownership of a hillside blasted into rubble by mining? The key was control of the site during production. And when a vein ran continuously below the surface, and various individuals claimed parts of the surface, who owned the vein itself? The improvised answer was that ownership hinged on the apex; whoever held the area where the vein ran nearest the surface, owned the vein. The apex law produced more lawsuits than clarity—not unusual for ideas of property stressed by the vagaries of geology and geography.

Cattle and grazing territory. The longhorns of the early cattle business were nearly wild; how was one to establish ownership of a supposedly domesticated animal that persisted in behavior appropriate to wildlife? And beyond the problems presented by property on the hoof with a will of its own, how did one assert property in grass? Ownership of the land itself was secondary to securing access to the grass; it is hardly surprising that rangeland eventually came under a net of leasing arrangements. More directly, the aspiring cattle grazer could, by claiming the water supply, control the surrounding terrain.

Timber. If the goal was short-term use—the lumbering equivalent of extraction—permanent ownership of the land was again secondary, as it was in mining and grazing. When the pressure for long-term use through sustained-yield forestry emerged, permanent ownership of trees and the soil beneath them would acquire new meaning.

Transportation routes. Free mobility may have been an American right, but the routes themselves were not necessarily free. Toll bridges and toll roads, stagecoach franchises, and mail contracts were themselves forms of property. nothing made this more dramatic than the nineteenth-century licensing and subsidizing of railroads.

Oil. As a resource, oil had the distinctive quality of fugacity—the capacity to move around—and this led to the "rule of capture." If a variety of wells were sunk into the same oil field, like straws into a soda, the oil belonged to the party that first removed it from the earth. This was an improvident rule that could not remain the only guide to ownership of oil. Proper alternatives took decades to devise.

Water. Here was the key aspect of property in an arid or semiarid region. The development of most of these other resources depended on the control of water. Though officially inanimate, water gives all the signs of having a life of its own—and a mobile, restless, and irrational life at that. If it is conceptually difficult to think of stepping into the same river twice, it is an even more remarkable feat to think of owning the river or a certain percentage of acre-feet or miner's inches of that river's flow. It is even more difficult to discover a principle of priority in all the varied uses of water—in farming, mining, ranching, recreation, and town services.

White reformers commonly lamented the failure of Indians to understand the white American's idea of property. If one works for a bit of anthropological distance and then surveys these different forms of property, one can understand the Indians' bewilderment. What is this variable and arbitrary relationship between human and matter, called "property"? White Americans may have felt that property was a sacrosanct value, but the diversity of Western resources put that stable and unchanging value through a dance, which left the concept looking flustered and in some disarray.

IV

Cases of conflict in which two individuals made competing claims for the same property for the same purpose were troubling but comparatively simple matters. Two California miners might converge on the same site; prior appropriation and the local mining code could usually sort out the conflict. Once mining involved the manipulation and redirection of water, conflicting claims could involve land, water, and the various needs of hydraulic mining (water directed against a hillside to dislodge and pulverize rock) and river mining (water channeled away from its usual course to expose the riverbed). Then, in turn, miners' use of water came into conflict with the operations of downstream farmers; carried by floods, the tailings and detritus of mining buried farmers' fields and clogged river ways and ditches.[20] This was no longer a matter of two individuals with similar purposes competing for the same resource; these situations now involved groups with different livelihoods, each feeling itself to be the possessor of the right to use its property to its best advantage.

If anyone had a chance to learn how complicated these matters could become, it was Joseph Lippincott, an engineer for the newly created Reclamation Service, whose activities have been captured by the historian William Kahrl. Charged with evaluating and developing the best prospects for federally sponsored dams and irrigation systems, Lippincott earned a position in the center of the fabled conflict between the city of Los Angeles and the Owens Valley. East of Los Angeles, the Owens Valley was a promising site for an irrigation project. As Reclamation Service engineer, Lippincott scouted out the valley and concluded that a project to develop the Owens River was justified. Where Lippincott swerved from the expected track was in identifying the beneficiary of that project as Los Angeles, not the Owens Valley. Trusted by the valley residents as an agent of the Reclamation Service, Lippincott took the results of his investigation and used them to direct the attention of the Los Angeles water engineers toward the Owens River.

Lippincott traveled on the borders between public and private enterprise, working as a federal engineer and as a paid consultant for the city of Los Angeles. His recommendations were acted on, and Los Angeles launched the major aqueduct project that replenished the city while depleting the valley. The valley residents felt tricked and betrayed; Lippincott had embarrassed his superiors and discredited the Reclamation Service while it was still in its early, precarious years. An official inquiry condemned his behavior. "Not only is private work in violation of law and regulation," it held,

but Lippincott's acts as a private consultant are peculiarly repugnant to his duties in the Reclamation Service. At the present time it is understood that the City of Los Angeles desires the Reclamation Service to relinquish an attractive irrigation project on which extensive investigations have been and are being made, and Mr. Lippincott, while acting as the Government adviser on this project, is accepting pay from the city for his services, including the exertion of his inflence to have the Government retire from the field.[21]

Was Lippincott repentant? Not at all. When found out, Lippincott defended himself vigorously. He was, to his own satisfaction, yet another Western injured innocent. In the prolonged controversy over the aqueduct, the charges against him reappeared. Each time, he struck the time-honored pose of the misunderstood victim. "It is a pretty severe thing," he said, "for a man to spend 25 years in building up a reputation and then have it destroyed in an unnecessary and ruthless way."[22]

Divided in his institutional loyalties, Lippincott had steered consistently toward two compatible goals: the growth of the region and the growth of his own income. Combining the goals, Lippincott was certainly not original; he was quite in line with the driving forces of Western history. If the national mandate was to use Western resources, especially water, to benefit the greatest number, then Los Angeles was the appropriate destination for the Owens River water. In several key transactions, Lippincott had behaved with something other than honor, but he was hardly the first Westerner to find that personal and regional economic growth required a few compromises with impractical morality. To his own mind, Lippincott had simply had the wit to join forces with the winners in one of California's major property conflicts. He saw no reward or purpose in wondering how the losers might feel.

In Western America, neither loser nor winner wasted much time in wondering how the other party felt. Western property users developed a style of maneuvering that made them resemble drivers who plunge into intersections, uninterested in the presence or intentions of other drivers. Given the limits of the Western environment and especially of water, there have been only so many avenues to prosperity. Users of those avenues have always encountered each other at intersections; hydraulic miners got in the way of farmers; farmers got in the way of cattle ranchers; urban water users got in the way of irrigators; dam builders got in the way of recreational river rafters. Collisions have occurred, but for most of the nineteenth century, and for much of the twentieth, traffic has been unevenly distributed, and sequentially jammed intersections—an effect urban dwellers know as gridlock—have not been much of a risk.

In our own times, the calculation of risk changes. Mining, oil drilling, farming, recreation, tourism, fishing, hunting, lumbering, manufacturing, power generating, and real estate developing—all the Western routes to power and prosperity are heavily traveled. At their intersections, the tension builds. Regulatory devices—courts and executive agencies—have attempted to keep traffic flowing, while the habit of blaming the traffic cop for the traffic jam has provided another source of resentment directed at the federal government. The multitude of intersections where interests conflict are not guaranteed to produce compromise. Property and profit have been for decades, and remain today, very sensitive subjects.

The commerce at the center of Western settlement: Granada, Colorado.
Courtesy Colorado Historical Society

Neither the Western past nor the Western present will make sense until attachment to property and attraction to profit find their proper category as a variety of strong emotion. Take the example offered by an injury suffered in the course of pioneering in Dakota Territory. Later active in Dakota politics, W. W. Brookings was caught in a blizzard in 1859; he suffered frostbite and then underwent a partial amputation of his feet. What errand in the wilderness left Brookings partially crippled? He had been "racing to the Missouri River to establish a townsite claim for his company.[23]

Disillusioning? One's first response is that, to court such danger, Brookings should have been up to something better than townsite speculation. In Western America (and elsewhere), the dominance of the profit motive supported the notion that the pursuit of property and profit was rationality in action, and not emotion at all. In fact, the passion for profit was and is a passion like most others. It can make other concerns insignificant and inspire at once extraordinary courage and extraordinary cruelty. It was the passion at the core of the Western adventure.

Three

Denial and Dependence

DURING ANY WEEK, some Western politician or businessman will deliver a speech celebrating the ideal of regional independence. Westerners, the speaker will say, should be able to choose a goal and pursue it, free of restriction and obstacle. They should not have other people telling them what to do. If authority must be used, it should be their own authority imposed on those who try to block the path toward progress. In a one-to-one correspondence between nature and politics, the wide open spaces were meant to be the setting for a comparable wide open independence for Westerners. This independence, the speaker will assume, is the West's legitimate heritage from history.

In our era of global interdependence, that traditional speech seems to be out of place, for other people's actions affect our lives in an infinite number of ways. The repeated invocation of the Westerner's right to independence begins to sound anachronistic, opposed to the reality of a more complex time. In fact, the times were always complex. At any period in Western history, the rhetoric of Western independence was best taken with many grains of salt.

In 1884 Martin Maginnis, the delegate to Congress from Montana Territory, geared up for a classic denunciation of a travesty against Western independence. Territorial delegates could speak, but not vote, in Congress, and a sense of oppression did not make Maginnis shy about exercising his right to speak. "The present Territorial system," he said, ". . . is the most infamous system of colonial government that was ever seen on the face of the globe." Territories "are the colonies of your Republic, situated three thousand miles away from Washington by land, as the thirteen colonies were situated three thousand miles away from London by water. And it is a strange thing that the fathers of our Republic . . . established a colonial government as much worse than that which they revolted against as one form of government can be worse than another."[1]

The colonies and the Revolution gave Westerners an irresistible analogy. Denouncing the territorial system required no originality. One simply matched up the parallels: London and Washington, D.C.; George III's ministers and the secretaries of the interior; appointed royal governors and appointed territorial governors; and beyond that, many terms did not even need translation—inadequate representation, violated sovereignty, unrecognized rights.

In fact, there were parallels between British colonies and American territories; the framers of the Northwest Ordinance had the colonial precedent in mind. It is still not easy to think of an alternative way to manage a newly occupied region. Maginnis's stridency aside, he was right in thinking that the territory, the primal political reality of most early Western development, did involve a limit on local sovereignty. But the difference between a British colony and an American territory was so enormous, and of such practical and philosophical significance, that it put something of a dent in Delegate Maginnis's argument. Colonies were to remain colonies, but territories were to become states, and thus, as the historian Howard Lamar has summed it up, the problems of liberty and empire were reconciled.[2]

Territories were transitional, even if the transition came in all lengths—no time at all in California, four years in Nevada, and sixty-three years in Arizona and New Mexico. Before statehood, even though they had elected representatives, residents in territories were under the authority of federally appointed governors and judges. Some of those men were perfectly competent; others were party hacks of limited charm and skill, to whom the office was only a reward for political services and not an opportunity to serve the nation, much less the territory. In Congress, a territory had only a solitary delegate, entitled merely to speak, and no senators or representatives.

"Citizens resented the territorial status," the historian Earl Pomeroy has pointed out, "not only because they were Westerners, but also because recently they had been Easterners." They had vivid memories of what it was to be citizens in an established state, and from that point of view the move to a Western territory did not heighten one's independence, but lessened it.[3]

An arbitrarily appointed governor, descending from outside, brought to mind other wars of independence besides the Revolution. The term "carpetbagger" became almost as much a favored epithet in the West as in the South. The imposed governments of Southern Reconstruction did resemble the territorial system, and that resemblance could make it look as if the West was receiving gratuitously what the South earned as punishment—a forced cutback in state sovereignty.

Were Westerners truly at the mercy of these appointed invaders? Were they, as a Dakota paper put it, "not even wards of the government, but a party subject to the whims of political leaders, the intrigues of schemers and the mining of party rats"?[4]

In territorial histories, one plot repeats. The territorial governor arrives. He is not a talented man, but he has some hopes of doing his job. He has a modest salary, less modest expenses, and some interest in his own political and economic advancement. He knows the territory's affairs are not in good order, and he would like it to be to his credit that he restored order and created a climate conducive to investment and prosperity.

In six months the fray is on. Petitions travel regularly to Washington, demanding the governor's removal. He has been pulled by one group of residents into a scheme for local development that will benefit them to the exclusion of others, and those others prove to be a resourceful group of opponents. Factions and feuds preceded the governor and will outlast him; in the meantime, though, he provides the handiest target for the discontented. With a salary limited by an economy-minded Congress and with living expenses inflated by territorial isolation, the governor's economic dilemma is soon a moral one. If the governors "starved," Earl Pomeroy has pointed out, "they showed that they were driven West by their incompetence; if they prospered, they showed they were dishonest." Under these pressures, "nearly all tried to retain business connections in the states or to invest in the territories." Territorial legislators were not unaware of the governor's financial vulnerability; it was a frequent strategy to supplement the official's salary with "increased compensation," a gesture of less than pure altruism. When one adds up the opportunities for Westerners to resist or to counterattack, the picture of appointed tyrants bullying the vulnerable, authentic Westerners appears to be a bit overdrawn. In 1862, the New Mexico legislature printed the "governor's message with a preamble referring to the 'false erroneous absurd and ill-sounding ideas therein contained.' " Victimized Westerners evidently retained a few powers of self-defense.[5]

Given little respect from their constituents, territorial governors could not hope for much more from Washington. Because authority was split between the Department of the Treasury, in charge of funds, and the Department of State and, after 1873, the Department of the Interior, it was not always clear who was in charge. No department went to much trouble to consolidate authority over the territories or to direct their operations with any guiding philosophy. Appointed officials found their supervisors reluctant to give advice; governors were often dispatched without instructions, and the Washington office was even known to refuse advice on particular matters. Even when the supervising department had a policy to pursue, its enforcement over the Western distances was hard; until the arrival of the telegraph, it was difficult to discover—much less prevent—absenteeism in officials. The standing rhetoric of the oppressed West aside, the territorial system's methods were more "ineffective" than "tyrannical."[6]

To say that the system was inefficient is not too say that it was insignificant. The territory guaranteed that a degree of dependence on the federal government would be central to every Western state's first years. This was a matter not simply of power but of its cousin, money.

In the early development of the Far West, five principal resources lay ready for exploitation: furs, farmland, timber, minerals, and federal money. Territorial experience got Westerners in the habit of asking for federal subsidies, and the habit persisted long after other elements of the Old West had vanished.

Nothing so undermines the Western claim to a tradition of independence as this matter of federal support to Western development. The two key frontier activities—the control of Indians and the distribution of land—were primarily federal responsibilities, at times involving considerable expense. Federal subsidies to transportation—to freighting companies and to railroads, to harbor improvement and to highway building—made the concept of private enterprise in transportation an ambiguous one. Even apparent inaction could in a way support development. Failing to restrain or regulate access to the public grazing lands or to the timber lands, the federal government in effect subsidized private cattle raisers and loggers with unlimited access to national resources.

Within the terrorial framework, the significance of federal money was often dramatic. Federal office provided a valued form of patronage; appropriations for public buildings offered another route to local income. Official government printing, entrusted to a local newspaper of the proper political orientation, could determine a publisher's failure or success. Territorial business involving Indians was another route to federal money. Volunteers in Indian campaigns would expect federal pay. Local Indian hostilities were a mixed blessing; forts and soldiers meant markets for local products and business for local merchants. Similarly, once conquered and dependent on rations, Indians on reservations became a market for local grain and beef.

In its early years, Dakota Territory gave the purest demonstration of this economic dependence. With the delayed development of farming and mining, Dakota settlers rapidly grasped the idea "of the federal government not only as a paternalistic provider of land and governmental organization but also as a subsidizing agency which furnished needed development funds in the form of offices, Indian and army supply orders, and post and land office positions." When Indian troubles increased, white settlement became risky, and hard times came to Dakota, "the federal government remained the only source of revenue and sustenance." In those rough times, "Washington was in essence subsidizing a government which had few citizens, no income, and a highly questionable future." Agricultural development and the mining boom of the Black Hills later relieved the pressure on federal resources, but in the meantime the precedent had been well set. It had become an "old Dakota attitude that government itself was an important paying business."[7]

Nonetheless, Dakotans also took up the standard cry of the oppressed colony. "We are so heartily disgusted with our dependent condition, with being snubbed at every turn in life, with having all our interest subjected to the whims and corrupt acts of persons in power that we feel very much as the thirteen colonies felt," a Dakota newspaper declared in 1877. As they asserted their rights to statehood, Dakota residents did not give much support to the idea that political innovation emanated from the frontier. They used the familiar states' rights arguments; their political ideas were "so much those of the older sections" that "they had not developed any indigenous ones of their own since coming to Dakota." After a close study, Howard Lamar found in the Dakota activists "a singular lack of political originality."[8]

Frederick Jackson Turner's idea that the frontier had been the source of American democracy did receive some support from pioneer rhetoric. Politically involved residents were often gifted speechmakers and petition writers, even if they lacked originality. Western settlers were so abundantly supplied with slogans and democratic formulas that putting our trust in their recorded words alone would be misleading. Only close archival research can reveal what those gifted speakers and writers were actually doing. An early event in Dakota history demonstrates the problem.

In 1857, in unorganized territory to the west of Minnesota, American citizens took part in what appeared to be a classic exercise in frontier democracy. Having moved beyond Minnesota's limits, the settlers in Sioux Falls organized their own government, elected officials, and began to petition Congress for territorial status. Acting to protect their lives and their property, they had fashioned a temporary political order to suit their unique needs. The whole exercise would surely have warmed the heart of Frederick Jackson Turner, and a number of local historians happily took the Sioux Falls "squatter government" at their word.

The risk came with a closer look, provided by Howard Lamar. Those self-reliant squatters were, it turns out, agents of a land company, financed and organized by Minnesota Democrats. Their plan was to get to Dakota early, create paper towns, organize a government, persuade Congress to ratify their legitimacy, and then enjoy the benefits of dominating a new and developing region. They were, at least, willing to work for the appearance of political legitimacy. "Electing" their first legislature, "the citizens of Sioux Falls split into parties of three or four and traveled over the countryside near the settlement. Every few miles each party would halt, take a drink of whiskey, establish a voting precinct, and then proceed to vote several times themselves by putting the names of all their relatives or friends on the ballots. After a reasonable number of fictitious voters had cast their ballots, the party would travel to the next polling place and repeat the process."[9]

The lesson of the Sioux Falls squatter government, of Dakota Territory, and of the other territories as well, was a simple one: in Western affairs, business and government were interdependent and symbiotic, and only a pathologically subtle mind could find a line dividing them. Petitioned to grant a railroad charter, the first Dakota Assembly members were cautious and reserved—until the railroad agreed to make "every member of the Assembly a partner!" True to their insight into government as a paying business, "the assemblymen had not hesitated to use their office to get in on the ground floor of what they considered a very good business deal."[10]

It does not take much exposure to Western political history to lead one to a basic fact: "conflict of interest" has not always been an issue of political sensitivity. The career of Senator William Stewart of Nevada has already provided us with a case study in overlapping loyalties in public officials—in Stewart's case—to the railroads and mining companies. Other Nevada senators of the same era could hardly criticize Stewart on this count. They were themselves officials and owners of banks and mines. Similarly, New Mexico Territory underwent years of domination by the Santa Fe Ring, a combination of lawyers, businessmen and politicians prospering from the territory's abundance of land. In Montana, politics paralleled the fortunes of copper, leaving Anaconda by 1915 in a position that "clearly dominated the Montana economy and political order."[11]

There was, of course, a difference between the sporting and energetic use of government in Dakota, and the corporate domination of Montana, between the individual initiative shown by Horace C. Wilson, territorial secretary of Idaho, who departed in 1866 with $33,550 of the territorial legislature's funds (he "seems to have been of a very selfish nature," as a contemporary put it), and the coordinated, legally sanctioned enterprises of the Santa Fe ring. But it was a difference of scale, not of kind. Companies as well as individuals followed narrow self-interest, failing to perceive "any separation between government and private enterprise." In every newly settled area, one of the first political questions concerned the location of the territorial capital or, one level below, of the county seat. These struggles came out of a full recognition on the part of the contestants that securing the seat of government also meant securing financial opportunity through a guaranteed population and a reliable market.[12]

Looking over his political history of Nevada, Gilman Ostrander summed up its message: "Actually, almost everyone knows that businessmen are out to make money and that politicians are out to gain office and that much history has been made in this nation by businessmen and politicians helping each other out." Ostrander's only error of phrasing was the suggestion that businessmen and politicians were different people; in fact, they were often the same. This interpenetration of business and government is too easily defined as "corruption." Like "speculation," "corruption" suggests that a practice, actually the product of an obvious opportunity and overlap of interests, is an anomaly or social illness. The essential project of the American West was to exploit the available resources. Since nature would not provide it all, both speculation and the entrepreneurial uses of government were human devices to supplement nature's offerings.[13]

Consider the dominant political figure of Wyoming, before and after statehood. The imagination supplies a tough and self-reliant rancher—a Cincinnatus in this case leaving his horse, not his plow, to go to the aid of his homeland. The picture is partly true. Francis Warren did invest in ranching, but also in utilities, banks, railroads, and, at first, merchandising. Like many Westerners, he pursued two interchangeable goals—"his own enrichment and the development of Wyoming." What made him a leader in the territory, governor for a time and senator after statehood? "His ability to construct a political machine dedicated to the efficient acquisition of federal subsidies," the historian Lewis Gould has explained, "set him apart from his colleagues." Wyoming "could not rely solely on its own economic resources for growth." Aridity and a short growing season limited agriculture, and cattle raising did not lead to either stable or widely distributed prosperity. Compensating for nature's shortages, Warren's pursuit of federal money—for forts, public buildings, and other improvements—met the hopes of his constituents, who "were more concerned with economic development than with social protest and as a result favored policies designed to increase their stake in society."[14]

Warren and Wyoming were beneficiaries of the Great Compromise of 1787, by which the American Constitution gave "equal representation to all states, regardless of the disparity of their populations." Proclamations of powerlessness aside, Western states had huge areas of land, few people, and two senators apiece. Given equal standing with their colleagues from more populous states, Western senators had the additional "advantage of representing relatively few major economic interests. They were therefore in a position to trade votes advantageously, in order to pass the relatively few measures which the interests they represented wanted badly." Senator Warren of Wyoming, as his biographer has put it, "left scant positive imprint on American life. He rarely looked up from his pursuit of influence for himself and riches for his state to consider the pressing questions of his time." The opportunity to take up a concern for national affairs always existed for Warren and his Western counterparts, but the workings of Western politics did not push them to it.[15]

II

Western dependence on federal resources did not end with the territories. Neither did the accepting of help—with resentment. Far from declining in the twentieth century, federal participation in the Western economy expanded. The Reclamation Act of 1902 put the national government in the center of the control and development of water, the West's key resource. President Theodore Roosevelt and Chief Forester Gifford Pinchot pressed the cause of expert management of the national forests, using federal powers to guide resource users toward a longer-range version of utility. The Taylor Grazing Act of 1934 finally centralized the control of grazing on the public domain. Beyond the Taylor Act, many New Deal measures framed to address the national problems of the Great Depression were especially rewarding for the West.

In early June 1933, Wyoming was proud of its status as "the only state or territory which had not asked for or received any federal assistance for its needy." In late June 1933, the state changed course and took its first federal relief check. Wyoming's "late start," T. A. Larson has pointed out, "proved to be no deterrent. . . . The federal government's nonrecoverable relief expenditures in Wyoming between July 1, 1933, and June 30, 1937, amounted to $330.64 per capita compared with $115.18 in the United States. Meanwhile, per capita internal revenue collected in Wyoming for the years 1934–1937 amounted to $28.94 compared with $109.43 in the United States." This was not an imbalance unique to Wyoming; Colorado "received twice as much as it sent to a government which it considered meddlesome and constitutionally threatening." The New Deal, Leonard Arrington has found, "benefited the West more than other sections of the nation. Indeed, when one lists the states in the order of the per capita expenditures of the federal economic agencies, the top fourteen states in benefits received were all in the West."

The West got "sixty percent more" on a per capita basis than the impoverished regions of the South. "Per capita expenditures of federal agencies in Montana from 1933 to 1939, for example, were $710, while they were only $143 in North Carolina."[16]

The New Deal was a good deal for the West. The Civilian Conservation Corps did much of its finest work in the West; the farm credit programs saved numerous farmers and cattlemen from bankruptcy; the Soil Conservation Service tried to keep the West from blowing away; the Farm Security Administration built camps to house the impoverished migrant workers of California. And yet many Western political leaders complained. They took advantage of programs that helped their local interests, and they spent much of their remaining time denouncing the spread of bureaucracy and the give-away quality of the New Deal. The case of the cattlemen was representative: hit by drought, the consequences of overgrazing and of dropping prices, Western cattlemen needed help. But aid "brought regulation, and regulation the cattlemen could not abide." In 1934, in a Drought Relief Service program, the federal government began buying cattle. The sellers "had to agree to any future production-control plans which might be started," and "the prices paid were not high." Still, federal money to the amount of "nearly $525 million" went "to save cattlemen from ruin and starvation," the historian John Schlebecker has written. "For this salvation, many cattlemen never forgave the government. Large numbers of them resented the help."[17]

New Deal assistance went against a number of Western values. T. A. Larson's description of Wyoming residents applied to many other Westerners: "Although they had always been dependent on various types of federal aid, they wanted as little government as possible, and preferred most of that to be in state or local hands. Professing independence, self-reliance, and dedication to free enterprise, they served as vocal, aggressive custodians of what remained of the frontier spirit." In fact, a fair amount of that "frontier spirit" lived on. Parading their independence and accepting federal money, Westerners in the 1930s kept faith with the frontier legacy.[18]

It is common to associate the American West with the future, one of independence and self-reliance. The future that was actually projected in the Western past is quite a different matter. It was in the phenomenon of dependence—on the federal government, on the changeability of nature, on outside investment—that the West pulled ahead. In the course of American history, the central government and its role in the economy grew gradually; years of nonintervention were succeeded by the growing power of the federal government in the Progressive Era, the New Deal, and Word War Two. In the West, in land policy, transportation, Indian affairs, border regulation, territorial government, and public projects, it has been possible to see the future and to see that it works—sometimes. Heavy reliance on the federal government's good graces, the example of the West suggests, does expose the two principals to substantial risk—to inefficiency and mismanagement on the part of the benefactor and to resentment and discontent on the part of the beneficiaries. To a striking degree, the lessons of the problems of the American welfare state could be read in the nation's frontier past.

III

As powerful and persistent as the fantasy that the West set Americans free from relying on the federal government was the fantasy that westward movement could set one free from the past. The West, for instance, was once a refuge for people who had trouble breathing. Sufferers from asthma, bronchitis, and even tuberculosis believed they chose a therapeutic environment when they chose the clean, dry air of the West.

Respiratory refugees particularly favored Arizona. Tucson's population jumped from 45,454 in 1950 to 330,537 in 1980, in large part an accretion of people who liked the climate—the clear air, the direct sunlight. Understandably, many of these new arrivals missed their homelands. Ill at ease with the peculiar plants and exposed soil of the desert, they naturally attempted to replicate the gardens and yards they had left behind. One popular, familiar plant was the magnificently named fruitless mulberry, the male of the species, which does not produce messy berries. What the fruit-free mulberry produces is pollen.

Re-creating a familiar landscape, Tucson immigrants had also re-created a familiar pollen count. Allergies reactivated. Coping with all the problems of Sun Belt growth, the Tucson City Council found itself debating in 1975 a resolution to ban the fruitless mulberry.[19]

Tucson citizens with allergies had taken part in a familiar Western exercise: replicating the problems they had attempted to escape. It was a twentieth-century version of the Boone paradox. Daniel Boone found civilization intolerable and escaped to the wilderness. His travels blazed trails for other pioneers to follow, and Boone found himself crowded out. His fresh start turned rapidly stale.

Of all the meanings assigned to Western independence, none had more emotional power than the prospect of becoming independent of the past. But Western Americans did what most travelers do: they took their problems with them. Cultural baggage is not, after all, something one retains or discards at will. While much of the Western replication of familiar ways was voluntary and intentional, other elements of continuity appear to have caught Westerners by surprise—as if parts of their own character were specters haunting them despite an attempt at exorcism by migration. No wonder, then, that emigrants made so much of their supposed new identity; no wonder they pressed the case of their supposed adaptations to the new environment, their earned status as real Westerners. Accenting the factor of their migration and new location, Westerners tried to hold the ghosts of their old, imported identities at bay.

The West had no magic power for dissolving the past, a fact that Americans confronted at all levels, from the personal to the national. A tragic demonstration of this came in the pre–Civil War relations of North, South, and West. The West might have seemed to be a route of escape from the struggles between the two other sections; in fact, the West brought those struggles to their most volatile peak. The process came to a focus in the life of Stephen Douglas, portrayed in a telling biography by Robert W. Johannsen.[20]

Widely remembered for his debates with Abraham Lincoln, Douglas was a congressman and then a senator from Illinois. He made his first great impact on the national scene by responding to the crisis posed by the acquisition of new Western territories in the Mexican War. The open question of slavery in the new territories had brought a congressional deadlock, which Douglas's maneuvering managed to break.

Douglas succeeded because he broke the compromise into pieces and passed these individually. Reassembled, the Compromise of 1850 gave, to the North, California as a free state and restrictions on slavery in the district of Columbia; to the South, it gave a tighter Fugitive Slave Law and the federal assumption of Texas's debts, left over from the republic. And, in a plank that was officially neutral and a concession to no one, Utah and New Mexico were organized as territories—with the right to make their own decisions before statehood on whether they would have slavery. This doctrine of "popular sovereignty," with which Douglas was particularly associated, played a political version of "hot potato," removing the inflammatory issue of slavery from Congress and tossing it to the territories; they would make a decision on slavery before statehood, but Congress gave no indication of just when, or by what mechanism, that decision would be made.

Senator Douglas was so delighted with the peace he thought he had achieved in the Compromise of 1850 that he declared a determination "never to make another speech on the slavery question." Douglas, like many Americans, cared more about making a living than about slavery. And he, like many other Americans, had some of his economic hopes attached to the project of a railroad to the Pacific.[21]

Douglas loved the American West and the possibilities for economic expansion and profit it presented. In various set speeches given throughout his career, he compared America to a young and growing giant. "I tell you," he would say,

increase, and multiply, and expand, is the law of this nation's existence. You cannot limit this great Republic by mere boundary lines, saying, "Thus far shalt thou go, and no further." Any one of you might as well say to a son twelve years old that he is big enough, and must not grow any larger, and in order to prevent his growth put a hoop around him to keep him to his present size. What would be the result? Either the hoop must burst and be rent asunder, or the child must die. So it would be with this great nation.[22]

It no doubt added to the effectiveness of this speech that Douglas's own appearance complemented the metaphor. He was very short—and did not grow longitudinally over time—but he did, through the 1850s, encapsulate the drama of national expansion through the middle. No one put a hoop around Stephen Douglas; no one said, "Thus far and no further," and, judging from the photographs, a hardworking tailor evidently performed for Douglas's waistlines the same function Douglas performed for the nation—freeing it of the constrictions and boundaries of earlier compromises.

A good Illinois man, Douglas wanted Chicago to enjoy the prosperity of becoming the Eastern terminus of the Western railroad. To support this patriotic project, Douglas had invested in Chicago real estate. But the Pacific railroad and the related increases in Chicago real estate had to face their first obstacle in the territory immediately west of Missouri and Iowa, the area known as Permanent Indian Territory. In 1830, with the Indian Removal Act, the federal government had relocated Eastern tribes in the areas that would become Kansas, Nebraska, and Oklahoma, and the proper promises were made that all this was a permanent arrangement. Thus, in the early 1850s, as Pacific railroad fantasies proliferated, it looked as if the United States might have hemmed itself in.

Douglas began introducing bills to organize Nebraska Territory. By the conventional pattern of territorial organization, there would be an accumulation of white settlers in a new region; they would call Congress's attention to themselves; and then they would receive territorial status. Douglas's efforts thus were, from the beginning, peculiar, because there were hardly any white people in what would become Kansas and Nebraska, and the ones who were there—a few missionaries, traders, and advance squatters—were not much concerned with their official status.

Douglas wanted the new territory in order to do away with the lingering fiction of a permanent Indian territory. "The idea of arresting our progress in that direction," he said, "has become

so ludicrous that we are amazed, that wise and patriotic states-
men ever cherished the thought. . . . How are we to develop,
cherish and protect our immense interests and possessions on
the Pacific, with a vast wilderness fifteen hundred miles in breadth,
filled with hostile savages, and cutting off all direct communication. The Indian barrier must be removed."[23]

To get Nebraska and a railroad route, Douglas had to con-
ciliate the South. That turned out to mean creating two territories, so that one territory could be a free state and one a slave
state. Nonetheless, the Kansas-Nebraska Act of 1854 left that
decision, by the doctrine of popular sovereignty, to the settlers
themselves.

Douglas thought in 1854 that he had arranged for peace and
prosperity again. Instead, he became a widely hated man as the
struggle over Kansas became a national nightmare. Douglas was
vilified so often, he said, that he "could travel from Boston to
Chicago by the light of [his] own effigy." Without realizing it,
Douglas had selected the best possible stage to make national
melodrama out of the slavery controversy, as Northerners and
Southerners contested—both in Congress and on the site—for
control of Kansas. Newspapers made the most of the violent
events, in which the issue of slavery and the acquisition of land
together created the worst social tinder.[24]

The frontier, far from being a refuge from the problems of
"civilization," became the symbolic source of disunion. In Kansas, Americans made the prewar transition to the dehumaniza-
tion of opponents, to the preparation to wage a justified war
against savages and barbarians, and the creation of a climate where
verbal violence could suddenly turn into physical violence.

Douglas had just wanted peace and a railroad and a decent
return on his real estate investments. He thought he had found
a way to maximize the profits of American expansion and to
minimize, or even dispose of, the costs.

On June 3, 1861, only forty-eight years old and deeply in
debt, Douglas died of causes that are hard to figure out from the
terms of nineteenth-century medicine: "rheumatism 'of a typhoid
character,' " an "ulcerated sore throat," and " 'torpor of the liver.' "
Just before his death, Kansas was finally admitted to statehood,

in one of those congressional acts that had to await the removal of Southern opposition—through secession. Douglas's very enthusiasm for the future of the Union had led to its collapse.[25]

IV

A troubling decade of history taught Douglas the cruel but common lesson of Western history: postponements and evasions catch up with people. An apparently successful evasion, more often than not, turns out to be a greater obligation contracted to the future. Douglas's personal act of evasion reenacted in miniature a national attempt at postponement. Planning the future of the Republic, Thomas Jefferson had hoped that America could avoid the problems of mature or declining societies by developing through space, not through time. Westward expansion would keep Americans in possession of property, agrarian, independent, and responsible. To maintain the vision, Jefferson looked away from crucial aspects of expansion. The dreams of the Jeffersonians aside, Drew McCoy has written, "the system of commercial agriculture that expanded westward across space entailed an exploitative cast of mind that could not be eradicated—a cast of mind well revealed in the rampant land speculation and profiteering of nonslaveholding Americans in the West, but undoubtedly best exemplified in the most vicious form imaginable of exploiting both land and people, the institution of slavery."[26] The price of the Jeffersonian evasion would finally have to be paid, and Douglas, going about his business in the happy faith that personal improvement and national improvement ran on parallel tracks, found himself presented with the bill.

The Civil War posed no permanent obstacle to fantasies of Western independence and fresh starts. Into our own time, they have continued to appeal to Westerners at all positions on the political spectrum. Ernest Callenbach's popular utopian novel, published in 1975, sketched life in Ecotopia. Innovative in detail, *Ecotopia* was nothing if not traditional in its basic motif: the West as a place secure from the corruptions and decadence of the East. The familiar faith in boundaries persisted; Callenbach had his Ecotopians fight a war of independence and then maintain a policed border, protecting them from the moral, economic, and ecological contagions emanating from the East. The Ecotopians, and Callenbach, were well advised to select the well-watered Pacific Northwest for their nation; drawing their borders carefully, they eliminated the troubling problem of Western aridity. Feminists ruled Ecotopia; patriarchy and all its futile dreams of mastery and conquest, the narrator discovered to his initial alarm, had been put in their place—and that place was outside Ecotopia's well-policed borders. Economic freedom and fulfillment had risen to fill their place. In sensuality and personal development, Ecotopians had at last found an unending frontier. With the contagions of the East suppressed, Ecotopians could make the West what it was supposed to be in centuries of imaginings: a place where nature would restore Euro-Americans to their senses.[27]

Other strains of Western utopianism in the 1960s and 1970s showed a similar debt to the past. In college in 1971, in a class in American history, we were treated to guest speakers from a New Mexico alternative community. For half an hour, our two visitors bragged to us of their freedom from the corruptions of modern industrial society. While the two men spoke, we couldn't help noticing that their women stayed on the side with the children. In the classic Western fashion, the commune had replicated a few old traditions. The community, the speakers told us, had declared its independence from a sick society and now celebrated its self-sufficiency. A member of the audience, interested in their farming methods, asked how they had achieved their self-sufficiency in food. They were, it turned out, a little short of the goal. And what did they get by with in the meantime? Food stamps.

The hippies from the New Mexico commune were secure participants in Western tradition: living in a rugged environment, putting on magnificent verbal displays on the subject of fresh starts and autonomy, and still solidly connected to the system they had supposedly left behind. Independent living is hard work, after all; one needs all the help one can get.

There is nothing wrong with human interdependence; it is, among other things, a fact of life. A recognition that one is not the sole captain of one's fate is hardly an occasion for surprise. Especially in the American West, where the federal government, outside capital, and the market have always been powerful factors of change, the limits on personal autonomy do not seem like news. And yet humans have a well-established capacity to meet facts of life with disbelief. In a region where human interdependence has been self-evident, Westerners have woven a net of denial. That net, it is clear in our times, can entrap as well as support.

Four

Uncertain Enterprises

WHEN ADAM LIVED IN EDEN, he lived off the bounty of nature. After he sinned, his conditions of employment took a turn for the worse: he had to earn his bread by the sweat of his brow. If the fall from Eden had followed the patterns of Western American history, Adam would have carried a further burden: he would have sold the crops he produced at an unpredictable, often disappointing price—or he would have worked for wages.

Only a few Americans, utterly lost in myth and symbol, could have imagined that life in the West was labor free. Certainly, all opportunity involved work, but the Western ideal set limits to that labor. Frontier opportunity was supposed to permit a kind of labor by which one simply gathered what nature produced. The laborer was to be self-employed; and the status of laborer was to be temporary, left behind when the profits made escape possible.

The ideal only hinted at the more important point. To be moved from natural resource to commodity to profit, the West's holdings clearly had to be transformed by an investment of capital and labor. This was the elemental fact obscured by the myths and romances: in its essence, Western expansion was a lot of work.

The West of work: coal miner's residence, Colorado. *Courtesy Colorado Historical Society*

While much of that work was done by individuals laboring on their own, a great deal was done for wages. And when people worked for their wages and for another person's profits, myriad questions opened up, questions not put to rest by any end to the frontier. What was a fair profit? What was a just distribution of rewards? Why was it that the man who worked the hardest—the man who dug the earth, shoveled the rock, sorted the ore—often earned the least? And how much did a man give up—in dignity, in autonomy, in freedom—when his livelihood depended on wages, when other people's decisions controlled his labor?

Political independence was long in coming to Westerners, but economic independence was even more elusive. Success in Western businesses and industries depended on variables subject to little human control. Economic fortunes rose and fell with variations in nature's cooperation, with changes in the capital avail-

able to run the business, with the accessibility of markets, with
the reliability of prices, and with the supply of labor. No Western industry illustrates this multiple dependence more clearly
than mining.

Moreover, no industry had a greater impact on Western history than did mining. When it came to expansion, farmers moved
fast—but miners moved faster. Mining took a comparatively
gradual process and accelerated it, drawing thousands to California and then scattering miners, merchants, camps, towns,
mines, mills, smelters, trails, and roads throughout the interior
West. Short-term and transitory, catapulted from boom to bust,
mining nonetheless had important long-range effects on the West.
Mining placed settlements of white people where none had been
before. It provoked major conflicts with Indians. It called territories and states into being and forced them to an early maturity.
It drew merchandising and farming in its wake. As it changed
rapidly from individual enterprise to a consolidated, industrial-

The West of play: tourists in snow cut on Rollins Pass, Colorado. *Photo by
L. C. McClure, courtesy Denver Public Library, Western History Department*

ized business, mining threw the West into the forefront of indus-
trialized life. Perhaps most important, mining set a mood that
has never disappeared from the West: the attitude of extractive
industry—get in, get rich, get out.

The geographer Wilbur Zelinsky has explained "the Doctrine of First Effective Settlement": "Whenever an empty territory undergoes settlement, or an earlier population is dislodged
by invaders, the specific characteristics of the first group able to
effect a viable, self-perpetuating society are of crucial significance for the later social and cultural geography of the area."[1]
For mining, the doctrine requires a bit of modification. That
unstable industry was by many standards something other than
"effective settlement," but it nonetheless had a lasting effect on
regional character. Rather than "settling" the region, mining
rushes picked up the American West and gave it a good shaking—and the vibrations have not stopped yet.

Mining rushes shook up not only the region but also the participants themselves. As a way to earn a living, mining rarely
made men into secure captains of their destinies. Even in the
placer phase, when surface gold could be gathered by individual
effort, circumstances buffeted the miners. Consider location.
Minerals appeared in places not chosen for convenience. Suc-
cumbing to the lure of fortune, the prospective miner first faced
the trying and unsettling business of getting to the site.

In 1849, Bernard Reid thought he had found an easy answer
to the question of how to get from St. Louis to the gold in California. A restless young man of twenty-six, uncertain of his career,
unwilling to settle down, Reid responded warmly to the appeal
of the gold rush. But was he to buy a wagon and a team of draft
animals, load the wagon with food and supplies, put his faith in
a guidebook, join a company of fellow travelers, negotiate
mutually agreeable rules, and then drive the wagon twenty miles
a day—through rain, mud, and dust, keeping an anxious eye out
for water and grass needed to keep the animals alive and pulling—for at least three months or more of unrelenting exertion?

Reid thought he had found the alternative. California gold
spawned entrepreneurship of all varieties, and one team of businessmen seized on transportation. The founders of the Pioneer

Line offered a speedy wagon service to California. Passengers would pay $200, and the company would assume responsibility for providing wagons and carriages, driving and caring for the animals, carrying the passengers and their luggage, and serving food for a journey they estimated to be, as Mary McDougall Gordon has put it, "a mind-boggling 55 to 60 days." One rumor even suggested the likelihood of valet service. At the price of $200, it seemed to Reid and his fellows, one could buy one's way out of a great deal of trouble.[2]

Expectations, as usual, met a rough reality. The company had greatly underestimated the difficulty of the trip. Within days, it was clear that the wagons were badly overloaded. The "passengers," it soon turned out, would have to walk. Several clients held out, sticking to the letter of the contract and insisting on their right to ride. Until the group voted to require walking, Reid noted in his journal, "many of them had persisted in riding, though the mules could scarcely drag their loads." The patrons of the Pioneer Line repeatedly had to face the consequences of overloading, discarding luggage to make the loads manageable. Floundering on every count, the managers of the Pioneer Line could do nothing to fend off the diseases of the overland trail. At the start of the trip, several members of the party died from cholera; at the end, men were dying from scurvy, brought on by a terrifying lack of food. Like many overland diaries, Reid's became a litany of deaths recorded and of graves glimpsed along the way. No one could feel immune to these illnesses; the suffering of others could clearly become one's own. Stricken by scurvy, Reid's fellow traveler Niles Searls considered his prospects: "Judging from the effects of scurvy on others, I am good for about three weeks—and then—and then— . . . ." A day later, one man died but Searls himself began to improve: "Hutton is dead. Others are worse. I am better."[3]

Arrived in California, through with his journey ("a long dreadful dream"), Bernard Reid was not through with hardship. He inspected the gold diggings and found the prospects mixed: "Some of the miners are making good wages—others barely making expenses. All seems a lottery." "Felt lonesome," he wrote. "Hard to realize my present condition." He traveled on to San

Francisco, where he fell seriously ill. Here the ties formed in the rough journey proved their worth. Fellow passengers took care of him, though he still had occasion to remark, "It is a hard thing to be sick in this country." Recovered, he tried prospecting in the mines—and ended up in debt to the partner who financed his expedition. After a few more failed efforts, Reid could remark, "Oh! how bitterly do many curse the day they left home, and swear vengeance upon the whole tribe of editors who deceived them!" With their "high hopes" wrecked, Reid said, California miners were "in the condition of convicts condemned to exile and hard labor."[4]

Back in San Francisco, Reid took any job he could find, shoveling sand or working "as a 'roller boy' in a newspaper office." At last, Reid found his opportunity in "teaching mathematics, English, and Spanish" at the newly founded Catholic university, Santa Clara College. He paid off his mining debts and then set himself to saving for the passage home. He had, it turned out, paid heavily to go to California, in order to work to earn the money to leave California. In 1852, he sailed for the Eastern United States.[5]

Reid's frustration with California mining was by no means exceptional. Having endured the hardship and expense of two thousand miles of travel, overland travelers straggled off the trail into California in the fall, usually too late too dig or pan gold for another seven months. To have traveled so far only to kill time, waiting for the end of winter, was a great frustration. Even in the proper season, miners could spend weeks building a flume or ditch to redirect a stream, then watch their work dissolve in an unexpected flood. Even when things went well, placer mining was hard and wearing work that entailed standing in cold water and repeated stooping and bending. It was labor that most of the ambitious miners would never have chosen as wage work. The conditions were particularly frustrating as crowds made it difficult to find unclaimed locations. And illness persisted after the overland trail; an irregular diet made many susceptible to disease and even death. Disease was certainly the deathblow to the romance and glory of California mining: "diarrhea," reported a doctor in Sacramento, "was so general during the fall and winter months and degenerated so frequently into chronic and fatal malady that it has been popularly regarded as the disease of California. . . ."[6] One moment's empathy with a dysentery-plagued forty-niner, far from home and unsure of his recovery, counteracts any envy for thrilling days of adventure in the goldfields.

Perhaps, one might think, people then were different—psychologically tougher, anesthetized against frustration and sorrow, calloused against illness and death. The best corrective for that notion is J. S. Holliday's wonderful edition of William Swain's gold rush diary and letters. As a young man of twenty-seven, Swain left his wife, infant daughter, and aged mother behind on a farm in upstate New York, all in the care of his trusted brother George. Swept away by the stories of California gold, William Swain went as the family's agent, expecting to return with a minimum of $10,000 as a secure base for the family's fortunes.

Giving the lie to notions of untrammeled Western freedom, Swain's family sent him off with a package of restraints and instructions: stay pure; do not fall prey to strange vices, like drink, gambling, or others even less mentionable; and read the Bible regularly, especially the preselected appropriate verses. Swain and his hometown travelers followed orders. They spent their first Sabbath evening "debating upon the moral binding force of conscience and in reading the Bible." Months later in California, Swain was still writing his brother, "I thank Heaven that *we* had parents who taught us to stand upon *principle* . . . [and] to rely upon ourselves and choose our own course of conduct irrespective of the influence and opinions of others. . . . I shall read the passages in the Bible you have pointed out with great pleasure."[7]

Swain stayed on track, and yet his hard work and dedication went unrewarded. He tried mining; he and his partners selected a site and then took up the exhausting work of river mining, removing the river from its bed with flumes and ditches. He stayed away from formal gaming tables, but river mining was essentially gambling. Only after all the work was done could Swain and his fellows find out whether their bet had been worthwhile. "[It] is a fact," Swain soon learned, "that no energy or industry can secure certain success in the business of mining; and it may perhaps be my lot after a summer of hardship and exposure to be but little better off than I am now."[8]

That did indeed prove to be his lot. Swain then had to struggle with the decision: After all the work and trouble of getting to California, could he just give up? Would he be leaving too soon? If he stayed and tried a little longer, would the rewards finally come? By the fall of 1850, Swain concluded he had gambled enough. With money sent by his brother, he bought his ship's passage home.

Swain's letters, both the ones he wrote to his family and the ones they wrote to him, make a point often lost in Western history. These were psychologically complex people, not two-dimensional "noble pioneers." Swain's wife, Sabrina, used techniques of matrimonial communication that seem strikingly modern. "O William," she wrote, "I wish you had been content to stay at home, for there is no real home for me without you." She told him of their daughter Eliza's health: "While I am writing to one she has already forgotten," Eliza "is better but still very unwell." "As to my own health," Sabrina went on,

it is no better. . . . Not only my back, but my stomach troubles me very much; also I have a great deal of pain in my head, particularly on the top. . . . The fact is, William, I feel bad every way, not only poor health but low spirits which I cannot get rid of. I cannot be reconciled to my lot. If I had known that I could not be more reconciled than I am, I should have tried hard to have kept you at home. My feelings are such that I cannot describe them, and more than that, I try to conceal them as much as I can. I am quite confident that it wears on me.

The catalog of ills completed, Sabrina twisted the knife: "But let my feelings be what they will, I hope it will not trouble you."[9]

Most wearing on both sides was the delay in communication. Swain's family went without news of him for seven months and did not even know if he had survived the trip. Swain himself endured "almost a year" without news from home. His mother had been in poor health when he left, and the consequences of distance and delay became clear in his letters. "Give my love to Mother," he had to write, "if she is yet living. . . ." The uncertainty worked from the other direction as well. "It is a most affecting thought to me and one that strikes me very forcibly, too," Sabrina wrote William, "that while I am writing these lines to you, your body may be moldering back to its mother's dust from whence it came."[10]

"I am sure you will realize our anxiety to hear from you," Sabrina wrote. "The time during which we have had no correspondence has been a vexatious and tedious one!" William wrote, "—and one of anxiety to us all." One might have thought that the word "anxiety" came into its own in our stress-ridden, post-Freudian times, but the word is omnipresent in the Swain letters. Fueled by the uncertain mails, anxiety could circle back around on itself: "I have felt the greatest anxiety," William wrote to George, "to get a letter stating that you have got my letters!" "My anxieties for you are beyond description"; "I never dreamed that I could feel such anxiety"; "we are thus left to live on anxiety"; "at times my anxiety so gets the mastery that I can hardly control myself"; "you have no idea of the anxiety we feel"—in that steady refrain, the lives of the Swains and others long dead regain immediacy, and the psychological reality of the California "adventure" becomes clear.[11]

Reporting the discovery of gold in 1848, the California military governor had given the quintessential good news of mining. "No capital is required to obtain this gold," he said, "as the laboring man wants nothing but his pick and shovel and tin pan with which to dig and wash the gravel." However long it might last, the first phase, in which the resource was abundant and theoretically accessible to all, yielded to a second phase, in which access to the resource required capital, technology, and coordinated effort. In California, hydraulic mining and underground quartz mining soon replaced the first, egalitarian "placer gold" phase. Once past that first phase, the expenses of mining could go wild, giving rise to the proposition "It takes a mine to run a mine." Underground mining meant shafts, tunnels, tracks, carts, hoists, blasting equipment, and paid labor. Minerals encased in or bonded to rock then had to be removed by expensive crushing and refining techniques. Even in the earliest phases, mining required some expertise; rewards fell to those who knew enough to choose good claims and to develop them appropriately. As mining developed, expertise became more and more vital to success, and

Hydraulic miners transforming a mountain landscape. *Courtesy Denver Public Library, Western History Department*

mining engineers with special training began to challenge the dominance of experienced amateurs.[12]

Most significantly, the growing complexity of mining left the individual small operator rapidly outmoded. Power shifted to companies and corporations with large labor forces. The financial focus of ambition for most miners who stayed in the West shifted from windfalls to wages.

All this happened so rapidly that there was a lag in perception. As reality moved on, the old image blazed still, an image of the mineral West as a free-for-all, an open season on natural resources. Well into the 1880s, for instance, the term "miner" included all levels of the industrial hierarchy. Everyone called himself a miner—prospectors, vestigial placer miners, partners working small claims, mine foremen and managers, small capitalists, bonanza kings, *and* mine laborers. The universal adoption of the title marked the delayed recognition of the economic stratification built into large-scale mining, but the recognition could not be avoided forever.

Beginning in 1859, the silver and gold of the Comstock Lode, in Nevada, inspired a short, classically egalitarian mineral rush. By the mid-1860s, underground mining had reoriented the Comstock economy to large companies, absentee owned, sometimes verging on monopoly. Workers in these large Nevada mines could have had few illusions about their place in the hierarchy or their status as independent, autonomous fortune hunters. Each shift began with the workers assembled for inspection, which one newspaper described as follows:

The transition to underground mining: miners in Colorado. *Courtesy Colorado Historical Society*

The operatives . . . were collected in a large room connected with the engine-room, waiting for the roll-call, which took place at 5 o'clock, each man answering to his name as the same was called by the time-keeper, and immediately after starting to his place—and as the last name was called, those that had been at work passed out, each one giving his name as he passed, which was checked by the time-keeper. By this means no mistake is made, and punctuality is secured which otherwise could not be done.

This version of life in the Wild West did not strike the imagination of the time or appeal later to the novelists or moviemakers; the scene made it too clear that the West was hardly a refuge from industrialism.[13]

In the early years of Western industrial mining, workers like those in Nevada did organize unions and workingmen's associations, but these cooperative groups served most often as mutual aid societies. Rather than seek power through strikes, the early unions tried to compensate for an inappropriate legal code, one that usually held mine injuries and accidents to be the responsibility of the worker.

American law was not well prepared for the questions raised by industrial conditions in any form, but it was particularly unprepared for mining, a point brought out in recent books by Mark Wyman, Richard Lingenfelter, and Ronald Brown. Mining was peculiar in the very nature of the workplace; it was itself always changing, as new tunnels were blasted out and the walls of existing tunnels came under steady attack. Given the unpredictability and uncertainty intrinsic to the place itself, the question of accident liability would always be complicated, even with appropriate laws. As it was, the early premises of a rudimentary legal system drew attention away from the workplace and the company and toward individual responsibility.

If an injured miner in the late nineteenth century decided to present his grievances by lawsuit, he faced a set of preliminary, situational obstacles. The aggrieved miner had first to reckon with high legal costs, with his own ignorance of court procedures, with his fear of losing his job, and with similar fears on the part of supporting witnesses. He also had to anticipate a long waiting period for getting the case to trial and then through appeals.

If the injured miner faced up to these obstacles and went ahead with the suit, he encountered three main legal obstacles— three variations on the reverence for individual responsibility. Common law gave judges and juries in industrial liability cases three ways of clearing companies of responsibility. First, the "fellow servant" tenet held that an accident caused by a fellow worker's negligence or error was not the company's responsibility. For several decades, the courts would take the job foreman to be in the category of a fellow servant; the company could escape liability even when the worker was following a direct order from his supervisor. Second, the tenet of "contributory negligence" covered many other situations, in which the slightest contribution of the worker to his own injury cleared the company. For any situation not covered by the first two tenets, the third— "assumed risk"—could generally apply. By this principle, the miner voluntarily entered what everyone knew to be a risky occupation. In going underground, in riding the cage two thousand feet or more down into the shaft, in working with dynamite, the worker knew what he was getting into; only in very exceptional situations could he later claim to be a victim of unanticipated risks. With these three concepts, and with the "nature of the workplace" argument to suggest that, since the mine was a constantly changing workplace, companies could not be expected to maintain perfect safety conditions, one begins to understand the miner's sense of helplessness.[14]

Even the best mines were poorly ventilated and seldom contained any provision for sanitation. They often smelled of human excrement and discarded food. Miners in some mines worked in temperatures exceeding 120 degrees Fahrenheit, only to ascend the shaft and enter a bitter winter. Technological improvements were a mixed blessing; the air drill, for instance, released workers from the hand labor of hammer drilling but created much more lung-clogging dust. The inhalation of rock particles abraded lung tissue and left a multitude of minuscule scars, bringing on the widespread problem of silicosis. Along with long-term health risks, more dramatic opportunities for injuries came with every descent into and ascent out of the mines, as workers trusted their lives to the cables, hoisting engines, and platform of the cage and to the responsibility of the hoisting engineers. The cages were often just platforms without sides, and every year saw a share of accidents like this one in 1889, described by the historian Mark Wyman: "A crew in the St. Lawrence Mine in Butte was riding up at the end of a shift when one miner put out his shoe to shove his dinner bucket back from the edge. His foot was caught between the rising cage and the shaft and was suddenly drawn and ground through the narrow opening. Although his fellow workers held him on the platform, his leg was pulled from its socket and he died soon afterwards."[15]

Dizziness was a frequent cause of cage injury and death. Having worked long hours in the hot and fetid lower areas, breathing only bad air, workers would lose their balance and fall from the platform or against the shaft wall. Sometimes equipment problems or the incompetence of a hoisting engineer would cause a mass accident, dropping ten people at a time to the bottom of the shaft. There were cave-ins and rockfalls; many companies admitted to economizing on timbering to support the mine walls.

Dynamiting accidents played a part, primarily in premature or delayed explosions. One shift would plant charges, and then, as the next shift came on duty, the departing foreman would fail to inform the new team of the location of the undischarged blasts waiting below. A man named Joseph Adams in Montana in 1900 had exactly that experience. He drilled his way into an undisclosed dynamite charge set by the preceding shift. The explosion "blinded Adam's left eye and damaged his right eye, fractured his jaw, knocked out most of his teeth," blew off his left hand, and crippled his right hand. This was not, the courts decided, the company's fault. The mining workplace was always changing. One could not expect complete safety. Joseph Adams died before the final decision on his case, but his survivors received no compensation.[16]

In 1884, in Montana, William Kelley lost both his eyes and one ear in a similar explosion, and the Montana supreme court announced the usual decision: "Notwithstanding the progress and advancement in the art of mining, it yet remains a hazardous and dangerous occupation, which, in spite of the many obligations of the owner of a mine to the employees, embraces other risks which the servant assumes as incident to the calling." Kelley's injury, then, was "the result of an unforeseen and unavoidable accident incident to the risk of mining" and entitled him to no compensation.[17]

The "assumed risk" argument rested on the idea that the miner could refuse dangerous assignments, something an utterly job-dependent worker was unlikely to do. The legal theorists also assumed, as one contemporary put it, that the worker met almost superhuman standards for alertness. The worker presumed by the law "never relaxes his vigilance under the influence of monotony, fatigue, or habituation to danger, never permits his attention to be diverted, even for a moment, from the perils which surround him, never forgets a hazardous condition that he has once observed, and never ceases to be on the alert for new sources of danger." Conjuring up this ideal worker and then holding real-life workers to that standard, the courts embraced the notion of individual responsibility and, in the process, set up a perfect climate for corporate irresponsibility. The lag in perception was at work here: the old times of individual opportunity still set basic attitudes, and the new times of corporate centralization of power still waited for recognition.[18]

In the nineteenth century, those miners who tried to work within the legislative system had little success. Most laws to improve safety conditions were dismissed as "class legislation," resisted on the grounds that it was inappropriate to pass laws favoring the interests of one class over another. Of course, nearly all the laws covering mining could fairly be labeled "class legislation," favoring the property-owning class over the laboring class. This proposition, visible in hindsight, was not on the minds of the mineowners of the time.

II

If so many in the game of mining lost, or at best held even, who won? Despite their common membership in the property-owning class, the winning mineowners came in a variety of forms. Some had been lucky enough to rise from the ranks of prospectors. Many were former merchants whose stores gave them the capital to invest in mining. Some were gifted at litigation, parlaying their skills as "courtroom miners" into power and fortune. And then, as the years passed, many owners were Easterners, men who added Western minerals to their expanding industrial empires. Local residents or Easterners, rising from the ranks or investing from outside, mineowners moved power around as emphatically as their mines rearranged the earth.

The configurations of power in Butte, Montana, showed the process at its starkest, as the historian Michael Malone has demonstrated in a recent book. A gold rush hit the region in 1864. The happy placer phase had a fevered heyday and a rapid decline. After 1870, the minerals came locked in difficult underground quartz veins. Montanans knew that the earth at Butte "held some combination of precious and base metals; but they had no idea how to work them." The first round of pioneers had been stymied; the mines had to wait for the second round—"shrewd merchant-financiers who moved in during the hard times, bought [the mines] up cheaply, and had the capital and the ability to develop them." At Butte, these financiers would also direct mining away from the precious metals and toward copper, for which the rising business of electricity had created a new need.[19]

Butte had one of each type of the mining capitalist. Marcus Daly represented the self-made man, risen from the ranks. An Irish native of humble origins and little education, Daly came to the United States, by himself, at age fifteen. He moved from New York to California and then on to the Comstock Lode in Nevada, where he became a foreman and a person of considerable mining expertise. Sequential moves—mining was nothing if not a mobile profession—through Nevada and into Utah finally landed him in Butte in 1876. Working initially as the agent for a group of Utah capitalists, Daly took over a silver mine and helped to set off Butte's second boom. With a new set of partners, including George Hearst, Daly in 1880 acquired the Anaconda mine outside Butte. This placed him at the forefront in the production of copper rather than silver. With the Anaconda mine as his base, Daly oversaw the construction of an entire industrial complex: mines, a railroad, a smelter, and a town.

Meanwhile, representing a second type of mining entrepreneur, the merchant with little direct experience with mining, William Andrews Clark had equally humble beginnings. The child of small farmers in Pennsylvania, Clark moved with his family to Iowa and then chose to participate in the Colorado gold rush rather than in the Civil War. In the uncertain early days of Montana mining, "Clark made huge profits by buying up large stocks of goods and freighting them to the right places at the right times." He secured the local mail contract, built a store in Helena, bought gold dust, made loans, and took up banking. Then, in the early 1870s, Clark turned to Butte, where he found that hard times had reduced the price of many claims. Clark took the opportunity. As his investments multiplied, Clark became a model of the nineteenth-century "robber baron." Not everyone found this charming. "[H]is heart is frozen," one Clark watcher wrote, "and his instincts are those of the fox: there is craft in his stereo-typed smile and icicles in his handshake. He is about as magnetic as last year's bird's nest."[20]

Augustus Heinze provided a third variation on the theme, becoming a masterful courtroom miner. His origins were far from humble; his father, a German immigrant, made "a modest fortune as a New York-based importer." Heinze was much better educated and far younger than Clark and Daly. In 1889, not quite twenty years old, he came to Butte and immediately began work as a mining engineer. He soon concluded that his greatest opportunity lay in the refining end of the business. By 1894, Heinze and his family money had produced a pace-setting smelter in Butte. A hearty man, legendary for his capacity to fraternize both in Butte saloons and in New York salons, Heinze would become more and more a courtroom miner, gifted at finding legal cases ripe for profit.[21]

Finally there was Henry Rogers, the Eastern capitalist. Having risen through the ranks of Standard Oil, Rogers was a principal in the formation of the Amalgamated Copper Company in 1899, later known as Anaconda, an enterprise launched toward the never quite realized goal of becoming the copper trust just as Standard Oil was the oil trust. Rogers was himself a type of the "robber baron," "a brutal, tooth-and-claw infighter" in business, who meanwhile "lavished millions on churches and public buildings for his hometown, Fairhaven, Massachusetts"—and not for Butte.[22]

Through three decades, like dinosaurs, mastodons, and

sabertooth tigers squaring off for a fight, these copper kings confronted each other in Butte. Massive in the scale of their influence and power, they were not equally grand in motive or method. On that count, the contest more nearly resembled a confrontation of alley cats.

William Clark wanted badly to be a senator. With an equal passion, Marcus Daly wanted to keep Clark from becoming one. For a time, Montana politics became the battleground for those conflicting ambitions. Having found money to be an effective instrument in business, Clark expected it to work as well in politics. In 1898, he tried to buy the number of state legislators needed to elect him senator, while Daly endeavored to buy them back. Elected in 1899, Clark underwent the humiliation of a Senate refusal to seat him. The bribery and corruption Clark had used tainted not only his own name but also that of Montana. In his own defense, Clark reportedly said, "I never bought a man who wasn't for sale."[23]

Meanwhile, Henry Rogers began laying his plans for a copper empire, and Marcus Daly sold his Anaconda interests to Amalgamated Copper. As the Amalgamated expanded, Augustus Heinze went to work as a "court-house miner," employing as many as thirty-seven lawyers. The apex law, awarding ownership of a particular vein to the party owning its nearest approach to the surface, proved particularly fruitful to Heinze. In one case, securing the rights to two slivers of unclaimed land nestled in the midst of Amalgamated holdings, Heinze sued for the whole. With a barrage of similar claims, and with the support of local judges known to be in his pocket, "Heinze-inspired litigation threatened hopelessly to ensnarl the giant Amalgamated Copper Company." With creative use of the lawsuit, Lilliputians could still tie up Gulliver.[24]

In 1900, Clark's senatorial ambitions rose again, and a curious set of alliances resulted. In the campaign, Clark wanted a legislature receptive to his senatorial plans, Heinze wanted to keep control of the locally elected judges, and those disparate aims induced them to work together. Playing on their status as outsiders from the Amalgamated trust, Clark and Heinze mined a rich vein of local sentiment, casting themselves as defenders of

Montana's frail integrity against rapacious outsiders. The Amalgamated and its officers were tyrants, colonizers, and foreigners, tainted by their association with the most ruthless trust of all, Standard Oil.

A gifted entertainer, Heinze brought in vaudeville shows, clowns, and cartoonists to fight the trust and win the voters. One cartoonist offered a glimpse of the Amalgamated "as a rapacious gorilla stalking up a mountainside carrying the fainted maiden Montana in its arms"—and this long before Fay Wray and King Kong met at the Empire State Building. Both sides engaged in the spirited acquisition of newspapers, which they put "into position much like opposing armies would mount artillery." Heinze himself took to the stump, explaining to Montana's workers their common cause: "My fight against the Standard Oil is your fight. In this glorious battle to save the State from the minions of the Rockefellers and the piracy of Standard Oil you and I are partners. . . . If you stand by me I shall stand by you." To make the point more immediate, Heinze and Clark both granted their workers "the eight-hour day while maintaining the prevailing $3.50 daily wage." By casting the East as the headquarters of corporate villainy, Heinze and Clark temporarily succeeded in obscuring the class differences that divided Montanans. In the election of 1900, Clark and Heinze won. Celebrating, Heinze said the victory "had given the death-blow to tyranny and despotism, to coercion and blackmail."[25]

Not long after victory, however, the actions of the defenders of Montana conveyed a different message. Fearful of challenging the Amalgamated people nationally, and especially fearful that they might cause the Senate to question his credentials again, Senator Clark made an early peace with his much-denounced enemies. Some years later, he went further and sold the Amalgamated his own holdings. Heinze himself for a time kept up his legal and political harassment of the company. Then secret negotiations began, and in 1906 Heinze sold his properties to a holding company in the control of the amalgamated. The Amalgamated "people," Heinze had instructed Montanans, "are my enemies, fierce, bitter, implacable; but they are your enemies, too. If they crush me today, they will crush you tomorrow." All of Heinze's doings, Michael Malone has suggested, may well have had the "primary objective all along" of securing a higher price for his surrender. If the Amalgamated "crushed" Heinze, it evidently paid him and his partners ten to twelve million dollars for the privilege.[26]

For all their differences, the copper kings all held some principles to be self-evident. Though they might not have said it so bluntly, neither Daly, Heinze, nor Rogers could have disagreed much with William Clark's classic statement against Rooseveltian conservation. In response to the idea of conserving for posterity, Clark cheerfully spoke for his contemporaries. "Those who succeed us," he said, "can well take care of themselves." The same could have been said for the copper kings' employees.[27]

The arena where giants struggle—or even the alley where cats fight—is seldom a safe or pleasant place for bystanders. In 1903, for instance, cornered by Heinze's lawsuits, the Amalgamated shut down its operations in Montana, throwing "nearly 6500" men into immediate unemployment and eventually, as the effect rippled through the supporting coal, timber, and railroad businesses, creating a total of 15,000 out-of-work men. The unemployed and their families, the bulk of Montana's population, endured a month of misery while the copper kings sulked.[28]

At the other end of the hierarchy was a different stratum of history—a matter of strategy and organization as complicated as the maneuverings of the owners. In the years before the victory of the Amalgamated, Butte miners could benefit from the upper-level struggles. Courted as voters, workers could be the recipients of bonuses, turkeys, entertainment, free drinks, and wage and hour concessions. Moreover, Marcus Daly remembered his origins as a working miner and felt some residual solidarity with his employees. But when the Amalgamated took over, the workers' maneuvering room contracted, as labor appeared increasingly as a cuttable cost in the ledgers of New York offices. It was true that workers and owners retained a common interest in the industry's prosperity. When the government stopped purchasing silver, or when prices for copper dropped, this was bad news at all levels of the mining hierarchy.

Although industrial relations never settled into an utterly clear case of opposed class interests, the Western mining industry, like the Western timber industry, could provide situations that closely resembled the Marxist model of class struggle. To the owners, property came first. Unions and collective bargaining represented an intolerable intrusion on their right to use their property on their own terms. Discontented individuals could present their own complaints, the theory went; if they did not like the job, they could quit. With their massive investments, the mining capitalists assumed the greatest risk and thus were entitled to set the terms for labor. They were running a business, after all, not a charity; unionization, they could argue, interfered with the worker's individual independence, and individual independence was what made the whole system work.

Like everything else in Western history, labor activism did not follow any simple pattern. But one main current began in the familiar turf of Butte. In the late 1870s, a union began to grow "by fits and starts." Ethnic tensions—between Irish and Cornish miners—plagued the Butte Miners' Union; once again, Western history provides few instances of fully realized class solidarity. Factionalization aside, the Butte union became "the most powerful union in the western mines," "the center of the western mining labor movement." With Butte in the lead, Western workers in 1893 formed the key organization, the Western Federation of Miners.[29]

The timing was appropriate. A rapid decline in silver prices led companies to make wage cuts all over the West, "triggering widespread lockouts and strikes in the bitterest and most violent mining war." In the ruthless use of power, the companies held the commanding position. As in Montana, elsewhere in the West mineowners held great political power; when mining was a state's major source of income, its legislators had no interest in scaring away investors by seeming to support labor's side of the struggle. The political power of mineowners led to the intervention of the state militia in strikes, ostensibly to maintain order, but frequently to break the strike. Mineowners also had the support of the judges, as the conservative judicial temperament of the times ratified the rights of property. As in Montana, mineowners often held a direct financial interest in newspapers, so that the power of the press could be added to the forces against strikers. Companies often employed their own network of spies to report on union and strike activities, of armed guards, and of strikebreakers. Moreover, the blacklist was commonly used to keep known union supporters out of the mines. While the owners might decry the illegitimacy of associations of workers, they could on occasion suppress their own competition to form mineowners' associations—to combat workers' associations.[30]

In this situation, Western labor activists could hold little faith in the craft-based tradition of the American Federation of Labor. To have small decentralized locals face off against powerful national companies seemed to invite defeat. Accordingly, Western labor activism had a strong impulse toward broader, industry-wide unions, including workers at all levels of skill, who could then provide a large base of resistance to large employers.

But even with effective broad-based organization, the realities of power kept Western unions off balance. Consider the two principal Cripple Creek strikes, portrayed in a study by the historian James Wright. In 1894, the mine operators declared that they would lengthen the working day from eight to nine hours, without raising wages. The recently formed union of the Western Federation of Miners responded with a strike. Troops entered Cripple Creek—not to break the strike but genuinely to enforce order and bring a negotiated peace. This anomaly stemmed from the fact that a Populist, Davis Waite, sat in the Colorado governor's chair. While the lesson of the 1894 strike might have been encouraging to labor, the 1903–4 strike taught an opposite lesson. This time the goal was to get smelter workers an eight-hour day, with Cripple Creek miners in a sympathy strike against the mines that shipped ore to the smelters. The state troops returned, but now the governor was no Populist. Determined to keep labor under control and to prove that Colorado was supportive and protective of its businesses, Governor James Peabody used his troops to intimidate workers and even to deport leaders. Governor Peabody had his own explanation for his actions:

It will be a matter of great regret to me if the laboring men of this state fail to see that I am fighting their battle, for I sincerely believe that organized labor has no more dangerous enemy than the Western Federation of Miners, which is seeking, under the cloak of organized labor, to protect itself alike in the promulgation of its dishonest socialistic theories, which recognize no right to private property, and from the result of its anarchistic tenets and tendencies.[31]

The defeat at Cripple Creek convinced some activists that Western conditions required a new, more radical organization. Accordingly, a diverse group of the discontented met in Chicago in 1905 to form the Industrial Workers of the World (IWW). The Western Federation of Miners constituted the largest already organized supporters of the IWW, but that did not guarantee the organization a smooth start. The IWW was, in its first years, racked with feuds, some of them ideological, but most of them bitterly personal.

Once the Wobblies, as its members were known, had survived their first round of factionalization, the organization kept a regional split: an Eastern wing involving mostly immigrant factory labor; and a Western wing, more widely celebrated in folklore, of primarily single, male, often almost migratory workers in the mineral, timber, and agricultural businesses. The timber camps of the Pacific Northwest formed an especially appropriate recruiting ground. Working long hours in isolated camps, distant from the centers of company power, housed in primitive and crowded barracks, subject to seasonal layoffs and vulnerable to corrupt employment recruiting, timber workers were a fitting target for the Wobbly vision of one big union taking a stand against an inhumane distribution of work, power, and profit.

For a small, disorganized group, Western Wobblies got a great deal of public attention. Some of that, they asked for directly. Beginning in 1910, in rebellions that started as protests against manipulative employment agencies, the Wobblies staged a series of free-speech fights along the Pacific Coast. Seeing the Wobblies as the embodiment of social disorder, city governments passed ordinances prohibiting their public speeches. Some of these ordinances were extraordinary in their nullification of civil liberties. Consider one from Los Angeles: "It shall be unlawful for any person to discuss, expound, advocate or oppose the princi-

ples or creed of any political party, partisan body, or organization, or religious denomination or sect, or *the doctrines* of any
economic or social system in any public speech, lecture, or discourse, made or delivered in any public park in the city of Los
Angeles."[32]

Combatting these ordinances, Wobblies would sweep into town
and begin giving street speeches; arrested in bulk, they hoped
to clog the jails and the judicial system. In this pioneering use of
civil disobedience and passive resistance, many speakers found
themselves on soapboxes but unsure of what to say. One sym-
pathizes with the fellow in Spokane who began with the traditional Wobbly salutation, "Friends and Fellow Workers." He was
not immediately arrested and therefore continued his speech by
shouting, "Where are the cops?" To avoid this problem of
speechless speakers, the Wobblies took to reading the Declaration of Independence or the Constitution, a practice that could
on occasion only infuriate their enemies more.[33]

Although their popular image centered on violence, Wobblies talked about violence a great deal more than they committed it. "[N]o Wobbly," the historian Joseph Robert Conlin has
emphasized, "was ever proved to have committed an act of violence." When they praised the value of sabotage, they most often
meant not the use of dynamite but the use of slow, inefficient
work to undermine industrial operations. Violent or not, the
Wobblies had by the time of World War One acquired a violent
public image. That image, coupled with war fever, patriotism,
and a distrust of anyone living on the fringe of society, brought
the Wobblies a fresh wave of persecution, a wave that turned
them into an organization depleted by its need for self-defense.
The same process had the side effect of discrediting mainstream
labor movements as well.[34]

Events in Bisbee, Arizona, in July 1917, described in a book
by James Byrkit, showed the process at work. Three large copper companies ran the mines of Bisbee; rising wartime profits
and the need to confront labor with a united front made the
companies more cooperative than competitive. As copper prices
went up, workers were told that war necessity required their
cooperation; when they asked for a share of the companies' ris-

ing profits, they were told that they were undermining national strength and the war effort by their selfishness.[35]

In 1917, Bisbee's copper miners delcared a strike for higher wages. Participating in the strike were around one hundred Wobblies. Some of the IWW members may in fact have been company agents. The use of the spy and of the agent provocateur—to foment the violence that would then discredit the union and justify a crackdown—had become so widespread that this matter of uncertain identity could never be completely dismissed.

Company managers and owners, and local officials, tolerated the strike briefly, then took extraordinary action. On the morning of July 12, 1917, vigilantes—supported by the local sheriff and other officials—rounded up 1,186 men, including merchants and lawyers who had sympathized with the strike, along with strike leaders and IWW members, leaving many wives and children behind in panic and disorder. With incidents of beating and brutality, but with only two deaths, the deportees were placed in train cars and taken out of state to Columbus, New Mexico, where federal officials finally quartered them at an army post. Individuals could return to Bisbee, the vigilantes indicated, *if* they gave up on the union and the strike and went back to work.

Later investigations and lawsuits brought the vigilantes no penalties. When this massive assault on civil liberties reached the U.S. Supreme Court, the justices graciously deferred to states' rights, returning the matter to Arizona's jurisdiction, though the deportation had clearly crossed state boundaries. Released by the local courts, copper company officials and the Bisbee middle class could even appear as patriots who had saved an important industry from the threat of a seditious rebellion. Newspapers across the nation supported the Bisbee deportation by a margin of two to one, and President Woodrow Wilson, increasingly intolerant of dissent, saw no reason to reverse the direction of a national opinion that cast the Wobblies as the villains and not as the victims of the incident. Their defeat—at Bisbee and in popular opinion—did a great deal, James Byrkit has shown, to discredit the labor movement in general. William Andrews Clark, the copper magnate familiar from his Butte activities but also an

owner of Arizona mines, captured the attitude: he would rather
flood his mines, he said, than concede to union demands. The
anti-Wobbly hysteria of World War One and the immediate
postwar years made Clark's threat unnecessary. He could live
undisturbed in the New York mansion he had built, an elabo-
rately ornamented structure of 131 rooms, reportedly costing
three million dollars. A poet captured the message of the house:

> "How," says the Senator, "kin I look proudest?
> "Build me a house that'll holler the loudest."

While Clark lived in his mansion and collected fine art, the Bisbee deportees undertook to reunite their families and find some
way to make a living.[36]

In his riveting book on the Bisbee deportation, James Byrkit
takes a peculiar tack at the end. Byrkit there calls the incident a
study in the "powerful colonial relationship [that] existed between
the East and the West, the old and new." The story, he says,
involved "the sponsorship and manipulation of the American
frontier by East Coast political and economic figures." With the
full story in mind, a regional distribution of good and evil is
unconvincing. Arizonans—in the legislature, in the governor's
office, in the courts, in newspaper offices, in the town of Bisbee—all played their part in supporting and even implementing
the deportation. The long-range effect may have suited the
interests of Eastern capitalists, but Western mining history, in
Bisbee and elsewhere, is by no means a clear morality play of the
conviving, manipulative East against the innocent, victimized
West.[37]

Whether or not they succeeded, Western entrepreneurs
showed essentially the same motives as Eastern entrepreneurs.
There were, as Richard Peterson had pointed out, a significant
number of mining entrepreneurs who concluded that decent
treatment of workers paid off, since "uninterrupted production
was preferable to reduced labor costs." Those comparatively
humane employers still had profits in mind, but more important, as Peterson has said, the employer's place of residence was
not necessarily the determinant of his labor policy:

[A]n argument which attributes worker exploitation and discontent to
absentee ownership overlooks the fact that such resident western own-

ers as the Colorado Springs entrepreneurs who confronted rebellious workers at their Cripple Creek properties in 1894, were at times just as likely to have trouble with their employees as were absentee eastern owners. The Leadville strike of 1896, for example, occurred when the industry was largely under the control of resident owners.

When Augustus Heinze undertook to direct the anger of Montana workers away from himself and toward the wicked East, he was not offering them an accurate view of their complicated world.[38]

An even more significant blow to the image of the vulnerable West in the tentacles of a tyrannical East comes from the actual operations of investment. In his illuminating book *A Mine to Make a Mine: Financing the Colorado Mining Industry, 1859–1902,* Joseph King shows the process at work. The placer phase of mining in Colorado proved very short; complicated ores and underground mining created an urgent need for capital. After rushing to Colorado and picking up claims, Western entrepreneurs reversed directions and rushed East—to the capital lodes of New York, Boston, and Chicago. A distressing proportion of their mining schemes were fraudulent; persuading Eastern fools to invest in an unseen mine two thousand miles away was, for some, a much more agreeable way to make money than actually working the mine. Even genuine, working mines were often overcapitalized, issuing stock at values considerably greater than the mine's actual value. The blind faith that Western mines created fortunes, the remoteness of Colorado, and the unscrupulous exaggerations of many mine promoters left many Eastern investors burned. They hardly saw themselves as the manipulators of the West; they felt far more like the manipulated. This form of mining—finding one's reward in the manipulation of stock sales— was yet another Western enterprise that failed to observe an end to the frontier. In 1920 at a convention of mining men, a parody captured the essence of this aspect of the business:

> There are mines that make us happy,
> There are mines that make us blue,
> There are are mines that steal away the tear drops
> As the sunbeams steal away the dew.
> There are mines that have the ore chutes faulted,
> Where the ore's forever lost to view,

But the mines that fill my heart with sunshine,
Are the mines that I sold to you.[39]

III

Western mines had created a social condition that would have
been abhorrent to the framers of the Republic. Westward
expansion was supposed to create a land of independent, agrarian landowners and to prevent the rise of a wage-dependent
laboring population. In mining, the opposite happened. This
was only one way that mining ran counter to the ideal expectations for the westward movement.

It was a contradiction little analyzed by Americans at the time.
As mining set the pace and direction of Western development,
Americans concerned with Indians continued to insist that agriculture was essential for their assimilation; to sow and to reap
was the true route to permanent prosperity and good character,
to civilization. It did not occur to the reformers of Indians that
their own countrymen in mining were also in need of programs
in civilization; agriculture and agrarian values were as under-
practiced in mining camps as on reservations.

Even so, mining appeared to be the social and economic
opposite of farming. Mining meant sudden riches for some and
hard and unrewarding labor for most; settlements suddenly
thrown together and as suddenly abandoned; rootless male populations; dependence on imported provisions; and extraction of
a resource that could not be replenished and would eventually
run out. In farming, the theory went, both labor and rewards
were distributed evenly through the population; permanent,
responsible settlement resulted; families anchored people in space
and through time; farm products provided an essential self-sufficiency; and an unlimited cycle of planting and harvesting ran
no risk of depletion.

And yet, from other angles, farming and mining did not
appear to be so different. The same factors of dependence—on
capital, nature's good behavior, transportation, markets, and a
labor supply—left farmers frequently discontented with their
"independent" lives. In their haste to produce marketable crops,
farmers did not necessarily work with long-term stability in mind;

getting crops in and out could become something close to an extractive industry—another way of mining the soil.

"Farming," as the historian Gilbert Fite has put it, "has always been a risky, uncertain, and sometimes heartbreaking business." The expansion of Western farming after the Civil War confirmed this proposition. In the new farms of the Western prairies and plains, hardship was more than a poignant, transitory chapter of pioneer life; hardship instead put a spotlight on the uncertainties and risks intrinsic to the farming life.[40]

Agrarian expansion onto the Great Plains went forward amid high hopes and expectations. Railroads wanted settlers, both as purchasers of their land grants and as future freight customers. In the United States and Europe, railroad advertising promised emigrants the finest of opportunities—fertile land, guaranteed access to markets, the amenities of nearby towns, and the security of one's own home and farm. As competition between railroads picked up, the fervor of the promotion increased proportionately, supplemented by the state boards of emigration. Once again, business and politics merged. Recruitment of settlers was so obviously in everyone's interest that promotional literature and agents were naturally taken to be within the legitimate sphere of government.

Set against this background of frenetic promises and publicity, the actuality of farming had to be disillusioning. Despite the promises of the Homestead Act, much good land was already in the possession of railroads and states, and purchase "continued to be the most usual means to obtain a farm after 1865." By the Homestead Act itself, one historian asserted, "[t]housands were deceived into thinking that securing a piece of land was all that was necessary to make a competence for the owner," just as descriptions of the mines had assured forty-niners that success was available to anyone who would work. Once settled on their new land, farmers faced both substantial expense and an urgent need to plant a first crop. The cost of a house, draft animals, wagon, plow, well, fencing, and seed grain could be as much as $1,000; many farmers succeeded on less than that, but they made up the difference in privation and hard labor. They were left especially vulnerable in delays to the first crop. If they arrived in late summer or early fall, without time to plant, if the first crop suffered from any of the numerous hazards of nature, hard times were certain. Jefferson's dream of the independent yeoman farmer had made no allowance for natural disaster or for the bankrupt position of a newly arrived farmer.[41]

In early Plains farming, hardship was extreme. The grasshoppers would have been nightmare enough. They came in clouds, sounding like hail on a house, sometimes covering the ground four to six inches deep; they could stop trains; and they ate indiscriminately. They immediately set to "devouring everything green, stripping the foliage, and off the bark, from the tender twigs of the fruit trees, destroying every plant that is good for food or pleasant to the eyes, that man has planted." Hailstones, drought, prairie fires, and failed adaptations to the semiarid West brought periodic disaster.[42]

These trials left a painful record in letters written to farm state governors, asking for relief. Private, voluntary help simply could not meet the seriousness of the problem, and in newly settled areas county governments had a tax base too limited to support extensive relief. Farmers turned to the state government as the only practical recourse. Quoted individually, the letters would seem melodramatic if they were not so numerous:

I have been trying to live on my place and with sickness and bad luck in crops have well nigh run out of everything—I have been sick for months and my wife is not well from exposure and hunger and I thought that there was no other way than to ask you to help me—If you can let me have $25 and some close *[sic]* for my wife and daughter and myself as we have not close to cover our backs or heads—And if I can't get the money I shall lose my place after livin' from hand to mouth for three years on the frontier.[43]

From 1873 to 1877, a grasshopper plague in Minnesota unleashed a flood of these letters. Some farmers lost their crops four years in a row. The state legislature made gestures of assistance, offering some direct relief in the form of food and clothing, but preferring to provide limited amounts of seed grain for the farmers' next crops. In practice, this did not work out to much aid: while requests for seed grain totaled "over sixty thousand bushels" in one year, the relief commission "had funds to supply less than one-third of the demand." Direct aid could be even skimpier: one family—"husband, pregnant wife, and six children—received only $5.95 worth of flour, sugar, dried apples, and tea" in a typical allotment.[44]

Why such a stingy response? The attitude of John Pillsbury, who became governor of Minnesota in the midst of the grasshopper crisis, illuminates the reasoning behind the grudging help. To Pillsbury and most of his contemporaries, there were two kinds of people: hardworking, self-reliant individuals and poor, dependent, chronic beggars. Farmers were supposed to be in the first category; as Jefferson had said, they should be the most self-reliant and independent of all citizens. When Minnesota's farmers asked for help, they were threatening to give up their proper moral character and become beggars and dependents. For their own good, for society's good, they could not be encouraged in this surrender of their virtue. Charity, Pillsbury felt, reduced its recipients to "habitual beggary" or "confirmed mendicancy." Encouraging this was a "deplorable mistake." Government help, a Minnesotan of like mind explained, could "undermin[e] the spirit of self-dependence so essential to a pioneer life, and arous[e] hopes of future aid in every little emergency." Even loans, the *St. Paul Daily Pioneer Press* argued, would "bankrupt all the moral resources of the State; [they] would sap and destroy those vital energies of self-reliance and self-helpfulness on which the physical and social progress and prosperity of a people depend."[45]

It was all right, Pillsbury thought, to instruct farmers on technique. Proper assistance meant distributing information on how best to kill grasshoppers, especially on how to construct futile devices called hopperdozers, instruments to be dragged through fields, catching bugs on their sticky surface. Each man meeting his own farm's grasshoppers in direct, one-against-a-million combat—that, Pillsbury thought, was the proper response to a plague of locusts.

In her study of the Minnesota grasshopper crisis, Annette Adkins skillfully analyzes the attitudes at work. Even when aid was offered, it came with a demanding "means test"—the farmer had too certify that he was truly desperate and not simply exploiting a free supply of grain. The ownership of a team of oxen, mules, or horses indicated that the owner was still a man of means; but if a man surrendered his team in order to qualify for aid, he was unable to plow and prepare for next year's crop. Government assistance, Adkins notes, came with "blatant suspicion" approaching "contempt." Officials had other reasons for downplaying the disaster; it was, after all, bad publicity, and bad publicity could cut off the stream of immigration that all boosters saw as essential.[46]

Even the suffering farmers themselves showed these widespread attitudes. Their writing, Adkins remarks, showed "how dearly they held the notions that charity was ill advised and demoralizing, that assistance rewarded the unworthy, and that poverty resulted from personal failure." "David if possible do not beg," wrote Mary Jones, whose husband was off seeking work. "I should be so ashamed to face people after begging my way to them. . . ." But the problem remained: when grasshoppers ate the crops, labor had been robbed of its legitimate connection to success. "I think we are both striving with all our might to better our condition," Mary Jones wrote her husband, "shall we succeed that is the question. . . ." In 1877, the grasshoppers left and put these maddening questions to rest. Like the locusts, the questions might be dormant but certainly not dead.[47]

A good crop with adequate prices could rescue a family and a region from desperation, but Western farming reached no plateau of contentment. The agrarian protest movement of the 1880s and 1890s, Granger activism and populism, made it clear that discontent lived on. After the first, desperate years, most Western farmers still felt a "constant worry over having enough money," a concern kept alive "by the uncertainties of crops and prices." This was no proof of improvidence on their part. The costs and expenses of farming caused an "almost constant need for credit."[48]

Because the consequences of widespread debt can be so grim, its meaning can easily be mistaken. As the farmer took up the costs of starting his business, it was an act of optimism to go into debt in order to raise capital and finance a happier future. When those happy expectations proved misleading, the debt became a source of despair, a mechanism for entrapment. In the late nineteenth century, a deflating currency meant that farmers usually borrowed inflated, cheap dollars and repaid deflated, more valuable dollars. Currency thus became the agent that delivered to farmers the message of their victimization.

Significant costs also came from railroad freight charges. Once again, a vehicle of optimism had become a trap; farmers who had been confident that prosperity would arrive with the railroad found that they had given their prosperity as a hostage to the railroads' rates. Farmers, it was said, raised three crops: corn, freight, and interest. Agrarian radicals logically concluded that life could be much improved by the control of railroads and currency, the two variables most unheeding of their wills.

Where, among the discontented groups of the West, would the farmers find their place? Were farmers a variety of oppressed workers? Certainly, they were often people working too hard for too little reward. But they were also small businessmen, clinging to the status and dignity of those who worked for themselves and not for wages. That split character curtailed the radicalism of their protests. Western workers might ally themselves to fight against property and privilege; but Western farmers, as property owners and entrepreneurs, were at once in the system and against it. A degree of returned prosperity would indicate that the system was finally going to work in their favor, and radical protest would subside until the next setback.

Just as the term "miner" could cover everyone from bonanza kings to wage laborers, so the term "farmer" could be misleading. What measures would benefit "the farmer"? Which farmer? Early in American history, English settlement had spawned a wide range of sizes in the category "farm" or "plantation." In the West, these differences hardly disappeared. In Minnesota and South Dakota in the 1870s and 1880s, bonanza wheat farming demonstrated the further reaches of large-scale farming. Absentee owners hired managers to run huge operations. In the mid-1880s, A. R. Dalrymple managed 34,000 acres, employing seasonally as many as one thousand men, "recruited from the itinerant farm labor force." The same pattern of large-scale wheat farming appeared in the Central Valley, in California. There, estates from the Spanish and Mexican eras set a pattern of large-scale landholding. The economy of scale required by certain kinds of irrigation confirmed the pattern. Large-scale farming, rechristened agribusiness, dominated California farming, relying on seasonal migrant labor of varying nationalities—men and women representing the exact opposite of the Jeffersonian agrarian ideal. In the twentieth century, the rest of the West leaned toward California's pattern. "For most farm operations," Gilbert Fite has said, "the needed efficiency required larger units." The "idea of bigness and efficiency" had become "a competing and even more compelling tradition." In a Western pattern of thought that had clearly not been much dented by the passing of the frontier, "[m]any farmers who had not become big operators retained the hope that some day they might achieve such a status," and accordingly showed no enthusiasm "for limiting the size of farms."[49]

Throughout the twentieth century, the familiar frustrations have reappeared: low crop prices, large debts and high interest rates, the fear of foreclosure, and problems in regulating production, varying from crop failure to price lowering overproduction. Today's family farmers rarely face starvation, as did those of the 1870s, but the farmer fed and clothed is nonetheless tied to a business foundering in debt in the 1980s. In their effort to help, government and technology have joined the many outside forces that farmers cannot fully control, sources of frustration and annoyance as much as aid.

By the nature of their enterprise, farmers sell at wholesale and buy at retail, which usually means selling low and buying high. Despite dreams of independence, farmers have become doubly dependent—on the behavior of both nature and markets. This dependence and the numerical dominance of urban, nonagrarian America, where the vast majority have an interest in cheap food, and the many complications of the international character of agricultural trade make it unlikely that agrarian discontent will disappear. Farmers will continue to feel at the mercy of outside forces—because, in fact, they are. Western farmers in the late nineteenth century lived with a sense of being squeezed by history, in a vise built by dropping prices on one side and high costs on the other. The same feeling can be found in farmers today. The time when America treated its farmers right must be in the past; few farmers could place it in the present.

Percentages might give the sentiment of nostalgia plausibility. American urban dwellers did not outnumber rural residents until 1920, but by 1981, farmers were less than 3 percent of the population. The loss of power implicit in that percentage could not escape anyone. Farmers had the unnerving experience of sinking from a majority to a minority, of missing the golden age and landing instead in an age turned dreary.

When, however, was this golden age—and where? A nostalgic sense of lost rural prosperity is by no means unique to the United States. In his book *The Country and the City*, Raymond Williams finds rural nostalgia in many places and times. Moving back through the centuries, Williams tracks laments for "recently" lost rural virtues—from Hardy to George Eliot, Cobbett, Goldsmith, Thomas More, and, at last, Virgil and Hesiod. As Williams points out, the lesson of this prolonged regress has to be qualified by the fact that each lament mourned a specific rural life. But it is nonetheless a pattern in Western civilization, long preceding Jefferson, to attribute ideal values to rural life that reality cannot match.[50]

When the twenty-two-year-old Howard Ruede left Pennsylvania for Kansas in 1877, he was not burdened with Jeffersonian illusions. He wanted a free homestead; he wanted to get a farm started so that his parents and siblings could join him; and he knew that this would mean a lot of work. He did not have much money (before leaving, Ruede "went to the bank and drew $75— all [he] had"—and then bought his train ticket for $23.05), and he knew that he would have to compensate for shortage of capital with an abundance of labor.[51]

Once Ruede had his homestead, his situation was still more notable for the things he did not have. He did not have a well. He did not have an auger, or even a pick, with which to dig a well. He did not have a team of oxen, mules, or horses, a plow, or any other farm machinery. He did not have a stove. He did not have a house in which to put a stove. He did not have meat—

except when he could kill a jackrabbit, find the money to buy beef or pork, or board with a better-established neighbor. He did not have firewood. He did not have a second pair of shoes, but he did, in his first pair, have a full share of holes. Ruede did have stamina and a skill—experience with printing. In a few weeks, his life in Kansas was structured by a network of jobs. He worked part-time for the printer in town thirteen miles away; that, in the absence of horse or wagon, meant an enormous amount of walking, though it also meant a gradual accumulation of cash. He worked for neighboring farmers in a variety of tasks: well digging, plowing, corn hoeing, harvesting, threshing, stripping sorghum cane, quarrying rock, cutting firewood. When they could not pay his wages in cash, they paid in bartered goods and labor. Ruede's neighbors may have lived on separate farms, but they were all pulled into a network of goods and services rendered and received—and remembered.

"I wanted to go to work on my claim," Ruede wrote in the middle of this whirl of jobs. But he still needed money. "I must let my own work lie at present," he said, "to do other people's work." Nonetheless, he managed to build a sod house; when the first one collapsed, he built another. He began digging for a well: "Talk about hard work will you? Just try digging in the ground out here. . . . The ground is packed just as hard as could be, and it is no fun to pick and shovel it." Repeatedly he struck shale and had to begin again on another site. He took up sewing and biscuit making, tasks forced on him by the absence of women: "I got out the needle and thread, and then 'stitch, stitch, stitch' till my back was nearly ready to break. . . ." On the matter of a team of animals, Ruede thought, planned, investigated, calculated, considered, postponed, and brooded. Right after his arrival, he had written, "[T]here is one thing we need very much—a team." The matter reappears constantly in his diary. "Without a team," he said, "you must depend on others and pay accordingly." As much as he needed the animals, he would not consider going into debt. And through it all, he added to his walking mileage by going after the mail and, like William Swain and thousands of miners, feeling deep disappointment when none came.[52]

Ruede's diary does inspire in the historian one futile wish:

that Jefferson, before penning his stirring words on the charm
and contentment of the farming life, could have spent one day
in Ruede's well-worn shoes. Reading his daily entries, one becomes
vicariously tired, worn down simply by thinking about his endless walking and working. After receiving a letter from his aunt,
Ruede wrote his family, "I never was so much surprised as when
I got Aunty Clauder's letter a couple of weeks ago. She tries to
make me out a hero, but for the life of me I can't see anything
heroic in coming out here to do farm work—do you?" Heroism
may not be the exact term, but to an empathetic reader, Ruede's
persistence and pluck are astonishing. Recording one of many
failed attempts at digging a well, Ruede wrote, "The chance was
for water, but fortune did not smile upon us. There's 3 ¼ days'
work for nothing." But he kept trying: "This failure to get water
does not discourage me in the least." Ruede showed a similar
determination in refusing debt and in saving his earnings. By
the end of the first year, joined by his father and little brother,
Ruede had acquired the longed-for team and wagon. His well
digging at last brought water. He had purchased "a number 8
cook stove and outfit for $24.25." His first year's work did not
earn Ruede leisure, but it did earn a reunion of the family, with
Mother, Pa, Ruth, Syd, and Bub all in one place, and with no
need to live on the tenuous connections of the mails. The family
reunited, their work went on.[53]

In Western businesses, in farming and in mining, as well as
in logging, oil drilling, and cattle ranching, labor and reward
were like an erratic couple—sometimes united, more often separated and uncertain of their future together, but never quite
divorced. Bernard Reid, William Swain, Marcus Daly, William
Andrews Clark, Howard Ruede, and millions of others all took
their chances in the lottery and drew wildly varying results. But
in the late twentieth century, when it has become commonplace
to hear denunciations of the despoiling of Western resources,
the rape of the land, the ecological and moral horror that was
Western expansion, it is important to remember this widely
varying cast of characters, and to recall that many of these
"despoilers" wanted, primarily, to find a job and make a living.

Five

The Meeting Ground of Past and Present

IN JULY 1986, in Aspen, Colorado, "a horse-drawn carriage went out of control and collided with a compact car." Meant to carry tourists, the carriage was, happily, tourist free when it knocked over a Volkswagen Rabbit. The occupants of the car "were treated for cuts and bruises"; the horse was fine.[1]

When horses met Volkswagens in what had once been wilderness, it was obvious that a great deal had changed in the American West. Ranchers used pickup trucks, farmers used home computers, and condominiums spread where fur trappers had once held their rendezvous. Horse-drawn carriages and other relics of the past were there for the tourists, part of a major, modern commercial enterprise for trading on the charms of a dead past. But the differences between the nineteenth century and the twentieth were so dramatic that they distracted us from the many elements of continuity holding the centuries together. Many of the basic issues and qualities of the nineteenth century were still dominant, even if they came in different clothes and in different vehicles. In the region's dependence on federal money, instability in business cycles, and inconsistent enforcement of laws, the twentieth-century West bore a strong family resemblance to that theoretically dead past.

The clearest and most persistent case of continuity involved disputes and conflicts over water. Aridity is, after all, the quality that most distinguishes the West (with the exception of the Pacific Northwest) from the rest of the country. Men and women on the overland trail to California in the mid-nineteenth century knew that water was a scarce resource as they crossed the deserts at the end of the journey. They had to make hard choices of loyalty, determining how much of their water to keep for their own survival and how much to share with their family and friends, and even with strangers in need. For a few weeks of difficult travel, those pioneers could not look away from the problem of aridity. They could not hope to conquer the desert, only to survive it and escape it. It took a few more years for another vision to grow—a vision that Western water, too, might finally submit to the masterful American will.

The poetry and power of dams, canals, ditches, and sprinklers do not strike every observer. Most people fail to see transcendent meaning in irrigated agriculture, but the idea came easily to William Ellsworth Smythe, one of the most articulate and tireless advocates of irrigation. A transplanted New Englander, Smythe was a journalist in 1890 when drought hit Nebraska. The experience of watching farms wither from lack of rain, while water flowed in untapped streams, changed the direction of Smythe's life. He converted to reclamation.[2]

Smythe saw two tracks of trouble converge in American history. On one, American expansion proceeded westward until it reached the ninety-eighth meridian, where precipitation becomes insufficient to support agriculture. Hitting that line, the "army of settlers" fell back, apparently defeated. Meanwhile, on a second track, the growth and consolidation of big business seemed to set up another kind of barrier. Their position threatened from below by immigrants and from above by big business, the native middle-class professionals were at risk, Smythe thought, of becoming "surplus men," outmoded by the trends of the time.

Where those two barriers intersected, Smythe saw opportunity and a second chance. God had left the West arid in order to challenge and reform America; the irrigated agriculture necessary in the West would force Americans out of their isolated, individualistic enterprises and seduce them into cooperation to build and maintain the necessary dams and ditches. In finishing what God had begun, transforming desert into garden, Americans would usher in a new era of human partnership with God. And, in a happy overlap with America's other social problem, the displaced native white middle class, the "surplus men," could find their opportunity in the desert West. It would be a new frontier both in geographical expansion and in opportunity for those penned up and in need of a refuge.

Smythe leaped into the crusade for federal support for irrigation. As was usual in Western history, schemes for a new independence rested on the old federal dependence. Since efficiently managed water would require healthy watersheds, reclamation fit easily into the conservation strategy of Theodore Roosevelt and Gifford Pinchot, and the Newlands Reclamation Act of 1902 was an early achievement of Roosevelt's presidency. Federal money would build dams. Established on their new farms, settlers would repay the government for its investment. The farms served by federal water were to be small family operations, under 160 acres. The dams would store formerly wasted water and send it to formerly useless lands, making the desert bloom. The vision couldn't have been happier—or harder to put into practice.

The 160-acre limit was almost immediately breached. Federally subsidized water irrigated large farms as well as small. A "hard-fought, impassioned controversy," in the historian Donald Worster's words, lasted until 1982, when "the old 160-acre homestead principle was dumped for a new standard, one six times larger than its predecessor."[3] Similarly, the idea of settler repayment worked far better in theory than in practice. Responding to settler complaints, Congress repeatedly passed acts extending the period of repayment. Meanwhile, Smythe's vision of independent small farms providing a haven for the beleaguered middle class produced the unexpected: agribusiness and suburban sprawl.

Smythe thought he served a clear and easily identified public interest, but the actuality of the Western water business proved to be a multitude of different interests. Water-use decisions involved the same repeating riddle: Which user of water most served the public good? Small family farmers? Corporate agriculture? Ranchers? City dwellers, with their needs for drinking, cooking, washing, and lawn watering? Mining companies? Fishermen? Companies supplying hydroelectric power? Military installations? Recreational river runners? Hispanic descendants of the old Spanish and Mexican settlers? Indian people on reservations? Hikers and tourists who simply wanted to see the rivers running in their appointed channels? Native animals and plants dependent on traditional water resources? Raise the question of water use, and the situation resembles an old-fashioned showdown, but with the rivals converging from ten different directions instead of the more traditional two.

If the West had unlimited quantities of water, the question would be abstract. Instead, the choices are as concrete as the dams that have changed Western rivers into giant plumbing systems. Increasingly, experts say that agriculture is a wasteful, inefficient use of managed water, which could more effectively support people in cities. History has played roughly with the vision of William Ellsworth Smythe.

Beyond these conflicts based on use, water has brought on plenty of disputes involving borders and sovereignties. States negotiate delicate compacts, very much like international treaties, to allocate rivers that cross state boundaries; when compacts will not work, states go to court. Arizona sues California; Kansas sues Colorado; states from the Upper Colorado Basin, where development was comparatively slow, look enviously at the Lower Basin, where reclamation got an early start. Even within particular states, regions compete; transmontane diversions in Colorado pit the Western Slope against the Front Range; comparatively well watered northern California faces off against endlessly thirsty southern California. The conflicts reach beyond the nation's borders; the Colorado River delivers a depleted, terribly saline flow to Mexico, despite an agreement to deliver 1.5 million acre-feet a year, an agreement in which American officials carefully skirted the question of water quality. The concerns over Western water extend to regions it never touches. If, for instance, American farmers frequently suffer from low prices caused by overproduction, why should the federal government subsidize a cheap supply of water to give Western farmers a competitive advantage? Why should the nation's taxpayers pay to improve the prospects of one small, regional group of entrepreneurs?

The problem is not solely one of overallocated rivers; much Western development has also rested on the pumping of subsurface groundwater. To earlier Western historians like Walter Prescott Webb, the use of windmills to raise the water seemed an intelligent adaptation to an arid land. But accelerated pumping eventually began to deplete the groundwater, only slowly replenished by rainfall and drainage. While experts disagree on the exact rate of depletion, the Ogallala aquifer underneath much of the Great Plains is shrinking, facing exhaustion sometime in the next few decades.[4] Depletion at least holds the prospect of putting competing uses to rest: there will be no point in fighting when the resource is no longer there.

Like William Ellsworth Smythe, many Westerners looked to the federal government to solve these problems of scarcity. The use of federal money as compensation for the West's failings brings us to a major issue of continuity—the key role of federal money in the Western economy. From the beginning of Western development, federal goodwill (manifested concretely in the form of cash and indirectly in the form of a permitted access to land, grass, water, or timber) had been one of the West's principal resources. When the other resources faltered or collapsed, federal support often turned out to be the crucial remaining prop to the economy. If anything, the twentieth century reinforced this "frontier" characteristic; Progressive conservation and reclamation, New Deal public works, the World War II expansion of defense spending, and Great Society welfare only added to the federal government's central role. In countless ways, Westerners of all persuasions had all or part of their welfare resting on federal goodwill: from Indian reservations to national parks, from grazing permits on the public lands to reclamation and hydroelectric projects, from defense contracts to shale oil subsidies, federal resources had become vital supplements to local economies. If Western economies suffered from a systemic imbalance—a sort of economic diabetes—then federal money was the insulin that kept the system working, making up for the shortages in the system itself.

The West, then, remained delicately sensitive to any proposed change in federal spending. A cutback, or even the threat of a retreat, could bring on an economic equivalent to insulin shock. In 1977, Jimmy Carter in apparent innocence suggested a review and reconsideration of Western reclamation projects, recommending that at least nine Western water projects be dropped entirely. "If Carter has his way," said the *U.S. News and World Report* in May of 1977, "the long era of massive water projects, approved by trade-off votes in Congress and paid for by federal tax billions, is nearing an end."

Western politicians responded with what Donald Worster has called "shocked, spluttering wrath." The threat to cut back the giant Central Arizona Project, designed to pump water over mountain ranges to Phoenix and Tucson, giving Arizona its last share of Colorado River water, brought an especially strong response. "The news," said the eloquent co-owner and operator of Arizona's largest cotton-gin firm, "was like having your dad die when you're 17. You just aren't ready for it." Neither, it turned out, was Jimmy Carter. Alarmed by the reaction, Carter backed off. He canceled his "hit list" and made modest proposals to raise user fees for federal water and institute tougher review procedures for new projects. "We're not out to put an end to dam building," said Carter's secretary of the interior. "High noon" at "the pork barrel" did not produce clear or immediate results, but a new and unsettling phase of federal policy was bearing down on the West. In the Reagan years, an odd coalition of fiscal conservatives and environmentalists created the necessary pressure to cut back the number of projects and to require a significant degree of locally derived financing. The change signaled an interruption in the West's "great tradition," as *Newsweek* called it, of stretching a "meager supply of water" by "adding liberal amounts of money—frequently the Federal government's."[5]

Beyond reclamation, the situation of farmers raised many of the same issues. If only the government would help out, the Grangers and Populists of the nineteenth century had thought, then farmers could be protected from the cruelties of nature and the vagaries of the market. The Populists had proposed a subtreasury plan, to help farmers regulate production by making it possible to hold crops until market conditions were favorable and to secure credit in the meantime. By the end of the New Deal, much of the desired legislative machinery was in place: production control systems through crop subsidies, devices to keep farm prices at parity, government-supported loan programs, bureaus for technical advice and guidance. The government had intervened to make farming stable, and yet the maddening result was that farming fortunes remained uncertain and changeable. Government intervention had, in some ways, simply added another villain to the already well-filled ranks standing between the farmer and his desired reward. Now, in rough times, the farmer could blame the weather, the market, the middleman, the banker, or the government, but not necessarily in that order.

As usual, optimism had laid the groundwork for disappointment. In the 1970s, amid "widespread feelings that land values would never stop rising and demand for farm goods would grow endlessly," farmers negotiated loans and expanded their operations. Large debts had, after all, become "a standard part of the farm gamble." Then, in 1979, the downturn set in. With "falling land values, slumping market prices, high interest rates and dwindling exports," overexpansion caught up with the farmers. The change from boom to bust came fast. "It was as if suddenly someone had flipped a switch," said a hard-hit merchant in a farm town. Farmers found themselves "heavily in debt for land no longer worth what they paid for it," forced to "spend more to grow the crop than it will bring in income." Estimates of the proportion of farmers in serious financial difficulty ranged from one-fourth to one-third; the total farm debt was over $200 billion, far beyond the individual debts of Third World nations. Merchants and towns depending on the farmers shared in the crisis; whole towns faced the possibility of disappearance. The farmers and their allies found themselves in a familiar position "at the whip end of a bewildering set of circumstances [they] cannot control." The headlines of the 1980s looked as if they had been recycled from the 1880s: "Hard Hit Farmers Hope to

Find National Voice" (February 1983); "Despair Wrenches Farmers' Lives As Debts Mount and Land Is Lost" (January 1985); "Agriculture's Bleak Outlook" (August 1985).[6]

During the Reagan presidency, anxiety about the federal deficit and a desire to cut federal spending led to a public debate that was a curiously reversed echo of the Populist Era. In a time of financial trouble, the Populists had argued for government involvement in the farm economy; in a later time of financial trouble, the Reagan forces argued for a retreat. "We've had 50 years of Government intervention," said Secretary of Agriculture John Block, "that hasn't solved the old problems"—a proposition that did seem to have history on its side. The free market, Block and Reagan concluded, could best regulate farm prices and, at the same time help farmers stand on their feet—a proposition history was less willing to support. It was like watching while someone plays with the rewinding switch on a movie projector: first the government moves forward to help the farmers and then the film reverses and the government begins to back away. The retreat was by no means a total one; despite repeated declarations of retrenchment, Reagan did not lead the way to a full overhaul of the system, and the 1985 farm bill proved to be "the costliest in history." But during the debates, hard-hearted statements were widely voiced. David Stockman, Reagan's main budget cutter, put it most bluntly; he could not understand, he said, "why the taxpayers of this country should have the responsibility to go in and refinance bad debt that was willingly incurred by consenting adults."[7]

"Farmers, ultimately, are businessmen," argued a Stockman sympathizer, "no more and no less, no more noble or wicked than other entrepreneurs. And judged as entrepreneurs, farmers seem to have done a shoddy job." Small family farms, partisans of this order held, were outmoded, economically inefficient, and too numerous; a shakeout in their numbers would be, in the long run, a social good. Government funding to keep them operating began to look like an equivalent to the funding of zoos or wildlife preserves, a way of keeping an interesting but endangered species alive under protected circumstances.[8]

And yet these farmers were also, as an Iowa newspaper put

it, "human beings whose lives are falling apart." It was hard to shrug off the words of farmers losing their land. "We worked like fools all our lives," said one. "And we wound up with nothing." This was, everyone acknowledged, a deeply emotional issue, in which public sympathy demonstrated the continued power of the agrarian ideal. "If we fail with agriculture," said a Republican senator from South Dakota, "we will have a rural America without economic purpose and an America without its heritage." How much was the preservation of this heritage worth to the nation? When businessmen and workers in other industries simply sank or swam, "should taxpayers continue to subsidize agriculture?" Should the federal government continue to support the habit of what one headline called "the Greatest Federal Aid Junkie of Them All"—rural America?[9]

II

Federal money, the theory had gone, could be deftly inserted into the Western economy to stabilize otherwise rocky enterprises. But the price of stability was higher than government spending could go; in fact, the vagaries of federal spending, with appropriations followed by cyclical cutbacks, became themsevles a source of instability. The American West remained a region where cycles of boom and bust played games with human hopes.

Consider Colorado's Western Slope. After the 1859 rush to the Front Range, the Western Slope had its own mineral rushes. They did not, however, lead to financial stability. The development of silver mining in Leadville and Aspen left the region vulnerable to the "terrible silver panic of 1893," Duane Vandenbusche and Duane Smith have noted. "Only then did Western Colorado realize that silver could not permanently sustain the region." Cattle ranching and tourism came to fill in some of the economic gaps but still left the region vulnerable to the whims of outside markets and prices. Feeling remote not only from Washington, D.C., and the nation's center of power, but also from Denver and Colorado's center of power, the Western Slope seemed handicapped by a late start in development and by its physical remoteness. Local frustration grew as the Western Slope in the twentieth century saw part of its water supply diverted

In Western boom/bust economies, abandonment and decline have proven nearly as significant as growth and progress. Mill in ruins, St. John, Colorado. *Photo by Muriel S. Tolle, courtesy Denver Public Library, Western History Department*

across the Rockies to the farms and the growing cities of the Front Range. "In time Denver may learn that she is not the state," the *Silverton Standard* remarked in 1893; nearly a century later, the Western Slope still felt cheated.[10]

Prickly as ever, a few Western Slope leaders continue to speak grumpily of seceding from Colorado and forming their own state. Certainly, the most recent economic events have done little to improve their mood. In the early 1980s, the Western Slope had a whirlwind courtship with the new industry known as shale oil, a synfuels romance that left the region feeling jilted and betrayed. The romance began in 1980, when the Carter administration created the federal Synthetic Fuels Corporation "to provide financial incentives, such as loan guarantees and a guaranteed purchase price, to the private sector for creation and production of synthetic fuels." The Western Slope's sizable deposits of oil shale attracted the attention of the Synfuels Corporation, and the relationship got off to the happiest start, when Exxon (in partnership with the TOSCO Company) set up the Colony Oil Shale Plant near Rifle, Colorado, and Union Oil of California was at work on the Parachute Creek Plant nearby. Anticipating an eventual population of 25,000, Exxon set to building a new community, Battlement Mesa, to house the work force of the extensive project. "We believe," a company spokesman announced with the usual boomtown confidence, "that all the factors necessary for a successful commercial shale oil operation are presently in place." Extracting oil from shale would still be expensive, costing roughly $30 a barrel. But with federal subsidies, with a barrel of oil valued in the high $30s and $40s in 1981, with prices expected to rise, this seemed a worthwhile gamble.[11]

On May 2, 1982, after investing millions in the effort, Exxon abruptly announced the closing of the Colony Plant, putting hundreds of people out of work and destroying the local dreams for an economic renaissance. Oil prices were falling, not rising, as had been expected; the technology for processing oil shale proved elusive and frustrating; and even the federal funding began to look doubtful. In an era of budget cuts, Congress reduced the Synfuel Corporation's funding, and then, on December 19, 1985, it signed the agency's "death certificate," giving it 120 days to close up shop. The oil shortage had ceased, and the mandate for alternative energy had withered. "I looked at all the money being spent and I said to myself, 'this time it's going to last,'" remembered a Western Slope leader in 1986. "I thought there was no way the oil companies could pull out after all the money they put into oil shale." The governor of Colorado, Richard Lamm, tried to achieve philosophical distance: "This is just part of the boom-and-bust cycle the West has been experiencing throughout its history. Colorado is going to take this blow and accept it the best we can." Philosophical distance, once again, was considerably aided by geographical distance. It helped to be in Denver and not in Rifle. It helped to be the governor, and not Dee Martin, aged twenty-five, who suddenly learned he had lost his job. "Man," he said, "I had the American dream. A wife, 2½ kids and two cars. Now I have an empty pocket. We came in sunny side up this morning and the world turned upside down."[12]

From its origins in the western Pennsylvania fields, the oil industry has swung from boom to bust, scarcity to glut, as supply and demand reached for each other with the grace of clumsy trapeze artists. Since 1859, oil prices have plunged and soared and plunged again, sometimes with a safety net and sometimes without. Nonetheless, the notion of progress persuaded believers that the oil business had, in some basic way, finally settled down. As knowledgeable a man as Robert O. Anderson, chairman of the board of the Atlantic Richfield Company (ARCO), could begin a book, published in 1984, with this confident line: "The industry has come of age during my lifetime." Part of that maturity derived from the federal government's retreat from the regulating of prices and production. Now, thought Chairman of the Board Anderson, "opportunities over the next twenty years appear to be unlimited. Careers in the petroleum industry offer great prospects for young people today."[13]

Conditions in the American West seemed, for a time, to bear out Anderson's confidence. In 1973, the embargo imposed by the Organization of Petroleum Exporting Countries (OPEC) meant opportunity for domestic oil production. Throughout the 1970s, Western states—especially Texas, Oklahoma, New Mexico, Wyoming, Montana, Colorado, and Alaska—found a blessing in the same oil shortage that seemed an affliction to the rest of the country. The opportunity ignited an explosion in speculation, in the founding of new companies, and in borrowing to finance speculation and future production. "Oil fever roared through downtown Denver," the *Rocky Mountain News* reported, and " 'the town went oil crazy.' " "In those days you could have sold stock in a pile of manure," reported one observer. "And some did." A thoughtful observer in Wyoming summed it up: "We were riding so high. . . . Who in his right mind was going to worry about a future?"[14]

Only a few years later, the old alchemy went to work, and boom was transformed into bust. Oil prices began to decline in

1982; then, in late 1985, the Saudi Arabians undertook to reshape the market by massively overproducing oil, forcing prices down, and undermining competitors. Instead of climbing to the $40, $50, or $60 range, as optimists had anticipated, prices dipped as low as $10 a barrel. American oil producers, especially operators of the numerous and expensive "stripper wells" producing under ten barrels a day, were utterly at the mercy of foreign competition; the expense of producing the oil could easily exceed the revenue from selling it. The "rig count" (the number of oil rigs in production) plummeted; the companies cut back in exploration; many workers lost jobs; and a vicious "ripple effect" set in, as oil equipment and service businesses, restaurants, retailers, banks, real estate companies, city, county and state governments, schools, and social service agencies felt the consequences of the price drop. Regions had built their "future on energy, only to find it a very slim reed." "One day you're sitting on top of the world," said a suddenly unemployed oil worker. "The next day, you have nothing to live for. You're starting all over again." Oil-dependent towns had "the forlorn feel of places that bet heavy, but bet wrong."[15]

What was an appropriate national response to this latest Western cycle? Devastating to some regions of the West, low oil prices were considered a great boon by other parts of the nation. When the oil-producing states asked for help, as the *New York Times* put it, they found "sympathy in short supply." The dilemma did, however, have implications beyond sectional relations. Should the United States simply "enjoy today's cheap oil—even at the price of greater dependence on foreign fuel—or try to help its foundering oil industry"? Would an import tariff, to keep prices high and undermine the threat posed by cheap foreign oil, serve the long-range purposes of national security? Oil businessmen were, some of them admitted, in a tough position to argue for government help. "We in this business have cried forever, 'Washington, please leave us alone,'" said one operator. "God knows it's hypocritical to say stay out of our business till we get our tail in a crack." From the national vulnerability brought on by dependence on imports to individual bankruptcies, the risks of resting one's fortunes on oil were as clear in 1986 as they had ever been. "I never want to go through another boom, and I never want to go through another bust," said one bankrupt businessman in Texas, "because both of them are equally distressing." But the chances of a new stability in oil seemed remote. "Buried in the oil glut of today may be the seeds of shortages tomorrow," the *Rocky Mountain News* said in June 1986. Lower prices lead to increased demand; increased demand exhausts the oversupply; prices rise and shortages reappear. The roller coaster moves on.[16]

But conventional roller coasters run continuously and, with very rare exceptions, safely; the track may pitch up and down, but the car remains on the track and in motion. For the proper economic analogy, one must imagine a roller coaster where the motor periodically shorts out, where the cars lurch to halts at unlikely places and then just as suddenly start up again, and where the safety bars and safety catches that hold riders in their cars and cars on the track have been eliminated from the design. A Colorado farmer, hit by both the decline in agriculture and the drop in his oil and gas royalties, explained what the ride felt like under those circumstances: "It's spooky. Everybody's sitting on the edge of their seat waiting to see who's gonna be next to fall."[17]

This vulnerability, regional as well as individual, leaves the prospect of growth a subject of considerable public testiness. Copper smelters, for instance, may seem to defile the environment, ruining the air and the land. And yet they also mean jobs. When they protest the damage smelters do to air and water, environmentalists can seem to be the enemies of the job-seeking Western folk. Clean-air standards thus seem to be the final blow to an industry already near collapse because of low prices and foreign competition. Casting environmentalists as the principal enemy, anxious Westerners can distract themselves from the intrinsic instability and "treachery" of extractive industries dependent on prices set by outside forces.[18]

In 1982, an enterprising writer codified this grumbling into a 300-page polemic, entitled *Progress and Privilege: America in the Age of Environmentalism.* Progress, William Tucker said, was simply "the process whereby each generation tries to make life better for itself and for the next." And standing in the path were environmentalists, "a social group that opposes *every form* of economic growth and progress as a *general* policy." Environmentalism was aristocratic, privileged, and conservative in the worst sense: "At heart, environmentalism favors the affluent over the poor, the haves over the have-nots." Like aristocrats through the ages, "having made it to the top, [environmentalists] become far more concerned with *preventing others from climbing the ladder behind them*, than in making it up a few more rungs themselves." Tucker drew a picture as clear as a face-off in a boxing ring: in one corner, the *"privileged* minority"; in the other, the earnest Americans who believed in progress and opportunity and merely wanted their share.[19]

The state of Oregon, meanwhile, showed that these matters did not have the simplicity Tucker and others tried to give them. Elected in 1968, Oregon's Republican governor, Tom McCall, put environmental issues at the top of his agenda. Under his guidance, Oregon passed "the most stringent environmental and land-use laws in the nation." McCall, moreover, took on the Willamette River—by all accounts, a "sewer"—and made it safe for spawning salmon and swimming humans alike. Although at least one local group, a coalition of labor and industry, denounced Oregon's new "environmental hysteria," "environmental overkill," and "environmental McCarthyism," Governor McCall earned considerable popular support with his defense of environmentalism's long-range economic benefits: "It doesn't really hurt me that we've lost a factory, or three or four, because in a very few years there will be a queue of applicants stretching miles into the distance because we will have preserved the environment—the only thing that really matters." Oregon's experiment was one of the most significant events in Western American history: an apparent reversal of the ruling trend toward ardent growth. The state was "a testing ground for environmental concepts of reduced, rechanneled growth," the *New York Times* said. "It has challenged the doctrine of the infinite good of infinite expansion, the spiral of more people, more industry, more pollution." Governor McCall had brought full national attention to the experiment with his famous 1971 statement to conventioneers: "Come and visit us again and again, but for heaven's sake, don't come here to live." It was an innovation Oregon could afford, the *New York Times* explained in 1973, because there was "more stability in Oregon's industry" than in that of other Western states.[20]

Nearly a decade later, Oregon had taken the usual Western roller coaster ride. With agriculture and, most important, lumber and construction in decline, Oregon no longer had its cushion of economic stability. "Blessed as it is with bountiful natural resources, Oregon came to depend on them"—and even to imagine that it could selectively protect and preserve them. In the 1980s, facing intense competition from Canadian imports, the timber industry was cutting back, closing mills, and shaking the regional economy. The situation in timber was similar to that in oil: a drop in demand, overproduction, foreign competition, and cries for protection through an import tariff. Unlike oil, the timber business got the first step toward trade protection—a tariff on Canadian cedar products, which then threatened to ignite a trade war with an affronted Canada. Solutions, as usual, generated their own problems.[21]

Just a few years before, optimism had been high. "We began to believe that making a profit was built into the system," said one businessman. "I think Oregon's Golden Age is over," said a laid-off sawmill worker in 1986. At the start of his second term, in 1982, Governor Victor G. Atiyeh told the Oregon legislature that it was time to declare a "statewide economic emergency" and devote the state's effort to fighting "the miserable image Oregon has with the national business community." To Governor Atiyeh, the *Christian Science Monitor* reported, "one of the most imposing roadblocks" to recovery "was the state's reputation for being self-satisfied, isolationist, and anti-business." Yesterday's attempt at utopia was today's embarrassment, and the governor worked full steam to repair the financial damage wrought by his predecessor's efforts to repair environmental damage. Ideological clarity, from William Tucker's standpoint, was in short supply. The remark made by a Pacific Northwest timber specialist captured the essence of the region's rough times: "Nobody is winning."[22]

In the 1970s and 1980s, when Western regions dependent

on a single industry perceived their vulnerability, they pinned their hopes on an utterly new solution: high-tech industries. When logging, mining, farming, ranching, or even (in Nevada) gambling seemed to provide an unreliable foundation for a local economy, California's Silicon Valley became the focus of envy. If it worked so well for California, then Oregon wanted to be Silicon Forest; Arizona, Silicon Desert; Colorado, Silicon Mountain; Las Vegas, Silicon Strip; along with, presumably, a whole set of less publicized Silicon Prairies, Plains, Foothills, Mesas, Canyons, Coulees. High tech, the theory went, would provide stable, clean industry and, thus, a permanent, thoroughly modern means of escape from the uncertain and anxious past of extractive enterprise.

The high-tech myth had joined the oil, mining, ranching, and agrarian myths; to believers, it was an "economic holy grail that could put people back to work and revitalize depressed communities." Like the other myths, the high-tech myth would soon betray its faithful. The new business, as the *New York Times* put it in late 1985, proved "just as vulnerable to the unpredictable forces of the marketplace as copper mining," or as farming, ranching, and all the other key Western businesses. It was the West's old story: a boom atmosphere generated overconfidence and overproduction. An overproduction of silicon chips had the same effect on the market as overproduction of grain; when "chip supply grossly exceed[ed] chip demand" in the early 1980s, high tech went through the familiar process of cutbacks, layoffs, closures, and consolidations.[23]

Even before the rough times hit, high-tech operations had revealed their strong family resemblance to other Western enterprises. Development required capital, and that meant the usual combination of dependence on and resentment of outside financiers ("vulture capitalists," in one popular phrase). Like other varieties of Western enterprise, high tech featured a myth of widespread success and a reality of a few winners and many losers. "If failed business ventures leave ghosts behind," *Business Week* said, "then the air in Silicon Valley must be thick with the phantoms of departed start-ups." Rapid change brought an almost immediate nostalgia for "the good old days" (a few months or years in the past) of *real* adventure and innovation.[24]

The sudden development of the industry meant a legislative and judicial lag, comparable to the lag in the regulating of mining, cattle, and oil. How was society to define, allocate, and protest this form of property, when "the goods" were easily concealed silicon chips or, worse, intangible ideas? The lag created, as it had in the other cases, bursts of opportunity for lawyers and for thieves who prospered in the shadowy borderland between the legal and the illegal. "When the valued object is as small and light as a chip, and when security is more cavalier than secure," Judith Larson and Everett Rogers note in their study of Silicon Valley, "the only question is how long until the next heist occurs." Trouble came in forms other than theft; expected to be a "clean" alternative to "smokestack" industry, high tech proved to have unexpected environmental consequences in the form of toxic waste. And a high-tech boomtown found itself with most of the problems familiar from other eras of Western history: congested, overburdened housing and city services; "extreme socioeconomic inequality," with low-paid workers at a considerable social and economic distance from the engineers and managers; a high rate of mobility and job turnover; and strains on mental health and family life. At the higher levels, ambition and competition thickened the tension. "Nothing's happening unless you're a little frantic," said one engineer. Finally, high-tech workers had all the tensions of living with "a dramatic boom-and-bust cycle." Moreover, in the low part of that cycle, an old Western labor issue returned to fuel anxiety: fear of Asian competition.[25]

When journalists referred to the "high tech gold rush," they chose an appropriate figure of speech. The downturn in high tech led people to ask a question raised thousands of times in gold and silver rushes: "Did we stake too much of our future on this?" "The whole industry," as Judith Larson has said, "is one of instability." The machines were certainly new, but the basic story was a terribly familiar one: "To dream great dreams is to invite great disappointments." "Failure," said Colorado's governor, Dick Lamm, "is as American as apple pie"—a truth that lacked the power to console.[26]

To Oregonians unemployed in the timber business, to em-

ployees in the volatile Silicon Valley industries, to former shale
oil workers in Colorado's Western slope, to farmers, ranchers,
and even bankers and businessmen whose trade depended on
the fortunes of the farms and ranches, to people who lost property and security in the periodic storms, earthquakes, floods,
winds, and droughts of the West, expectation and actuality made
a maddeningly poor match. We are willing to work hard, many
of these people thought, and hard work ought to earn us a fair
reward. The end of the Western rainbow was supposed to hold
at least a modest reward, but for many Westerners the pot with
the treasure seemed to have been ransacked sometime before
their arrival.

III

It was and is common in the West to believe that the times of
scarcity were a fairly recent phase, that in the immediate past
luckier arrivals got what they wanted from the West. But that
was, in fact, one of the longest-held beliefs of the West. The fur
trappers coming into the Rockies in the mid-1830s could regret
having missed the real boom times of the decade before; the
forty-niners in California could look back with envy to the forty-
eighters, those who arrived when times were really good and
opportunity was genuine and open. That sentiment—of having
arrived a few moments late for the party—was well established
by the mid-nineteenth century. Yet, each individual and group,
into our own times, experienced it as if it were new and novel, a
frustration particularly designed for them, a product of their
particular ill luck.

To many Americans, the West promised so much that the
promise was almost sure to be broken. It was a regional pattern
closely connected to a national one: the United States itself carried a comparable promise of freedom and opportunity, along
with a comparable set of frustrations. The West was the national
region most associated with optimism and opportunity. The
Western gap between expectation and results was thus a version
of the national gap, a version written in bigger, boldface, exaggerated type.

Certainly, many things had changed between the times of the

gold rush and Silicon Valley. The technology of communication and production presented a whole new world, a new "frontier," as the headlines often termed it. But the pattern that shaped nineteenth-century stories continued to give shape to the stories of our time. Americans continued to try to conquer nature, transforming a variety of resources into profitable commodities, but the effort at mastery continued to trigger unintended, troubling consequences. The pattern was hardly unique to the American West, but, as usual, the ironies of attempted conquest appeared here in an exaggerated, spotlighted form.

Consider, for instance, the problem of agricultural pests. When a farmer labors to produce a crop and bugs then eat the crop, it seems a very unjust allocation of labor and reward. Think of the futile "hopperdozers" (sticky surfaces to be dragged through the fields), recommended as the solution for the grasshopper plagues of the nineteenth century, and the appeal of powerful pesticides becomes clear. Naturally, farmers took to using them enthusiastically. Protecting the crop was the obvious priority. Even when the bad news began to come in, farmers—supported by the agricultural chemicals industry—held out for crop protection.

In 1962, the scientist Rachel Carson published *Silent Spring*, one of the most important books of the twentieth century. "Before her book," the *New York Times* environmental reporter Philip Shabecoff has written, "pesticides were regarded as the equivalent of miracle drugs. They could eradicate disease-carrying pests and sharply reduce crop losses without any apparent negative effect for human beings." Carson's warnings introduced caution to the issue, leading to the 1971 banning of DDT, the worst of the threats. Events over the next generation, however, indicated that society could not simply recognize error and reverse it. DDT and other prohibited chemicals "continue to show up in the environment long after being banned, in part because they persist so long," because other countries still use them, and because there might well be illegal use in this country. Moreover, a whole host of new legal pesticides took their place: the use of pesticides has more than doubled since the publication of *Silent Spring*. Pesticides accumulated in rivers and lakes, farmworkers took a heightened risk in direct exposure to toxic chemicals, and residues added a potential poison to commercial food. Rachel Carson had "warned that insect pests would develop immunities to pesticides over time, requiring more and more sprayings. In fact, dozens of species have developed such immunities." An even greater irony lay in the Department of Agriculture's figures on crop loss: "32 percent of crops were lost to insect, disease and weed pests in 1945, while in 1980 such crop loss was 37 percent."[27]

From time to time, the insects made their own statement— more forceful than those of scientists and statisticians—that they had not submitted to conquest. In 1985, areas of the West met the region's familiar plague, "a relentless onslaught of grasshoppers." " 'The ground's alive,' " a farmer in Idaho "said as he walked through knee-deep wheat, with nothing but grasshoppers left on the ravaged stalks." In the established patterns of Western history, "farmers blame[d] the Federal Government for the severity of the grasshopper infestation." These were, Idahoans argued, "Federal grasshoppers" from land under control of the Bureau of Land Management. But what were government officials to do? "If they don't spray, the farmers sue the Government for not controlling the problem," said an agricultural extension agent; if they do spray, environmentalists and beekeepers will sue. In the environmental muddles of our times, the federal government's efforts to "manage" nature have pinned it square in the center of the controversy, perfectly sited for blame and resentment.[28]

Every sort of Western enterprise offered its own case study of solutions creating new problems, answers posing new riddles. In its elemental sense, freed of an exclusive association with the nineteenth-century frontier, pioneering involved just this process of introducing new variables into an already complicated setting, and often inaugurating a process that transformed the pioneers' initial optimism into consternation. Whether they worked in the most traditional and apparently most natural of Western pursuits, like cattle ranching, or in the most radically innovative and unnatural, like atomic energy, Western pioneers undertook journeys into uncertainty. North America before Columbus had been a continent without domesticated grazing animals and without artificially manipulated radiation. The introduction of both factors set off unpredictable, long-range consequences, which experts in our time struggle to control. The introduction of cattle, sheep, and goats was, in many regions, a shock to the ecological system from which it never quite recovered. Wild animals roam, rotating their grazing pressure from place to place; domestic animals, according to the wills of their herders, often stay too long in one place, depleting the plants and their capacity to regenerate. Wild animals, if their range becomes drastically overstocked, will die off until the numbers and the resource rebalance; domestic animals can have populations maintained too long at artificially high levels. Sustained, intensive grazing can rearrange the basic workings of an ecosystem.

In a valuable recent case study, William deBuys follows the history of the northern New Mexico mountains, where Hispanos have been maintaining herds since the early nineteenth century. It is now popular to see the folk cultures of the West, both Indian and Hispanic, as beneficiaries of an enlightened and sensitive relationship to nature, until the disruptive deus ex machina, the cash market, entered the picture, making the folk into pawns of a heartless capitalist system, a system as oppressive to the land as to the folk. But deBuys's New Mexico findings point in a rather different direction.

Hispano villagers did (and do) have a warm and close attachment to the environment, and yet their livestock were still grazing too intensively and thereby eradicating native plant species and opening the way for exotics and, by altering the ground cover, creating problems of erosion and an erratic stream flow. This, deBuys found, *preceded* the arrival of that culprit among social forces—the cash market. "It would certainly be wrong to laud the early-day subsistence villagers as guardians of a careful balance in their use of the land," he concludes. "The severely eroded hills surrounding the older mountain villagers testify eloquently enough that land abuse predated the advent of the cash economy." The demands of a commercial market accelerated overgrazing, but "they did not invent the disease." A sensitive *feeling* for the land did not necessarily ensure a sensitive *treatment* of the land. "If there is a flaw in the relationship of the villagers to their environment," deBuys suggests, "it is that they, like the people of pioneer and subsistence cultures everywhere, have consistently underestimated their capacity for injuring the land."[29]

In the same way, the hardy and independent Anglo cattle rancher, symbolically at peace with and close to the land, could also prove to be an agent of inadvertent ecological injury. In the 1880s, overstocking and overgrazing had led to the disaster of 1887, in which the cattle, already weakened by drought, died in massive numbers during a severe winter. Apparently more stabilized after that calamity, the cattle business even submitted to the leasing of the public lands, under the Taylor Grazing Act of 1934.[30] Grazing permits on the public lands became yet another variation on the Western theme of property, with the permits forming part of the rancher's assets, salable along with his land. And yet, government regulation notwithstanding, livestock grazing could still injure the ecosystem, in ways that finally injured the livestock business itself by reducing the value and productivity of the land.

In 1985, this dilemma emerged in the question of the fee charged to those who leased the public lands. The federal government had, as the *Washington Post* put it, "kept this grazing fee artificially low to help cash-poor ranchers." Environmentalists would have phrased it a bit differently—the Bureau of Land Management had simply deferred too much and too long to the ranchers who dominated the local advisory boards for the grazing districts. In a related failure of bureaucratic integrity, the BLM knew the range was in trouble from overgrazing but did not press for reform. A 1979 study revealed that 135 million acres out of the 170 million acres of BLM land were "only in fair condition, or worse." Most studies had "recommended sharp reductions in the number of cattle," but the BLM still had "not asked ranchers to adjust cattle numbers." Instead, environmentalists argued, livestock grazers' dominance of the BLM permitted overgrazing, deterioration of the range, erosion and declining stream quality, and injury to fish and wildlife. Under these circumstances, setting a low fee for use of the public lands (roughly one-fourth that charged by private landowners) was not only a subsidy, said Maggie Fox, a Sierra Club spokesperson, but "a direct incentive to a rancher to overgraze." America's traditional hero on a horse seemed to stand revealed as a federally subsidized ecological threat.[31]

In an article entitled "Even the Bad Guys Wear White Hats: Cowboys, Ranchers, and the Ruin of the West," the environmental activist Edward Abbey took the quarrel as far as it could go. Some Western cattlemen, he announced, "are nothing more than welfare parasites." A form of "cowboy welfare" gave them "a free ride on the public lands for over a century." The problem goes beyond unfair subsidizing: "The cattle have done, and are doing, intolerable damage to our public lands," an injury for which "overgrazing is much too weak a term." Ranchers replaced wildlife with "ugly, clumsy, stupid, bawling, stinking, fly-covered, shit-smeared, disease-spreading brutes." Contrary to the popular image, Abbey claimed,

the rancher (with a few honorable exceptions) is a man who strings barbed wire all over the range; drills wells and bulldozes stock ponds; drives off elk and antelope and bighorn sheep; poisons coyotes and prairie dogs; shoots eagles, bears, and cougars on sight; supplants the native grasses with tumbleweed, snakeweed, povertyweed, cowshit, anthills, mud, dust, and flies. And then leans back and grins at the TV cameras and talks about how much he loves the American West.[32]

And yet, many Western ranchers continued to see themselves more as victim than as villain. Ranchers in the 1980s shared many of the farmers' problems: "surplus supplies, declining demand and, the bane of all agricultural operators, high interest rates." Cattle ranchers also faced their own marketing nightmare in a widespread consumer perception that eating red meat had an undesirable impact on health, a perception that had led to a 25 percent decline in consumption since the mid-1970s. Long-term Western ranchers also faced competition from wealthy new ranchers, who had made their money in other businesses and simply wanted the ranch for romance or a tax loss. And competition in the traditional form of cattle rustlers persisted. "A century ago," reported the *Denver Post*, "rustling was a big concern of ranchers, and many believe that it is an even bigger worry today." Trailers and trucks provided criminals with a more rapid and efficient method to escape, while ranchers and law enforcement agencies tried to fight back with the new technology of computerized information to track cattle and thieves.[33]

Ranchers also faced pressures from urban and recreational developers and from expanding coal companies. There was no clear and consistent line of conflict between ranchers and environmentalists; rather, the two groups sometimes united to hold the line against the spread of condominiums or strip mines. In the familiar method of borrowed identity, some ranchers cast themselves as the natives resisting invasion. "I have become, for all practical purposes, an Indian," said one white Montana rancher. "Like the Indian, I am standing in the way of progress because I live and work above part of the world's largest known reserves of fossil fuel." Ranchers, he argued, "are the new vanishing race."[34]

The temptation to vanish voluntarily by selling out to the developers was a strong one. Just as in farm country, the early 1980s were a financially troubled time in cattle country: "foreclosures, forced sales, failing banks, cattle-town economies strangled by surplus production and low beef prices." "That's how people are staying in business these days," said one rancher, the president elect of the formerly imperial Wyoming Stockgrowers Association. "You live on borrowed money." In his nineties, the Arizona cowboy poet Gail Gardener captured the nonmythic qualities of the cattle-raising life:

> If you ever have a youngster
> And he wants to foller stock,
> The best thing you can do for him
> Is to brain him with a rock.
> Or if rocks ain't very handy
> You kin shove him down the well;
> Do not let him be a cowboy,
> For he's better off in hell.

Confronting the possibility of a higher fee for public-land grazing, the Colorado rancher John Nieslanik expressed the problem more prosaically: "I'm getting $10 less (per 100 pounds) for beef than I was a year ago, I'm getting $2 less for milk than three years ago. So why do you want to sock me now?"[35]

The federal fee problem, it turned out, was the only one that consented to go away. In an era of massive budget cutting, President Ronald Reagan chose not to raise the grazing fee. To conservationists, this was "a political giveaway to Western livestock interests at a time when most other Federal programs were being slashed to reduce the budget defincit." The low fee, said one conservation leader, "was an unfair subsidy to a tiny minority of livestock operators in the West," a small pool of businessmen getting a special favor from their government. Cowboys, evidently, had not lost all of their charm.[36]

While the political squabbles went on, the large environmental question remained unsolved. A giant ecological niche had changed personnel; sheep and cattle and replaced buffalo and had largely supplanted elk and antelope. What had that done to the land? Was the process, as the *New York Times* suggested in 1979, one of "desertification"—"the desert creeping up on the rangelands"? How much of the change was progress and how much injury?[37]

And yet, the cattle business had only a few decades before seemed to be the solution, not the problem, for Western land use. If farming demanded more soil quality and water than the arid and semiarid West could provide, ranching was the appropriate adaptation, a way to utilize the land with an appropriate reduction in pressure. But from the introduction of cattle into Spanish Mexico to the Long Drive from Texas to Kansas in the 1860s, the cattle trade inaugurated a chain of unforeseen consequences, a chain by no means at an end.

However, in unforeseen consequences, nothing could beat the newest of Western industries. Certainly, no location on the planet is remote enough to escape the troubling issues of nuclear power. But the American West has been particularly close to the power of the atom, in ways that followed directly in the established themes of Western history. Moreover, if the unleashed atom introduced a new era in human history, the American West has been at the center of modern history, not left behind to dwell on a quaint and irrelevant past.

The ideal vision: cowboys and cattle in Gunnison County, Colorado. *Courtesy Colorado Historical Society*

Western locations played nearly every possible role in nuclear history. Los Alamos, in northern New Mexico, was remote enough to sequester the scientists who invented the bomb. At once desert and deserted, Alamogordo, New Mexico, offered an ideal place to test the first bomb. Into the Cold War, the Nevada Test Site provided the remoteness and aridity to make a permanent test site. Throughout the 1950s, nuclear tests went on over Nevada, and winds carried the fallout around the planet. After 1963, the tests went underground, but they persisted, with occasional leaks and accidents. Remote Western sites provided prime locations for Minuteman missile silos and, military planners thought, for the mobile MX system. Hanford, in the desert interior of Washington, became the site for plutonium processing and for a while constellation of nuclear services. Livermore, California, emerged

The ideal meets the passage of time: reunion of old cowboys at the XY Ranch, Colorado. *Courtesy Colorado Historical Society*

as a center for nuclear research and design. The Rocky Flats plant in Golden, Colorado, became a center for nuclear production, and the Pantex plant outside Amarillo, Texas, evolved into the place of final assembly for all nuclear weapons. Hidden in Cheyenne Mountain, near Colorado Springs, was NORAD (the North American Aerospace Defense Command), the command post for an actual war.

Areas of the West—especially the Colorado Plateau in the Four Corners area, and the Black Hills in South Dakota—proved to be rich in uranium ore, and the late 1940s saw a rush and boom in domestic uranium production. Separated by a century from the California gold rush, the uranium rush replicated many of the familiar patterns, even if jeeps had replaced burros and Geiger counters had replaced pans and rockers. Just as in conventional mining, the rush to make the initial claim meant opportunity for individuals, but actual production required large-scale investment, equipment, and hired labor. Uranium mining, however, added a whole new level of risk for workers and local residents. Miners working underground exposed themselves to, and even inhaled, radioactive dust; meanwhile, on the surface, radioactive tailings piled up, exposing residents to contaminated dust and water. Finally, when it came to the "peaceful" uses of nuclear energy, the West got—along with its share of nuclear power plants—the major attention of Project Plowshare. In this operation, scientists dreamed up ways to put atomic and hydrogen bombs to work—deepening harbors, loosening oil shale, removing poorly placed mountains, and breaking up arid lands, so that the pulverized earth would retain, in underground storage chambers, water that would otherwise run off unused.[38]

Fortunately, a sense of the serious health effects of radioactivity became widely distributed before Project Plowshare could begin the final mastery of nature in the West. The consequences of exposure began to appear in a variety of populations: in Navajo men who had worked as uranium miners; in army veterans who had been stationed at the Nevada Test Site and commanded to run toward ground zero in order to develop skills and strategies for combining nuclear explosions with conventional infantry war; in the "downwinders"—the patriotic, mostly Mormon good citizens of small towns in Utah and Nevada placed squarely in the path of fallout and repeatedly assured by test site officials that they were at no risk.

The serious aftershocks of the nuclear frontier began to be heard in the courts, as lawsuits recorded the injuries and suspicions of men and women exposed to Western radioactivity. In 1953, a herd of sheep had died in prodigious numbers after crossing the path of fallout and eating brush coated with radioactive dust. The sheep lost appetite; their wool fell out; the ewes delivered deformed and moribund lambs. The sheep were victims of malnutrition, the government insisted. Losing their case in the 1950s, the ranchers tried to reopen it in the 1980s. The Supreme Court declined to hear their appeal in 1986, allowing "cold weather and malnutrition" to stand as the official cause of death.[39]

Human victims, however, seemed to fare better in litigation, in spite of the difficulties involved in adapting law to the new problems of the nuclear age. The relation between exposure to radiation and the development, years later, of malignant tumors was a difficult problem of causation, with no clear way to connect criminal, crime, victim, injury, and punishment. Nonetheless, in May 1984, in *Irene Allen* v.

United States, Judge Bruce Jenkins in Salt Lake City ruled in favor of ten downwinders (or their survivors), cancer-plagued residents of the towns in the path of the Nevada Test Site fallout. By its "negligent failures" to warn the locals, Jenkins ruled, the federal government had "unreasonably placed" the plaintiffs "at risk of injury and, as a direct and proximate result of such failures . . . plaintiffs suffered injury." Judge Jenkins's decision marked "the first time the federal courts have recognized a clear link between US nuclear testing and cancer." Although the federal government would appeal the decision, the ruling had still opened "the Pandora's box that the Government thought it could close." What was the next step? Should Congress act to compensate the many victims of radiation? Once again, the Western past refused burial; the Jenkins decision, as the commentator Daniel Schorr put it, meant that the Atomic Energy Commission's "casualness [was] coming back to haunt the government."[40]

Western American history was offering another course in its standard curriculum, another case study in the conquest of nature and the unforeseen, maddening, and persistent side effects of that conquest. It was thus perfectly appropriate to find the West playing the principal role in the most unsettled issue of the nuclear business, the problem of storing the waste left over from fuel plants and military weapons production.

Where was the nation to store its nuclear wastes? Spent fuel from operating nuclear plants had been accumulating for years, with no permanent place of storage. Why not the West? Since the days of Indian removal and the Mormon flight from persecution, the West had appealed as a potential dumping ground, a remote place to which to transplant people whose presence annoyed, angered, or obstructed the majority. Why not apply the same strategy to toxic substances? Aridity left vast areas where humans had not settled densely. "Nuclear waste," one news story pointed out, "is a problem that most people want buried in someone else's back yard." Why not select the most remote back-yard of all?[41]

In 1982, Congress initiated a selection process to find a site for a permanent nuclear-waste dump. Initially, the search included the East Coast and the Middle West. When, in May of 1986, the list of three finalists was announced, the headlines made it clear which regions had won and which had lost: "United States Suspends Plan for Nuclear Dump in East or Midwest," reported the *New York Times*. "I am absolutely delighted," said a Republican congressman from Maine. "A dark cloud of uncertainty and doubt has been lifted."[42]

The cloud, of course, had lifted in the East and settled on the West: on Hanford, Washington; on southern Nevada; and on Deaf Smith County, in Texas. "You damned Yankees got what you wanted, to dump your nuclear trash on the West," said a Texan who operated a seed farm in Deaf Smith County. The Department of Energy had, improbably, targeted Texas's most productive agricultural county; the radioactive waste, more-over, would have to be buried in salt formations *below* the Ogal-lala aquifer, the lake of underground water that supported High Plains agriculture. The prospects for water contamination seemed enormous—"the worst kind of littering," as the Texas state attorney general called it. There was widespread resistance to the prospect of playing host to a hazard lasting thousands of years. "All three Western states," the *Christian Science Monitor* reported, "either have filed suit against the federal government or are planning to."[43]

And yet, true to the workings of anxious Western boom/bust economies, some Westerners saw a happy opportunity in nuclear litter. Some Texans regarded the dump "as a potential savior for the region's economy, slumping under the weight of sagging prices for oil, crops and cattle." In all three targeted states, the question of the dump divided "those attracted by the money the project would bring and others who fear contamination." "We need the jobs," said one resident near the prospective Nevada site. "Any way you look at it, it's death," said a fellow resident. "It's death for you or your children or your grandchildren, because nobody knows what that stuff does to you in the long run." The people who worked at Hanford, Washington, which had long been involved with the atomic industry, were the most enthusiastic. Since residents there had "lived and worked in and around the country's nuclear industry since the early days of the atomic age, the idea of a nuclear waste dump nearby seems less daunting," the *New York Times* reported. The dump, the mayor of a town near Hanford said, "would be a real shot in the arm for the city." The Washington site had the handicap of potential "earthquakes and volcanic activity," but many of the local residents had long made their peace with atomic risk, as had a variety of other Westerners. "If that plant blows up," said the owner of the bar nearest Colorado's Rocky Flats nuclear facility, "my worries will be over forever. So, why worry now?" The fabled Western tough guy, immune to fear and indifferent to risk, had assumed a new and terribly modern form.[44]

IV

As one set of obstacles and risks retired from Western history, another rose to take its place. Railroads eliminated the test of endurance, the thirst, and the physical exertion of the overland trail, and automobiles eliminated the railroad's's restrictions on individual choice and freedom of movement. With automobiles, Western freedom and independence seemed to take a leap upward, but the risk of death and injury from accidents, the dependence on fuel, the vulnerability to changing oil prices, and the expenses of road building and maintenance all took parallel leaps. Westerners had a well-established sense of their right to unrestricted, even impulsive mobility, but the collective product of these multiple individual choices was, for many Western cities, an ever-increasing problem of congestion and smog.

Los Angeles had led the way. As Robert Fogelson has shown, early-twentieth-century Los Angeles had a dominant population of newly arrived, native-born, middle-class white Americans. They had a clear "conception of the good community": single-family homes, large lots, lawns, residences isolated from businesses. To these settlers, cities were "congested, impoverished, filthy, immoral, transient, uncertain, and heterogeneous," while suburbs were "spacious, affluent, clean, decent, permanent, predictable, and homogeneous." Initially, street trolleys made it possible to build this decentralized vision; then the crowding, delays, and inflexibility of the trolleys made the automobile an attractive alternative. By the 1920s, the conviction was widespread that "motor cars provided better service at lower cost than electric railways." Los Angeles residents had, moreover, "formed intangible but by no means unimportant attachments" to their cars; "they wholeheartedly accepted dependence on the motor car without fully comprehending the implications of this commitment." In the 1930s, despite "extensive highway construction," automotive "traffic was highly congested and delays very common," but Los Angeles was "too firmly committed to the automobile by now to essay any alternatives." The city was set in its pattern of decentralization and fragmentation, and by the 1940s it was also set in its patterns of air pollution. The industrialization of Los Angeles played its part in the creation of smog, but the dependence on automobiles was unquestionably a prime contributor.[45]

If Los Angeles taught a lesson, it was not a particularly persuasive or effective one. Phoenix, in 1986, appeared to be "making many of the same mistakes Los Angeles made decades ago," developing "a low density sprawl of freeways and shopping malls that is at once dependent upon and victimized by the automobile." Traditionally considered a refuge for respiratory sufferers because of its "fresh and clean" air, Phoenix was now sometimes "shrouded in a thick cloud of smog," earning it, at least temporarily, the distinction of being the American city with the highest level of carbon monoxide. Denver gave Phoenix keen competition. Denver at rush hour, the *New York Times* reported in 1985, had developed "the kind of bumper-to-bumper fuming that newcomers had come West to escape." For days on end, Denver's smog—cheerfully nicknamed the Brown Cloud—interfered with the area's famous view of the Rockies. Along the Front Range, reaching south to Colorado Springs, "feverish development" without "central planning" threatened the "very qualities—clean air, open space, little congestion and mountain vistas—that made the area attractive in the first place."[46]

Prosperity seemed to hinge on the region's continuing growth, but growth would undermine the region's original attractions. How could Western boosters sort out the problem? How could they take their own contradictory regional identity and repackage it as an attractive, consistent image? Promoters and boosters were as active in the twentieth-century West as they had been in the nineteenth; their task had, if anything, become more challenging. Western towns, cities, and states have always tended to watch over their "images" as hypochondriacs watch over their health.

"War Declared on City Image as Cowtown," read a typical headline in the *Denver Post* in 1985. Many out-of-state businessmen, it seemed, harbored the dangerous misconception that Colorado was "not a good place to do business." On one side, the state's image was "anti-growth" and "anti-business," "too environmentally conscious," too willing to restrict business for the benefit of nature. Resisting progress, Denver, especially, appeared to be stuck with an antimodern identity—that of a "cow town." But then, on the other side, boosters worried about an opposite image—the picture of the Brown Cloud of smog dwelling over the city. The two bad images seemed to cancel each other out: if Denver was trapped beneath machine-produced smog, it could hardly be considered an anti-industrial backwater overzealously protecting its natural environment and its lost cowboy past. But boosters did not pause over these contradictions. Trying to overcome an image problem, Denver in the 1980s launched a "major media campaign," fervently wooing outside business with "speakers bureaus, newsletters, and a flurry of mile-high propaganda" aimed at dispelling both the cow town and the Brown Cloud images.[47]

In a way, Denver had an advantage over other Western communities. Albuquerque, for instance, seemed to carry a greater burden. In an opinion poll, the city proved to be "little known"; a survey of businessmen revealed "that the name Albuquerque conjured up no particular image." For many Western towns, having no image at all seemed a worse affliction than having a mistaken image to correct. Nonetheless, Albuquerque still had the familiar problems; though it grew more slowly than Denver or Phoenix, "congestion and pollution" were still catching up with it. As city after city, town after town, squirmed to fit itself into the proper image, the pressures on the Western environment built up a stockpile of problems that a refashioned image would not solve and might even make worse.[48]

In all these environmental muddles, the same question reappears, one just as difficult to answer in the nineteenth century as it is today: Can any force effectively police development, even when restraint seems to serve the general good? The list of history's failures provides few models for the present: futile efforts to restrain squatters on Indian lands, to oversee and license the fur trade, to make Mormons give up polygamy and to make the Indians assimilate, to transfer land into the hands of the small family farmers and avoid monopolies and concentrations of landed power, to subsidize the railroads and to combine their private corporate interests with the public good. All of the various efforts to make the West and Western enterprise "behave" seemed to stumble over this problem of enforcement. If the locals resisted the attempted reforms, what was the government to do? Deploy federal troops, at considerable expense and political injury, to enforce compliance? The solution was not popular in the nineteenth century, nor did it appear more attractive in the twentieth. And so, even when it seemed to many that it was time for restraint, those who chose defiance had an easily available retort: How are you going to make us stop?

This defiance took direct and literal form in the matter of the 55-mph speed limit. Instituted by Congress in 1974 to save fuel, the 55-mph limit endured because lower speeds saved lives. But by 1985 the restriction had earned a reputation as "the most widely broken national law since Prohibition." Defiance focused in the West. "For reasons that have to do with its wide open spaces, long distances between settlements and a traditional dislike for Federal meddling," the *New York Times* explained, "the West has long been the flashpoint for anti-55-an-hour sentiment." Many Western state legislatures tried "to get Washington to let them once again set their own speed limits of up to 70 miles an hour." The original justification for the law was gone, they argued; the energy crisis was over; Western distances created unique driving conditions; to drive from Reno to Las Vegas was to cover the distance from New York to Cleveland, but "on the emptiest and straightest roads in the country," where "boredom" was a greater danger than speed. "There is a sort of feeling here," said the governor of Montana, "that of all the stupid rules coming out of Washington, 55 was the stupidest." To engage in a kind of borderline nullification, Western states used "various ploys and stratagems designed to let their drivers exceed 55" without the states' risking the penalty of losing "highway money from Washington." "The most common detour around the lower speed limit in western states," the *Washington Post* reported, "has been the replacement of stiff speeding fines with mild, no-point tickets for drivers caught traveling between 55 and 70 mph." It was an issue of states' rights, argued Western rebels; the regulation might suit some regions but did not suit the West. In the meantime, the majority of Westerners driving on highways had become outlaws, persuaded that their own local needs and conditions set them free of national law.[49]

One distinctive minority made the same assumption, freeing itself for a course of outlawry at once very modern and very traditional. A loose organization named Earth First! publicized the rebellion. Loyalty to unchanged nature was its passion, a passion frustrated by laws to encourage development. The ecodefenders were thus forced, by their own logic, to go outside the law. The wilderness is under attack, Edward Abbey explained; "international timber, mining and beef industries are invading our public lands . . . and looting them"; the "jellyfish Government agencies" are aiding the looters. Since "self-defense against attack" is a basic law of life, ecodefenders are obligated by this higher law to act, engaging in practices technically defined as criminal in order to fight off the greater criminality of wilderness development.[50]

Introduced by Abbey's remarks, an extraordinary book provided a strategy, technique, and philosophy for these outlaws. *Ecodefense: A Field Guide to Monkeywrenching* began with a "Standard Disclaimer": this book "is for entertainment purposes only. No one involved with the production of this book . . . encourages anyone to do any of the stupid, illegal things contained herein." Disclaimer out of the way, the text provided down-to-earth (for-the-earth, the authors would claim) advice and step-by-step, illustrated instructions for ecosabotage. The instructions cover many approaches: how to put nails and spikes in trees to deter timber cutting; how to dispose of surveyor's stakes in order to disrupt road building ("once the road is in, a host of other evils will follow") and how to spike roads to puncture tires if the road is already built; how to bring down powerline towers and how to shoot out insulators ("with a shotgun") or electrical conductors ("a high-powered rifle is best"); how to interfere with seismic exploration for oil and gas ("a box of straight pins and a few tubes of super glue" can take care of the essential cables); how to disable bulldozers and helicopters; how to escape detection; how to keep quiet if the worst happens and arrest results. Repeatedly, the book's authors declare that the intention is to damage property, eventually making development too expensive and troublesome, and not to threaten human life (when disabling vehicles, *do not tamper with the brake systems*"). However they might appear to the Forest Service, the Bureau of Land Management, the timber, oil, gas, livestock, and mining companies, the eco-outlaws could see themselves as defenders of high principle, maneuvering in the freedom of the wilderness to ensure that the wilderness always remained free.[51]

In the twentieth century, the monkeywrenchers recognized, it was still very difficult for the agents of law to be everywhere at once. Combine the gap between law and enforcement with the push to profit intrinsic to Western history, and the recent past provides a full array of case studies in outlaw continuity. Oil companies smuggled oil out of an Indian reservation, avoiding royalty payments to the tribe.[52] The Bureau of Indian Affairs, true to nineteenth-century patterns, still struggled with corruption and misuse of official funds.[53] The Penn Square Bank in Oklahoma engaged in questionable, inflated financing of oil and gas development and came down in a mighty crash of scandal in 1982.[54] A county in Nevada recently plunged into a controversy over rival establishments of prostitution, when one entrepreneur tried to drive out a competitor—by arson.[55] "California supplanted New York as the nation's capital of confidence artists," marketing improbable investment schemes by playing on the "obsessive search for a good life," the hope for "an instant solution" that fueled much of Western expansion. The incentives for investment crime were enormous: "In just a few months," an assistant U.S. district attorney told the *Christian Science Monitor,* "depending on the pitch, they can rake in millions of dollars." "The real problem," said one expert, "is a manpower problem" especially at the federal level, as it had been throughout the West's struggles over enforcement. In 1986, "one CFTC [Commodities Futures Trading Commission] investigator and three lawyers" were "charged with monitoring hundreds of legal and illegal commodities firms in 13 western states," a weakness that spelled opportunity to the unscrupulous.[56] And bank robbers, as well as con men, continued to find the West the environment of preference. "Regionally, the West accounted for more bank holdups" in 1984 "than the other 37 states combined," evidently a response to the "West's proliferation of isolated branch banks." Even technique showed more continuity than change: "Modern-day bank robbers operate much the same way the Daltons and the James gang did. They usually rely on a gun and a lot of nerve."[57]

A prime case study in the persistent problem of defiant lawbreaking concerns the cash crop of marijuana. At a time when the Reagan administration was trying to cut down on the smuggling of foreign drugs, "the marijuana plantations of California" and the "booming nationwide industry" they represented were an "increasing embarrassment." And yet, the illicit enterprise had its own local logic. Areas of rural northern California had been through "years of setbacks for the local logging and fishing industries." Young people from the counterculture moved into places like Humboldt County in the 1960s, planting occasional marijuana patches. Following patterns set by other Western businesses, what began "as a backyard enterprise" gradually "evolved into large commercial operations." Marijuana growing not only "pumped up" local business but even became "the mainstay of the local economy" and "one of California's largest cash crops." "When they come in here with cash," said a northern California real estate agent, "we don't ask, 'Where'd you get this money?' " Marijuana, remarked a *Washington Post* reporter, "is against the law in the United States, but you would never know it here"—in Garberville, Humboldt County, California.[58]

The situation did not, however, make for tranquillity. Conflict between armed marijuana growers and armed "pot pirates" raiding their remote plots could make the wilderness into "a vicious battleground." In the squatter tradition, some growers used the public lands for their plantations. In 1982, marijuana plots were found at six thousand sites in national forests. "With a little bit of seed and the use of somebody else's land," said one law enforcement agent, the planter was on his way to "high profit and no taxes." In protecting their "property," wilderness planters sometimes set booby traps or conducted armed patrols. "Many innocent people" were thus "terrorized and brutalized" by these modern-day outlaws.[59]

The greatest disruption came from periodic attempts to control the problem. Organized as a coalition of law enforcement officials, the Campaign Against Marijuana Planting (CAMP) tried its best to interfere with the thriving northern California business. Raiding in the harvest season, commando teams arrived by helicopter, wielded automatic weapons, confiscated the crop, and destroyed it—often in large bonfires. The operation reminded many people of the Vietnam War; local residents felt their rights of privacy violated by the surveillance of spy planes, helicopters, and roadblocks. The CAMP people felt beleaguered, resented by law-abiding citizens as well as by the marijuana growers. It was a predictable collision "between a community that has come to rely on marijuana growing" and the law. "Contrary to popular opinion," said one CAMP official, "we're the good guys." The lawmen were "wag[ing] a probably futile effort to stamp out" the business; "most of the locals," noted one reporter, "love the big pools of cash the industry generates." Certainly, the outlaws of the late twentieth century used expressions unfamiliar to Billy the Kid. "This had been a very stressful afternoon," said one young woman after losing $200,000 of her crop to CAMP raiders. But this case study in contemporary outlaws was eminently serious business. "The economic and political impact of the illegal industry," according to the administrator of the California

Bureau of Narcotics Enforcement, "is enormous."[60]

The West was once the Wild West, the old image held, and then, heroically, law and order were introduced and the wilderness was mastered. But that image both exaggerated the significance of lawbreaking in the past and underestimated its significance in the present. With or without an open frontier, Western outlaws lived on, to a large degree preying on the trusting optimism, the vulnerability of strangers, the passion for profit, and the overstrained enforcement that had brought opportunity to their nineteenth-century predecessors. If the environmentalist outlaw or the marijuana grower seems too modern, there are also varieties closer to tradition.

From time to time, the old drama is played again: the act of violence followed by a retreat to the wilderness, capped by a manhunt. In 1981, a trapper in the border country between northern Nevada and southern Idaho killed two game wardens, set off an eighteen-month-long manhunt through the wilds, and was finally run to ground. Tried and convicted for manslaughter, Claude Dallas was sentenced to serve thirty years in an Idaho prison. Then, in 1986, "he slipped out of the prison after dark on Easter Sunday, cutting his way through two fences and disappeared into the surrounding desert outside Boise." Search teams looked for him in his old territory—"the place he knows best," the prison warden said—but "there was no way to search all of the region because of its vastness." Claude Dallas was once more, in the words of his biographer Jeff Long, "at large and repeatedly outwitting the twentieth century."[61]

In a considerably less successful venture in 1984, two "mountain men" in Montana kidnapped Kari Swenson, an athlete training for the Olympics. Don and Dan Nichols, father and son, wanted a woman to live in the mountains with them. "We don't get many women up in the mountains we can talk to," the father told Swenson. When rescuers followed them, the Nicholses shot one man, wounded their captive, and fled. A sheriff with a name ready for inclusion in Western folklore stayed on their trail. Five months after the crime, Sheriff Johnny France walked alone into their camp and arrested both men. To the judge, the trial was "a simple, kidnap-homicide case," but the press found "pathos,

sex, death, stunning scenery and a cast of picture-book characters playing out their story in one of the most colorful locales of
the American West." The Nicholses went to prison, Swenson
recovered from her injuries, and Sheriff France acquired an agent
"to handle book, television and film offers." The father and son,
however, were singularly short on cinematic charm: extremely
"dirty," Swenson had said—a parent-child team locked in family
pathology. ("I would hit him on the forehead with my fist," Don
Nichols said, in explaining his system of discipline. "That's the
safest place to hit a kid.") Viewed from the distance of a century,
violent individuals pursuing antisocial goals evidently have a great
deal of quaint appeal; Western booksellers report that books on
the old outlaws remained their most popular items. Take away
that comfortable remoteness in time, and spontaneous, individualistic crime loses a great deal of its charm.[62]

Even less appealing than the individuals were the outlaw
groups who joined together to fight for their own version of
principle and who found the West a congenial location. An organization called the Aryan Nations, headquartered in Hayden Lake,
in northern Idaho, proved a major producer of "racism and
extremist political rhetoric." Richard Butler, the leader of the
group, was an "inspiration" to many younger protégés, who prized
his attacks on "Jews, Catholics, blacks, Mexican-Americans,
homosexuals, communism, and the American economic system."
Splinter groups, however, would come to the conclusion that Butler was failing to act against these urgent threats. In the 1980s,
one group, known as the Order or the Silent Brotherhood, went
into action to overthrow the enemy they called ZOG—the Zionist
Occupation Government of North America. The resulting "trail
of violence" across the West included an armed robbery of $3.6
million from an armored car in northern California (to finance
the revolution), a plan to undermine the national currency with
counterfeiting, the suspected killing of a controversial Jewish talk
show host in Denver, and, finally, a shoot-out, in December 1984
on Whidbey Island, in Washington State, in which the Order's
charismatic leader, Robert Mathews, burned to death in a house
from which he held "almost 100 FBI agents at bay with automatic weapons fire for 36 hours." Prosecuted on racketeering

charges in Seattle, five members of the Order in February 1986 received "stiff sentences" (forty to one hundred years), which failed to diminish their sense of their own heroism. "Whatever I did," said Bruce Carroll Pierce, suspected of killing the Denver talk show host, "I did to bring honor to myself and glory to my brothers and glory to God." Their goal was not, after all, unprecedented in Western history: they had "sought the ultimate establishment of a 'racially pure' white supremacist state in the Pacific Northwest." "The whites are self-evidently the leaders, the light bearers of the world," said Richard Butler of the Aryan Nations. "The white race has been the culture bearers; they have been the civilizing influence of the world."[63] One hundred and forty years earlier, Butler's sentiments would have been standard refrains in the chorus of Manifest Destiny. It was only a further twist on the many ironies of Western history that the mainstream patriotism of the nineteenth century had become the rallying point for the latest variety of Western outlaw.

Part **2**

The Conquerors Meet Their Match

Six

The Persistence of Natives

IN 1992, THE UNITED STATES will take part in a touchy ceremony. Until quite recent times, the anniversary of Columbus's arrival in the New World seemed to be a simple holiday. At the Chicago Columbian Exposition in 1893, the four hundredth anniversary provided the occasion for a straightforward celebration of all the progress made since Columbus launched the conquest of the Western Hemisphere. But the five hundredth anniversary will come at an awkward point in our changing perception of history. The cult of "progress" has lost believers. The idea of a North America without industrial machinery, pollutants, pesticides, or nuclear waste does not immediately call to mind the words "primitive," "backward," or "savage." But more important, the 1992 commemoration planners must take into account that the natives did not vanish; the descendants of the pre-Columbian Americans are very much alive—as are, in many cases, their memories and resentments of the conquest. In an age of attempted civility toward minorities, it seems poor taste, at best, to celebrate an invasion, a demographic catastrophe, and a conquest.

Since Columbus, Euro-Americans have received, recorded, and acted on a great many impressions of Indian Americans. A dominant image cast the Indians as passive, acted on, pushed

White man and Indian in mock confrontation, presenting an atypical moment of clarity and simplicity in Indian/white conflict. At Pine Ridge Agency, South Dakota. *Morledge Photo, courtesy Denver Public Library, Western History Department*

about by the more forceful white men. It is one of the recognitions of our times that the Indians have been as much actors as the acted on; they, too, have gathered their impressions of Columbus's diverse fellow immigrants. It is important—and unnerving—to realize that ethnic stereotyping can work both ways.

The Western Apaches engage in a form of linguistic play in which one person will interrupt an everyday scene and imitate "the whiteman." Consider this example—an impression of a Bureau of Indian Affairs bureaucrat, recorded by Keith H. Basso:

Setting: A drinking party in an Apache home at Cibecue.

Participants: Nine adult Apaches, including M (male, age 47) and N, M's brother-in-law (age 35); at least five children; and KHB [the anthropologist].

Scene: M, who is standing unobtrusively in a corner, takes a piece of paper from his shirt pocket and begins to read it. N observes this and calls out to M in a loud voice.

N: You got trouble reading, my friend? Lemme see. I going to help you.
   [N walks to where M is standing and takes the paper from him. He holds it out before him and pretends to study it carefully. Then he turns and addresses M.]

N: This your form one hundred. No, maybe one hundred forty-three. Maybe thirty-six. I just don't know. You got to make application for seventy-two, seventy-three, seventy-four. You get it tomorrow, my friend, deadline pretty quick. Hurry up!
   [M smiles and shakes his head in amused resignation. N then launches into nonsense.]

N: No occupation steps . . . benefits line right here . . . qualification experience . . . work training function. See my friend, like that! Just you read instructions. Real easy. Now you know it, see? I help you out.
   [M reaches for the paper N is holding and takes it back.]

M: [in Apache] ('Enough. Whitemen are stupid.')[1]

"Whitemen are stupid"—to hear one's people spoken of so harshly may not be agreeable, but it is instructive. One gets a glimpse of how it feels to be judged from a distance, to be categorically considered limited and inferior by people whom one has never even met. Scholars have long been preoccupied with the image of "the Indian" in the Euro-American mind; now, it is clear, others must make comparable studies of the image of "the white man" in the Indian mind. In thinking about American Indian history, it has become essential to follow the policy of cautious street crossers: Remember to look both ways.

II

In the 1830s, the painter George Catlin devoted himself to preserving the Indians. Not to preserving them physically; he thought that was a lost cause. Although he found them fascinating, colorful, and often noble, he also considered them fragile.

Noble savages could not coexist with civilization. Their decline was fated; Catlin could do nothing about that. But he could preserve them—in paint and in words. He flew "to their rescue— not of their lives or of their race (for they are *'doomed'* and must perish), but to the rescue of their looks and their modes, at which the acquisitive world may hurl their poison and every besom of destruction, and trample them down and crush them to death; yet phoenix-like, they may rise from the 'stain on a painter's palette,' and live again upon canvass, and stand forth for centuries yet to come, the living monuments of a noble race."[2]

On the Plains in the 1830s, the "acquisitive world" was most actively represented by the fur and hide trade, particularly by the American Fur Company. The arrival of steamboats on the Missouri River made the transportation of heavy buffalo hides more economical, and the American Fur Company was encouraging hunting of the buffalo, with the Indians themselves enlisted to hunt in return for trade goods, including alcohol. Catlin knew that the Plains Indian way of life rested on the abundance of buffalo; the hide trade was the most direct way to make them a "dying race." With no restraint, he denounced the trade in buffalo robes: to cater to "white man's luxury," the "Indians of the great plains" would be "left without the means of supporting life." "Civilized" reasoning might argue "that *power* is *right,* and *voracity a virtue,*" but Catlin, for one, felt otherwise. "Oh insatiable man," he would say to the acquirer of buffalo robes, "is thy avarice such! wouldst thou tear the skin from the back of the last animal of this noble race, and *rob thy fellow-man of his meat, and for it give him poison!*"[3]

With this sentiment in mind, one would expect that when Catlin encountered representatives of the American Fur Company, the fur would fly. Conversations beginning "Oh insatiable man" might be expected to conclude in blows. Catlin did record a great many encounters with American Fur Company personnel, but the tone was not what one would predict. At the mouth of the Yellowstone, Catlin met a "Mr. M'Kenzie" who seemed "to have charge of all the Fur Companies' business in this region." Did Catlin denounce him for his avarice and for his cruel role in the decline of the Indians? On the contrary, he thanked him for his hospitality, his "spirit of liberality and politeness," and the "luxuries of the country" provided at meals. Staying at M'Kenzie's fort, Catlin enjoyed the benefits of "a bottle of Madeira and one of excellent Port [which] are set in a pail of ice every day, and exhausted at dinner." How had he reached this outpost of civilization? Catlin traveled as the guest of the American Fur Company; in contemporary terms, the company would have been the corporate sponsor of Catlin's arts project. Moreover, he traveled on board the first steamboat to ascend the farther reaches of the Missouri River—the steamboat that would make possible the increased export of buffalo robes. Denouncing the "white man's cupidity" and expressing his gratitude to Pierre Chouteau, the partner in American Fur who had given him a free trip on the company's steamboat, Catlin simply showed that, on the subject of Indians, he was, like many white Americans, a very emotional man. His emotions carried him to places where logic could not follow.[4]

Catlin lamented the dilemma of the Indians. "[M]y heart bleeds"—he had an instinct for the right phrasing, long before it was a cliché—"for the fate that awaits the remainder of their unlucky race." Even sadder than their eventual extinction was the transitional phase visible farther to the east. In settled areas, the "contaminating vices and dissipations" of civilization left Indians "tainted." But farther to the west, out on the Plains, the Indians were "yet uncorrupted" and "uncontaminated."[5]

A great deal of Catlin's sentiment for these properly noble Indians had more to do with what they were not than with what they were. It especially gratified him that they were not businessmen. They had "no business hours to attend to, or professions to learn"; they had "no notes in bank or other debts to pay—no taxes, no tithes, no rents." "Joint tenants" in natural abundance, they were "free from, and independent of, a thousand cares and jealousies, which arise from mercenary motives in the civilized world." Real Indians were, in other words, a great reproach to civilization; ostensibly describing the Indians, Catlin was actually saying more about his discontent with American society. He handled Indian virtues like darts thrown to deflate American pretensions. When it came to social customs, "the sys-

tem of civilized life would furnish ten apparently useless and
ridiculous trifles to one which is found in Indian life; and at least
twenty to one which are purely nonsensical and unmeaning."
The contrast, one begins to think, stems from the fact not that
Indians were so wise but that white people were so silly.[6]

Perhaps most enviable for the white person held captive to
his mercenary society was the Indians' capacity to have a good
time. Untroubled by acquisitiveness, "their inclinations and faculties are solely directed to the enjoyment of the present day,
without the sober reflections on the past or apprehensions of the
future." Without history and, as Catlin repeatedly reminded his
readers, without much of a future, they could afford to be happy,
with nothing "to do in the world, but to while away their lives in
the innocent and endless amusement of the exercise of those
talents with which Nature has liberally endowed them, for their
mirth and enjoyment."[7]

With so little to recommend civilization and so much to make
savagery attractive, one might expect Catlin to convert. On the
contrary, he remained quite certain that conversion should run
the other way. When it came to religion, Indians—even the
"uncontaminated"—were sincere but wrong. Allowed to watch
the sun dance, in which Indian men hung suspended by pins
stuck through their chest muscles, Catlin found it "too terrible
or revolting," "barbarous and cruel," "remarkable and appalling," "shocking and disgusting." The custom, he thought, "sick-
ens the heart and even the stomach of a traveller in the country,
and he weeps for their ignorance—he pities them with all his
heart for their blindness."[8]

"Many would doubtless ask," Catlin thought, whether the
Indians "could be made to abandon the dark and random channel in which they are drudging, and made to flow in the light
and life of civilization?" His answer was a solid and unambigu-
ous yes, but the reader 150 years later, remembering Catlin's
other sentiments, does not make so easy an escape from ambi-
guity. Did Catlin want to convert the Indians to civilization—
when he thought that civilization was contamination and corruption? If civilization was "a pestilence," and if the noble Indians
"lived with the genius of natural liberty and independence," why

on earth "divert them from their established belief" and "convince [them] that they are wrong"?[9]

Catlin's admiration for the Indians and his dislike for American commercial activity give, in the 1980s, a misleading impression of him as a cultural relativist, aware of and respectful of the viability and integrity of other ways of life. In the 1830s, Catlin made no more use of cultural relativism than of the automobile; for both, he had simply arrived too early. He enjoyed denouncing the vices of "civilization," but he was fully loyal to its virtues. The unwieldy world divided into the dual categories of virtue and vice. "Contaminated" Indians on the frontier were in the unfortunate situation of learning only the vices of "civilization" instructed by the all too qualified white frontiersmen. If the Plains Indians could be kept "severed as they [were] from the contaminating and counteracting vices . . . along the frontier," then, in moral quarantine, missionaries could fashion "a nation of a savages, civilized and christianized (and consequently *saved*), in the heart of the American wilderness."[10]

The Indian's "mind," Catlin said, "is a beautiful blank on which anything can be written if the proper means be taken." This Lockian ideal did not, of course, describe any actual Indian mind, then or now, but it accurately captured what Catlin wanted of his Indians. When he undertook to rescue them by preserving their image, he was acting with perfect consistency. The image—the noble, happy, pristine, uncontaminated Indian—had always been a great deal easier to live with than the diverse and complicated human beings who had come to be known as Indians.[11]

A complicated human being himself, Catlin was also an influential man. He wrote many books and, perhaps more significantly, took his gallery of Indian paintings—sometimes supplemented by living display Indians—on a tour of the United States and Europe. More than influential, Catlin was emblematic. In history, Catlin stands midway between the first encounters between natives and intruders and our own times. Many of his attitudes had a long history, and yet many of his assumptions still play a large role in Indian / white relations today.

First, to Catlin, Indians came in two categories: contaminated and uncontaminated. Demoralized and ruined, the tainted

Indians were mockeries of real Indians. They were, in any case, on their way out. The Indians on the Plains, however, were "entirely in a state of primitive wildness, and consequently [were] picturesque and handsome, almost beyond description." Untainted Indians were not only far ahead in moral terms; they were also the only really interesting and attractive "specimens," a word Catlin used frequently.[12]

Second, these untouched Indians were a lesson and reproach to civilization. Catlin, like multitudes of whites later, would structure his comparisons of Indians and whites by the measures of "better" or "worse." To this day, the competition goes on. Implicit in much formal Indian history is a Catlin-like set of questions. Did Indians live better than whites? Were they more honorable? Did they treat nature with more wisdom? Were Indians more at one with themselves than were their driven, fragmented, mercenary conquerors? The Catlin arrangement, by which Indians are most significant as their existence spotlights the flaws and failures of white people, persists with undiminished vigor.

Third, in Catlin, admiration and concern came mixed with plans for remodeling. As appealing as he might find some Indian customs, Catlin saw others he liked considerably less. The "disgusting" and "cruel" customs, he thought, had to be changed. Moreover, Indians simply could not survive, unadapted, in the modern world. In Catlin and his emotional descendants, the depth of one's concern for Indians correlated to the intensity of one's desire to remake them according to one's own standards of improvement.

Fourth, Catlin's Indians, once in contact with the course of white settlement, became helpless and passive, acted on and never acting. They were solely victims, utterly at the mercy of either white cruelty or, less likely, white benevolence. Their destiny would be determined by whites; if any Indians survived, it would be by the good graces of white people and not by Indian resourcefulness.

Finally, Catlin's Indians were a "doomed" and "dying race." Their "term of national existence" having "nearly expired," those still around were "remnants" or "relics." It was terribly sad but unavoidable. Catlin replayed this lament tirelessly. Reading his narrative is very much like attending an endless funeral service; one drifts off for a moment and returns to find the eulogy still in progress.[13]

Nineteenth-century European and American Romantics, of which Catlin was certainly one, found emotional gratification not only in contemplating the sublime ways of nature and nature's noblemen but also in contemplating mortality—in savoring the "sweet melancholy" (Catlin's phrase) of ruins and relics and graves. In the vigor and life of the Western Plains, Catlin was drawn to the thanatological. The Indians' immersion in the "real and uninterrupted enjoyment of their simple natural faculties" was surely made all the more moving and poignant by the idea of this celebration taking place at graveside, as Catlin's own words indicated. "My Heart has sometimes almost bled with pity for them," he wrote, "while amongst them, and witnessing their innocent amusements, as I have contemplated the inevitable bane that was rapidly advancing upon them. . . ." Unmistakable in his insatiable grieving is the emotional stimulus of savoring mortality, of looking over the edge of the abyss, aware that others are about to go over it.[14]

What would Catlin have made of the prediction that, in 1980, one and a half million Indians would appear in the U.S. census? Mark Twain's story of a frustrated coffin maker comes to mind. Jacops the coffin maker "used to go roosting around where people was sick, waiting for 'em," with a coffin "that he judged would fit the can'idate" ready at hand. When an old man named Robbins fell ill, Jacops spent three weeks—"in frosty weather"—camped outside Robbins's place. When Robbins "took a favorable turn and got well," Jacops sulked. When Robbins next fell ill, he made a bargain with Jacops: "he bought the coffin for ten dollars and Jacops was to pay it back and twenty-five more besides if Robbins didn't like the coffin after he'd tried it." At the funeral, Robbins rose out of the coffin and collected the bet; he had not been dead, but only in a trance. "It was always an aggravation to Jacops," the story concluded, "the way that miserable old thing acted."[15]

Like Robbins, Indians survived their much-predicted death.

Nonetheless, had George Catlin been persuaded to believe that
Indians would persist into the twentieth century, he would still
have known one thing for sure: they would not be "uncontaminated" Indians. They would not have "the bold, intrepid step—
the proud, yet dignified deportment of Nature's Man, in fearless
freedom, with a soul unalloyed by mercenary lusts." They would
not be real Indians, Catlin and his heirs could be certain, and
the proof of their fraudulence would be this: they would not
match the stereotype that Catlin himself had enshrined.[16]

III

Between 1845 and 1848, another artist, the Canadian Paul
Kane, traveled in the Northwest to observe and record Indian
habits. Staying with the Chinook Indians, he experienced first-
hand the linguistic diversity of North America. The Chinook
language was so foreign to English that Kane was both shocked
and disapproving, finding it impossible "to represent by any
combination of our alphabet the horrible, harsh, spluttering
sounds which proceed from their throats." It was, Kane claimed,
"so difficult to acquire a mastery of their language that none
have been able to attain it, except those who had been born
amongst them." The Chinooks, however, met the Europeans
halfway. From their exchanges with "English and French traders," the Chinooks had synthesized an intermediate language, "a
sort of patois" that permitted trade. "[T]heir common salutation," Kane noted, "is Clak-hoh-ah-yah," which apparently originated "in their having heard in the early days of the fur trade,
a gentleman named Clark frequently addressed by his friends,
'Clark, how are you?' This salutation is now applied to every
white man. . . ."[17]

The greeting "Clak-hoh-ah-yah" suggested not only a trace
of Brooklynese in the wilderness but also the flexibility and
adaptabilty of Indians. For centuries in North America, Indians
had been exchanging customs, words, and material goods; after
white people entered the picture, Indians continued to adapt
and borrow. Contrary to the image of a pristine, unchanging,
pure Indian, actual Indians changed and yet remained distinctive.

A few years ago, a visitor from Montana told several of us the story of a Crow dance he had attended. At this supposedly "traditional" dance, he said, the Crow Indians had been wearing Lakota headdresses, Pueblo moccasins, and Levi-Strauss jeans. We were all clearly meant to join him in his conclusion "And they call *that* 'traditional'!"—which it was. Adaptation and borrowing were far more central to Indian tradition than was any imposed notion of purity.

Tradition and change combined in other ways, initially startling to outsiders. At the turn of the century, a young Winnebago went on a raid. The young man, given the initials S.B. by the anthropologist who recorded his autobiography, had heard from his father and other relatives that raids against other tribes were a crucial way to develop and prove one's manhood. S.B. and his friends decided to go on a raid for horses. Seventy-five years earlier, in the context of frontier Wisconsin, this would have been appropriate Winnebago behavior, a route to honor and prestige. Closer to 1900, the event's meaning became cloudier. S.B. and his comrades traveled to Nebraska, where they killed a Pottawattomie Indian. The peculiar arrangements of persistence and change came into the spotlight. The deed now was murder, not heroism; and the raiders had not traveled by horse. "We took the train," S.B. said, "carrying some baggage."[18]

The train ride might seem peculiar at first, but it carried its own logic. At least three centuries earlier, Indians had adopted metal pots, knives, and even guns and used them to pursue traditional ends. The purchase of a railroad ticket did not require an individual to give up his past and adopt the goals of the railroad age. The horse, as well as the railroad, had been brought to North America by Europeans. Fully incorporated into Plains, Prairie, and Plateau Indian life, the horse was itself—by the standards of pre-Columbian purity—not "really Indian." The adoption of new transportation, whether horse or railroad, carried a simple meaning: Indians, like white Americans, like Asians, like Europeans, both changed and stayed the same. Tradition and innovation were by no means mutually exclusive. If anything adds a distinctive edge to the Indian pattern of persistence and change, it is that few other groups faced such a combination of violence, property loss, and systematic, coercive campaigns for assimilation.

In the mid-twentieth century, historians found in the concept of culture a new way to analyze the workings of white / Indian relations. Without the concept of culture, Euro-Americans and Indians found the reasons and meanings behind each other's way of life opaque and bewildering. The very idea of "culture"—as a whole system of ideas and behavior—was a creature of the late nineteenth and early twentieth centuries, slow to move from professional anthropological circles to popular thought. Euro-American ways of thinking were dominated by the ideas of civilization and savagery. Carrying associations of both nobility and violence, savagery was mankind's childhood, a starting stage in which society drew its shape and order from nature. Savagery meant hunting and gathering, not agriculture; common ownership, not individual property owning; pagan superstition, not Christianity; spoken language, not literacy; emotion, not reason. Savagery had its charms but was fated to yield before the higher stage of civilization represented by white Americans.

Interpreting Indian / white relations in these terms, Euro-Americans seldom glimpsed the complexity and integrity of Indian cultures. This misunderstanding was certainly significant. Nonetheless, overstressed, it draws our attention away from the essential matter of property. All the cultural understanding and tolerance in the world would not have changed the crucial fact that Indians possessed the land and that Euro-Americans wanted it.

From the beginning, the usual justification was that Indians were not using the land properly. Relying on hunting and gathering, savagery neglected the land's true potential and kept out those who could put it to proper use. A sparse Indian population wasted the resources that could support a dense white population. The argument thus shifted the terms of greed and philanthropy: it was not that white people were greedy and mean-spirited; Indians were the greedy ones, keeping so much land to themselves; and white people were philanthropic and farsighted in wanting to liberate the land for its proper uses.

Philanthropy went even further, to the idea that this was all in the Indians' interest. The instincts of humanity required that Indians be liberated from savagery and advanced to civilization. It was the only way to rescue them from their otherwise fated decline. Causing them to give up hunting and gathering and to adopt farming would reduce the amount of land they needed. Liberating Indians from savagery thus had the happy side effect of "liberating" their land and resources as well. In the mission to civilize the Indians, benevolence and acquisitiveness merged; the interests of missionaries who wanted to acquire the souls of Indians and the interests of settlers who wanted to acquire their lands found a paradoxical harmony.

The sources of so many American ideals, Jeffersonians held out considerable hope for the civilizing of the Indians. Intensely interested in the relation between nature and humanity, Jefferson and his colleagues had considerable faith in the capacity of changed environments to reshape humans. Instructed and retrained in a secondary social environment that encouraged farms and Christianity, Indians could change rapidly from savages to citizens.[19]

Expecting rapid and happy change, the Jeffersonians were predictably disappointed. The pattern of their hopes and failures would reappear in Indian / white affairs. Expecting too much in the way of rapid assimilation, completely misjudging the Indians' loyalty to their own ways of life, benevolent white people would repeatedly try to rush change, fail, and then embrace an easy resignation and disillusionment. They had tried to help the Indians, it would seem to white philanthropists, and the Indians had failed them—failed to seize the opportunities they offered, persisting in their ways like a patient willfully remaining ill to frustrate the doctor who tried to save him. Meeting resistance on the part of the beneficiary, shallowly rooted optimism prepared the ground for a deep-rooted pessimism.

The two causes—disillusionment in the humanitarians and desire for more land in settlers—combined to produce Indian removal in the 1830s. A third factor—states' rights and the threat of disunion—clinched the deal. In 1802, the problem of Georgia's refusal to cede its western lands to the Union prompted the United States to agree, eventually, to extinguish all Indian title

within the state. As years passed and that promise went unfulfilled, white Georgians could put themselves in the familiar role
of the injured innocents, waiting for the national promise to be
kept.

Georgia's Indians, meanwhile, appeared to be fulfilling
another sort of promise—becoming "civilized." By the 1820s, the
Cherokees had a written alphabet, a newspaper, good relations
with missionaries, and, sometimes, plantations and slaves. Neither they nor the neighboring "civilized tribes"—the Creeks,
Choctaws, Chickasaws, and Seminoles—appeared to be on their
way to removal.

The idea of removal, however, had had a considerable appeal
to presidents before Andrew Jackson. If the Southeastern Indians exchanged their lands for trans-Mississippi lands, a terrible
problem in race relations and in state sovereignty would go away,
accomplishing at once the removal of the Indians, of the potential for violence between settlers and Indians, of Georgia's irri-
tation over the unfulfilled 1802 compact, and of the federal
government's embarrassing inability to control its own citizens.
Undoubtedly, a demonstration of the government's ability to
enforce Indian territorial boundaries would have been a very
good thing for tranquil and stable Indian relations. But the power
was simply not there. In 1796, George Washington had sized up
the situation. Considering the policing of a line between Indian
land and white settlers, Washington felt it was the right thing to
do: "The Indians urge this; The Law requires it; and it ought to
be done; but I believe scarcely anything short of a Chinese Wall,
or a line of Troops will restrain Land Jobbers, and the Incroach-
ment of Settlers, upon the Indian Territory." Rather than the
government controlling the people, the people—or at least those
on the far fringes of settlement—had the power to control the
government, which is what, after all, democracy is supposed to
mean.[20]

Earlier presidents might have approved of the idea of removal,
but they held to the qualification that it should be voluntary,
occurring when Indians realized that it was in their interests to
escape their white neighbors and start fresh in the West. But the
presidential election of 1828 gave the issue a new orientation;

President Andrew Jackson was not likely to hold up "progress" while waiting for a voluntary relocation. With Jackson's sponsorship, it was possible to pass the 1830 Removal Act and then to secure removal treaties, with tactics ranging from coercion to bribes and fraud.

The removal policy had the support of Northern humanitarians to whom relocation seemed the only way to save Indians from their predatory neighbors and from the contagion of white vices. "While I am writing to you," said Thomas McKenney, superintendent of Indian affairs, whose conversion to removal may have hinged on a recognition of the dangers Southeastern Indians faced or on a recognition that government bureaucrats who wanted to keep their jobs were wise to follow the lead of the popular General Jackson, "the paths of the wilderness are pressed by the fallen bodies of *starved* and expiring Indians!" The Southeastern Indians, McKenney and others had decided, either moved or perished. They could still be saved, but only if they were fast removed from the scene of their victimization.[21]

With men like McKenney available, no one—least of all President Jackson—had to advocate removal as a cold-blooded effort at land acquisition. Jackson himself compared Indian removal favorably to white westward migration. White settlers, he said,

remove hundreds and almost thousands of miles at their own expense, purchase the lands they occupy, and support themselves at their new homes from the moment of their arrival. Can it be cruel in the Government, when, by events which it cannot control, the Indian is made discontented in his ancient home—to purchase his lands, to give him a new and extensive territory, to pay the expense of his removal, and support him a year in his new abode[?] How many thousands of our own people would gladly embrace the opportunity of removing to the West on such conditions?[22]

The posture was a remarkable one, but for whites intent on "helping" Indians, it was more the rule than the exception. From the helper's point of view, the ignorance and inexperience of the Indians made them incapable of deciding their future for themselves. Like Andrew Jackson, Indian reformers took it upon themselves to determine the Indians' best interests and then to act—coercively, if necessary—to pursue those interests. It was, of course, paternalism, but given their widely used comparison of Indians to children, paternalism was exactly what the officials had in mind.

Put in practice, Indian removal in the 1830s found its place as one of the greater official acts of inhumanity and cruelty in American history. The impulse to economize characterized much of removal's implementation. Shoddy contractors delivered inadequate food and supplies, while the summer heat and winter cold made the emigrants vulnerable to disease. It was in no official's interest to keep thorough records on deaths; thus, estimates of how many died are still matters of dispute. How many Cherokees, for instance, died during the "Trail of Tears"? The most recent answer takes into account all the contributing factors: "adverse weather, mistreatment by soldiers, inadequate food, disease, bereavement, and loss of their homes," noting hardships in the new territory as well as on the trail. Defining population loss as "the difference between actual population size (after removal) and what population size would have been had removal not occurred," Russell Thornton has raised the numbers of Cherokees lost from the often estimated four thousand to eight thousand.[23]

No one will ever determine the exact numbers, but the undoubted devastation of removal still makes official statements of contentment surprising. "The generous and enlightened policy," Secretary of War Joel Poinsett called it, "ably and judiciously carried into effect." Succeeding Andrew Jackson, Martin Van Buren was equally cheerful in appraising removal. "The wise, humane, and undeviating policy of the government in this the most difficult of all our relations foreign or domestic, has at length been justified to the world in its near approach to a happy and certain consummation."[24]

Affecting tribes in the North as well as the South, removal was of unquestionable significance in Indian policy, overruling Indian wills with federal plans, asserting Congress's "plenary power"—unilaterally to set the terms of Indian affairs in defiance of treaties. Once one's attention has been caught by removal, curiosity naturally draws one on through the following phases of federal policy: concentration (relocating Western Indians into two broad areas to the north and south of the principal overland trails); confinement to reservations, through both negotiations and military force under Grant's peace policy; assimilation and allotment (division of tribal lands into private property) under the Dawes Act; the Indian New Deal; the attempt in the 1950s at termination (withdrawing the federal government from responsibility for Indians); and then, in our own times, the multiple meanings of self-determination.

The temptation is to overplay the significance of federal policy, for one, seductive reason: it makes things seem simple. Following federal policy is, in fact, the only route to a clear, chronological, sequential overview of Indian history. Step away from Washington, D.C., and you face a swirl of distinctive regional, tribal, factional, and personal histories, in which origins, white contact, cooperation, conflict, assimilation, and resistance in these varying groups defer to no definite chronological sequence. Most unsettling is the experience of reading an Indian autobiography and finding in the details of the individual's life no mention of the federal policies that were supposedly the key determinants of Indian life.

Irrelevant to many aspects of everyday life, federal Indian policy nonetheless deserves close attention. It did shape the context of individual lives, and it provides essential information about the relations between the natives and the invaders. But one must still beware of the illusion of a purposeful sequence of events. When the Apache in the "whiteman joke" made fun of the Bureau of Indian Affairs, mocking its senseless jargon, he was in many ways proving the proposition advanced in 1828 by Henry Schoolcraft, the Western traveler and Indian expert. Legislation in Indian affairs, Schoolcraft said, is "only taken up on a pinch. . . . Nobody knows really what to do." The attempt to reconcile American ideals of fair and humane treatment of other humans with American impulses to acquire more land and get on with progress made Indian policy the record of a persistent muddle, an ongoing struggle—on the part of white Americans—with the fact that conquest left a troubling legacy and that no end to the frontier could do away with that legacy.[25]

As the Indian wars drew to a close, a group of white reformers stepped forward to offer their permanent solution to the
Indian problem. Every October, starting in 1883, concerned citizens would gather at Lake Mohonk, in New York, at an attractive resort hotel. This annual conference functioned as a kind of
think tank and lobbying group, from which congressmen received
many of their ideas.

Calling themselves "the Friends of the Indian," the Mohonk
activists drew frequent parallels between the emancipation of black
slaves and their intended liberation of Indians. The comparison,
however, required an odd twist of logic. Freeing blacks meant
freeing them from slavery and from the slaveholders. If the
reformers wanted to free the Indians, from whom did they want
to free them? To free the slaves, reformers had to defeat the
slaveholders; and to free the Indians, reformers had to defeat—
the Indians.

Something had been holding blacks back, and that oppressive force was slavery. But what was holding Indians back, preventing them from taking the opportunity to adopt civilized ways?
The Mohonk reformers gave white people some of the blame;
Indians had been held back by the failure of white Americans to
give them the help and opportunity they needed. But the main
force of oppression in Indian life, the reformers concluded, was
tribalism.

Loyalty to the tribe kept Indians entrapped in savagery and
communalism; it prevented them from developing the individ-
ualism and "manhood" that characterized modern civilized
Americans. The Indian reformers felt that they had to kill Indianness so that individual Indians might live; they had to destroy
savagery in order to liberate the human beings trapped in it.
They acted on the assumption that inside every Indian was a
white American citizen and property holder waiting to be set
free; the job of reform was to crack the shell of traditional tribal
life and thus free the individual.

Acting on these assumptions, the so-called Friends of the
Indian acted in ways that one might more logically expect from
enemies. But they remained, in their own eyes, utterly well
intentioned, hating Indianness but believing in the potential of

individual American Indians to become Indian-Americans and then simply Americans. The means to this end might have to be coercive, but the reformers were convinced that the urgency of the situation made gradual compromise intolerable.

In 1887, in the Dawes General Allotment Act, the reformers got their victory. Allotment meant the breaking up of the reservations into multiple tracts of land, owned by individuals; land left over after the allotments was to be sold to whites. Reformer idealism had thus intersected with settler practicality; liberated Indians also meant liberated land. Allotment was by no means a new idea; Jefferson had believed that individual property and a change to farming would be the key to the civilizing of Indians. What made the Dawes Act distinctive was the breadth of its application and the conviction of its backers that allotment would, in a single stroke, solve the complicated problems of Indian / white relations.

Like the humanitarian advocates of removal, the reformers of the 1880s saw the situation as urgent, even apocalyptic. In their speeches and essays, they repeated certain themes endlessly. The Indians faced "this stern alternative: extermination or civilization." Civilizing them, "once only a benevolent fancy," Carl Schurz wrote, "has now become an absolute necessity, if we mean to save them." The past, the reformers were the first to admit, had been dreadful. Indians had been "tricked out of" their land "by unscrupulous white men, who took advantage of their ignorance." "When we were weak and [the Indian] was strong, we began by deceiving him," and once stronger, "we thought we would exterminate him if we could not civilize him." All this was dreadful and inhumane, a stain on the American past. The government simply could not control its own people; it was "impotent to protect the Indians on their reservations, especially when held in common, from the encroachments of its own people, whenever a discovery [was] made rendering the possession of their lands desirable by the whites." Once they had become assimilated, voting property holders themselves, the Indians would be able to protect themselves as white Americans did. But their large communal landholdings were obviously obstacles to progress and development, property that the government could not defend either in theory or in practice.[26]

The Dawes Act reformers, with a typical American faith, believed they could declare their independence of a flawed past and make a fresh start. The treaties and reservations had been a bad idea, they thought; the lines of the reservation fenced in Indians, under the control of despotic agents, and fenced out civilization, Christianity, and economic opportunity. Throwing down the barriers of the reservation was one of "the duties that the strong owe to the weak." Rations and annuities, promised in treaties, had made the Indians into dependent "paupers," taken away their will to work, and encouraged them in their "lazy, indolent, vagabond life." To escape this dependence, the Indian had to be made into modern economic man. He had to become aware of "broader desires and ampler wants"; he had to be "touched by the wings of the divine angel of discontent. . . . Discontent with the tepee and the starving rations of the Indian camp in winter [was] needed to get the Indian out of the blanket and into trousers—and trousers with a pocket in them, and with a *pocket that ache[d] to be filled with dollars!"*[27]

The Indians' economic dependence wore away at their moral fiber; it also wore down the national treasury. Allotment not only taught "the Indians habits of industry and frugality, and stimulate[d] them to look forward to a better and more useful life" but would also "relieve the government of large annual appropriations." A program that could in one stroke reduce federal spending and erase the errors and injuries of the past appealed both to American idealism and to American practicality. Henry Dawes, sponsor of the Dawes Act, summed it up: "[A]t last in the philosophy of human nature, and in the dictates of Christianity and philosophy, there has been found a way to solve a problem which hitherto has been found to be insoluble by the ordinary methods of modern civilization, and soon I trust we will wipe out the disgrace of our past treatment, and lift [the Indian] up into citizenship and manhood, and co-operation with us to the glory of the country." The Indians, all the reformers agreed, had been "wronged long enough."[28]

The wronging was not, however, quite over. Indians held 138 million acres in 1887. In the next forty-seven years, 60 million acres were declared, after allotment, to be surplus land and "sold to white men." Also in the next forty-seven years, 27 million acres left the Indians' possession through allotment to individuals and then sales to whites. The Friends of the Indian had initiated a process that took nearly two-thirds of tribal land away, without doing much to assimilate Indians into a homogeneous mass of American property holders.[29]

The same pattern continued to plague Indian affairs: optimism and good intentions brought muddled consequences more often than success. Consider the telling case study in Clyde Milner's portrait of Quakers working with the Pawnees in the 1870s. Quaker enthusiasm for "anti-slavery activity and aid to the freedmen" carried over after the war into enthusiasm for helping the Indians along the road to assimilation. When President Ulysses S. Grant attempted to solve the problems of Indian affairs by appointing religious men as agents and superintendents, the Quakers saw a happy opportunity to put ideals into practice. But it was not long before these philanthropists began to catch glimpses of the limits of their power. The Pawnees, for instance, never fought against the United States, and, as allies, they felt justified in expecting the government to protect them against their common enemies, especially the Sioux. In 1871, their new Quaker superintendent assured them that the government would protect them if they traveled with a proper pass. "At the mention of government protection," Milner tells us, " 'a derisive laugh passed around the council.' " "My situation was embarrassing," the superintendent reported. Relations between Quakers and Pawnees hardly improved over time, as the Quaker commitment to assimilation led to heightened conflict. By "the end of the Quaker's work," the Pawnees "had left Nebraska for the Indian Territory—in part, to escape their Quaker agents."[30]

The campaign for assimilation that brought the Dawes Act had also drawn on optimism and a faith in Indian potential. Many of the reformers genuinely believed that Indians could escape their initial stage of civilization and move upward to meet whites. Compared with blacks, Asians, or southern and eastern Europeans, as the historian Fred Hoxie has noted, "Native Americans posed the smallest threat to existing social relationships," since they were located in remote places, present in limited numbers, and endowed with an appealing aura of romance and nostalgia. "It appeared," Hoxie has written, "that incorporating native people into the larger society would displace no one; it would carry few political costs," and the experiment could confirm the viability of American ideals. "If every Indian child could be in school for five years," predicted an education journal in 1893, "savagery would cease and the government support of Indians would be a thing of the past." By the early 1900s, though, disillusionment had again replaced confidence; "optimism and a desire for rapid incorporation were pushed aside by racism, nostalgia, and disinterest." Influential scholars and policymakers gave up the push for assimilation and relegated Indians to the periphery of American life. The attention of white Americans returned to Indian land and resources, and, in Hoxie's words "a campaign for equality and total assimilation had become a campaign to integrate native resources into the American economy."[31]

IV

In 1920, the reformer John Collier met the Taos Indians and was most impressed. Collier did not come from the happiest background himself; he grew up in Georgia, where his mother had died young and his father had committed suicide. Since then, Collier had been on a quest, hiking in the woods, studying in New York, traveling in Europe, working with communities in New York's ethnic neighborhoods and in California adult education. The quest was supposed to lead to community and fulfillment, but by 1920 it had reached only disillusionment. The Indian people of Taos seemed, by contrast, to have had a far more satisfactory history. Since their pre-Columbian origins, Taos Indians had enjoyed a fulfilling communal spiritual life; despite Spanish and American conquerors, they kept their traditions alive. When Collier witnessed their ceremonies in 1920, he saw "a whole race of men, before [his] eyes, pass[ing] into ecstasy through a willed discipline, splendid and fierce, yet structural, an objectively impassioned discipline which was a thousand or ten thousand years old, and as near to the day of first creation as it had been at the prime."[32]

True to Catlin's formula, Collier saw Indian strengths as a counterpoint to white weaknesses: "They had what the world has lost. What the world has lost, the world must have again, lest it die." Like Catlin, Collier lamented the basic propositions of commercial society: "The nature of man was believed to be founded in traffic and acquisition of goods—and the human personality was therefore base, calculating, and shallow. . . . Man had always been," in this system, "an isolate, an address, a role in a competitive society." For human societies, the results of these attitudes were as grim as the causes: "the uprooting of populations, the disintegration of neighborhoods, the end of home and handcrafts, the supremacy of the machine over the man, the immense impoverishment of the age-old relationships between the generations, the increased mobility of the individual. . . . All this confused, degraded, and even sometimes destroyed the societies utterly."[33]

In forcing their grim ways on the Indians, Collier thought, white Americans had been not only cruel to others but also self-destructive, ruining the very tradition that could save them. Collier thus tied white salvation to Indian salvation: white Americans had to put Indian people back on their feet so that they could in turn instruct and redeem their conquerors. Meeting the Indians after years of disillusionment, Collier reported, led him to say to himself, "with absolute finality about the Indians: *This* effort toward community must not fail; there can be no excuse or pardon if it fails."[34]

In the 1920s, Collier assumed the role of the advocate for Indians. He helped to fight off a plan to take Pueblo lands. He took up the cause of religious freedom, fighting the efforts of the Bureau of Indian Affairs and of missionaries to suppress native religion. The suppressers were distressed by the sexual content of native dances; defending his chosen people, Collier asserted that the Pueblos were "sexually the purest and sweetest people" he had ever known. There were, apparently, no limits to his conviction that he fully understood the Indians.[35]

The election of Franklin Roosevelt opened the door to a new regime in Indian affairs. Although he later claimed to have been reluctant to take the office, Collier was a willing candidate for the post of commissioner of Indian affairs. Appointed to office, Collier went instantly from being the bureau's main critic and gadfly to being its director. He faced an extraordinary challenge in translating his criticisms into positive action. As he remarked many years later, in one of his humbler moments, "even blunderingly making dependent people free to grapple with real emergencies is hygienic, life-releasing and life-saving. . . . Imperfect action is better for men and societies than perfection in waiting. . . ."[36]

Submitted by Collier and then revised quite heavily by Congress, the Indian Reorganization Act of 1934 did represent a significant break with the past. Under the IRA, the Indian New Deal set out to reverse the loss of Indian land set off by the Dawes Act, to organize the tribes into self-governing political units, and to provide for their economic rehabilitation through conservation programs and loans from a revolving credit fund. The program was voluntary; tribes had to vote in favor of participation before the act applied to them, although this was a provision added by Congress and not chosen by Collier.

To this day, evaluating the merits of John Collier and the Indian Reorganization Act can be an exercise in bewilderment; his story certainly is yet another contribution to Western history's bulging file of case studies of good intentions and ironic results, of a simple vision crashing into a complex reality. One can sort the complications into several categories: the opposition groups Collier faced from the beginning, the dilemmas that put an unexpected strain on Collier's ideals, and the conceptual weaknesses that those dilemmas exposed.

From the beginning, Collier met opposition. He had, after all, been an outspoken, often abrasive critic of the Indian affairs power structure, and the legacy of that conflict did not disappear when he assumed office. Many missionaries were already familiar with him through the issue of religious freedom; their hostility could only increase as Collier set about cutting federal support for church-run Indian schools and implementing a program that could appear to be reversing "progress" in favor of "paganism." Similarly, career employees of the Bureau of Indian Affairs could feel that any changes at all meant disruption and more work for them, while Collier's changes could make the Indians unruly and difficult to manage. On another front, white businessmen in mining, cattle raising, or farming who had arranged to use Indian resources could feel that Collier threatened those arrangements. Meanwhile, the members of Congress had other matters—and other expenditures—on their minds; their occasional fits of concern for the Indians were likely to be followed by indifference or even hostility.

And then, on the other side, Indians themselves had their reasons to question yet another white-initiated version of "help." As Collier himself said, many Indians approached his proposals "amid a cloud of grimly silent fears," "under the shadow of many betrayals of past years." The text of the IRA was long and complicated, a further reason for distrust and uncertainty. And then there were the particular situations leading Indians to question the reform. Some Indians who had acquired and held allotments of land under the Dawes Act were reluctant to contribute their personal holdings to Collier's ideal of a reconsolidated tribal land base. Collier might have preferred to believe in universally noble Indians, eager to share with their fellows, but reports from some reservations suggested a more recognizably human model. "[T]hose now owning lands," the Pawnee superintendent reported, "were of the opinion that they should not be penalized for having kept their property intact, and as a result do not desire to pool their interests in community holding and let others who have dissipated their funds and property, share and share alike with them."[37]

Some Indians had converted to Christianity, and resented Collier's efforts to return them to a traditional past. "We do not want [our children] to be turned back forty years to take up the old communal life which never made for progress," a group of Nez Percés said. One opposition group, given considerable credibility by frequent appearances at congressional hearings, was Joseph Bruner's American Indian Federation, a group of acculturated Indians, many from Oklahoma, who persisted in declaring that Collier was "seeking to frustrate the opportunity of the Indian to enter American life as a citizen, and, instead [was] perpetuating an in[i]quitous, un-American Bureau, and forcing a

subdued, Bureau-controlled . . . people into a segregated serf-
dom, continued to be ruled by the dictatorship of a Government
Bureau, which has held the American Indian in chains. . . ." Collier, they said, had handed the Indian office over to the "Christ-
mocking, Communist-aiding, subversive and seditious American
Civil Liberties Union." Meanwhile, beyond the reach of the
American Indian Federation, on various reservations where the
group was split, minority factions could oppose the IRA out of
the fear that under its auspices the majority could overrule the
minority. Perhaps most dramatically, Indians could oppose Collier when his ideas of proper natural resource conservation con-
flicted with their own.[38]

With that cast of characters, dilemmas were guaranteed to
result. Consider the following:

• The annual appropriations fight. Once his bill had become
law, Collier's struggle was by no means over. Year after year, he
had to return to Congress to fight for money for his programs,
sacrificing ideological purity and clarity to the demands of politics.

• The required referenda. By congressional mandate, each tribe
had to vote on the IRA, and those elections had to occur within
a limited time. As a result, the bureau had to shift into immediate action, persuading and pressuring Indians for the upcoming
vote. The results, moreover, were not overwhelmingly encouraging to Collier: "181 tribes (with a population of 129,750)
accepted the law and 77 tribes (86,365 Indians) voted to reject
it."[39]

• The problem of the constitutions. Under the IRA, Collier said,
each tribe "drew up a constitution fitted to its own needs, and
according to its cultural patterns and traditions." But few human
groups are instinctually constitution writers, and the Bureau of
Indian Affairs ended up preparing a model constitution, which,
with a few minor revisions, the participating tribes adopted.
Beyond this standardization, the bureau did on a few occasions
reject constitutions that Collier and his staff deemed unsatisfac-
tory. The IRA constitutions may well have represented tradi-

tional government, but they tended toward the Anglo-American tradition.[40]

• The power of review. Rhetorically in favor of full Indian self-government, Collier held back on a full grant of autonomy. In a variety of matters, the constitutions kept a right of review for the secretary of the interior, on issues ranging from "the establishment of civil and criminal codes by the tribe" to the "levying of taxes on tribal members and non-members residing on the reservation" and the "issuance of permits and setting of fees for hunting, grazing, and fishing."[41]

• The problem of communication. The language of the IRA was legalistic and technical, not the language of laypeople of any ethnicity. When many members of a tribe still spoke the traditional language, communication became even more problematic. The Papagoes, for instance, had "no equivalent words for terms like *budget* and *representative,*" and "the same word was applied to *president, Indian commissioner, reservation agent* and *king.*"[42]

• The limits on credit. Because of the IRA and its revolving-credit fund, Indian people had far better access to loans than ever before. But once again, because of close supervision from Congress, the project could not fail; the loans had to be repaid; and the administrators could not take much risk. The loans had to go to good credit risks—to people and programs already supplied with collateral and experience, not to those in the greatest need.

• The problem of peyote. Formally organized in the early twentieth century, the Native American Church combined native and Christian elements with the ritual use of peyote. On certain reservations, tribal elders and authorities could match white missionaries in their disapproval of peyote and its accompanying church. When the tribal council persecuted members of the Native American Church within their own tribes, what was Collier to do? He had defended both religious freedom and tribal self-government; if it was wrong for the U.S. government to suppress an individual's free religious practice, why was the same act legitimate when Indian leaders were the oppressors?

In these various dilemmas, one can see hints of the general fault lines in Collier's thought and programs. The IRA directed itself to the reorganization of "tribes," and yet the unit of the tribe was far better established in Collier's imagination than in actuality. It was a common pattern in white / Indian relations; Euro-Americans would see a tribe as a political unit, whereas tribalism might be much more a matter of shared language, culture, and system of subsistence, the meaningful political units being at the village, band, or clan levels. In asking Indians to organize as tribes, Collier was not necessarily restoring a lost unity, but asking for something entirely new.

Moreover, Collier's vision of a latent harmony was unrealistic on other counts. Lines between mixed bloods and full-bloods, between wealthy families and poor ones, between acculturated individuals and those holding to tradition, divided groups on many reservations. Requests to conduct a referendum, write a constitution, and elect a tribal council were not going to heal those divisions; instead, on a number of occasions, reorganization actually increased the tensions, providing more opportunities for conflict.

Collier was certain that all Indians held within them a latent impulse for unity and tribalism; he was equally certain that Indian ways represented the true spirit of conservation, the "reverence and passion for the earth and its web of life." This was the core of what white people should borrow from Indians: "Will we learn from the Indian the age-old knowledge we now, through our acts, reject—the knowledge of the interrelatedness of life, of reciprocity and cooperation between man and nature, and between man and man?" If Indians were what Collier wanted them to be, the scenario should have been a very happy one: Indians would provide the warm fellow feeling with the earth, government experts would provide technical assistance in restoring the "web of life," and nature in the United States would be restored and regenerated.[43]

The case of the Navajos illustrated what could go wrong with Collier's plans. In a classic instance of Indian adaptability, the Navajos had shifted to herding the sheep, goats, and horses introduced by the Spanish. Placed on a reservation, they were encouraged to develop even larger herds. But by the 1930s the range was badly overgrazed and contributing to the general problems of Depression era dust storms. The historian Richard White has pointed out a further implication: erosion on the Navajo Reservation was threatening the newly constructed Boulder (Hoover) Dam on the Colorado River. "Too much silt," White has written, "was coming down the river from the reservation"; if not stopped, "it would pile up behind the dam and destroy its usefulness." Reservation silt, the Soil Conservation Service reported in 1936, was "thus threatening the enormous Federal, State, municipal, and private investments involved in, or directly or indirectly dependent on, the maintenance of the storage capacity of the reservoir."[44]

To Collier and his experts borrowed from the Soil Conservation Service, both the problem and the solution seemed clear: the herds had gone past the carrying capacity of the land, and the herds had to be reduced. But there clarity ceased. In a hurry to solve the problem, Collier leaped in; there was no time to develop a thorough understanding of what the herds meant to the Navajos or to conduct an open dialogue on the reasons and strategies for reduction.

To the Navajos, sheep and goats were the basis of identity and security. Isolated from the official conversations with the tribal council (a council that preceded the IRA and was not organized under its tenets), many Navajo people experienced Collier's stock reduction program as a sudden, arbitrary, and very threatening seizure of their most valued possessions. Families had to give up animals at a set rate; if an owner of a small herd gave up 10 percent, it was bound to be far more devastating than if large owners surrendered the same percentage. Collier's people had in fact proposed that the owners of huge herds should give up a greater percentage, and thereby absorb more of the loss, but those large owners squashed that proposition. Meanwhile, many Navajos felt that the solution to the problem was to expand the reservation, rather than to force the people to give up the basis of their wealth, security, and prestige.

In the abstract, the situation could not have been more harmonic: the Navajos cared deeply about nature; Collier cared deeply about nature; administrator and administrated could proceed in unity to set an example for the rest of the world. The actual results, however, left Collier frustrated and the Navajos bitter; many of them vilified the name "Collier," and chose, in the referendum, not to participate in his Indian Reorganization Act.

John Collier, it now seems clear, had remained a paternalist. He was aware of the history of white paternalistic meddling in Indian affairs; that was exactly the pattern of American history that he wanted to end. This was, of course, an irony with a long pedigree in Western civilization; the oracles warned Oedipus of the sin he would commit, and then, in the process of avoiding that sin, he committed it. Collier did help the Indians, but like his bureaucratic forefathers, he helped them on his own terms and with his own goals. His language makes that point clear: "The establishment of a living democracy, profound democracy, is a high art," he wrote; "it is the ultimate challenge to the administrator." This was, in other words, a project in design, in sculpting living human material. Collier's assumption of the role of director was even clearer. "Responsibility," he said, echoing the theme of school vice-principals addressing the student council, "is necessary to freedom," and that carried a special application to the Indians: "one responsibility is perpetuation of the natural resources, and conservation must be made mandatory on the tribes, by statute."[45]

Indian affairs provided Collier with, in his phrase, "an ethnic laboratory of universal meaning," and he was determined to see that his experiments in that laboratory worked out as he wanted. With unrelenting congressional supervision and criticism, Collier could not allow the experiment to go awry; he had to ensure that the Indians used their freedom appropriately.[46]

To this day, the results of the experiment remain difficult to determine. Is an IRA tribal government genuinely representative of the tribe, or is it a puppet government run for the benefit of a small elite? Was Collier really an assimilationist, permitting a superficial indulgence of cultural traits, while requiring an economic and political standardization? Was he fundamentally a careerist, hitching his own interests and influence to the role of

"Interpreter and Protector of the Indian"? How much room for genuine Indian reform does a government employee have, when he must continually answer to Congress? John Echohawk, director of the Native American Rights Fund, has provided a good summation. "The Indian New Deal wasn't perfect," he said, "but its results were fundamentally beneficial for Indian people. The Indian Reorganization Act reversed the direction of American Indian policy. The pattern of history changed from the erosion of Indian sovereignty to its restoration and revival."[47]

There was, in any case, little doubt that Collier's regime was a great deal better than the following one. In Cold War America, "an intolerance toward anything that deviated from mainstream values" influenced Indian affairs, as well as foreign policy and domestic civil liberties. To conservative white Americans preoccupied with communism, "traditional Indian communal social structures . . . seemed too similar to the dreaded socialist systems" the United States was determined to fight abroad. In a "conservative reaction" against the New Deal, many congressmen and senators wanted "to end the trend toward enlarged federal budgets and mushrooming bureaucracies," and the Bureau of Indian Affairs seemed to them an appropriate target.[48]

"Out of this situation," the historian Larry Burt has explained, "emerged a bloc of conservative congressmen known as terminationists who advocated an end to trust arrangements and any remaining tribal sovereignty, the integration of Native Americans into the dominant culture, and federal withdrawal from all Indian affairs." The new movement produced House Concurrent Resolution 108 in 1953:

. . . it is the policy of Congress, as rapidly as possible to make the Indians within the territorial limits of the United States subject to the same laws and entitled to the same privileges and responsibilities as are applicable to other citizens of the United States, to end their status as wards of the United States, and to grant them all of the rights and prerogatives pertaining to American citizenship.

The ostensible purpose, as usual, was to "liberate" the Indians; the hope also was to get the federal government released from the trouble and expense of the Indian business. Implemented with the Menominees in Wisconsin, termination succeeded in turning a moderately prosperous reservation into the poorest county in Wisconsin. The Menominee Restoration Act of 1973 was a sign of both a new era of rising Indian activism and a formal federal retreat from the policy of termination. But there was no reason to think that the issue was finally settled; any new era of social conservatism might again bring congressional attempts to cut the ties of history in the interests of homogenizing the American population and saving money.[49]

One can ponder the history of federal Indian policy and still not feel wise enough to choose a course for the future. To this day, if one resolves to "help the Indians," it is not at all clear what one has resolved to do. "Helping the Indians" still puts the beneficiaries at risk of paternalistic interference, the imposition of the helper's standards of improvement. Cease meddling, and just let them alone? This suggests termination—the old impulse to cut the obligations and contracts of the past, reject the guilt for past injuries, and let the Indians look out for themselves. In a nation fond of simple solutions, loyal to an image of itself as innocent and benevolent, Indian history is a troubling burden. What balance of assimilation and tradition could restore morale to a demoralized people? Temporary expedients drift into permanence; in recurrent cycles, officials search for a way to end the government's obligations.

Indian policy offers a case study in the problems of dependence: the providers felt drained and exploited, while the recipients felt cheated and exploited. Considered in these terms, Indian policy could pass for a dress rehearsal for the New Deal and the welfare state. After the conquest, Indians were a population in trouble, with massive unemployment and poor prospects for economic recovery. Having lost many of their opportunities to pursue their traditional subsistence, Indians had literally lost their jobs, and, as every recent case study shows, unemployment can devastate both individual and group morale.

The federal government acted on an obligation to provide compensation and protection for a people who had obviously been hit hard by history, who had lost their earlier ways of getting by. The New Deal and all the subsequent welfare legislation followed the pattern but widened the scope, to include the American people in general who had been devastated by the Depression.

The lessons were there, in Indian history, if anyone had wanted to see them. Helping the afflicted, federal paternalism had demonstrated, was not a simple matter of aid efficiently given and cheerfully received. Aid, from a centralized national agency, was inevitably aid with strings attached. Federal funds meant federal supervision, which then meant compromised autonomy for the recipient. Dependence was thus as likely to provoke resentment as gratitude. Conservatives in the 1980s, lamenting the quagmire of welfare, sounded as if they had cribbed their language and sentiments from the Indian reformers of the 1880s.

Indian history may have prefigured the welfare state, but it never lacked distinctive and unique features. There is no Bureau of Italian-American Affairs, no Bureau of Mexican-American Affairs, no Bureau of Black-American Affairs. There is, and perhaps there will always be, a Bureau of Indian Affairs, an institutionalized statement that American Indians are not like any other minority. The difference is a study in the power of origins. A minority by conquest is not the same as a minority by immigration, and four centuries of history have not blurred the difference.

In treaties and agreements, the federal government agreed that Indians would have special services, special lands, and a special trust relationship, a bewildering combination of protection and lost independence. Tribal sovereignty was unlike any other element of the American political structure, a fact still true today.

Would it endure forever? In different phases of history and in different moods of prophecy, white people have predicted the same solution to "the Indian problem": a melancholy disappearance through disease, wars, and demoralization or a happy disappearance through assimilation, which would make Indians just another minority.[50] One begins to think of George Catlin and his anticipation of Indian disappearance as a relic or remnant of the 1830s, and then one's morning newspaper provides evidence that Catlin's point of view is far from dead.

"By the end of the nineteenth century," wrote a Colorado

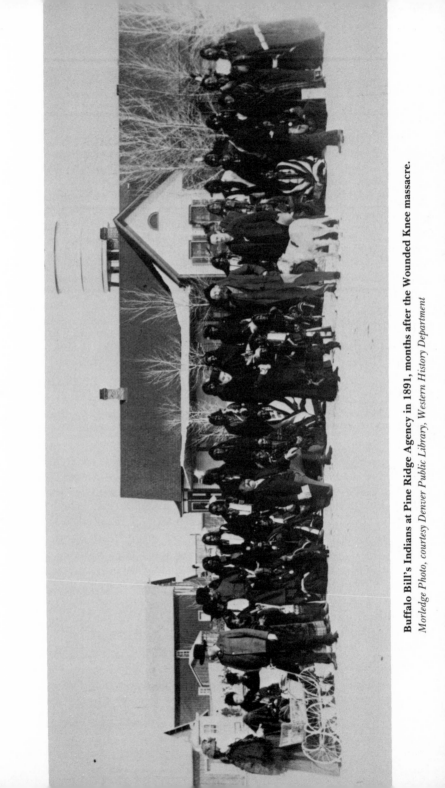

Buffalo Bill's Indians at Pine Ridge Agency in 1891, months after the Wounded Knee massacre.

Morledge Photo, courtesy Denver Public Library, Western History Department

reporter on August 12, 1984, "the process of tribal relocation was complete, and Indians had become part of a generalized nostalgia for an American frontier. When it closed, it took whole native tribes with it." The article, ironically, was about a show of Catlin drawings, but the conclusion unknowingly mimicked his sentiments. Despite a vision of the closing frontier as a sinkhole, pulling structures and people into its collapse, no "whole native tribe" disappeared in that fashion. But the predictions had become so familiar that they were taken to be true. Told so often that the Indians were vanishing, many Americans—and some reporters—assumed that it was true.[51]

Similarly persistent was the power of the Indian image, popping up in the most unlikely places. The *Boston Globe* in 1981 ran a front-page story on the Senate confirmation hearings of the first female Supreme Court justice. "Sandra Day O'Connor," the article began, "sat before her questioners, erect, like an American Indian." The spirit of Catlin lived. The image, of course, was supposed to be positive—noble and stoic. It was disorienting only if the reader happened to know actual Indians, who were noble and stoic in roughly the same proportions as other humans. But the surprise came in imagining other possible phrasings: Sandra Day O'Connor sat before her questioners "like an American Jew," or "like an American Black," or "like an American WASP," which is how, one suspects, O'Connor actually sat.[52]

With any other group, the journalist would have recognized that they—blacks, Jews, WASPs—are still alive, diverse, and sensitive to stereotyping. Struck by an impulse to indulge in ethnic stereotyping, the writer would have flinched, anticipated the angry letters to the editor, and chosen another phrase. But the "noble, vanishing Indian" was another matter.

The power of the stereotype can be partly explained: most white Americans have gained their impression of Indians through the printed word or through film, not through personal experience. This, too, has deep historical significance. One of the few things that characterized all Indian tribes north of the Rio Grande was the practice of an oral culture. Europeans and Americans seemed, by contrast, to be compulsively literate, pausing in the midst of their exploring and colonizing for frequent journal

entries, letters, and reports. The result was a vast imbalance in
the production of records: a flood of words in which white people said what they thought of Indians, and few chances for Indians to reciprocate. That imbalance of records is only one aspect
of Indian history that makes the historian feel, periodically, at
sea.

V

In 1763, Father Juan Nentuig wrote of his experiences with
the Opata Indians in northern Mexico. He valued their willingness to farm and raise cattle, but he found one of their habits
maddening:

. . . it costs infinite trouble and anxiety to make them get rid of a phrase,
which certainly must have been invented by the enemy of the human
race. It is this. To everything they hear (no matter from whom), not
having seen it with their own eyes, they say: *Sepore ma de ni thui*. Perhaps
thou speakest truth. Until the ministering Father is able to banish this
phrase from his neophytes they cannot have the faith required by the
infallible authority of God and Church.[53]

Two hundred years later, the Western historian finds many
occasions in which the Opata attitude can be profitably imitated.
Indian history is so complex, and involves such a proliferation
of points of view, that an open mind is essential. Attempting to
reassemble the lost past—like the Opatas, "not having seen it
with their own eyes"—historians have to be adept at putting
together diverse versions of the same events. Confronted by the
enormous diversity of Indian cultures, with conflicts both between
and within tribes, with the multiple perspectives of Spanish,
French, and Anglo-Americans, of explorers, traders, settlers,
soldiers, and bureaucrats, one could certainly do worse than
invoke the Opata slogan, *Sepore ma de ni thui*.

Traditional frontier history flattened out Indians, rendering
them insignificant both before and after conquest. "Within the
zone of the United States, where Indian population was sparse
and at a low level of culture," claimed a textbook published in
1978, "it could be simply brushed aside by the frontier." Significant only as they proved a "barrier" to white expansion, Indians

figured in history for the brief, "colorful" phases of war and then vanished. Civilization had driven out savagery; the West was opened; and the Indian side of the story engaged, at most, the tender feelings of a few sentimentalists.[54]

Once the conquest was secure, sentiment became a luxury more people could afford. Romantics like George Catlin had already made use of noble savages to point a contrast with the vice and artifice of civilization. This strategy actually gained power in the twentieth century. Since there was no chance of reversing the conquest, it was safe to regret it. Discontent with modern industrial society led to an interchanging of the usual terms: white Americans were the barbarians, savage and unprincipled, possessed by primitive greed; Indians were the genuinely civil people, who lived with an ecological wisdom and saintliness that made white Americans look like childish brutes.

Even when reversed, the abstractions of savagery and civilization did not do much to illuminate history. Shifting sentiment to "the Indian side" assumed that there was such a unitary thing. Given endless reinforcement in Western novels and movies, the stereotype of the unitary, simple, pristine, and victimized Indian had gained even more power in the twentieth century. That power was curiously unaffected by the image's inability to fit the facts.

The very word "Indian" rests on an act of the mind and not on pre-Columbian actuality. In his study of Euro-American images of Indians, Robert Berkhofer, Jr., quotes an important passage from Roger Williams's 1643 study of New England Indians. The natives, Williams wrote, "have often asked me, why we call them *Indians*."[55] It was a good question. The word, of course, only enshrined Columbus's error; where he landed was not the Indies, and the people were not Indians. The term remains misleading: "Crisis in Indian Leadership," the headline will read, and in the article the reader will find Sikhs and Gandhi, instead of the expected chiefs and tribal chairmen. Most misleading is the impression of a single, homogeneous group identity. Kept narrow, used for the minimal meaning of "human beings indigenous to America, and their descendants," the term has a basic practical use. But stretched to mean much more, it goes past its breaking point. Anytime one is tempted to refer to "the Indian," two considerations should hold off the temptation.

First, one must remember the diversity of language, culture, and economy. Anthropologists have divided America north of the Rio Grande into at least twelve cultural regions, and even those are units of meaning far narrower than the diversity they attempt to embrace. In the Pacific Northwest, the coastal people benefited from an abundance of food from the ocean, did not farm, prized wealth, practiced a variety of slavery, and had a clearly hierarchical society; in the Northeastern woodlands, groups raised corn and squash, hunted seasonally, and gave their loyalty to social units ranging from the band to the intertribal league of the Iroquois. In the Southwest, some of the people were nomadic hunters, while others farmed and lived in villages hundreds of years old, practicing a complex religion. None of these ways of life matched the Plains Indian model enshrined in novels and movies as the "real Indian" way of life. Within some culture regions, there was considerable linguistic diversity; California alone had representatives of all the major language groups. Moreover, cultural similarity cannot be mistaken for political solidarity. Neighboring tribes, with what would appear to out-siders as utterly similar ways of life, still directed their loyalties to different leaders and different ethnicities.

Second, one must keep in mind the variations in historical development. Tribes made contact with Euro-Americans at dif-ferent times and under different circumstances. Some experi-enced a prolonged period of trade and infrequent contact; others suddenly confronted a flock of permanent white settlers. Some tribes were removed repeatedly, undergoing what was essen-tially a refugee experience, forced to immigrate into the terri-tory of other tribes. A few groups, like the Pueblos, did not move at all and discovered ways to give first the Spanish and then the Americans a superficial compliance, while keeping up old ways in private. Some tribes followed the course of clear, armed resis-tance; others allied themselves with the Euro-Americans, fight-ing together against a shared Indian enemy.

Despite these variations, the historian, annoyed by the eth-nocentricity of earlier frontier history, might still have the impulse to "take the Indian side." But the impulse offers no escape from ethnocentricity; the very notion of "the Indian side to the story" requires one to hold resolutely to the Euro-American angle of vision, by which Indian diversity flattens out into one, simple story.

In southern California in 1846, Luiseño Indians killed eleven Californios (Hispanic Californians) who appeared to be intruding into their territory. With the aid of Cahuilla Indian allies led by Juan Antonio, a party of Californios sought vengeance. After a battle, the Cahuillas and the Californios took "eighteen to twenty" Luiseño prisoners and gave them into the keeping of the Cahuilla Juan Antonio. The Hispanic commander of the expedition reported on the next event: "we went back to Juan Antonio and found that he had killed all the prisoners. I reproached him for these acts of cruelty, and he answered me very cooly that he had gone to hunt and fight and kill Indians who would kill him. . . ."[56]

Incidents of this sort do not make it easy to locate "the Indian side." Intertribal rivalries both preceded white contact and followed it. The Crow Indians occupied the center of a much contested territory in the Northern Plains. Read a Crow autobiography, and you are in a densely peopled world of raids and counterraids, of alliances kept and broken, a world in which white people are surprisingly peripheral. In one remembered skirmish, the Crow warrior Two Leggings wounded a Piegan warrior: "He was almost dead and there was no reason to be afraid, so I suppose I played with him. He was my enemy and had probably killed some of my relatives." Once the man died, Two Leggings took his scalp. Remembering the incident, he summed up the good news of victory for his party: "The Piegans had been chased away and nobody was killed."[57]

"Nobody was killed"—which was to say, no *Crow* was killed. In this world of intertribal struggle, it was natural for the Crows, and for a great many other Indian groups, to see white people as promising allies against enemies. It was logical for Crow warriors to serve as scouts for the U.S. Army, to fight against the Sioux and Cheyennes. As Thomas Dunlay points out in his study of Indian scouts, "Indians often acted on the assumption that whites could be used to serve Indian purposes."[58] When tribe fought tribe, with or without whites in the picture, where was "the Indian side" to be found?

For much of American history, the "good Indians" were the collaborators—the Squantos and Pocahontases, who teamed up with the winners, the kind and helpful Indians who warned whites of impending attacks. Indians who died in heroic defense of their homelands might be individually admired, but it was not until the mid-twentieth century that the connotations of the terms reversed. The "good Indians" then became the patriots who had fought to defend the interests of their people, while the collaborators became the "bad Indians," the ones who sold out.

There is, however, a third perspective—which is to see Indian leaders as people steering their way through a difficult terrain of narrowing choice. George Phillip's *Chiefs and Challengers* provides a telling example of this third perspective. In 1851 one chief, Antonio Garra of the Cupeños, chose rebellion, creating a pan-Indian alliance to drive the Americans (though not the Hispanics) out of California. The coalition failed, and Garra was captured by another Indian leader, turned over to white authorities, tried, and executed. A second chief, Manuelito Cota of the Luiseños, though appointed to office by whites and remaining officially loyal to the Americans, still was able to retain considerable maneuvering room, playing off the American civilian subagents against the military officials. By "collaborating," Cota was able to unify his people and to see them become "the most prosperous Indian people in southern California." As Phillips notes, "one tends to see in Antonio Garra an individual who courageously resisted the American colonization of southern California and who bravely gave his life in the process," and to regard Cota as a mere "puppet of the government." And yet Cota was, by certain measures, far more effective in helping his people get the best that they could out of a bad bargain. In previous years, we might have bogged down in the question, Who was the real patriot? Now it seems far more productive to ask, What strategies did these leaders use, why did they choose them, and what were the results?[59]

But do these questions provide a sufficient corrective to the ethnocentric conventions of the past? The trained historian's response is to leap to the high ground of objectivity and neutrality. "We have changed," the professional historian wants to say to Indian people. "We have discarded the ethnocentric concepts of savagery and civilization and progress; we will not play favorites; we will be neutral cultural relativists. You can trust us now."

What in those assurances could persuade the distrustful that the conversion went beyond a change in manners, that the same old attitudes are not disguised under a veneer of tolerance? And what if neutrality was no longer enough—what if Indian people are now so certain of their injuries that they want condemnation and blame explicit in the writing of their history? How were white historians to respond when articulate and angry Indian people protested the fact that their history had been too long in the keeping of the outsiders and invaders?

In a talk called "Genocidal Aims toward Our Culture," delivered in 1974, Alan Slickpoo, director of the Nez Percé tribe's History and Culture Project, denounced the errors and "poor interpretation" of much Indian history written by whites. The popularity of Indian life as subject matter had created, he said, a situation in which "anyone who got on the 'bandwagon' of American Indian history became an 'expert' on the life of the Indian, all except the Indian himself." Ignoring Indian expertise and tribal interests, "too many books have been written without the expressed consent and endorsement of the Indian tribes concerned." After centuries of error and mishandling, "the Indian community," explained James Jefferson, tribal historian of the Southern Ute tribe, had become "suspicious of any type of study."[60]

The historiographic past does not, after all, provide the firmest ground for launching a defense of professional history. Much of what passed for objective frontier history was in fact nationalistic history, celebrating the winners and downgrading or ignoring the losers. Weighed down by decades of writing in which bearers of civilization displace unworthy savages, historians cannot overnight achieve a detached, nonpartisan inquiry. Defending the integrity of the profession, one can only hope that one's ethnocentric predecessors can be credibly and rapidly disowned.

The nationalism of conventional frontier history carried the assumption that history was itself a kind of property in which Americans deserved to take pride. Indians have put forth a counterclaim: Indian history is not solely *about* Indians; it is his-

tory *belonging* to Indians, in which the owners should take pride
and which should make them feel better about their inherited
identity. But this claim can only make contemporary historians
uncomfortable. Companies and corporations, government institutions and bureaucracies, and vain individuals have all, at one
time or another, recruited historians to write authorized histories, reconstructions of the past that confirm the institution's or
individual's faith. Religious belief makes this situation even more
of a trial to the professional. Leaders in the Latter-day Saints,
for instance, ask that Mormon historians write "faith-affirming"
history, avoiding inquiries that would reduce the sanctity of the
church's origins. All over the United States, religious and political fundamentalists make a similar demand of textbooks; history
taught to America's children, they say, should support and
encourage the proper pride in Christian values and American
nationalism.

Francis Jennings, whose position as director of the Newberry
Library's D'Arcy McNickle Center for Indian History put him in
frequent contact with Indian people, has written, "Traditionalist
Indians have different concepts of history from academics. Among
other differences, Indians generally deny that their forebears
crossed a land bridge from Asia. 'Our ancestors came out of this
very ground,' they will say, and discourse on this theme with
eloquence." The scholar might be sympathetic, but, as Jennings
has said, "no historian can afford to break free from Genesis in
his own culture only to adopt its counterpart in another."[61]

The historian, or any other American, who deliberates on
these matters loses a comfortable and settled point of rest but
finds a fresh angle on familiar subjects. In the late nineteenth
century, moving with his family from Ohio to Missouri to Kansas
to Montana, Thomas Leforge finally settled down—by joining
the Crow Indians, marrying into the tribe, and living with them
for twenty years. "The Indians liked to hear of the strange ways
of white people," Leforge remembered. "They wondered at these
peculiarities, the same as white people wonder at the customs
prevailing among Indians."[62]

Historians of the American mainstream who think they have
nothing to learn from Indian history are missing an important
opportunity. Take up this Indian perspective on the peculiar

ways of white people, and you are set free of the intellectually crippling temptation to take white people's ways for granted. Considered from this anthropological distance, white people are really quite interesting—and not simply creatures of economic self-interest, servants of the expanding world market, or cogs in a commercial system. Indian history inspired the development of ethnohistory, which places actions and events in a carefully explored context of culture and worldview. Ethnohistory reaches its peak when its techniques are applied across the board, when white people as well as Indians are cast as actors in complex cultural worlds, and when no point of view is taken for granted.

Consider, for instance, the refreshing angle of vision embodied in "The Well-Baked Man," an Indian tale in a collection of myths and legends assembled by Richard Erdoes and Alfonso Ortiz. The "magician, who was Man Maker," undertook to make human beings, shaping them out of clay and baking them in an oven. The first batch went into the oven, and the trickster Coyote soon declared them done. Man Maker looked at the product with disappointment: "Oh my, what's wrong?" he said. "They're underdone; they're not brown enough. They don't belong here—they belong across the water someplace. . . . I can't use them here." Another try proved more successful, the product coming out "neither underdone nor overdone." " 'These are exactly right,' " said Man Maker. " 'These really belong here; these I will use. They are beautiful.' So that's why we have the Pueblo Indians."[63]

Of course, Indian people can and should write their own histories according to their traditions, just as pioneers and their descendants have every right to publish books enshrining their own version of the past. For the sake of national and regional self-understanding, however, there should be a group of people reading all these books and paying attention to all these points of view. In that process, Western historians will not reach a neutral, omniscient objectivity. On the contrary, the clashes and conflicts of Western history will always leave the serious individual emotionally and intellectually unsettled. In the nineteenth-century West, speaking out for the human dignity of all parties to the conflicts took considerable nerve. It still does.

Seven

America the Borderland

IN THE AMERICAN SOUTHWEST, previously the Mexican North, Anglo-America ran into Hispanic America. The meeting involved variables of language, religion, race, economy, and politics. The border between Hispanic America and Anglo-America has shifted over time, but one fact has not changed: it is one thing to draw an arbitrary geographical line between two spheres of sovereignty; it is another to persuade people to respect it.

Victorious in the Mexican-American War in 1848, the United States took half of Mexico. The resulting division did not ratify any plan of nature. The borderlands were an ecological whole; northeastern Mexican desert blended into southwestern American desert with no prefigurings of nationalism. The one line that nature did provide—the Rio Grande—was a river that ran through but did not really divide continuous terrain.

If nature did not draw lines, human society certainly did. Friction and conflict begun in Europe were easily transplanted to the New World. England and Spain clashed in the maritime warfare of the Armada; Protestant Englishmen envied Catholic Spaniards their New World empire and especially their gold and silver. Economic competition mixed with religious conflict to fuel the English enthusiasm for *La Leyenda Negra*—the Black Legend, which portrayed Spaniards as particularly predatory, cruel, and malevolent in their dealings with Indians. That legend gratified both the conscience and the vanity of the presumably more humane English. With the Black Legend in their minds, some New England Puritans brooded over the presence of Spanish Catholics far to the south; the "New World" seemed less than pure if the papists had a more sizable empire than the Puritans. Two centuries later, Anglo-Americans moving into the borderlands encountered long-term Hispanic residents. Much modified by environment, time, and contact with native populations, northern and southern Europe met in odd circumstances, and conflicts between them, unresolved since the Reformation, surfaced again.

In 1528, the first Europeans to see the future borderlands began their unintended tour. After a Spanish expedition shipwrecked on the coast of the Gulf of Mexico, Álvar Núñez Cabeza de Vaca and three other survivors had one hope: to head west and south and eventually to find fellow Christians in Mexico. The Indians whom Cabeza de Vaca met spoke different languages, all foreign to him; the rivers, the mountains, and the plains were, to the Europeans, unmapped and untamed. The advantages of "civilization," of literacy, of connections at the Spanish court, counted for nothing. Over eight years, Cabeza de Vaca moved from tribe to tribe, working his way west and then south. He was lucky enough to develop a reputation as a healer, and by the time he headed into northern Mexico, he had become a regional celebrity, traveling with an entourage from one tribe to the next.

The proof that he was approaching the domain of his fellow Spaniards came in a disturbing form. Cabeza de Vaca reached a territory that was "vacant, the inhabitants having fled to the mountains in fear of Christians." He had entered the slave-raiding frontier. Rescue involved mixed sensations. "We gave thanks to God our Lord for choosing to bring us out of such a melancholy and and wretched captivity," Cabeza de Vaca said. But soon he and his party were in "a hot argument" with their rescuers, "for they meant to make slaves of the Indians in our train." In 1536, the border between Christians and Indians might not have been fenced or surveyed, but Cabeza de Vaca knew when he had crossed it.[1]

Four years after Cabeza de Vaca's return, Francisco Vásquez de Coronado saw no reason why the spirit of enterprise that brought Cortés the conquest of Aztec Mexico should fail to bring him a comparable empire. Why not anticipate a "Nuevo México" to the north, a prospective empire for Coronado himself? Cabeza de Vaca's reports had not been encouraging, but a preliminary expedition to the northern borderlands in 1539 had produced the happiest results. One Fray Marcos de Niza returned from the far north with reports of the Seven Cities of Cíbola, cities of gold and luxury, ripe for conquest. Well-connected to the Mexican viceroy and enriched by a prudent marriage, the thirty-year-old Coronado secured a commission to lead the conquest of Cíbola. In 1540, Mexico City held an abundance of adventurers, young men eager to follow in the tradition of Cortés and Pizarro, and Coronado had no trouble filling his ranks with fortune hunters.[2]

On the journey from Mexico City to present-day New Mexico, some fifteen hundred miles, conducting a party of more than a thousand, traveling by partially explored routes through deserts and rough mountains, Coronado paid the price of hardship that was sure to be the prelude to great rewards. His arrival at "Cíbola" thus ranked as one of the great disillusionments in Western history. When the Spanish found a humble pueblo with no traces of gold or other riches, the inexplicable Fray Marcos, originator of tales of golden cities and empire, became a very unpopular man and made an early return to Mexico City. A six-month journey had left the party nearly without provisions; from the Pueblo Indian point of view, the arrival of the Spanish was a nightmare of uninvited guests demanding food and insisting that the natives make unintelligible promises to become "Spanish vassals" and "Christians." Coronado's endless demands for food, clothing, and blankets drove the Indians into rebellion, and the winter of 1540–41 passed with raids, sieges, attacks, and reprisals between the Spaniards and the Pueblos.

In the spring, the Spaniards' hope for fortune revived with rumors of Quivira—another empire of gold, farther to the north and east, out on the Great Plains. They learned of Quivira from an extraordinary character in borderlands history, an Indian they called the Turk. Evidently a Plains Indian in captivity with the Pueblos, the Turk led Coronado out onto the Plains, weaving irresistible stories of the kingdom of Quivira, where gold bells hung from trees, lulling the Quiviran king to sleep.

Situated somewhere in present-day Kansas, Quivira turned out to be a village of Plains Indians, living in brush huts and earning their living with nothing more golden than corn. The extreme high hopes of Coronado and his men had put them at the mercy of the Turk's masterful trickery. In Kansas, the trickery exposed, Coronado killed the Turk. Vengeance did not make the expedition any less of a disaster.

Back at the Rio Grande, preparing for the trip back to Mexico, Coronado was thrown from his horse and severely injured. In 1542, carried in a litter part of the way, he returned to Mexico City with no good news to report. The conquistador tradition had run aground in the deserts and plains of the northern borderlands.

Almost sixty years later, in 1598, Juan de Oñate launched a second attempt at colonizing the far north. Expectations still ran surprisingly high; once in New Mexico, Oñate gave Coronado's Quivira another try, with a similarly unsatisfying result. Oñate's fortune hunters were not happy with the prospect of giving up on gold and settling for the pedestrian and unadventurous labor of livestock herding and irrigated farming. Facing friction with Indians and mutinies among his own settlers, Oñate gave up on his empire building, resigned as governor, and absorbed his losses. The empire's officials then looked at the colony of New Mexico: unproductive, isolated (a six-month journey from Mexico City), bogged down in factions and disputes despite the smallness of the stakes. Why bother to retain a colony that was in many ways a mistake?

Retreat, it turned out, was untenable, and for ironic reasons. The Franciscans who had accompanied Oñate claimed they had been able to convert some of the Pueblo Indians. Convert and baptize Indians in the true faith, and then abandon them? Few worse crimes were imaginable. New Mexico would stay a colony, and the Spanish crown would assume responsibility for it—on behalf of the Pueblos. If consulted, the Pueblos would have disagreed with this consideration of their spiritual needs; some decades later, they disagreed violently in the 1680 Pueblo Revolt, expelling the Spanish from New Mexico. Reconquered by 1694, New Mexico settled into its place on the periphery of the Spanish Empire. The settlers of New Spain's northern frontier, the historian Oakah L. Jones has shown, developed a "distinct" culture, with basic "institutions brought from Europe, yet modified to meet the challenge of different environmental conditions." The large majority of residents were neither soldiers nor missionaries, but civilian settlers—"the farmer, day laborer, stockman, and artisan." With little beyond agriculture and ranching to attract settlers, New Mexico remained "a remote, exposed, and isolated frontier, . . . similar to an island outpost." Still, with the bulk of the population "hard-working, individually employed small farmers and artisans," and with "[g]rowing numbers of people, mixing of races, and a blurring of class differences," New Mexico was "anything but static." It was not the hypnotized, stagnant, "sleepy" backwater Anglo-Americans would later imagine it to be.[3]

Spanish officials might have wanted a closely regulated, predictable empire, with individual will subordinated to imperial control, but New Mexicans often had other plans. Like many New England settlers, New Mexicans wanted "to live near their fields," creating "scattered settlements," despite "the Spanish government's desire to concentrate its people at a few major points for defensive purposes." The government's preference had a clear logic in New Mexico. Out on its northern periphery, the empire had encountered a troublesome population of nomadic or semi-nomadic Indians. In contrast to the Anglo-American "frontier of exclusion," the Spanish might well have had a "frontier of inclusion," incorporating Indians into the colonial economy and society. Nonetheless, the nomadic Indians of the northern borderlands made the distinction insignificant. Whatever the Spanish might have intended, the Apaches were not part of any "frontier of inclusion." They were instead a perennial administrative problem, respecting no directives and no boundaries, raiding both Hispanic settlers and Pueblo villagers, and reducing whole areas of New Mexico to uninhabitable war zones. The Spanish response was to build the presidio, a fort containing a small number of soldiers; the presidio might have served as a refuge from attack for its occupants, but its soldiers could do next to nothing to control the Apaches. Presidios were stationary and Apaches were mobile, having little to fear from these outposts of Spanish power.[4]

The Spanish northern borderlands thus became a defensive frontier, holding off Indian raiders and responding to the stimulus of imperial rivalry. Already overextended in New Mexico, Spanish colonial officials still felt compelled to respond to the challenge posed by the French presence in the Mississippi Valley. The Spanish colonization into Texas was an instance of this use of the borderlands as chessboard, in which a French advance had to be followed by a Spanish counteradvance. Similarly, the Russian and English interest in California provoked a Spanish countermove, extending the unwieldy unit of the borderlands to hold off a rival sovereignty.[5]

The colonization of California had been engineered by a particular individual, José de Gálvez, visitor general to New Spain. As visitor general, Gálvez was the king's official emissary, sent to assess and address the problems of the realm. A man of great will, certain of his abilities, Gálvez came to New Spain in 1767 and plunged into administrative reform of the unwieldy colonial bureaucracy. His plan for the northern borderlands was simple: to engineer the settlement of California in order to ward off English and Russian encroachment; to control the unsubdued, raiding Indians; and to speed up the whole business of civilizing and incorporating Indians into the empire.[6]

This seemed a workable plan, when the borderlands were viewed from a distance. On-site, the intractability of both the unconquered Indians and the Indians providing only superficial submission to the missionaries made a vivid impression. Gálvez nonetheless persisted in his plans, launching the settlement of California and then turning to mission problems in the border region of Sonora. And then, he leaped from his bed one night to announce that Saint Francis of Assisi had appeared to him, promising to take personal responsibility for controlling the nomadic Indians.

José de Gálvez made a slow recovery from his mental break-down; once recovered, he returned fully to administrative respectability. Later, even higher office made it possible for him to punish those who remembered his mental weakness and spoke of it too audibly. Gálvez no doubt had his personal reasons for madness, but the administrative problems of the borderlands were a sizable reason in themselves. The uncontrolled Indians, the disappointments and the failed expectations of gold and for-tune, and the unwieldiness of colonies ranging from California to Louisiana (acquired from the French in 1763) all frustrated the would-be masters of the borderlands.

II

The governing of the borderlands proved no more reward-ing for Mexico than it had been for Spain. Mexican independence in 1821 did not persuade the Apaches that a new era had dawned or that cooperation was now in order. The opening of the Mexican borderlands to American colonists and merchants made the region into what it remains today: a true frontier, in the European sense, in which two nations confront each other and compete for control of the local resources and routes to opportunity. For the first, imperial phase of the borderlands, Spanish authorities tried to hold the line against French, English, and American encroachment. In the second phase, Mexican officials tried to control the Americans who pressed for advan-tage both in trade and in land acquisition. In the third phase, following the conquest and transfer of sovereignty, Americans would superimpose their institutions on the Hispanic ones. And in the fourth phase, Mexican immigration would accelerate, as campesinos and craftsmen pursued jobs and wages north of the border, and Americans, like Spanish and Mexican officials before them, found that it was extremely difficult to maintain the sanc-tity of a line across the land when the "aliens" were convinced that opportunity lay on the other side.

Though most distant in time, the first was by no means the least interesting phase. For a century or more, remoteness was at once New Mexico's burden and its advantage. Then, in 1714, bad news appeared in the form of the French trader Louis Juchereau de Saint-Denis, who had traveled overland to forge a commercial connection between the French Mississippi Valley and the New Mexican settlements. Apprehended by Spanish officials intent on keeping the empire closed to foreigners, Saint-Denis followed in the best romantic tradition of the border agent, marrying into the Spanish commandant's family and returning to Plains exploration, this time as a Spanish agent. The individual intruder had been neutralized and assimilated; nonetheless, the border was breached. New Mexican isolation could no longer be taken for granted, as long as the vague borders of French Louisiana edged up on the equally vague borders of New Spain's northern territory.[7]

All this took a curious twist in 1763. Defeated by the British in the French and Indian War, France undertook to save Louisiana from the fate of Canada. Ceded to Spain, Louisiana could avoid becoming part of the British spoils of war. With a stroke of the pen, Spain's North American empire leaped eastward, reaching to the Mississippi River. As gifts go, Louisiana was more headache than boon; it added to Spain's administrative burdens and, most disturbing, presented Spain with new neighbors—the aggressive, land-grabbing, scheming Anglo-Americans on the other side of the Mississippi River.[8]

The schemes soon began. In the early nineteenth century, the open lands of Texas provided a temptation Anglo-Americans were ill prepared to resist; before 1821, American intruders and squatters—the "illegal aliens" of their day—were already troubling the Spanish officials of Texas. Schemes emanated as well from higher-ranking sources. The commanding officer of the army of the new American Republic, General James Wilkinson, allied with Aaron Burr, was a fountain of plots—to sever the North American interior from Spanish domination and even to create an empire and nation from the raw material of the continent's interior. When Lieutenant Zebulon Pike set out to explore the headwaters of the Arkansas River in 1806, he *might* have been acting as Wilkinson's agent; historical conspiracies are no easier to document than contemporary ones. In any case, the

Spanish had their reasons to bristle when Pike appeared on their turf, in the mountains north of Santa Fe. One might see the arrested and deported Pike as another innocent victim, led by curiosity and adventure into the domain of an early evil empire. Reverse perspectives, and Pike looks like an intruder, an alien, and a probable spy.[9]

Facing the external pressures represented by Pike, the Spanish borderlands also had their own internal pressures—most notably, a pent-up consumer urge that was apt to lead the border residents to welcome the foreigners the empire tried to keep out. In 1821, when Mexican independence inaugurated a second phase of borderlands history, that urge was unleashed. Mexico took off the restraints, allowing American traders into Santa Fe and American trading vessels into California ports, while permitting American colonists to settle in Texas. The hope was that foreign personnel could serve Mexican ends, that the commercial energy of Americans could bring a new vitality to the border economies. In Texas, especially, it was a risky experiment. The province, officials knew, was underpopulated and vulnerable. Where was Mexico to find new colonists who could hold Texas for Mexico? The Mexican frontier simply did not provide conditions attractive enough to pull settled Mexican people to the north. An abundant supply of colonists could be found in only one place—the United States.[10]

The theory, then, was that Texas could bring in Anglo-American colonists, give them land, and convert them—to Catholicism, to Mexican citizenship, and to Hispanic civilization. If Anglo-Americans found Indians resistant to "civilization," Anglo-Americans in Texas proved to be as stubborn as Indians in resisting efforts to remake them. Settled at a distance from the Hispanic Tejanos, Anglo-Texans kept to their own enclaves, becoming more and more resistant to the sovereignty of their host country. It did not help matters that the Mexican government remained unstable, taking a sudden turn in 1834 toward centralization under the recurrent leader Antonio López de Santa Anna. Organized around the issue of local self-government, accelerated by racial, religious, and language conflicts, Anglo-Texan discontent led to revolution and to the creation of the

Texas republic in 1836. Mexico did not, however, concede the question, refusing to recognize Texan independence and yearning for a reconquest. Mexico made at least two tries, temporarily recapturing San Antonio in 1842. Efforts at reconquest notwithstanding, the independent republic in the American interior, a creature of General Wilkinson's imaginings, had actually come to exist. Would the Texas Revolution set a precedent? Was California on its way to becoming "another Texas," to be stolen from Mexico by Anglo infiltration?[11]

In California, the experiment never had the opportunity to run to completion. Nonetheless, Anglo "infiltration" there started off in a direction very different from that in Texas. From the 1820s on, individual American trappers and traders settled in California, often marrying into Hispanic families, adopting Spanish as their principal language, and at least starting to become Mexicanized Americans. Cut short by the massive influx of Anglo-Americans in the gold rush, a degree of blending and assimilation began California's contact between Hispanic and Anglo. As in Texas, discontent with the Mexican home government ran high, especially following Santa Anna's 1834 move toward centralization. In California, however, those most actively discontented with Mexican government were Hispanics, not Anglos. Resistance to Mexican authority went so far, in 1836 (the year of the Texas Revolution), as a conditional declaration of independence. California, the legislature declared, shall be "independent of Mexico until the federal system adopted in 1824 shall be reestablished," a demand not unlike the initial demands made in Texas. With such a background in discontent, it took the Anglo conquest and political and economic disposession to provoke in Hispanic Californians a strong sense of identity with Mexico, a nationalistic sentiment not much in evidence in the years before the Mexican-American War.[12]

In those years, nationalism was certainly in full force on the American side. Desire for more territory, especially for the acquisition of a Pacific port, coincided with racism and condescension to produce a belief that Mexico could be easily persuaded to surrender territory to its clearly more powerful northern neighbor. The reasoning resembled the persistent way of thinking about Indians—that they were not using the land productively and properly and that, therefore, dispossession would be not only easy but also right. In pressing for the sale of California, President James K. Polk acted with little understanding of how the indignity of having lost Texas had become a sensitive issue in Mexico, making it political death for any faction in power to make further concessions to Anglo-America.[13]

Under those circumstances, with Mexico still denying Texas's independence, its annexation by the United States was a mortifying international insult. A disputed annexation then presented this practical problem: Where was the real border between the nations? The question had serious consequences. When U.S. troops arrived in the disputed territory between the Nueces River and the Rio Grande, war was unavoidable. That Mexico was impoverished and hardly capable of sustaining a war only dramatized the depth of resentment Mexicans felt. On April 25, 1846, Mexican troops attacked American troops in an area of unsettled jurisdiction. By the nature of border disputes, it was possible to say, as President Polk put it, that "American blood had been shed on American soil." It was also possible to say, as Polk's critics put it, that American blood had been shed in a Mexican cornfield.[14]

Today it is easy to forget that between 1846 and 1848 the United States invaded Mexico's heartland and occupied the capital city, that American troops—especially uncontrolled volunteers—served as ambassadors of ill will to Mexico's countryside and cities, and that Mexican powerlessness forced the surrender of half of the nation's territory—California, New Mexico, Arizona, and Texas and parts of Nevada, Utah, and Colorado.

Like many other episodes in Western American history, the Mexican-American War shifted meanings radically when viewed from different directions. It takes only a modest effort of the imagination to see America's grand venture in continental Manifest Destiny as it looked to Mexico: a shameless land grab and an aggressive attack on Mexican sovereignty.[15]

Carried away by the spirit of victory, some Americans spoke of taking "All Mexico," envisioning a scenario in which the Mexican people would either become uplifted, Americanized, and made ready for democracy or disappear, with the Vanishing Hispanic going the way of the Vanishing Indian. When the fervor of the "All Mexico" movement died down, the United States settled for the sparsely settled but immense northern borderlands.[16]

Innocent hopes that the new territory and people could easily be incorporated into the United States ran into a rougher reality. The problem was not simply one of friction between the United States and Mexico. Within the United States, too, sectional tensions frustrated the most basic stages of the process of incorporation.

The surveying of the new border, for instance, turned out to be a bureaucrat's nightmare. A flurry of appointments, resignations, and replacements punctuated the attempt to fill the position of border commissioner. The fourth appointee, John Russell Bartlett, set out with the happiest expectations. A Protestant Yankee himself, Bartlett was a bookseller, amateur scholar, and lay politician from Rhode Island. When his political connections secured him the boundary commission job, which assigned him to collaborate with Mexico in surveying the border, it seemed an ideal intersection of national need and personal opportunity. Bartlett read of the exotic landscape, flora, and fauna of the newly acquired Southwest. As a close observer and a competent artist, he relished this chance to add to the standing knowledge of the region.[17]

Begun in optimism, Bartlett's expedition soon became an ordeal. He and his party took a sea passage from New York to the Texas coast and then prepared to travel overland. The problems of directing and controlling a large group, ranging from other educated Eastern men to Texas teamsters, had not figured in Bartlett's hopes for adventure. Barely a week passed before an American in his party quarreled with a local Mexican. The American killed the Mexican, and Bartlett, fresh from his Rhode Island bookstore, found himself trying to compensate the murdered man's family.

Factions within the surveying party added to Bartlett's burdens. In part, Commissioner Bartlett and his official surveyor were simply a bad personality match; added to their imcompatible temperaments, the party represented all shades of section-alism. Hopes for a Pacific railroad had influenced the Mexican border survey; Southerners were determined to secure territory far enough to the south to provide a level, viable route for a railroad to benefit their section. As a Rhode Island Yankee, Bart-lett was immediately suspect; in fact, his agreeable relations—and willingness to compromise—with the Mexican commis-sioner made him unpopular with Southerners in general and with his surveyor in particular.

The party wrote letters prolifically, passing their complaints and quarrels on to Washington. Eventually, sectional tensions and Bartlett's apparent inefficiency would lead Congress to sus-pend his funds, and thereafter Bartlett would conclude his Southwestern adventure with an undignified retreat. In the meantime, the Southwestern terrain was difficult, water scarce, and food expensive. Midway through, Bartlett fell ill and spent months recuperating in Mexico. During his tenure, despite his frailties, much of the present border was mapped, but the trip had provided few of the expected pleasures.

Even so, John Russell Bartlett's relations with his Mexican counterparts were more agreeable than relations with American colleagues. In that brief phase of history, Bartlett suffered more from friction between the American North and South than from friction between Mexico and the United States. Bartlett's trou-bles were symptomatic of the larger struggle provoked by the Mexican acquisition: the near breakdown of the Union over the extension of slavery, avoided by the precariously stitched together Compromise of 1850.[18]

Compared with the battles in Congress, mapping the border was a minor matter. The exact location of the border did not stir up the international tensions of the region. A huge loss of terri-tory was the key blow to Mexican national dignity; locating the dividing line was far less significant. On that count, Bartlett was a lucky man. Beset by illness and attacks from his own forces, he faded away before the conflict grew between the diverse peoples of the Southwest. That conflict had come before and would come later.

III

Take the matter of Indian control in Arizona and New Mexico. During the Mexican period, relations between Hispanic settlers and Apaches and Comanches had reached their nadir. Well-used trails took Indian raiders hundreds of miles south into Sonora and Chihuahua. Governors of some northern Mexican states established scalp bounties, turning Indian scalps into commodities redeemable for cash. A diverse cast of characters, ranging from Hispanics to Anglos and other Indians, flocked to the opportunity. Of course, there was no certain way to distinguish an Apache scalp from any other dark-haired scalp; in the boom years of the bounty system, Hispanics and Indians other than Apaches were thus vulnerable to attack by scalp hunters.[19]

Against this violent background, the Treaty of Guadalupe Hidalgo at the end of the Mexican War committed the United States to controlling the nomadic Indians. By agreeing to prevent the Indians from raiding into Mexico, the United States had agreed to solve the principal border problem, the one the Spanish and the Mexicans had never mastered. A promise to control the Apache and Navajo was not, one would think, a promise to make lightly; it was, moreover, from the Apache and Navajo point of view, a promise without logic. If the Apache and Navajo had fought the Hispanics for years and if Americans entered the war and fought against the Mexicans, then surely the Americans were the allies of the Apaches and Navajos. Why would the Americans prevent their allies from raiding their common enemy across the border? A line through space could never look more arbitrary than it did to Indian people whose ancestors have moved unhindered in the region long before the line was even imagined.[20]

For Hispanic people north of the new border, the change in sovereignty could seem equally abrupt and arbitrary. The treaty allowed them to emigrate to Mexico or to stay in the United States, with their rights as American citizens ostensibly guaranteed. As Indians did with their treaties, so Hispanics had in the Treaty of Guadalupe Hidalgo a written guarantee of their rights to retain their legitimate land claims. Like Indian treaties, too, the 1848 treaty would be much violated but would nonetheless remain on the books as a promise awaiting fulfillment.[21]

Conquest was far more than a simple political and legal transaction. As the historian Deena Gonzáles has said, "Conquest affected everyone: Native, Spanish, mestizo, and mulatto; men, women, and children; old and young." The arrival of soldiers in the 1840s only capped the process begun earlier by the

Santa Fe in the late nineteenth century, center of the longest-lasting Hispanic settlement in the United States. *Courtesy Denver Public Library, Western History Department*

arrival of traders; from the 1820s on, Hispanic people responded with a complicated mixture of accommodation and resistance. Just as Indian women had, by marrying traders, bridged the meeting of cultures in the fur trade, so Hispanic women in New Mexico played a key role in introducing one group to the other. Intermarrying, "Spanish-Mexican women brought Euro-American men into their community, their homes, and their lives." Already Catholic, Irish men, in particular, were equipped to make the transition. For Euro-American males and Hispanic women alike, intermarriage was an innovative way of pursuing stability during an unsettling social transition. Occasionally, an even more enterprising individual could go even further in seizing new opportunity. The New Mexican businesswoman Gertrudis Barceló found her opportunity in the influx of Euro-Americans. The successful operator of a gambling saloon in Santa Fe, Barceló met the conquest head on, growing "wealthy," as her biographer put it, "on Euro-American money."[22]

Americans had promised to honor the legitimate land claims of Hispanics in the ceded territories. American land law, super-imposed on unsurveyed and unclaimed lands, was complicated enough; but when it met the legacy of Spanish and Mexican land law, it was a sure source of confusion. And to a certain sort of frontiersman, confusion presented a fine opportunity.

When Thomas B. Catron was immersed in the confusion of New Mexican land claims, he was a man in his element. A lawyer who arrived in New Mexico in 1866, Catron rose to a central position of influence in the Santa Fe ring, a group of lawyers and politicians at the center of New Mexico territorial politics. Catron and his fellows built "their own political and economic empire out of the tangled heritage of land grants." Following the promises given in the treaty, the United States set about clearing titles for Hispanic grants. "Naturally the lawyers of Santa Fe exacted their fees," the historian Howard Lamar has written, "for clearing titles. Being paid in land, they themselves gradually acquired ownership of the largest grants and became, as it were, their own clients. Eventually over 80 per cent of the Spanish grants went to American lawyers and settlers."[23]

No one played the game better than Catron. In his career,

he "owned entirely, or had an interest in, at least thirty-four land grants," thus owning "at one time or another more than three million acres." According to his biographer, Catron was without peer: "He was undoubtedly the largest individual landholder in the history of the United States, and also represented clients as an attorney in litigation for more land than any other person." Kit Carson got the publicity and became a household word; Thomas Catron remains known to few. Catron may have lost to Carson in color and adventure, but the lawyer nonetheless outweighed the scout in significance. "His methods were contentious and his conduct abrasive," his biographer has noted, "but they got results." True to the patterns of Western history, one of the results involved the high price of victory. In building his landed empire, nearly as large as Delaware and John Russell Bartlett's Rhode Island put together, Catron had to borrow heavily to acquire and hold property that was not yet producing much profit. Catron might have been one of America's largest landowners, but he was also a great debtor, a dilemma "which led to the ultimate loss of most of the property he owned." From 1890 on, Catron "was harassed almost unbearably by financial problems that hit him from all quarters." Coping with sons of the highest and most expensive educational ambitions and with a wife addicted to expensive travel, Catron seemed more the overworked and underrewarded husband than the villainous land baron. In 1908, the expenses of one of his wife's trips forced him to borrow money. "Mama," he explained to one son, "will need more money than I have to my credit."[24]

Like New Mexican Hispanos, Hispanic Californians (Californios) found Anglos in hot pursuit of their landholdings. The congressionally created Land Claims Commission set out in 1851 to review the Spanish and Mexican land grants. A variety of factors—from, as Mario Barrera has put it, "high legal fees and court costs, combined with a shortage of capital and the necessity to borrow money at high interest rates," to the pressures of American squatters indifferent to Hispanic claims—made it unlikely that the grants would remain in Hispanic hands. In noting these land losses, we should counter any nostalgic images of a pre-Anglo era of equitably shared property. "Many Californios," Barrera has said, "owned no land from which to be displaced."[25]

For the elite, a loss of political power paralleled the loss of land. This was often a transaction by demography; in northern California, for instance, the gold rush simply flooded the region with Anglos, immersing any remaining Hispanics in a sea of foreigners. These "foreigners," nonetheless, took little time in reversing the terms. In 1850, the California legislature passed the Foreign Miners' Tax, intended to drive non-Anglos out of the mines. "Foreigners" included Sonorans and, because of a failure to distinguish between the origins of individuals, most Hispanics as well. It was evidently an Anglo-American talent to change overnight from being intruders to being legitimate residents and, conversely, to turn the natives into "foreigners."[26]

The Treaty of Guadalupe Hidalgo obligated the United States to admit Mexican residents of the new territories to full citizenship. Californios did participate in the California constitutional convention, securing a provision to have the laws of the state printed in both Spanish and English. But take the case of one of those participants, Manuel Dominguez, a landowner. Eight years after the constitutional convention, Dominguez was prohibited from testifying in courts. The reason? Dominguez was a mestizo, with Indian blood, and Indians had no right to testify in California courts.[27]

In southern California, Anglo settlement proceeded at a gentler pace, awaiting the arrival of the railroads and allowing Hispanics to remain politically significant both as voters and as officeholders. This was also true of New Mexico, where Hispanics remained a majority until the twentieth century. Even in those regions, though, many Hispanic people could find themselves unrepresented in government, since the Southwestern Hispanic population was no monolith of clearly understood, shared interests. Class differences ran through Hispanic society, and Anglos in Texas, New Mexico, and California could usually find allies in the Hispanic upper classes, among *ricos* who would collaborate in the interests of property and social order, even at the expense of their lower-class countrymen. Anxious to win and keep the good opinion of Anglos, the postconquest Hispanic elite sometimes undertook to Europeanize or "whiten" themselves, accenting a Spanish line of descent to distinguish themselves from mestizos, people of mixed Spanish and Indian backgrounds. In New Mexico, some of the elite sympathized with white Southerners fighting off attacks on their "peculiar institution"; New Mexico had its own, in some ways comparable institution of debt peonage, which antislavery laws could threaten.[28]

Even with concessions and accommodations, Hispanics still lost power when the numbers turned against them. In southern California, as in New Mexico, the arrival of the railroad initiated that change, providing a means of comfortable immigration and hooking those remote regions into the national economy. The railroads, as a student of mine once put it, functioned as a pipeline, picking up white middle-class Protestants in their home territory of the East and Midwest and pumping them out the other end, into the formerly remote regions of the West. When, in the 1880s, the railroads discharged middle-class white Americans into southern California, Hispanic settlements changed from pueblos to barrios, from towns in which Hispanics were the majority population to segregated enclaves in cities in which Hispanics had become a minority. Reduced in power and property, Hispanics in the borderlands nonetheless remained an active and distinctive people. A number of recent historical studies reveal Hispanic communities maintaining their language and religious traditions, creating mutual aid societies, founding newspapers, and reinforcing their common identity.[29]

Confronting Hispanic people over the nineteenth century, Anglo-Americans demonstrated a standard set of responses. After visiting California in 1834, Richard Henry Dana offered an influential portrait of Californios in his widely read *Two Years before the Mast*. The Californios were festive and colorful, he thought, but improvident and undeserving of California's vast resources. Living in a promising country, they failed to use it properly. This led Dana to make his memorable declaration: the Californios

inhabit a country embracing four or five hundred miles of sea-coast, with several good harbours, with fine forests in the north; the waters filled with fish, and the plains covered with thousands of herds of cattle;

blessed with a climate than which there can be no better in the world; free from all manner of diseases, whether epidemic or endemic; and with a soil in which corn yields from seventy to eighty-fold. In the hands of an enterprising people, what a country this might be.[30]

Looking at upper-class Hispanics, Anglo-Americans like Dana saw wasteful, frivolous people; when they looked at the lower classes, their attitude could become even more contemptuous. On his tour of the Plains and Rockies in 1846, Francis Parkman wasted no time in trying to learn more about Hispanics; he had their category already prepared. He had no trouble evaluating the first Hispanics he saw in Missouri: "thirty or forty dark slavish-looking Spaniards, gazing stupidly out from beneath their broad hats." While Parkman could find a few things to admire in "untouched" Indians, he did not even imagine the possibility of merit in Hispanics. Mexicans, to his eye, were "squalid," "their vile faces overgrown with hair," "mean and miserable."[31]

By the 1850s, Anglos in Texas and California had added the stereotype of the Mexican bandito, the highwayman whose sneaky and treacherous ways of preying on innocent travelers were part and parcel of his ethnic character. In a fictional story offered as truth, the widely respected Clarence King, later to be the first director of the U.S. Geological Survey, described an encounter in California with two supposed bandits. Though at first he found "the stolid, brutal cast of their countenances . . . not worse than the average California greaser," closer inspection of one man, "a half-breed Indian," revealed "deep brutal lines" in his face "and a mouth which was a mere crease between hideously heavy lips." Instantly, King had "summed up their traits as stolidity and utter cruelty."[32]

Published in 1872, King's *Mountaineering in the Sierra Nevada* provoked no public outcry against such ethnic stereotyping. King's characterization of Mexicans was a perfectly acceptable component of the genteel literature of adventure. Outside of literature, such attitudes could inspire behavior that was hardly genteel. In southern California and especially in Texas, the years after the conquest saw frequent episodes of violence, approaching at times a state close to "race war." Lynching, it turned out, was not solely an attack by white Southerners against Southern blacks. Like blacks, Mexicans could be punished for suspected crimes, or simply encouraged to stay in their place, by the arbitrary, extra-legal actions of Anglo-Americans.[33]

In the years after 1848, a question remained open: Had the Anglo-American acquisition of Latin American territory reached the end of its trail? Even after the "All Mexico" movement died away, the notion of further expansion took control of individual minds. The tradition of filibustering went on, with adventurers leading free-lance armies into foreign territory in hopes of chiseling off a region for independent-nation status or for prospective annexation to the United States. The disappointments of gold rush California recruited ambitious and frustrated young men for the business of filibustering. Foremost in taking advantage of that discontent was the remarkable William Walker. Walker was small at five feet five inches and less than 120 pounds. A shy man originally from Tennessee, he went to gold rush California in 1850. Walker held in full measure, as the historian Charles H. Brown has noted, "the conviction that he was destined to achieve greatness." After a few years as a California editor and lawyer, his destiny turned toward Latin America. In October 1853, leading forty-five men, Walker left San Francisco to go redeem Baja California and Sonora. By November 3, he had occupied the capital of Baja and proclaimed his new sovereignty: "The Republic of Lower California is hereby declared free, sovereign, and independent, and allegiance to the Republic of Mexico is forever renounced." Walker thought he could liberate the northern Mexico provinces both from the Mexican government and from the attacks of the nomadic Indians. A man who took to the making of proclamations as ducks take to water, Walker told the people of lower California that his goal was "the amelioration of [their] social and political condition, and the improvement of the country, by all the arts which conduce to the civilization of people."[34]

His Sonoran invasion, however, disintegrated once he confronted some of the Indians he had declared he would tame and once he confronted the rought desert terrain. Indians stole, and the Colorado River drowned, Walker's livestock. His party was soon "in a most miserable and destitute condition," wrote one observer; Walker himself had "but one boot and a piece of a boot." Naturally, "there was much disaffection in camp, and in a barren country which they had invaded with hostile intentions, with few means of repelling attacks, exhausted, naked, starvation staring them in the face, many men prepared to abandon the waning fortunes of the expedition, and return to the settlements for an honest livelihood." Choosing retreat, Walker escaped north across the border to San Diego. The borderlands had defied another would-be master.[35]

The defeat did not stop William Walker. His second try at filibustering showed just how vulnerable Latin America was to the adventurer's scheme. American acquisition of the California coast, along with the population shift of the gold rush, had placed a new value on Central America. Overland travel from the East Coast to the Pacific Coast was expensive and time-consuming; shipping to Panama, taking the land-and-water route across the Isthmus, and then shipping north to California was equally expensive and troublesome. The idea of constructing a Central American canal carried an irresistible logic; in the meantime, the transit route across Nicaragua had become a significant and valuable appendage to American commerce. Thus, there was a curious logic to Walker's second plan. Thirty-one years old in 1855, Walker sailed from San Francisco in June with fifty-eight men, on a rickety ship. He arrived in Nicaragua, capitalized on the ongoing Nicaraguan civil war, and, incredibly, took over the country, still secure in the "delusion," as Brown put it, "that all his actions were motivated by the desire to bring law and order to an abandoned people." Walker's final defeat came from his struggles with his fellow American Commodore Vanderbilt. Vanderbilt's financial control over the transit route and Nicaragua, along with American investments in Mexico, would demonstrate that filibustering was unnecessary and unsubtle. Financial power could curtsy in the direction of national sovereignty and then go about its business, without the messy consequences of Walker's methods.[36]

IV

In the late nineteenth and early twentieth centuries, American business was finding many uses for the resources of Hispanic America, including uses for the labor of Hispanic people. As railroads pushed into the Southwest, their heavy labor demands led the companies into recruiting Mexican laborers, contracting with them, and transporting them to the United States, in cheerful defiance of the federal laws prohibiting the importation of contract labor. The availability of railroad transportation, especially of the refrigerated car, made the exportation of fruits and vegetables possible, and this, combined with the rise of Southwestern irrigation, set off a new phase of agribusiness. The growing of fruits and vegetables required intensive but seasonal labor; Mexican nationals supplied that seasonal labor, coming north for the harvest and other periods of peak demand, and returning home or at least moving elsewhere in the off-season. As the economy of the South rested for decades on the availability of black people's labor, so that of the Southwest depended on Mexican labor. Americans enjoying an affordable supply of fruits and vegetables in all seasons were pulled into this chain of dependence, regardless of their distance from the actual borderlands.[37]

On the other side of the border, because the Mexican economy was often unstable, jobs in the United States represented an essential economic supplement. People who could not make a living in the countryside could look for work in the crowded Mexican cities or head north to the United States. In interviews in the 1920s with the Mexican sociologist Manuel Gamio, Mexican immigrants told why they had come to the United States. Their reasons were fully in line with the traditional image of the nation, and especially the West, as a place of opportunity. "My intention," said Felipe Valdés, ". . . is to get a good job and save some money and start out for myself, for one can make good money here and there is always work." Many of the immigrants planned to return home once the reward was in hand, but in that, too, they resembled many Anglo-American participants in Western mineral rushes.[38]

Mexican immigrants had many motives and hopes in common with European immigrants, but they also had their differences. European immigrants crossed an ocean and thus put a sizable obstacle to continuing reinforcement of their traditions and cultural distinctiveness. For Mexicans, land contiguity between the nations made return far more feasible. Proximity to Mexico thus made it much easier to retain a traditional identity; immigrants living in Southwestern enclaves often found it unnecessary to learn English or to adapt to American customs in food or clothing, since they lived their lives in the company of other Hispanics. For understandable reasons, few Mexicans saw much attraction in American citizenship. Mexico remained their homeland. "I will never change my citizenship," said many of the people interviewed by Gamio in the late 1920s, "for that would be to deny the mother who has brought one into the world." Experiences with Anglo racism confirmed the inclination to withdraw from participation in American life. Anglos "don't like us," explained Carlos Almazán. "They think we aren't as good as they and as we are submissive they do whatever they want to with our labor. . . ." The immigrants themselves perceived the distinctions between them and long-term Hispanic residents of the United States. "[O]ur worst enemies," one man said, "are the Mexicans who have lived here for a great many years and have gotten settled and have become American citizens," and who thus resent the intrusion of these unassimilated Mexican nationals. But those distinctions, many recognized, were not visible from the other side. "We are all Mexicans anyway," said one man born in Arizona, "because the *gueros* [blonds, or Anglo-Americans] always treat all of us alike."[39]

The willingness to accept lower wages earned the immigrants the support of employers, but also the hostility of American labor. Even low American wages could be ten times greater than Mexican wages; moreover, workers who planned to return to Mexico with their savings could reconcile themselves to living under rough conditions as a temporary necessity. But this, of course, made them appear to be dangerous competitors for jobs, lowering wages and living standards for all.

Hostility to Mexican immigrants was, again, not solely a matter of Anglo attitudes. The Southwestern Hispanic population was no more a monolith of united interests in the twentieth century than it had been in the nineteenth century. Hispanics who had lived in the United States for a generation or more could

see recent arrivals as *cholos*—lower-class people, rough and unso-
phisticated. *Cholos* in large numbers might well increase the hostility Anglos already felt, and then that hostility would be applied
indiscriminately to all Hispanic people, the assimilated natives
of the United States as well as yesterday's arrivals. From the other
side, Mexican immigrants could see the adapted U.S. Hispanics
as *pochos*—people of compromised identity, Spanish-speakers
whose language was tainted with Anglicized words, "Mexicans"
only in a remote and diluted way. "The Mexicans who are born
and educated here," said one man interviewed by Gamio, "are
people without a country."[40]

In the early twentieth century, the complex matter of Mexican immigration was not much on the popular national mind.
The issue of European immigration aroused much more interest and controversy. In 1924, Congress finally passed a bill
bringing a broad policy of immigration restriction. The act set
quotas for European immigration but omitted the countries of
the Western Hemisphere from the quotas. Mexican immigration
was subject only to a literacy requirement, a prohibition on contract labor, and an eight-dollar head tax; none of those qualifications were much enforced.

American nativists, however, were not slow to react to the
omission of Mexico from the quota system. By putting a quota
on European arrivals and not on Mexicans, the United States, in
a common nativist refrain, was "barring the front door to America while . . . leav[ing] the back door wide open." Those who
would use the "back door" represented to the nativist a considerably worse threat than the southern and eastern Europeans.
Mexican immigration meant "a vast horde that spreads a brown
Aztec tint over large sections of our map." Uncontrolled, this
immigration could, the nativist thought, turn Western history on
its head. The population rush might "reverse the essential consequences" of the Mexican-American War. The recent Mexican
immigrants, one advocate argued, "are making a reconquest of
the Southwest." And the threat was not merely one of nationality. "More Indians have crossed the southern border in one year
than lived in the entire territory of New England at the time of
the Plymouth settlement. The movement," one observer felt, was

"the greatest Indian migration of all times."[41]

Nativists knew what they thought of impure races intruding into white America, but they did have to struggle briefly to fit "Mexican" into the proper category. The 1920 U.S. census was placing "Mexican" in the category "white." Sensitive to the currents of change, the census had by 1930 redefined "Mexican" as a separate racial category. But the confusion was hard to dispel; there were even proposals to allow white Mexicans the privilege of open immigration, while prohibiting the entry of dark Mexicans. Confronted with this proposal, Secretary of Labor James J. Davis took a stand. "[I]t would be impossible," he said, "for the most learned and experienced ethnologist or anthropologist to classify or determine their racial origin."[42]

Were Mexicans to be regarded as essentially Indian? As some variation on a colored race? Somewhere between Indians and blacks? Certainly, no enterprise in racialistic thinking had ever made the concept of race look more absurd and arbitrary, but such subtleties did not shake the faith of believers. A Texas farmer wrapped the situation up when he said, "We feel toward the Mexicans just like toward the nigger, but not so much."[43]

The advocates of restriction employed the usual arguments in defense of the fragile purity of white Americans. An increase in Mexicans would represent a "fearful racial problem," which would "plague future generations very much as the South has suffered from the presence of unassimilable negroes." To the nativists, keeping out Mexicans was in no way a violation of American ideals; instead, it was an essential defense of them. Incorporating a subordinate, laboring, racial caste, "[w]e would be sacrificing the ideals which our fathers worked so hard to establish and preserve and which we are morally bound to perpetuate." Joined by organized labor, the restrictionists declared their intention to keep out unfair labor competition and preserve American opportunity for white Americans. The strategies and arguments used to achieve Chinese exclusion reappeared in the arguments against Mexican immigration.[44]

Throughout the 1920s, with each charge toward restriction, the defenders of Mexican labor—Southwestern fruit, vegetable, and cotton growers, railroads, industrial employers of unskilled workers—countercharged. They sounded very much like the employers of Chinese labor forty years earlier. Mexican labor was essential to certain businesses in which labor was the only cuttable cost. Mexican workers were "docile"; they would work contentedly for low wages. They were unambitious; they did not aspire to leave unskilled labor behind and move on to greater rewards. They were, their defenders claimed, physically adapted to stoop labor in hot climates; they could perform tasks that would ruin white men. And, best of all, they were temporary; they could recross the border as easily as they crossed it; the United States was a place for only temporary, seasonal visits. They would return home of their own accord; they would not burden their host country past the period of their usefulness. And, as a final charm, if their own homing instinct failed, they were—unlike blacks, Puerto Ricans, or Filipinos—easily deportable.[45]

Restrictionists and antirestrictionists alike worked from a similar stereotype of the Mexican as a racially determined, "docile, indolent, and backward" peon. The question of identity was, to both sides, settled; the only remaining question was, as the historian Mark Reisler has summed it up, "whether permitting such people to labor in the United States would prove ultimately advantageous or disadvantageous to the national interest."[46]

In chronic fear of a labor shortage (or, more accurately, a cheap-labor shortage) at the crucial time of harvest, Southwestern growers could not bear the thought of border restriction. Lobbying against it was a matter of clear economic self-interest. In their cause, growers were joined by an influential ally. Diplomats in the State Department spoke up to oppose the inclusion of Mexicans in the quota system. The international price was simply too high, at a time when the State Department hoped for improved Pan-American relations. If politicians insisted on some form of restriction, then, in Reisler's words, "the State Department sought an inoffensive method of limiting Mexican immigration, one that would not precipitate ugly diplomatic repercussions."[47]

The constraints of diplomacy may have made a formal legislative act of restriction untenable, but they did not interfere with informal administrative methods. The State Department did initiate a tightening up on visas among the American consuls in Mexico; with the eight-dollar head tax, the literacy test, the contract labor prohibition, and the ineligibility of an individual judged to be at risk of becoming a public charge, consuls had no trouble refusing visas and cutting back substantially on legal immigration. A cutback in legal immigration reduced the officially reported statistics of immigration; there was no evidence that it had the same effect on actual immigration. With a sporadically policed, two-thousand-mile border ahead of them, Mexicans denied a visa always had a second chance at immigration.[48]

In 1924, Congress finally authorized the creation of a border patrol, for both the Canadian and the Mexican lines. Its 450 men distributed along those immense borders did not make a very powerful statement; increased to 800 men by 1928, the Border Patrol might have been efficient at particular times and places, but a solidly policed border would have meant enormous allocations of money and men. A variety of policy changes failed to resolve the problem. In the Depression of the 1930s, when jobless American citizens had a new interest in menial jobs, city and county governments initiated their own campaigns of repatriation, returning Mexicans to Mexico in order to reduce local relief burdens. Then, from 1942 to 1964, initially with the justification of wartime necessity, the bracero program permitted the legal importation of Mexican labor, involving over time "some 4.5 million Mexican workers." With or without the bracero program, illegal aliens came anyway, avoiding the control and regulation of the formal program and recognizing that the enforcement of regulations was, in the historian Juan García's words, "at best patchy and at times almost nonexistent." In Operation Wetback, a well-publicized series of raids in 1954, U.S. forces swept through the Southwest, deporting illegal workers. In the midst of the raids, citizens of Mexican descent could feel themselves at risk, vulnerable to incidents of mistaken identity. Operation Wetback, García has written, "reinforced the belief among Mexicans and Mexican-Americans that they were unwelcome and once again demonstrated the precarious status of Mexicans in this country." But Joseph Swing, commissioner of the Immigration and Naturalization Service, ended the year 1954

Workers from Mexico during World War II, contributing essential labor and restitching the ties between Anglo-America and Latin America. *Courtesy Denver Public Library, Western History Department*

with considerable satisfaction. "The so-called 'wetback' problem no longer exists," he announced. ". . . The border has been secured."[49]

Anglo-Americans looking at the Southwest had long imagined arriving at last at mastery. Nonetheless, whether they put their faith in conquest by traders, soldiers, or border patrolmen, whether they believed mastery lay in the future, present, or past, the conquered and controlled borderland continued to exist only in the imagination. When politicians in the 1980s bemoaned the fact that America had "lost control" of its border with Mexico, they dreamed up a lost age of mastery. In fact, from the Gulf of Mexico to the Pacific Ocean, the Mexican border was a social fiction that neither nature nor people in search of opportunity observed. That proposition carried a pedigree of decades, if not centuries.

V

If the first decades of the twentieth century saw some Anglo-Americans alarmed over the threat posed by Mexican immigration, at least something had happened to provoke a reaction. In the 1880s, Porfirio Díaz had settled into power in Mexico. His dictatorial policies may have pleased Americans by encouraging foreign investment, but they had the unhappy effect of consolidating landholdings and driving rural residents from their homes. A revolt against Díaz began in 1910. Remote from the centers of power, the northern borderlands were deeply involved in the Mexican Revolution. The region on both sides of the border provided a refuge and rallying ground for dissident movements. American border cities provided a prime location for the smuggling of arms and ammunition. And refugees driven out of Mexico by the fighting came to the United States, hoping to wait out the revolution and return when peace itself returned.[50]

The Mexican Revolution fractured amid struggles among rival groups led by charismatic but disunited leaders. Hence conflicts in the borderlands were only occasionally clear matches between Díaz's federal troops and the rebels. Rebels also fought each other, and border towns were tokens in a two- or three-way struggle among rival groups. These attempts to capture border towns provided Americans with a curious form of spectator sport; standing on roofs or plateaus, using spy glasses or the unaided eye, they could from El Paso watch a battle for Juárez on the other side, just as southern Californians could watch the battle for Tijuana.

All this generated considerable American anxiety. Would the chaos at the border flow north and engulf the United States? In October 1916, when the revolutionary leader Francisco (Pancho) Villa raided the American town of Columbus, New Mexico, those fears grew. Intent on punishing Villa, General Jack Pershing led American troops into northern Mexico on a fruitless search for the rebel leader. It was an exercise of questionable international legitimacy, with little respect for Mexican sovereignty. The days of 1846–48 seemed to have come again.[51]

The American jumpiness took a new direction with the famous "Zimmermann telegram." The United States's official neutrality in World War One was weakened by the discovery of a German message to Mexico. In the message, the German foreign secretary, Arthur Zimmermann, offered Mexico a deal: if Mexico joined the Germans and attacked the United States, the Germans would support the Mexicans in the reconquest of the territory lost in 1848. The scheme was, of course, unrealizable, but it nonetheless added the fear of Mexican collaboration with the kaiser to the other causes for agitation. In what the historian Richard Romo has called a "Brown Scare," the city of Los Angeles panicked. "Los Angeles police," Romo had reported, "began arresting Mexicans, and government agents stepped up their surveillance of the Mexican community." The city also put a "local embargo" on "gun and liquor sales to Mexicans." The alarmist and xenophobic Los Angeles Times saw a great threat to the border regions. "[B]order cities and towns," one editorial said, are at great risk because the Mexicans, a "desperate and despairing" lot, cannot resist the chance for "plunder." "If the people of Los Angeles knew what was happening on our border," warned the Times, "they would not sleep at night. Sedition, conspiracy, and plots are in the very air. . . . Los Angeles is the headquarters for this vicious system, and it is there that the deals between German and Mexican representatives are frequently made."[52]

On one point, the Los Angeles Times was correct—the questions raised by the meeting of Latin America and Anglo-America remained open and unsettled. The editors shared that awareness with many Mexican people. "These southwestern states," one immigrant said in Gamio's interviews in the 1920s, "were stolen from Mexico. But that isn't going to stay that way. Some day we are going to get back what was lost." This line of thinking received a great boost in the activist 1960s, as the Chicano Pride movement publicized the persistence both of Hispanic people's culture and of their injuries. Short of reconquest, there was the more limited question of justice under the Treaty of Guadalupe Hidalgo. Like Indians, Hispanics in the borderlands had been conquered. Like Indian treaties, their treaty had been much violated, especially in the loss of land claims. But unlike Indians, Hispanics did not benefit from a mid-century effort at restitution; there was an Indian Claims Commission, but no Hispanic Land Claims Commission. "The Congress of the United States," Victor Westphall concludes in his study of Hispanic land claims, "has been constantly and infamously remiss in implementing the obligations incurred as a signatory of the Treaty of Guadalupe Hidalgo." An Hispanic Land Claims Commission, then, could provide a way in which Congress could "legislatively redress its own wrongs."[53]

With or without a claims commission, the legacy of the conquest and the significance of the border show no signs of disappearing. Consider this remark from a Mexican newspaper: "Mexicans who live under poverty and ignorance on one side of the river cannot remain unaware of the fortune enjoyed by citizens of the United States who live on the opposite bank." Though published in 1825, the observation fully reflects reality 160 years later.[54]

VI

In no other field of Western history did the concept of the end of the frontier in 1890 carry so little meaning. Turner's frontier had no relevance to Hispanic borderlands history; Turner himself showed little awareness of Hispanic people's existence. Despite a prolific scholarship in Spanish borderlands history, inaugurated at the turn of the century by Herbert Bolton at Berkeley, Hispanic history remained on the edges of Western

American history. As late as 1955, in an otherwise brilliant critique of Western history, Earl Pomeroy dismissed the whole topic. "Local foreign groups have loomed over-large" in the writing of Western history, Pomeroy claimed,

whether because they were colorful or because they represented a more indigenous and environmental cultural ingredient than the Americans who moved in from the East. The role of Spanish culture in the Southwest has been exaggerated from the days of Helen Hunt Jackson and the Ramona legend to the day of the latest real estate speculator who manufactures Spanish-sounding place names. Actually the native Spanish and Mexican elements in many parts of the West—particularly California, where they are most revered today—were small and uninfluential, often fairly recent arrivals themselves; the typical American settler was ignorant of their language and despised their institutions.

Pomeroy was certainly on the right track in finding falsity in the enshrining of a romantic Spanish colonial past; but, it is clear to us now, false renderings of that past do not make it any less significant.[55]

If the seventeenth- and eighteenth-century Spanish borderlands were the only significant element of Hispanic history, they would still provide an essential study in comparative colonization. Similarly, the American conquest of the borderlands would be an essential element of the story of expansion, to be compared and contrasted with the conquest of Indians. But the relevance of Hispanic history does not end there. Mexican immigration, the reinforcement of a distinctive culture by proximity to the home country, control of the border, the challenge of bilingualism, the subsidizing of American business by low-paid Mexican labor—all of these issues and patterns originate in the past and arrive at full force in the present. Redefine "frontier" in the European sense, as the line dividing two nations, and the concept fits the American Southwest and the Mexican North. Moreover, it fits as well now as it did in 1714 when the French trader Saint-Denis made his way to Santa Fe, ending New Mexico's isolation and bringing it into the North American clash of empires.

The most enduring issue of this frontier is the question of legitimacy. Is today's Mexican immigrant an illegitimate intruder into territory that was for two and a half centuries a part of Mexico, before conquest made it American? In the 1960s and 1970s, reviewing the losses and injuries of the preceding century, angry Chicanos could call the Southwest "Occupied America"—a land that was legitimately and authentically Hispanic, and only by coercion American. But beginning the story of Occupied America in 1836, with the Texas Revolution, or in 1848, with the treaty, fudged a vital fact: the Hispanic presence in the Southwest was itself a product of conquest, just as much as the American presence was. The Pueblo Indians found themselves living in Occupied America long before the Hispanics did. Moreover, Hispanic culture and society in the borderlands was not an unchanging, pure monolith. In New Mexico, Texas, California, and Arizona, Hispanic ways had been changed by distinctive circumstances, and the resulting way of life was neither solely Mexican nor solely American—but Mexican-American.[56]

In a variety of ways, contemporary attitudes make it difficult to put Hispanic history in its proper place at the center of Western American history. On the Anglo side, attitudes have over the last century developed a peculiar split: one attitude toward Spanish borderlands history—conquistadores, missions, and rancheros viewed from a safe distance in time; and another, often very different attitude toward actual Hispanic people, especially people working at the low-paid jobs that were and are a key support of the Southwestern economy.

In his revolutionary *North from Mexico: The Spanish-Speaking People of the United States,* originally published in 1949, the southern California intellectual and reformer Carey McWilliams dissected "the fantasy heritage" popularized by Southwestern promoters. Anglo settlers in the Southwest had separated a glorified Spanish past from the ongoing Mexican-Indian presence. "The romantic-heroic side has been accepted and enshrined," McWilliams wrote: "the prosaic or mundane phase has been ignored and discredited." In the late nineteenth century, the business of romanticizing the Spanish past had gotten under way. Spanish place names took root in suburbs and subdivisions; haciendas and ranchos and *vias* and *calles* and *caminos* proliferated as they never had in the latter days of the Spanish Empire. The doings of the conquistadores acquired a status larger than life; Coronado's futile travels acquired a grandeur and glory denied them in his own time.[57]

Several levels below the romance of the Spanish past was the actuality of land acquisition—territory moved from Hispanic ownership to the possession of Anglos. And at the bedrock, as the most persistent dynamic of the border, was the dependence of American business on Hispanic labor.

Set against these elemental transactions in land and labor, the Anglo romanticizing of conquistadores and mission fathers broke apart the continuity of history. The distant past was colorful and appealing; the immediate past and the present were pedestrian matters of agricultural production, labor supply, and border regulation. Hispanic history came in two parts, and the parts did not connect.

The California missions particularly engaged the romantic sentiment of Anglos, inspiring an expensive campaign of historic preservation. Restored, mission buildings were picturesque and evocative, lovely sites for the imagination at play. The imagination could then people these tranquil places with gentle and dedicated friars and grateful, uplifted neophytes. Growing misty-eyed over the missions, one turns away from the unhappy facts of what missions meant to California Indians.

Missions rested on coercion; missionaries used whippings to enforce daily discipline and to keep neophytes from trying to escape the missions and find refuge in the interior. Even at the risk of severe punishment, "at any particular time approximately one person out of ten was undertaking to escape the mission environment." Relocated, forced to give up their native religion and their native subsistence, mission Indians were the perfect prey for diseases. "[C]ontagion," the historical demographer Sherburne Cook wrote, "was enormously facilitated by the custom of gathering large numbers of Indians in one place." Whatever ideals motivated Father Junípero Serra and the other mission founders, "[a] more perfect arrangement for the spread of gastrointestinal disorders could scarcely be devised." As neophytes died, the Spanish raided the interior to add to the converts, replenish the mission population, and supply the essential labor that underlay the mission's agricultural prosperity.[58]

It was certainly true that the rush of Anglos in 1849 was even more devastating to the native population than the Spanish missions had been. It was also true that, following the usages of the Black Legend, Anglos could condemn Spanish brutality toward Indians while they worked at their own variety of oppression. But studies in comparative sin are always difficult matters of judgment. Take the case of the California Indian slave trade. Arrived in gold rush California, Anglos appreciated the benefits of Indian labor. In part, that meant adapting the system of peonage by which coastal Indians, after the secularization of the missions, had been brought to perform the necessary labor on the Mexican ranchos. But it also meant slave raiding among the yet unsubdued tribes in the interior and targeting Indian women and children as potential servants. In newspaper accounts of that business, Hispanic surnames appear along with Anglo surnames, as entrepreneurs in the business that made Indians into commodities.[59]

In Hispanic history, as in every variety of Western history, one never has the luxury of taking point of view for granted. Hispanics—like Indians, Anglos, and every other group—could be victims as well as victimizers, and the meanings of the past could seem, at times, to be riding a seesaw. Consider, for instance, the dramatically different images of the Texas Rangers. Early in the Anglo colonization of Texas, the Rangers began "as something of a paramilitary force" for fighting Indians. As the threat from Indians diminished, the Rangers became a force for protecting the property of Anglo-Texans and for keeping Mexicans and Mexican-Americans subordinated. Surviving into the twentieth century as a kind of state police, the Texas Ranger had acquired a strong and positive standing in myth, "eulogized, idolized and elevated to the status of one of the truly heroic figures in American history." In 1935, the historian Walter Prescott Webb published an influential study that reinforced the image of the Texas Ranger as "a man standing alone between a society and its enemies," a law officer who was also "a very quiet, deliberate, gentle person who could gaze calmly into the eye of a murderer, divine his thoughts, and anticipate his action, a man who could ride straight up to death."[60]

The popular image of the Ranger had evidently not changed

much when President Richard Nixon spoke at the groundbreaking of the Ranger Hall of Fame in 1973. "For one and a half centuries," said Nixon, "the Texas Rangers have vividly portrayed the dauntless spirit of the great American Southwest, and relentlessly served the best interests of both their state and nation. I welcome this opportunity to express on behalf of all Americans the deepest admiration for the proud tradition of public service that has earned you such a splendid reputation ever since our frontier days."[61]

Apparently, neither President Nixon nor his speechwriters had consulted a study of borderlands folklore published by Américo Paredes in 1958. "The word *rinche,* from 'ranger,' is an important one in Border folklore," wrote Paredes. "It has been extended to cover not only the Rangers but any other Americans armed and mounted and looking for Mexicans to kill." Adopting the Mexican point of view, scholars who came after Webb drew a different moral and political portrait of the Rangers. "The Anglo community," Julian Samora, Joe Bernal, and Albert Peña have written, "took it for granted that the Rangers were there to protect Anglo interests; no one ever accused the Rangers operating in South Texas of either upholding or enforcing the law impartially." The Rangers, moreover, kept up their traditional role in the twentieth century, lending a hand in strikebreaking and in cracking down on "Mexican-American activism in politics and education."[62]

"[T]he Mexican-American side of the story," noted Samora, Bernal, and Peña in 1979, "has finally been brought to the attention of other Americans." The inclusion of these new angles of vision added vitality and depth to Western American history. Most important, the mestizo background of many Mexicans and Mexican-Americans made a crucial statement about the complex legacy of conquest. In the mestizo, Indian and Hispanic backgrounds met. Accordingly, as the historian George Sanchez has put it, the Mexican "presence in the Southwest is a product of both sides of the conquest—conquistador and victim."[63] It is surely one of the greater paradoxes of our time that a large group of these people, so intimately tied to the history of North America, should be known to us under the label "aliens."

Eight

Racialism on the Run

In 1871 an informal army of Arizona civilians descended on a peaceful camp and massacred over one hundred Apaches, mostly women and children. Who were the attackers at Camp Grant? The usual images of Western history would suggest one answer: white men. In fact, the attackers were a consortium of Hispanics, Anglo-Americans, and Papago Indians. However different the three groups might have been, they could agree on the matter of Apaches and join in interracial cooperation. Hostility between Apaches and Papagoes, and between Apaches and Hispanics, had in fact begun long before conflict between Apaches and Anglo-Americans.[1]

In the popular imagination, the frontier froze as a biracial confrontation between "whites" and "Indians." More complex questions of race relations seemed to be the terrain of other regions' histories. The history of relations between blacks and whites centered in the South, while "ethnic conflict" suggested the crowded cities of the Northeast, coping with floods of immigrants in the late nineteenth and early twentieth centuries. As blacks moved north and European immigrants crossed the Atlantic, new populations put the adaptability of American society to the test. Could native Americans of northern European stock tolerate these "others"? Was it better to deal with them through assimilation or through exclusion? How could old-stock Americans defend their valued "purity" against these foreign threats?

These are familiar themes in the history of the Southern and Northeastern United States, but ethnic conflict was not exclusive to the East. Western America shared in the transplanted diversity of Europe. Expansion involved peoples of every background: English, Irish, Cornish, Scottish, French, German, Portuguese, Scandinavian, Greek, and Russian. To that diversity, the West added a persistent population of Indians, with a multitude of languages and cultures; an established Hispanic population, as well as one of later Mexican immigrants; Asians, to whom the American West was the East; black people, moving west in increasing numbers in the twentieth century; and Mormons, Americans who lived for a time in isolation, evolving a distinctive culture from the requirements of their new faith. Put the diverse humanity of Western America into one picture, and the "melting pot" of the Eastern United States at the turn of the century begins to look more like a family reunion, a meeting of groups with an essential similarity—dominantly European, Judeo-Christian, accustomed to the existence of the modern state.

The diversity of the West put a strain on the simpler varieties of racism. In another setting, categories dividing humanity into superior white and inferior black were comparatively easy to steer by. The West, however, raised questions for which racists had no set answers. Were Indians better than blacks—more capable of civilization and assimilation—perhaps even suitable for miscegenation? Were Mexicans essentially Indians? Did their European heritage count for anything? Were "mongrel" races even worse than other "pure" races? Where did Asians fit in the racial ranking? Were they humble, menial workers—or representatives of a great center of civilization, art, and, best of all, trade? Were the Japanese different from, perhaps more tolerable than, the Chinese? What about southern and eastern Europeans? When Greek workers in the mines went on strike and violence followed, was this race war or class war? Western diversity forced racists to think—an unaccustomed activity.

Over the twentieth century, writers of Western history succumbed to the easy temptation, embracing a bipolar West composed of "whites" and "Indians." Relations between the two groups shrank, moreover, to a matter of whites meeting obstacles and conquering them. Fought and refought in books and film, those "colorful" Indian wars raged on. Meanwhile, the sophisticated questions, the true study of American race relations, quietly slipped into the province of historians who studied other parts of the country.

In 1854, in the cast of *People* v. *Hall,* California Supreme Court Chief Justice J. Murray demonstrated the classic dilemma of an American racist wrestling with the questions raised by Western diversity. Ruling on the right of Chinese people to testify in court against white people, Murray took up the white man's burden of forcing an intractable reality back into a unified racist theory.

No statute explicitly addressed the question of Chinese testimony, but Murray found another route to certainty. State law, he argued, already prevented blacks, mulattoes, and Indians from testifying as witnesses "in any action or proceeding in which a white person is a party." Although state law did not refer explicitly to Asians, this was, Murray argued, an insignificant omission. Columbus, he said, had given the name "Indians" to North American natives while under the impression that he was in Asia and the people before him were Asians. "Ethnology," having recently reached a "high point of perfection," disclosed a hidden truth in Columbus's error. It now seemed likely that "this country was first peopled by Asiatics." From Columbus's time, then, "American Indians and the Mongolian, or Asiatic, were regarded as the same type of the human species." Therefore, it could be assumed, the exclusion of "Indians" from testifying applied to Asians as well.[2]

Judge Murray found an even more compelling argument in the essential "degraded" similarity of nonwhite races. The laws excluding "Negroes, mulattoes and Indians" from giving testimony had obviously been intended to "protect the white person from the influence of all testimony" from another caste. "The use of these terms ["Negro," "mulatto," and "Indian"] must, by every sound rule of construction, exclude everyone who is not of white blood."[3]

Concluding that Asians could not testify, Murray spelled out the "actual and present danger" he had defused. "The same rule which would admit them to testify, would admit them to all the equal rights of citizenship, and we might soon see them at the polls, in the jury box, upon the bench, and in our legislative halls." With a smoke screen of scientific racism, using anthropology, Murray thus declared the essential unity of darker mankind. He did his best to keep power, opportunity, and justice in California in the hands of God's chosen, lighter-skinned people. And he did a good job of it.[4]

Faith could reach as far as intellect. "We believe, O Lord, that the foundations of our government were laid by Thine own hand," the Reverend Isaac Kalloch, Baptist minister in San Francisco, began his prayer at the city's Fourth of July celebration in 1878. ". . . we pray that our rules may all be righteous; that our people may be peaceable; that capital may respect the rights of labor, and that labor may honor capital; that the Chinese must go. . . ." One could use the verb "may" with the deity on lesser matters, but when it came to the Chinese, one shifted to the verb "must." The ambitious minister did in fact express his audience's feelings, with exactly the right verb form. By the next year, the Reverend Kalloch had become San Francisco's Mayor Kalloch.[5]

To white workingmen, post–gold rush California did not live up to its promise. Facing limited job opportunities and uncertain futures, white laborers looked both for solutions and for scapegoats. Men in California came with high hopes; jobs proved scarce and unrewarding; someone must be to blame. In California, capital had at its command a source of controllable, underpaid labor. White workers, the historian Alexander Saxton has said, "viewed the Chinese as tools of monopoly." The workers therefore "considered themselves under attack on two fronts, or more aptly from above and below."[6] Resenting big business and resenting competition from Chinese labor, frustrated workers naturally chose to attack the more vulnerable target. The slogan "The Chinese must go" could make it through Congress and into federal law; "Big business must go" was not going to earn congressional approval.

The issue of the Chinese scapegoat became a pillar of California politics, a guaranteed vote getter. In 1879, a state referendum on the Chinese question brought out "a margin of 150,000 to 900 favoring total exclusion." Opposition to the Chinese offered unity to an otherwise diverse state; divisions between Protestants and Catholics temporarily healed; Irish immigrants could cross the barrier separating a stigmatized ethic group from the stig-

White Californians focusing their frustration on the Chinese. *From Frank Leslie's* Illustrated News, *courtesy Denver Public Library, Western History Department*

matizing majority. Popular democratic participation in the rewriting of the California constitution showed this majority at work. "[N]o native of China, no idiot, insane person, or person convicted of any infamous crime," the constitution asserted, ". . . shall ever exercise the privileges of an elector of this State." Moreover, in the notorious Article XIX, the framers went on to prohibit the employment "of any Chinese or Mongolian" in any

public works projects below the federal level or by any corporation operating under state laws. These provisions, the historian
Mary Roberts Coolidge wrote early in the twentieth century, "were
not only unconstitutional but inhuman and silly." They were also
directly expressive of the popular will.[7]

"To an American death is preferable to a life on a par with
the Chinaman," the manifesto of the California Workingmen's
Party declared in 1876. ". . . Treason is better than to labor beside
a Chinese slave." Extreme threat justified extreme actions;
extralegal, violent harassment followed closely on violent declarations. In harassing the Chinese, white Californians did not seek
to violate American ideals and values; they sought to defend them.
"They call us a mob," a female organizer said, single-handedly
demolishing the image of women as the "gentle tamers" of the
West. "It was a mob that fought the battle of Lexington, and a
mob that threw the tea overboard in Boston harbor, but they
backed their principles. . . . I went to see every Chinaman—white
or yellow—thrown out of this state."[8]

California may have "catalyzed and spearheaded the movement for exclusion," but, as Stuart Miller has shown, this was not
a matter of a narrow sectional interest pushing the rest of the
nation off its preferred course. Negative images gleaned from
traders, missionaries, and diplomats in China predisposed the
whole country to Sinophobia; the use of Chinese workers as
strikebreakers in Eastern industries clinched the question. The
1882 Chinese Exclusion Act, a product of national consensus,
met little opposition.[9]

The opposition, after all, occupied a precarious moral position. Those who defended the Chinese were also those who
exploited them. Leland Stanford, one of the Central Pacific's
founding partners, characterized the Chinese as "quiet, peaceable, industrious, economical—ready and apt to learn all the different kinds of work required in railroad building." The Central
Pacific relied on Chinese workers in the Sierra Nevada, one of
its construction managers recalled, adding, "The snow slides
carried away our camps and we lost a good many men in those
slides. . . ." To the railroad builders, the Chinese were cheap,
expendable, and replaceable, performing a necessary but un-

attractive form of labor. "[If] you should drive these 75,000 Chinamen off," Charles Crocker, the Central Pacific partner in charge of construction, declared, "you would take 75,000 white men from an elevated class of work and put them down to doing a low class of labor that the Chinamen are now doing, and instead of elevating you would degrade white labor to that extent." Paying lower wages to Chinese workers had become essential to the profit structure of some businesses. "If the Chinamen were taken from us," a California textile millowner asserted, "we should close up tomorrow."[10]

Railroads and other large businesses had an obvious interest to protect in unrestricted immigration. Words of interracial tolerance thus flowed from men not renowned for humanity and compassion. When the most successful capitalists came to champion the Chinese, race and class became a perfect muddle. To members of the white working class, the Chinese were not fellow sufferers of oppressive labor conditions; they were the essential tools and pawns of the business elite. In the most persistent pattern of Western self-perception, the white workers saw the Chinese as effectively their oppressors and themselves as innocent victims.

True to another longtime pattern of Western history, President Grover Cleveland expressed his distress over the incidents of violence and offered his solution. Since the government could not control its citizens and since they persistently harassed the Chinese, there was simply no way to protect the Chinese in America. This was, in other words, the old "humanitarian" argument for Indian removal—the solution to crime was to banish the victim.[11]

The early goal of the white "Californians," a historian asserted in 1964, was "to extend the blessings of American culture to all Chinese as an answer to the challenge of their humanitarian concepts." One reads the chapter introduced by this claim with the deep hope that one will never inadvertently "challenge the humanitarian concepts" of a white Californian. Citing examples of missionary efforts and invitations to Fourth of July parades, Gunther Barth asserted that the Californians had before 1870 made an earnest effort to acculturate the Chinese. Seeing them-

The indispensable builders: Chinese men at work on the Central Pacific Railroad. *Southern Pacific photo, courtesy Denver Public Library, Western History Department*

selves as sojourners in America, earning money for an eventual return to China, the Chinese refused the invitation. These "discouraging results . . . predisposed disillusioned Californians to view the attempt to bring the Chinese into the realm of American culture as hopeless."[12]

Barth wrote of an era before the economic troubles of the 1870s brought out the full frustration and resentment of California workingmen. It was an era when, in fact, some "philanthropists, missionaries, public officials, and clergymen" did try to rescue the Chinese from their paganism and launch them toward Americanization. But it was also the era of the Foreign Miners' Tax, brought to bear first against Hispanics in the mines and then against the Chinese, the era in which the Chinese were denied citizenship, and the era of Judge Murray's ruling.[13]

"San Franciscans," Barth reported, "tackled the task of Chinese acculturation for the first time" in 1850, "when a shipment of missionary tracts," originally destined for China, reached the city. Community leaders decided to distribute the pamphlets in a public ceremony, the mayor and several clergymen officiating, speaking through an interpreter. When one minister held forth on life after death, he provided unintended amusement. "[T]he idea of the existence of a country where the China boys would never die," a newspaper reported, "made them laugh quite heartily."[14]

Such efforts at assimilation produced meager results, which in turn provided "evidence" for the "inability" of the Chinese to assimilate. An 1877 official statement from the California state senate made all the standard points in this argument:

During their entire settlement in California they have never adapted themselves to our habits, mode of dress, or our educational system, have never learned the sanctity of an oath, never desired to become citizens, or to perform the duties of citizenship, never discovered the difference between right and wrong, never ceased the worship of their idol gods, or advanced a step beyond the traditions of their native hive. Impregnable to all the influences of our Anglo-Saxon life, they remain the same stolid Asiatics that have floated on rivers and slaved in the fields of China for thirty centuries of time.

Once the failure to assimilate had been interpreted as racial character, anti-Chinese partisans joined the tide of scientific racism, freed from blame or responsibility for any injuries that followed.[15]

Along with scientific racism, the anti-Chinese advocates could draw on a familiar element of nineteenth-century American political thought. The arrival of the Chinese coincided with widespread controversy over slavery; almost immediately, the two matters were intertwined. Most Chinese immigrants had to borrow money for their passage; this credit-ticket system put them under the control of Chinese merchants. Control extended through their stay; to secure a return ticket, the Chinese immigrant had to present a release, certifying that he was debt-free.

To Americans both before and after the Civil War, this controlled labor carried strong associations of the ultimate coercion of slavery. Debates over Chinese immigration came to be dominated by the analogy of slavery: if an economy was built on cheap, racially distinctive, centrally controlled labor, the West would bring on itself the struggles and frustrations of the South. Indulging the "shortsighted and selfish policy on the part of men of capital" would mean, as the governor of California put it in 1867, "a curse upon posterity for all time." If white Americans saw Chinese labor as a variation on slavery, their version of abolition was to keep out the slaves.[16]

Unquestionably, the Chinese people exploited their own, though the analogy might have been closer to colonial indentured servitude than to slavery. Scorned and harassed by white Americans, in debt to merchants, unfamiliar with English, Chinese workers relied heavily on the Chinese elite. Struggles between the Chinese "companies" involved people at all levels of hierarchy and did away with any sentimental notion of solidarity among the oppressed. Class and race complicated matters within the Chinese population, as well as outside it.

The 1882 Exclusion Act recorded the paradox, by excluding *laborers* but permitting the continued influx of merchants and students. Merchants, after all, stood for a different China: the much-sought-after goal of the Northwest Passage, the China of commercial possibilities, the China with whom the United States negotiated formal treaties and trade relations. In the 1882 Exclusion Act, racial antipathy revolutionized American immigration policy, drawing for the first time a line based on race and nationality. In matters of trade, however, racial antipathy did not drive Americans out of their commercial senses.

Nor did racial feeling force Americans to forget recent history. In a classic, racially based reading of history, the official representative of San Francisco explained the global past and future to Congress:

The Divine Wisdom has said that He would divide this country and the world as a heritage of five great families; that to the Blacks he would give Africa; to the Red Man He would give America; and Asia He would give to the Yellow race. He inspired us with the determination, not only to have prepared our own inheritance, but to have stolen from the Red Man, America; and it is now settled that the Saxon, American or European groups of families, the White Race, is to have the inheritance of Europe and America and that the Yellow races are to be confined to what the Almighty originally gave them; and as they are not a favored people, they are not to be permitted to steal from us what we have robbed the American savage of. . . .[17]

II

Everyone knows that the nineteenth-century West was a rough place, where unfortunate and extreme acts of nativism occurred. But, conventional thinking would have it, the frontier eventually settled down, the wildness ended, and the twentieth century began. People soon behaved better.

This conventional image was reassuring, progressive—and inaccurate. If antipathy to the Chinese arose during the frontier phase of development, why did it reach a peak in the 1870s, when the California state government was already in its third decade? How could a distant frontier state of feeling translate into federal policy? The 1882 act had a ten-year duration; it was renewed in 1892 and made permanent in 1902. How can one hold the frontier responsible for those repeated national commitments?

In fact, frontier conditions had only a limited effect on national and local responses to the Western problems of race. Far more significant were two persistent factors. First, Americans came West with high hopes for improved personal fortune, hopes that carried both the seeds of disappointment and frustration and, not far beyond, the need for someone to blame. Second, scapegoats were everywhere at this crossroads of the planet, meeting ground of Europe, Asia, and Latin America. Frontier or not, the twentieth-century West made no peace with the problems of pluralism.

Anti-Oriental racism was not subtle, but it could make distinctions. In the nineteenth century, to many Americans, all Asians were not alike; the Japanese were better. Whereas the Chinese held to their ancient ways, the Japanese seemed adaptable and progressive, willing to modernize and Americanize, given the opportunity. Probably more important, before 1890, few Japanese people lived in the United States. The Chinese, to their peril, were far more numerous.

Even though the Chinese Exclusion Act permitted Chinese laborers already in the country before 1880 to remain, this was primarily a population of single males, one unlikely to generate the fear of a "horde" of aliens. At the turn of the century, the focus of fear shifted. As Japan became a significant military power, as Japanese numbers in the United States increased, Western racial resentment kept pace with those changes.

Anti-Japanese crusaders did not have to start from scratch; they could borrow much of their rhetoric and feeling from the earlier anti-Chinese movement. An early activist, James Duval Phelan, then mayor of San Francisco and later candidate for the Senate on the slogan "Keep California white," declared the essential continuity of the two threats: "The Japanese are starting the same tide of immigration which we thought we had checked twenty years ago. . . . The Chinese and the Japanese are not bona fide citizens. They are not the stuff of which American citizens can be made. . . ." They were not bona fide citizens because they were "aliens ineligible for citizenship." Their children, the nisei, born in the United States, could be citizens, but the first-generation Japanese, the issei, would stay trapped in this circular logic: prohibited from naturalizing, they remained aliens; as aliens, their loyalty would always be suspect.[18]

If the Japanese were sometimes found to be "more intelligent and civilized . . . than the Chinaman," the Japanese were correspondingly "more dangerous." Taken to be the "most secretive people in the world," the Japanese were caught in another rope of circular logic. Superficial docility and cooperation only made them more suspect; if they *appeared* to plan no trouble, they were all the more definitely up to something.[19]

Long before the attack on Pearl Harbor, ways of distrusting the Japanese in America had been virtually codified. In 1921, a conference of Western congressmen agreed that an invasion was already under way. It might be a "peaceful penetration," but it was nonetheless "an invasion by an alien people." Japan, in other words, was effectively colonizing the Pacific Coast, and especially

California, with a redistribution of numbers. It was, after all, the same process that Americans used in their own expansion; the Pacific Ocean would present no greater obstacle to Japan than the Atlantic had presented to Europe.[20]

Japan's emergence as a world power certainly precipitated much of this suspicion; the willingness to modernize, once admired by Americans, was suddenly unnerving when it resulted in a major naval power across the ocean. But Americans by no means confined their suspicions to the Japanese still in Japan. "[E]very one of these immigrants," the *San Francisco Chronicle* asserted in 1905, ". . . is a Japanese spy." William Randolph Hearst's *San Francisco Examiner* joined in during the next year. "Japan Sounds Our Coast," one headline ran; "Brown Men Have Maps and Could Land Easily." At its first annual convention, in 1908, the Asiatic Exclusion League of North America made a full statement of this apparent military threat, protesting the presence "in our midst of a large body of Asiatics, the greatest number of whom are armed, loyal to their governments, entertaining feelings of distrust, if not hostility, to our people, without any allegiance to our governments or institutions, not sustaining American life in times of peace, and ever ready to respond to the cause of their own nations in times of war. . . ." In their misplaced loyalty, these Asians made up "an appalling menace to the American Republic, the splendid achievements wrought by the strong arms and loyal hearts of Caucasian toilers, patriots and heroes in every walk of life." In the first two decades of the twentieth century, the historian Roger Daniels has shown, "yellow peril" propaganda had created a "conditioned reflex" on the subject of the Japanese: a belief in "the inherent and genetic disloyalty of individual Japanese plus the threat of an imminent Japanese invasion."[21]

On different occasions, anti-Oriental crusaders demonstrated that the example of the South weighed on their minds. "The menace of an Asiatic influx," a labor leader declared, "is 100 times greater than the menace of the black race, and God knows that is bad enough." California, said a member of the women's auxiliary to the Native Sons of the Golden West, was being "Japanized" just as the South was being "Negroized."[22]

These analogies with the South reflected a crucial fear of racial mixing. The familiar question worked as well in a Western setting. "Would you like your daughter to marry a Japanese?" the publication of the Native Sons of the Golden West asked. "Will you permit your daughter to marry a Jap coolie?" the organizers of the Asiatic Exclusion League asked. An "eternal law of nature had decreed," a speaker to the league warned, "that the white cannot assimilate the blood of another without corrupting the very springs of civilization." One of his neighbors, a California farmer declared at a public hearing, was a Japanese man. "With that Japanese lives a white woman. In that woman's arms is a baby. What is that baby? It isn't a Japanese. It isn't white. It is a germ of the mightiest problem that ever faced this state; a problem that will make the black problem of the South look white."[23]

The purity of white women, miscegenation as defilement, the dreadful but tantalizing idea of sex outside the usual boundaries—these Southern standbys also served the needs of the white West. This anxiety was clearly at the center of the repeated assertions that the Japanese were unassimilable, a claim that, given the actual behavior of the Japanese, otherwise made no sense.

Indeed, their very success in certain arenas of assimilation earned the Japanese even more hostility. From the beginning, they showed their own variety of "the Protestant work ethic." They, too, valued "honesty, industry, zeal, punctuality, frugality, and regularity." Unwilling to remain wage earners, many Japanese immigrants set themselves to acquiring property, becoming farmers instead of farmworkers. Their extraordinary energy was evident in the fact that in 1919 they "produced about 10 percent of the dollar volume" of California's crops, while working "only 1 percent of the state's land under cultivation." Far from refusing to participate in American life, many of the Japanese were acculturating too successfully, in the judgment of their white competitors. Once it became clear that the Japanese posed real competition, farmers joined with labor groups, the American Legion, and purity-preoccupied middle-class groups in the campaign to exclude them, as the Chinese had been excluded earlier.[24]

Western hostility to the Japanese created an awkward international dilemma for President Theodore Roosevelt. In 1908, Roosevelt and the Japanese government arrived at an informal solution, stopping short of official, federal law. In the Gentlemen's Agreement, the Japanese government agreed "not to issue passports to skilled or unskilled laborers" embarking for the first time to the United States. Then, in 1924, the new immigration policy in the National Origins Act gave the exclusionists what they wanted: a ban on further Japanese immigration, with exceptions for students, tourists, and certified merchants. Those already in the country remained, as did the residue of racial distrust and suspicion. It did not take a prophet to see the potential for trouble ahead. In 1937, a nisei student at the University of California asked and answered a rhetorical question: "[W]hat are we going to do if war does break out between the United States and Japan? . . . In common language we can say 'we're sunk' . . . our properties would be confiscated and most likely [we would be] herded into prison camps—perhaps we would be slaughtered on the spot."[25]

In the Japanese internment policy of World War Two, long-standing Western prejudice and immediate wartime panic made a perfectly tailored fit. Looking for justifications to remove the Japanese from the coast and relocate them in the interior, strategists found in history all they needed. Those advocating internment detected no actual incidents of sabotage to justify the removal. There were none. Without definite evidence, the headlines ran anyway ("Caps on Japanese Tomato Plants Point to Air Base," "Japanese Here Sent Vital Data to Tokyo," "Map Reveals Jap Menace: Network of Alien Farms Covers Strategic Defense Areas over Southland"). Without proof of actual treachery, officials and journalists had to call on the old pattern of thought: the fact that the Japanese *seemed* innocent proved that they were up to something. Earl Warren, at the time California's attorney general, demonstrated this logic at work: some people, he said, "are of the opinion that because we have had no sabotage and no fifth column activities in this State . . . that means that none have been planned for us. But I take the view that this is the most ominous sign in our whole situation." Saboteurs were simply planning with care: "I believe that we are just being lulled into a false sense of security and that the only reason we haven't had disaster in California is because it has been timed for a different date."[26]

In the face of this logic, how were Japanese-Americans to prove their loyalty? One year before Pearl Harbor, the largest organization of nisei had declared a creed of super-Americanism. Organized in 1930, the Japanese American Citizens League (JACL) offered its members this statement of faith in 1940:

I am proud that I am an American citizen of Japanese ancestry, for my very background makes me appreciate more fully the wonderful advantages of this nation. I believe in her institutions, ideals and traditions; I glory in her heritage; I boast of her history; I trust in her future. She has granted me liberties and opportunities such as no individual enjoys in this world today. She has given me an education befitting kings. . . . She has permitted me to build a home, to earn a livelihood, to worship, think, speak and act as I please—as a free man equal to every other man.

Acknowledging the existence of prejudice, the JACL creed did not compromise its optimism: "Although some individuals may discriminate against me, I shall never become bitter or lose faith. . . . I am firm in my belief that American sportsmanship and attitude of fair play will judge citizenship and patriotism on the basis of action and achievement, and not on the basis of physical characteristics." Faced with relocation, many Japanese clutched this faith, while JACL leaders held to a policy of accommodation and cooperation. Good behavior could not, however, extricate them from the circular logic of the camps' strategists.[27]

"There are going to be a lot of Japs," said General John DeWitt, head of the Western Defense Command, headquartered in San Francisco, "who are going to say, 'Oh, yes, we want to go, we're good Americans and we want to do everything you say,' but those are the fellows I suspect the most." As a career army officer far more experienced with paperwork than with combat, DeWitt took every opportunity to dramatize the seriousness of his command, treating the Pacific Coast as a potential war zone. Freely mobile Japanese-Americans, citizens or not, were an authentic military danger, he thought. His position, he felt, rested on evidence of the essential Japanese character:

In the war in which we are now engaged racial affinities are not severed by migration. The Japanese race is an enemy race and while many second and third generation Japanese born on United States soil, possessed of United States citizenship, have become "Americanized," the racial strains are undiluted. . . . It therefore follows that along the vital Pacific Coast over 112,000 potential enemies of Japanese extraction are at large today.

Although he was not an elected representative of the West Coast, DeWitt nonetheless expressed—and acted on—popular opinion. "There's a tremendous volume of public opinion now developing," he reported, "against the Japanese of all classes, that is aliens and non-aliens, to get them off the land. . . . They don't trust the Japanese, none of them."[28]

Public officials and, especially, journalists substantiated DeWitt's claim, fueling local panic with alarmist headlines and

The Ninomiya Family at the Granada Relocation Internment Center, Amache, Colorado. Internment, the theory went, protected the United States from sabotage by Japanese residents of suspicious loyalty. *Photo by Tom Parker, courtesy Denver Public Library, Western History Department*

proscriptive editorials. As usual, racism—even racism in the midst of wartime panic—showed itself capable of making distinctions. Take care, a *Los Angeles Times* columnist warned readers, "to differentiate between races. The Chinese and Koreans both hate the Japs more than we do. . . . Be sure of nationality before you are rude to anybody."[29]

Anti-Japanese feeling flowed beyond California. In April 1942, the first director of the War Relocation Authority, Milton Eisenhower, met with Western governors. Eisenhower had hoped for a program of individual resettlement, with the Japanese removed from the coast, but integrated into ordinary life in the interior. That hope, he learned from the governors, was futile, because of "the exceedingly hostile attitude demonstrated toward any resettlement." The interior states, the governors said, did not want to be "the dumping ground" for California's problems. Given the strong feelings of their constituents, some governors explained, they could not be responsible for the protection of the relocated Japanese. Accordingly, Eisenhower had to shift his plans, toward permanent, guarded camps, isolated from other populations.[30]

The national government, the governor of Utah complained, was "much too concerned about the constitutional rights of Japanese-American citizens." It is difficult to find evidence of this concern for Japanese rights. The relocation plan placed 110,000 Japanese people in camps, most of them for the duration of the war. Two-thirds of those moved were American citizens. Forty years later, that issue most clearly haunts the Americans who look back on the incident: the complete violation of civil rights under the pretense of wartime necessity.[31]

World War Two relocation set a precedent that might well haunt Americans. Probably most troublesome was the reluctance of the Supreme Court to act as a bulwark for constitutional rights. In several cases, the wartime court "carried judicial self-restraint to the point of judicial abdication." Obviously uncomfortable with many aspects of the decision supporting the government's actions, Justice William O. Douglas nonetheless expressed the key to the cases. "The point," he wrote, "is that we cannot sit in judgment of the military requirements of that hour.

. . ." In the majority opinion in *Korematsu,* upholding a "conviction for failure to report for evacuation," Justice Hugo Black went even further. "To cast this case into outlines of racial prejudice," he said, "without reference to the real military dangers which were presented, merely confuses the issue. Korematsu was not excluded from the Military Area because of hostility to him or his race."[32]

Forty years later, the dissenting opinion of Justice Frank Murphy makes more satisfying reading. There must be, he wrote, "definite limits to military discretion." In the case of relocation, "[a] military judgment based upon such racial and sociological considerations is not entitled to the great weight ordinarily given the judgments based upon strictly military considerations. . . . I dissent, therefore, from this legalization of racism."[33]

Murphy's opinion notwithstanding, the voices of the white West echoed in the Supreme Court; patterns of suspicion nurtured in the West redirected the justices's "reasoning." This time, in the 1940s, it was difficult to blame the frontier.

III

In their anti-Oriental crusading, white Westerners often referred to the South and its "problem." In a search for case studies of discrimination and conflict in black / white relations, they did not need to go so far afield. During the nineteenth century, black people were sparsely represented in the West. Their numerical insignificance, however, did not stop white people from being preoccupied with the issues of black migration. Despite visions of Western fresh starts and new beginnings, the South's "problem" had long ago moved West.

The extension of slavery into the Western territories had, of course, been a prime source of sectional tension before the Civil War. The struggles over the admission of new states, free or slave, had alarmed those concerned with the survival of the Union; "a firebell in the night," Thomas Jefferson called the conflicts preceding the 1820 Missouri Compromise. Fantasies of Western innocence aside, the Western territories were deeply implicated in the national struggle over slavery.

In 1850, California was admitted as a free state; in 1857,

Oregon was admitted with a similar status. That fact alone can give the impressions that the Westerners were, in some principled way, opposed to slavery. That impression needs closer examination.

Most white settlers in Oregon opposed the intrusion of slavery into their territory. However, they also opposed the intrusion of free blacks. Following on earlier territorial laws, the 1857 Oregon state constitution included a provision excluding free blacks and received heavy voter support. "The object," one early Oregon leader explained, "is to *keep* clear of this most troublesome class of population. We are in a new world, under most favorable circumstances, and we wish to avoid most of these great evils that have so much afflicted the United States and other countries." To the white Oregonians, this was a principled position. The project was to create and preserve a better social order and to steer clear of the problems and mistakes that plagued other, less pure regions. Oregon's exclusion of blacks thus appeared to be "a clear victory for settlers who came to the Far West to escape the racial troubles of the East."[34]

The particular conditions of Oregon added another reason for black exclusion. The question of the admission of free blacks, Oregon's delegate to Congress explained in 1850,

is a question of life and death to us in Oregon. . . . The negroes associate with the Indians and intermarry, and, if their free ingress is encouraged or allowed, there would a relationship spring up between them and the different tribes, and a mixed race would ensure inimical to the whites; and the Indians being led on by the negro who is better acquainted with the customs, language, and manners of the whites, than the Indian, these savages would become much formidable than they otherwise would, and long and bloody wars would be the fruits of the comingling of the races. It is the principle of self preservation that justifies the actions of the Oregon legislature.[35]

Beyond actual armed conspiracy, white Westerners saw in black rights the first link in a chain reaction. Permit blacks a place in American political and social life, and Indians, Asians, and Hispanics would be next. Western diversity thus gave an edge of urgency to each form of prejudice; the line had to be held against each group; if the barrier was breached once, it

would collapse before all the various "others." White Southerners could specialize, holding off one group; white Westerners
fought in a multifront campaign.

Post–Civil War Reconstruction thus posed a challenge to the
institutions of the West as well as to those of the South. Western
members of Congress could often join in imposing black rights
on the South; the South had rebelled, after all, and deserved
punishment. One punishment was black suffrage. But imposing
black suffrage on Western states that had not rebelled—that was
another matter, and the occasion for another round in the west-
ward-moving battle of states' rights.

Confronted with the Fifteenth Amendment, giving blacks the
vote, both California and Oregon balked. "If we make the African a citizen," an Oregon newspaper argued in 1865, "we cannot
deny the same right to the Indian or the Mongolian. Then how
long would we have peace and prosperity when four races separate, distinct and antagonistic should be at the polls and contend for the control of government?" In California, opposition
to the Fifteenth Amendment hinged on the prospect that suffrage without regard to "race, color or previous condition of servitude" might include the Chinese. The Fifteenth Amendment
became law without ratification by California or Oregon. The
Oregon legislature "in a gesture of perverse defiance rejected
the amendment in October, 1870, fully six months after its
incorporation into the federal Constitution." The amendment,
the state senate declared, was "in violation of Oregon's sovereignty, an illegal interference by Congress in Oregon's right to
establish voting qualifications, and a change in law forced on the
nation by the bayonet." White Southerners might have been
reduced to a state of temporary impotence, but they could take
comfort in the fact that others had adopted their favored arguments.[36]

In their ongoing preoccupation with purity, various Western
state legislatures also moved to hold the line against racial mixing. California, Oregon, and—most extraordinary, in light of its
current flexibility in matrimonial matters—Nevada all passed laws
against miscegenation. Below the level of law, white Westerners
practiced their own, more casual versions of discrimination. Labor

unions excluded black workers; owners of restaurants, inns, and hotels limited their clientele; housing segregation was common. Scattered through historical records are incidents in which individual communities abruptly resolved to expel their black residents. "In 1893," Elizabeth McLagan has reported, "the citizens of Liberty, Oregon, requested that all the black people leave town." In 1904, facing high unemployment, the town of Reno, Nevada, set out to reduce its problems by "arresting all unemployed blacks and forcing them to leave the city." "There are too many worthless negroes in the city," the Reno police chief explained.[37]

In the twentieth century, as black migration from the South to the West accelerated, Western states' discriminatory laws stayed on the books. Although never consistently enforced, Oregon's prohibition on free blacks was not formally repealed until 1926. California's ban on miscegenation lasted until 1948; Nevada's remained until 1959. Oregon and California finally consented to a symbolic ratification of the Fifteenth Amendment—in 1959 and 1962, respectively.

While relocation during World War Two moved the Japanese into the interior, jobs in the booming defense industries pulled blacks west. By 1950, Western states, especially on the Pacific Coast, had substantial black populations. When those people encountered discrimination and frustration, their discontent was not a simple matter of the South's problem transplanted west.

IV

Race, one begins to conclude, was the key factor in dividing the people of Western America. Its meanings and distinctions fluctuated, but racial feeling evidently guided white Americans in their choice of groups to persecute and exclude. Differences in culture, in language, in religion, meant something; but a physically distinctive appearance seems to have been the prerequisite for full status as a scapegoat. If this conclusion begins to sound persuasive, then the Haun's Mill Massacre restores one to a realistic confusion.

On an October day, the Missouri militia attacked a poorly defended settlement of the enemy, killed seventeen, and wounded fifteen more. One militiaman discovered a nine-year-old boy in hiding and prepared to shoot him. Another intervened. "Nits will make lice," the first man said, and killed the boy.[38]

Is this the classic moment in an Indian massacre? The murdered boy, like the other victims at the 1838 Haun's Mill Massacre, was white—and Mormon.

In the 1830s, Missourians hated Mormons for a variety of reasons. They had unsettling religious, economic, and political practices; they were nonetheless prosperous, did not hold slaves, and could control elections by voting in a bloc. They were a peculiar people, seriously flawed to the Gentile point of view. Mormons were white, but the Missourians still played on most of the usual themes of race hatred. When the governor of Missouri suggested a war of extermination against the Mormons, he made one point clear: the absence of a racial difference could not keep white people from thoroughly hating each other.

Mormonism, moreover, was an American product. In the 1820s, in upstate New York the young Joseph Smith had brooded about American religious diversity. With so many sects making competing claims to certainty, how was the seeker to make the right choice? "I found," Smith said, "that there was a great clash in religious sentiment; if I went to one society they referred me to one plan, and another to another. . . ." It was obvious that "all could not be right" and "that God could not be the author of so much confusion." Wrestling with this chaos, Smith began to experience revelations, he said, leading him to the acquisition of buried golden plates. Translated, the golden plates became the Book of Mormon, and the basis of a new American religion, offering the certainty of direct revelation in modern times. To its believers, Mormonism was not so much a new religion as an old one restored. Over the centuries, true Christianity had become corrupted and factionalized, broken into the competing sects that had once perplexed Smith. The Church of Latter-day Saints of Jesus Christ restored the lost unity.[39]

Against that backdrop of sects and denominations, Mormonism offered its converts certainty and community. In Mormon doctrine, earthly labors carried a direct connection to spiritual progress; one's exertions in the material world directly reflected one's spiritual standing. With nearly every daily action "mor-monized," as a later observer put it, Saints clearly had to cluster, constructing communities in which they could keep each other on track. In converting to Mormonism, one converted to a full way of life within a community of believers. In their first decade, Mormons were already on their way to becoming a new ethnic group, something new under the American sun.

As Mormon numbers grew, and the majority of the converts clustered in the Midwest, they came into increasing conflict with their Gentile neighbors. Their novel religion, their occasional experiments in communitarianism, their ability to vote in a bloc, their very separatism, made them targets for suspicion and hos-tility. When Joseph Smith summarized his people's experience, he could not be accused of much exaggeration: "the injustice, the wrongs, the murders, the bloodshed, the theft, misery and woe that has been caused by the barbarous, inhuman and lawless proceedings" of their enemies, especially in the state of Mis-souri.[40]

Nauvoo, Illinois, was the Saints' last attempt at a Midwestern refuge. In Nauvoo, the Mormons endured the ultimate perse-cution in the lynching of their prophet and leader, Joseph Smith. Under the leadership of Brigham Young, the Mormons gave up on living in Babylon and sought a new location in the remote West.

When the "Indian problem" grew heated in the early nine-teenth century, the remote and isolated West had presented itself as a geographical solution: place the Indians in locations white people would not want anyway, and end the friction by a strat-egy of segregation. Geography appeared to offer the same solu-tion to "the Mormon problem." Relocated in the remote and arid Great Basin, the Mormons could escape persecution by a kind of spatial quarantine; the dimensions of the continent itself would guard them. Even when the gold rush broke the quaran-tine and when Gentiles—and even Missourians—were suddenly provoked into crossing the continent, the Mormons had had the chance to reverse the proportions and become an entrenched majority in the territory of Utah.

To the Mormons, this relocation fit smoothly into their providential history: God's chosen people had once again undergone persecution and then been rewarded with a refuge and a homeland, a North American Zion. With the Saints saved by virtue and by isolation, the rest of the world could pursue its evil destiny. "While kingdoms, governments, and thrones are falling and rising; revolutions succeeding revolutions; and the nations of the earth are overturning," Church leaders said in 1849, "while plague, pestilence and famine are walking abroad; and whirlwind, fire, and earthquake, proclaim the truth of prophecy, let the Saints be faithful and diligent in every duty. . . ." To a remarkable degree, they were.[41]

The aridity of Utah meant that prosperity depended on a cooperation that the Mormons, uniquely, could provide. Land might be privately held, but water and timber were held in common and allocated by church authorities. The church leadership ordained the founding of towns and farms; communally organized labor could then build the dams and ditches that made irrigation possible. In their prosperity and good order, the settlements of the Mormons impressed even those who could find nothing else to admire in this peculiar people's way of life.

That peculiarity had become suddenly more dramatic. Established in their own territory, far from disapproving neighbors, leaders had felt empowered to bring the church's peculiar domestic practice into the open. In 1852, the Mormons stood revealed as practitioners of polygamy.

For the rest of the nineteenth century, the idea of one man in possession of more than one woman would strike most non-Mormon Americans as deviant, licentious, and *very* interesting—a shocking matter of sexual excess. In fact, Mormon polygamy was a staid and solemn affair. If the patriarchal family was a good thing, if bringing children into the world to be responsibly raised in the right religion was a major goal of life, then it was a logical—and very American—conclusion that more of a good thing could only be better. The Mormon family, properly conducted through this world, would reassemble in the afterlife. Adding more personnel to this sanctified unit gave Mormon patriarchs even greater opportunity to perform their ordained function.

The rest of the United States, however, kept its preference for monogamy. Savages, heathens, and pagans, Americans understood, practiced polygamy. The idea of white citizens' taking up the custom was profoundly unsettling.

In the 1850s, to Gentile Americans and to federal officials, especially, polygamy was only one of the ways in which Mormons defied American conventions. In 1850, Utah received the usual machinery of territorial government; for the first years when Brigham Young held the office of governor, the territorial judges were still outsiders, Gentiles, carpetbaggers. Many were not impressive moral specimens. The judges soon discovered that Utah society took its directions from the church and not from outside appointees. Their authority snubbed, the judges found their outlet in written complaint. "I am sick and tired of this place," wrote one judge, "—of the fanaticism of the people, followed by their violence of feeling towards the *'Gentiles,'* as they style all persons not belonging to their Church." Mormons, he complained, spoke of both the government and its officials "in the most disrespectful terms, and often with invectives of great bitterness." Mormons, another unhappy judge explained, "look to" Brigham Young, "and to *him alone,* for the *law* by which they are to be governed: therefore no law of Congress is by them considered binding in any manner." Federal officials were "constantly insulted, harassed, and annoyed by the Mormons": "the judiciary is only treated as a farce"; "it is noonday madness and folly to attempt to administer the law."[42]

An "irreconcilable difference" of "habits, manners, and customs" as well as religion lay between Mormons and Gentiles, a sympathetic army officer had observed in 1849. The poor fit between American territorial government and LDS theocracy, and especially the laments from the judges, convinced the federal government that Utah was in virtual rebellion. In 1857, the U.S. Army moved in to control the Mormons. "CITIZENS OF UTAH: We are invaded by a hostile force, who are evidently assailing us to accomplish our overthrow and destruction," Brigham Young told his people, then engineered a strategic retreat. With the Saints fleeing to the south, following a scorched-earth policy, the Mormon War was relatively eventless. In a negotiated peace, Brigham Young agreed to accept a territorial governor not himself. Despite the lack of direct combat, the 1857 war still represented an extraordinary case of the U.S. Army deployed against a church primarily composed of U.S. citizens.[43]

The "war" over, the battle over polygamy went on. In 1856, the newly formed Republican party had announced its intention to eradicate the "twin relics of barbarism": slavery and polygamy. Initially hitched together as public evils, Southern slavery and Mormon polygamy never fully separated in the minds of concerned reformers. Slavery oppressed blacks; polygamy oppressed women. Liberation, in both cases, meant abolishing the institution that kept its victims entrapped. Mormon women were held in a dreadful anachronism of a domestic institution; they must be set free, whether they wanted freedom or not. From time to time, Mormon women held meetings to declare their loyalty to the institution of polygamy. At one such meeting, "for nearly three hours one speaker after another defended polygamy, all believing it to be an inspired doctrine, given by God to aid in redeeming a sinful world from a condition of sin and pollution to one of holiness and purity."[44]

Those speakers, however, did not daunt their self-declared protectors. If oppressed women were deluded enough to embrace their chains, could that discourage their liberators? On the contrary, it only made the case more urgent. The situation did, however, involve Gentile reformers in uncomfortable paradoxes. The Utah legislature, hoping to increase Mormon voting power, gave women the vote. Antipolygamy reformers were thus in the peculiar position of fighting female suffrage in order to keep Mormon women from voting for their own oppression.

Gentile opinions of polygamy and Mormon peculiarity in general covered a wide range, from tolerance to desperate outrage. Mormons, wrote Mrs. Elizabeth Cumming, the wife of the first non-Mormon territorial governor, were "generally ignorant, fanatical, superstitious, and possessing a profound disdain for the religious belief of the rest of the world—but," Mrs. Cumming concluded in a surprising twist, "all these last qualities are their own business, not mine." At the opposite extreme of the even-tempered Mrs. Cumming was Mrs. Benjamin Ferris, wife of an early territorial secretary. Finally leaving Salt Lake, she wrote, "we turn our backs upon the Mormon capital, with its wretchedness, abomination, and crimes. . . . oh! how rejoiced to escape a region of human depravity. . . ." Other observers could betray ambivalence. The Mormons, as an influential Eastern journalist wrote in 1866, "wish us to know that they are not monsters and murderers, but men of intelligence, virtue, good manners and fine tastes. They put their polygamy on high moral and religious grounds. . . ." That acknowledged, the journalist went on to demand that the government face up to "this great crime of the Mormon church," a crime that should be "prosecuted and punished as such." The Mormons, he said, with few exceptions, showed all the qualities of "narrowness, bigotry, obstinacy."[45]

Obstinacy was certainly a key. For thirty years, Congress tried to make the Mormons behave. Antipolygamy laws added up to a sustained campaign to change personal behavior, a campaign without parallel except in Indian affairs. Through journalistic sensationalism, as well as congressional preoccupation, polygamy acquired great symbolic power as an intolerable deviation in American social behavior. "There is an irrepressible conflict," a journalist wrote in 1879, "between the Mormon power and the principles upon which our free institutions are established, and one or the other must succumb. . . . [I]f something is not done soon to stop the development of this law-breaking, law-defying fanaticism, either our free institutions must go down beneath its power, or, as with slavery, it must be wiped out in blood."[46]

It was an extraordinary claim—that untamed Mormonism could bring down America's free institutions. The center of the irony lay in the many ways that Mormonism was quintessentially American. Faith in progress, commitment to hard work, devotion to the family, careful attention to material prosperity—in all these qualities, Mormons could not have been more American. Their sacred text, the Book of Mormon, concerned the pre-Columbian history of North America; their effort to make the desert bloom was an archetypal episode in the American attempt to conquer nature; despite the elements of hierarchical authority, the lay priesthood in which all adult males participated was American democratic participation structured into the center of the church. Despite all these conventional American qualities, in the years of the polygamy persecutions, Mormons nonetheless appeared to be aliens, behaving in ways odd enough to rival the Indians and the Chinese. How, antipolygamists must have wondered, could white people have become so different so fast? And how could they be made to stop?

Antipolygamy laws finally drove the Mormon leaders into hiding, concealed—in defiance of federal law—by their loyal followers. The church had been placed in receivership; cohabitation prosecutions went on apace; zealous federal agents pursued the concealed leaders. Then, on September 24, 1890, President Wilford Woodruff of the LDS issued an official manifesto, advising the Latter-day Saints "to refrain from contracting any marriage forbidden by the law of the land." The year was 1890, and one kind of frontier opportunity had indeed closed.[47]

Why have your people been persecuted? Horace Greeley asked Brigham Young in 1859. Why have the Saints been regarded with such "aversion and hatred"? The question did not stump Young. "No other explanation" was necessary, he felt, beyond that "afforded by the crucifixion of Christ and the kindred treatment of God's ministers, prophets and saints, in all ages." Persecution, interpreted in that manner, served to unify the Saints, not to break them; persecution was clearly crucial in the formation of their emerging ethnic identity. For Gentiles, however, Young's explanation hardly settled the issue.[48]

Whatever else it tells us, the Mormon example shows that race was not the only provocation for strong antipathies and prejudices. White people could also become aliens, targets for voyeuristic exploitation, for coercive legislation, even for the use of the U.S. Army. But, the Mormon example also shows that in the long run it paid to be white.

At the Utah statehood convention in 1895, Charles S. Varian gave a speech of reconciliation. Varian had earlier been U.S. district attorney for Utah Territory "and relentless in his prosecution of polygamy." He had, however, found the convention to be an occasion of harmony. Every member, he thought, had "been taught by his fellowmen that, after all, we are very much alike, and that the same passions, and the same motives, actuate us all."[49]

"After all, we are very much alike"—it was a statement no

one at the time made to the Chinese or the Japanese. Once polygamy had been formally settled, the "differentness" of Mormons could be subordinated and their essentially American qualities celebrated. "[T]heir Mormonism has not impoverished them," Horace Greeley had noted, substantiating Brigham Young's words to him: "I believe I know how to acquire property and how to take care of it." Within a few decades after the 1890 manifesto, most Mormons in Utah were voting Republican—for the party that, for thirty years of antipolygamy legislation, had led in their oppression. "[A]ll the dead past has been buried," Varian had said in his speech at the statehood convention, and a shared respect for property had exorcised ghosts of resentment from that past.[50] Fond as it might be of its pedigree and traditions, with much of Utah solidly Republican, the Republican party of today would no more persecute Mormons than it would reconstruct the South.

V

When it came to pitting Western people against each other, politics and economics could work as well as race or religion. When white people appeared to threaten order and prosperity, the lesson was once again clear: race was no protector from vicious conflict. Consider three examples:

• In May 1912, the middle-class citizens of San Diego, California, forcibly expelled the anarchist speakers Emma Goldman and Ben Reitman. San Diego was, in that year, "an established city of more than 40,000 people," "progressive Republican" in politics. In their radicalism and also in their association with the Wobblies, the Industrial Workers of the World, Goldman and Reitman represented a threat that the city's boosters would not tolerate. Goldman "escaped violence only by the narrowest margin," a San Diego newspaper reported. But "treatment that the vigilantes would not give the woman was accorded to the man. Reitman was mysteriously spirited away from the hotel some time near midnight . . . and, it is reported, tarred and feathered and branded on the back with the letters 'I.W.W.' He is furthermore said to have been forced to kneel and kiss the American flag. The branding was done with a lighted cigar, which was traced through the tar. . . ." The concerned citizens and policemen of San Diego were not always so gentle. In other confrontations, "at least two radicals were killed."[51]

• On April 20, 1914, the Colorado militia attacked a tent colony of strikers and their families. Both sides had guns and used them, but bullets were not the major source of injury. In the middle of the battle, the tents burst into flames. Two women and eleven children burned to death. The Ludlow massacre "climaxed a labor struggle in Colorado which erupted into a civil war all over the state."[52]

• On November 5, 1916, two steamboats carrying Wobblies left Seattle for the town of Everett, to support a strike under way against the timber industry. Armed vigilantes and policemen tried to prevent them from landing; in the exchange of bullets, five workers and two vigilantes died, while over fifty were wounded and seven were reported missing. "The water turned crimson," one historian has written, "and corpses were washing ashore for days afterward."[53]

The conventional approach of blaming Western violence on the "frontier environment" does not explain these incidents. Although most of the strikers at Ludlow were of southern or eastern European origin, racial or ethnic explanations of conflict are also of limited help. Judging by the written record alone, a historian blind to actual physical characteristics might think that there were at least eight oppressed races in the West: Indians, Hispanics, Chinese, Japanese, blacks, Mormons, strikers, and radicals.

Exploring the ways in which "Mexicans, Chinese and Indians were shamefully abused by the Yankee majority," Ray Allen Billington in 1956 placed the responsibility on the "corrosive effect of the environment" and "the absence of social pressures." The abuse, he said, represented "a completely undemocratic nativism."[54]

This explanation has an innocent certainty now beyond our grasp. Nativism was only in an ideal sense "undemocratic." The California votes on Chinese exclusion and the Oregon votes on black exclusion made the voice of democracy in these matters

Red Cross members searching the ruins after the state militia attack on the Ludlow Tent Colony, where labor conflict escalated to war. *Dold Collection, courtesy Denver Public Library*

clear. Second, blaming "the corrosive effect of the environment" for nativism involved doubtful logic; white Americans brought the raw material for these attitudes with them, with little help from the "environment." And finally, on close examination, over the duration of Western history, the very concept of "the Yankee majority" was a coherent entity only if one retreated to a great distance, from which the divisions simply could not be seen.

Western historians, like Western people throughout the centuries of contact between formerly separate worlds, have been desperate for categories in which they could place these perplexing and unsettling "others" whose existence made life unmercifully complicated. For more than a century, Americans thought they had found the key in "race." Race would provide a filing system, a set of conceptual containers in which one could place troubling individuals, understand them as much as they needed to be understood, and get on with one's business. But the West, from the beginning, overloaded the concepts; Indian diversity alone would eventually have demonstrated the inadequacy of racial categories. Unsure of an alternative, Americans still held on to the filing system, as well to the faith that Congress could fine-tune the system and make it work.

When the weight of Southern civilization fell too heavily on Huckleberry Finn, Mark Twain offered the preferred American alternative: "I reckon I got to light out for the Territory ahead of the rest, because Aunt Sally she's going to adopt me and sivilize me, and I can't stand it. I been there before." The West, the theory had gone, was the place where one escaped the trials and burdens of American civilization, especially in its Southern version. Those "trials and burdens" often came in human form. Repeatedly, Americans had used the West as a mechanism for evading these "problems." Much of what went under the rubric "Western optimism" was in fact this faith in postponement, in the deferring of problems to the distant future. Whether in Indian removal or Mormon migration, the theory was the same: the West is remote and vast; its isolation and distance will release us from conflict; this is where we can get away from each other. But the workings of history carried an opposite lesson. The West was not where we escaped each other, but where we all met.

That has made for a very complicated history. The histories of minorities, written in the last few decades, have made those complications unavoidable. But how, with the addition of these various points of view, is Western history to regain coherence?

When the advance of white male pioneers across the continent was the principal concern of the Western historian, the field had coherence to spare. But two or three decades of "affirmative action history" have made hash of that coherence. Ethnocentricity is out, but what alternative center is in?

When it comes to centers, Western history now has an embarrassment of riches—Indian-centered history, Hispanic-centered history, Asian-centered history, black-centered history, Mormon-centered history, and (discredited though it may be) white-American-mainstream-centered history. If historians were forced to choose one of those centers, hold to it, and reject all others, we would be in deep professional trouble. But that is by no means the only choice available.

Take, for instance, a thoroughly un-Western metaphor for a complicated phenomenon—a subway system. Every station in the system is a center of sorts—trains and passengers converge on it; in both departure and arrival, the station is the pivot. But get on a train, and you are soon (with any luck) at another station, equally a center and a pivot. Every station is at the center of a particular world, yet that does not leave the observer of the system conceptually muddled, unable to decide which station represents the true point of view from which the entire system should be viewed. On the contrary, the idea of the system as a whole makes it possible to think of all the stations at once—to pay attention to their differences while still recognizing their relatedness, and to imagine how the system looks from its different points of view.

What "system" united Western history? Minorities and majority in the American West occupied common ground—literally. A contest for control of land, for the labor applied to the land, and for the resulting profit set the terms of their meeting. Sharing turf, contesting turf, surrendering turf, Western groups, for all their differences, took part in the same story. Each group may well have had its own, self-defined story, but in the contest for property and profit, those stories met. Each group might have preferred to keep its story private and separate, but life on the common ground of the American West made such purity impossible.

Everyone became an actor in everyone else's play; understanding any part of the play now requires us to take account of the whole. It is perfectly possible to watch a play and keep track of, even identify with, several characters at once, even when those characters are in direct conflict with each other and within themselves. The ethnic diversity of Western history asks only that: pay attention to the parts, and pay attention to the whole. It is a difficult task, but to bemoan and lament the necessity to include minorities is to engage, finally, in intellectual laziness. The American West was a complicated place for its historical participants; and it is no exercise in "white guilt" to say that it is—and should be—just as complicated for us today.

Nine

Mankind the Manager

IN 1891, GIFFORD PINCHOT—then a self-confessed "tenderfoot"—first saw the Grand Canyon. He was speechless, but his arbitrarily acquired traveling companion, an office boy named Doran, was not. While Pinchot "strove to grasp the vastness and the beauty of the greatest sight this world has to offer," Doran "kept repeating, 'My, ain't it pretty?' " Pinchot remembered, "I wanted to throw him in."[1]

A better reader of character than Doran might have seen two traits in Pinchot and avoided putting himself at risk: Pinchot was a man intensely drawn to nature and intensely repelled by fools. In his later career, no longer a tenderfoot, Pinchot was chief forester of the United States. In the interim, he had become the nation's leading apostle of resource management.

In 1897, Pinchot returned to the Grand Canyon with a more suitable companion, the naturalist John Muir. In the company of America's most persuasive nature lover, Pinchot found his admiration divided between his companion and the place. Muir was a preeminent storyteller, and although it risked alarming their traveling companions, Pinchot persuaded Muir to linger on an outing and camp at a distance, so that he would have a better chance to hear Muir's stories. During this agreeable time together, the only moment of disagreement came when they encountered a tarantula. Pinchot wanted to kill it, but Muir defended the spider, arguing that it had every right to be there.[2]

This spider and the conflict it triggered were more revealing than the harmony it interrupted. Muir's feeling for nature was all-embracing; to destroy the wilderness, even an unappealing and alarming creature, was sacrilege. Pinchot, undeniably fond of nature, had no objection to intervening in order to better it. Whether in the killing of tarantulas and rattlesnakes or in the managing of forests, Pinchot believed that nature could bear improvement.

Preservation, or nonintervention, was to Pinchot a curious sentiment; it was certainly what made Muir a fascinating specimen. But if it threatened to influence policy, preservation was certain to become a dangerous folly. In the American West, Pinchot felt sure, nature would inevitably be put to use. The forces for development would devour nature-loving opposition. The only way to avoid disastrous exploitation was to meet the impulse for development and channel it—to demonstrate to the developers the benefits of efficient, rational, sustained-yield use. The choice, Pinchot thought, was between wise use and wasteful use. In light of that alternative, the preservationist advocating "no use" was simply another variety of fool. Pinchot liked Muir personally, but in the elemental struggle of resource politics, Muir's sentiments echoed the refrain of Doran the office boy at the Grand Canyon: "My, ain't it pretty?"

Offspring of a patrician Northeastern family, young Gifford Pinchot "loved the woods and everything about them." As he contemplated college, his clear preference for the outdoors led his father to make an inspired suggestion. "Would you like tb be a forester?" the senior Pinchot asked, and thereby, as his son was the first to admit, he changed American history.[3]

Gifford Pinchot had, to that point, been undecided between medicine and the ministry. By choosing forestry, he kept to the· spirit if not the substance of the rejected professions. In natural resource management, he found a cure for a national illness; and in persuading the nation to take the cure, he proselytized with an energy any evangelist could envy.

In America in the 1880s, resolving to be a forester was easier than becoming one. American schools, like American society in general, did not recognize the professional category. Following family tradition, Pinchot went to Yale and pieced together appropriate courses from botany and geology. But this did not add up to training in practical forest management; for that, Pinchot had to go to Europe, where a need to manage limited resources had inspired a breakthrough into techniques of using forests while keeping them healthy.

The confident Gifford Pinchot, chief forester and believer in man's mastery and management of nature. *Courtesy Oregon Historical Society*

After a year's training, Pinchot returned to America, eager to apply his lessons. The year was 1890, but to Pinchot's eye—and regret—the frontier and its behavior patterns were far from over. American expansion, he thought, added up to "the greatest, the swiftest, the most efficient, the most appalling wave of forest destruction in human history." Worse, this "massacre," this "fury of development," carried popular support. Theft was a matter of indifference; stealing timber from the public lands was treated as "common and perfectly normal"; resources were wasted as much as used; and the government did nothing. Buried in the Department of Agriculture was a small and ineffective Department of Forestry, functioning at best as a bureau of information, not of action.[4]

Playing a "lone hand," blazing his own trail, Gifford Pinchot set out to get forestry (always with a capital *F* in his autobiography) established. There were two possible approaches. "One was to urge, beg, and implore; to preach at, call upon and beseech the American people to stop forest destruction and practice Forestry; and denounce them if they didn't." That technique could get forestry "into the papers" but never "into the woods." The alternative was to demonstrate forestry in action, to persuade by showing that it paid. This method would make only a delayed impact on news stories, but an immediate impact on the woods. Private consulting allowed Pinchot to get to work; rather than move the leviathan of government, he could demonstrate his program in workable units of private land. And, at the same time, he could travel. Europeans, Pinchot reported, had been shocked and disappointed to learn that he had never even seen Niagara; for a person of his continental ambition, it was an even greater embarrassment never to have seen a forest—or any other terrain—in the West.[5]

In 1891, President Benjamin Harrison began the process that would eventually bring Pinchot and the national forests together. Harrison began withdrawing certain public lands and reclassifying them as national forest reserves. In 1898, after serving on a presidential commission to review the status and purpose of the forest reserves, Pinchot accepted the position of head of Agriculture's Division of Forestry.

A few pieces needed yet to be put in place. The forester was in the Department of Agriculture, and the forests were in the Department of the Interior. Their administration, by a subdivision of the General Land Office, left Pinchot deeply frustrated. Everything he learned and saw of the Interior appointees left him in despair; at best, they were ignorant; at worst, corrupt; they were patronage appointments, relatives and friends of politicians, and city men who administered their forests from a safe distance (it is better to live in town, one told him; that way he was better able to spot distant fires); they were also invalids and weaklings sent West for their health. One forest superintendent Pinchot met in California was "a timid little man," who "wore a white lawn tie and a shawl around his shoulders." Forest management was a job for well-trained, vigorous, tough *men*, not these sad creatures so short of physical strength and moral vigor.[6]

In the meantime, separated from the forests by a bureaucratic canyon, Pinchot took up his earlier strategy. If he could not manage the public lands, he could persuade private owners to adopt his rational techniques. Pinchot's bureau thus began a publicity campaign, offering a consulting service free to small landowners and at the price of expenses to large companies. While Pinchot lobbied for the transfer of the responsibility for the national forests from Interior to Agriculture, work with privately owned forests kept his staff occupied, added to their experience and knowledge, and, not incidentally, helped accumulate goodwill in the private sector.

In one official domain, Pinchot found an inexhaustible supply of goodwill. During one of his first meetings with Theodore Roosevelt, Pinchot and the future president—not uncharacteristically for either—engaged in athletic struggle. "T.R. and I did a little wrestling," Pinchot wrote, "at which he beat me; and some boxing, during which I had the honor of knocking the future President of the United States off his very solid pins." The friendship never lost its vigor; on one occasion, Roosevelt took the chief forester on a November walk in Washington, a walk that eventually led them to swim a river. When Pinchot arrived home, his clothing was still wet. A lifelong servant drew the obvious conclusion: "You've been with the President again."[7]

Their shared dedication to physical action meshed perfectly with Pinchot's aggressive plans for resource management. Deeply fond of Pinchot, Roosevelt gave him unwavering support. They saw each other once a day, and sometimes more often. "I believe it is but just to say," Roosevelt wrote of Pinchot in his autobiography, "that of the many, many public officials who under my administration rendered literally invaluable service to the people of the United States, he, on the whole, stood first."[8]

Neither Pinchot nor Roosevelt could be comfortable with passivity, and forestry, Pinchot always made clear, was no passive matter of drawing lines around the woods and guarding them from use. Real forestry was "Tree Farming," a process in which trees were harvested, replanted, and harvested again. Trees were a crop, like "corn," though crops of trees took "more time and less attention" than corn. The purpose was to "make the forest produce the largest amount of whatever crop or service will be most useful, and keep on producing it for generation after generation." "The job," Pinchot insisted, "was not to stop the axe, but to regulate its use." This proposition carried partic-ular force if one granted Pinchot's assumption that the axe could not be stopped anyway. The American public, and especially the Western public, had to learn that efficient forest management was not only morally sound; it also paid financial rewards.[9]

In 1905, Roosevelt and Pinchot succeeded in having the national forests transferred from Interior to Pinchot's domain in Agriculture. Authority, Pinchot was sure, had reached its proper place. "While we could still say nothing but 'Please' to private forest owners," he wrote, "on the national Forest Reserves we could say, and we did say, 'Do this,' and 'Don't do that.' " With such an increase in power, Pinchot obviously needed a comparable increase in staff. Where could he find knowledge-able helpers? American educational opportunities in forestry were still inadequate. What could be done? To a less advantaged per-son, this might have been a problem without a solution. Pinchot, by contrast, went to his parents, presented the problem, con-tacted Yale, and matched parental funds with institutional back-ing to create the Yale School of Forestry. He also began recruiting college students for seasonal work, persuading the fittest to take up forestry as a profession. In short order, the U.S. Forest Ser-vice had built up a team with extraordinary morale and dedi-cated both to the principles of forestry and to their charismatic chief.[10]

Pinchot expressed unending faith in his young men. They knew not only the technicalities of forest management but also how to take care of themselves in the outdoors. In reading con-servation literature of the period, it is always a good idea to look at the pictures—of stalwart young men, vigorous, healthy, with clear intelligent eyes directed at the camera, radiating integrity and purpose. If one contemplates the pictures for a moment, one begins to share in the faith: find solid young men like that, train them professionally, appoint them to office, and put the

West in their hands, and an age of waste and error will come to an end.

What were these young men to do? In phrasing that Pinchot clearly enjoyed, they were to pursue the "public interest," "applying common sense to common problems for the common good." In each forest, they would study the trees, discover the particular reproductive behavior of those plants, then methodically mark mature trees for harvest, oversee the harvest and sale of those trees, and replant—preparing for a second growth forest that would be far more orderly, productive, and manageable than the initial virgin stand. The foresters would also educate the local public, helping them to realize that sustained-yield forestry was far more in their interest than short-term extraction. Established in the forests, this program would spread to privately owned land and to other public lands, and the long-range consequences would be of immense national benefit. With rational management, natural resources would serve to keep the nation permanently strong; management, Pinchot believed, would also fight the power of monopoly and promote the cause of equal opportunity.[11]

This was, Pinchot repeated endlessly, a program to support democracy and the rights of the average citizen. And yet, it was also a program directed by an elite group of professionals. The foresters might make decisions to suit their idea of the public interest; but it would still be their decision and not the public's. Pinchot was determined to court the goodwill of the people, especially of Western American people, but he was also determined to educate them and redeem them from their mistaken and shortsighted opinions. Management, by definition, was a social process in which experts were to set the course and the grateful people, recognizing their true interests at last, were to follow.

The elitism of management posed no conceptual problem to Pinchot. His privileged childhood had left him at ease with the notion of his own preeminence. Moreover, to intervene when a nation risked serious injury was perfectly proper; if one could distinguish the route to disaster from the route to recovery, it was criminal not to act. Conservation, Pinchot said, "is a question of right and wrong, as any question must be which may involve

the differences between prosperity and poverty, health and sickness, ignorance and education, well-being and misery, to hundreds
of thousands of families." With such an issue at stake, one did
not stand by politely respecting the majority's right to choose
misery.[12]

In speeches, articles, and pamphlets, Pinchot gave his earlier
aspiration to the ministry a healthy outlet. Right against wrong,
the corrupt special interests against the American people,
monopoly against the average citizen—Pinchot loved his broadly
stated contrasts. Practice, however, was a more subtle matter.
Business must be separated from government, Pinchot would
say grandly; this, of course, was the same man who had earlier
devoted his government bureau to helping private landowners.
In his first years in Washington, D.C., Pinchot remembered, he
learned a number of lessons: he "saw how trying to bull things
through may cost more than it comes to; learned to keep [his]
temper and be thankful for half a loaf; . . . and had to make
plans for handling millions of acres of public forest, and defend
them when made." These lessons reinforced Pinchot's original
conclusion: commercial use of natural resources was inevitable.
The problem, as he had said, was not to prohibit the axe but to
regulate its use, to accept half of what one wanted when the
whole could not be had. Livestock grazing in the national forests, for instance, might contribute to erosion and to the destruction of seedlings, but it had to be permitted since it could not be
prohibited. Ban stock grazing in the national forests, and the
well-organized growers associations would be in arms, inciting
their representatives and senators to put the Forest Service in its
place. It was far better, Pinchot thought, to let the sheep keep
their place in the forests and to make sure that no Westerner fell
into the delusion that conservation meant the locking up of
resources.[13]

Steering through stormy waters, Pinchot never wavered. The
problem was to get the cooperation of public opinion and of
Congress; once given a mandate, genuine forestry and Pinchot's
carefully selected young men could cope with any challenge. What
Pinchot wanted and thought did not shift much over the years.
He wanted centralized authority over natural resources. He
thought that timber harvesting would be a clear and rational

process of selecting the appropriate trees and selling them to deserving purchasers. He thought that government could be freed from the pernicious influence of big business. He thought that the "public interest" and the "common good" could be defined, located, and pursued, as clearly as if they were tangible targets and not abstractions. He thought that productive, well-managed forests would provide the happiest model of humans and nature in cooperation. He thought that the Forest Service, starting fresh and without "entrenched habit," could avoid the traps and snarls of red tape.

Each article of faith tarnished in the course of the twentieth century. Government control over natural resources remained divided among multiple bureaus, services, and divisions. Each unit was potentially the kingdom of its own appointed ruler. Timber harvesting and sales became a matter of accelerating controversy. Business and government remained locked in an intimate, often unhappy relationship. The identity of the "public interest" remained a matter of dispute, the sought-after trophy in an ongoing interest-group game of "capture the flag." Managed forests also became, for some opponents, unfortunate models of humans misunderstanding and misusing nature, trying to treat forests as crops when nature intended them to be the antithesis of domestication. Moreover, to critics of all persuasions, red tape threatened to engulf the whole operation.

In Pinchot's time in office, the conflict seemed to lie between those engaged in quick, wasteful extraction for short-term profit and those committed to careful, long-term use. People committed to the preservation of pristine wilderness, and thereby opposed to any use beyond recreation, seemed at first to be an eccentric and ineffective minority. Standing at the Grand Canyon in 1891, Gifford Pinchot could not have imagined that "My, ain't it pretty?" would evolve into a significant and influential political force. Extended to its logical conclusion, "Ain't it pretty?" becomes "So leave it like it is.'"

II

"We have so many different objectives," a Forest Service employee said in January 1985, "we are like a yo-yo on a string." The beleaguered employee was the "acting ranger of the Wind

River District of the Gifford Pinchot Forest."[14]

It was not that the issues suddenly became complicated; they were already that in Pinchot's time. But each solution Pinchot saw as final turned out to raise new problems; practiced widely in the twentieth century, systematic forestry provided a sustained yield of conflicts as well as timber. The greatest source of conflict was the rise of recreational interest in the forests. More and more articulate voting Americans valued the forests for hiking, camping, fishing, and hunting. The Multiple Purpose Act of 1960 wrote this interest into federal law, directing the Forest Service to provide for "outdoor recreation, range, timber, watershed, and wildlife and fish purposes." The act of 1960 showed an undiminished faith in management, mandating the "harmonious and coordinated management of all the various resources, each with the other, without impairment of the productivity of the land." Aesthetic scenery and scientific forestry could coexist, Congress still thought. Even if lions would not lie down with lambs, wise management could turn loggers, stockmen, downstream water users, hikers, campers, fishermen, hunters, trout, elk, deer, bears, coyotes, domestic cattle and sheep, and wild sheep and mountain lions into a latter-day peaceable kingdom.[15]

The kingdom predictably fell into factions and struggles, and the record of a fallen utopia accumulated in newspapers, in the disputes over deficit timber sales, over increased harvests and clear-cutting, and over wildlife policy.

Even if one agreed that putting resources to efficient use was the greatest good, the Forest Service still came in with a flawed performance. Many timber sales, especially in the Rocky Mountains, turned out to be deficit sales—that is, they cost the government more than they earned. Because the government was responsible for selecting trees to be cut, for administering the sale, and—most expensive—for building roads to provide access to the timber, its expenses frequently exceeded the price of the timber. The Forest Service, in other words, often subsidized the timber industry, letting taxpayers provide a kind of "woodlot welfare" for private enterprise.[16]

The financial workings of the forests might engage the attention of few Americans, but when harvesting affected the appearance of a forest, public opinion became more audible. Clear-cutting (cutting all the trees in a plot instead of cutting only mature, diseased, or dead trees) could trigger the greatest outrage. To timber companies and to Forest Service experts, clear-cutting had undeniable charms; building one road to one site for one big haul certainly meant less expense and trouble. Moreover, clear-cutting left a plot of land in which trees could be scientifically replanted. To the commercial forester, old-growth virgin stands were troublesome, diverse in species and age, unmanageable. For management, progress meant getting rid of the old unplanned forest, planting intelligently, and thus starting fresh with an orderly, sensible stand of trees. The hiker, the environmentalist, and the local tourist promoter, however, saw clear-cutting in different terms. In was an affront, a violation of the forest's integrity, an intrusion of ruthless industrialism into what should be a sanctuary, or a potential blow to local tourist income. Ugly and disruptive to its opponents, efficient and direct to its advocates, clear-cutting illustrates an axiom of Western history: one man's improvement is sure to be another man's defilement.[17]

Short of clear-cutting, the appropriate rate of timber harvesting was also a matter of unlimited dispute. In 1984, the Forest Service released fifty-year plans for individual forests. Many of those plans involved an increase in cutting. Others might protest the prospective injury to nature and recreation, but John B. Crowell, the assistant secretary of agriculture in charge of forests, saw things differently. "From an economic standpoint these trees are doing nothing but standing there rotting," he said. "We could get more value by cutting them down and growing a new crop."[18]

Government enthusiasm for cutting left every policy open to suspicion and distrust. In 1984, a tree population in Colorado hit troubled times. To many enthusiasts, aspens represented the essential charm of the Colorado mountains. But, Forest Service experts announced, many aspen stands were of a uniform advanced age; the established trees were not allowing a following generation to grow. The trees required "treatment"—a synonym for "extensive cutting."

Distrust came not only from the fact that Forest Service experts seemed like overeager surgeons, offering amputation as the solution to any illness. Aspen is low-quality wood, of value only if used in wood products like waferboard. Certain companies had recently developed an interest in setting up waferboard plants in Colorado. One of those companies was Louisiana Pacific, for whom John Crowell, the bureaucrat in charge of the forests, had formerly been general counsel.[19]

"Multiple purpose" use at least distributed anxiety generously. Timber companies worry about the "locking up" of resources if sentimental nature lovers have their way. Livestock grazers worry about a possible loss of access to grazing lands. Towns near the forests worry about the loss of timber industry jobs, in the event of reduced cutting, and about the loss of income from tourism, in the event of increased cutting. Hunters, hikers, and nature appreciators worry about losing the natural abundance and beauty they want to keep in the forests. State officials worry about the authority lost to a centralized, uncooperative Washington bureaucracy. Any proposed change in policy could be guaranteed to alarm someone; for that matter, the determination *not* to change policy would also alarm. The system of conservation that Pinchot had imagined—a smooth cycle of selection, harvest, sale, replanting—joined an ever-growing number of plans that optimistically marched on the West and then stumbled over reality. Pinchot had counted on the rule of reason over practical matters. But those "practical matters" were in fact tied to strong emotions. The profit motive itself involved as much emotion as rational calculation.

Even if human conflicts and complexities could have been suppressed in a less democratic society, nature alone would have kept the managers unsettled. Take the matter of fire. Pinchot's opinion, as always, was clear. Forest fires were a terrible but preventable form of waste. "I recall very well indeed," he wrote, "how, in the early days of forest fires, they were considered simply and solely as acts of God, against which any opposition was hopeless and any attempt to control them not merely hopeless but childish. It was assumed that they came in the natural order of things, as inevitably as the rising and setting of the sun." Those foolish ideas now stand discredited, he asserted. "To-day we understand that forest fires are wholly within the control of men." The prevention of forest fires fit smoothly into what Pinchot felt was "the first duty of the human race"—"to control the earth it lives upon."[20]

Self-evident propositions, however, have a limited shelf life. Pinchot pinpointed the misguided folly of the past assumption that forest fires were an inevitable part of nature. Half a century later, his own assumptions were under attack. Fires, most foresters now believe, are an essential part of natural cycles. Humans can control them for a while, but multiple small preventions build up the tinder for later massive fires. Moreover, cyclical fires burn over forests, clearing out the old, diseased, or over mature timber and giving fresh growth a chance to start. Some nuts and seeds cannot sprout without benefit of fire. Fire now appears as an essential tool of restoration; it is certainly not "wholly within the control of men."

Does that mean that the best management policy is acquiescence—accepting fire and letting it have its way? Such "wisdom" is nearly beyond human reach. A forest in flames is one of the most frightening phenomena on the planet. And, fires are terrible destroyers of property.

In the late summer of 1984, "more than 5,000" men and women fought a multifront battle against fires in Montana, started by lightning and spread by high winds. For several days, the fire seemed to be winning. Fires burned in sparsely populated territories, but they did not confine themselves to trees, brush, and grass. One "swept through a subdivision, destroying 34 homes, and damaging another six." On top of property damage, fighting the fire cost "more than a quarter-million dollars a day." The fire fighters, a newspaper story noted, work on "carv[ing] a broad line of dirt around the fire. But there are fires within fires, fires behind fires and fires outside the major fire. There are even fires underground, which can burn out a white-hot cavity beneath a seemingly normal forest floor and then cave in beneath an unwary foot."[21]

"To-day we understand that forest fires are wholly within the control of men," Pinchot said in 1910. "Tonight, there is fire all over the wilderness," a Montana state official replied seventy-four years later. In Montana, Forest Service experts agreed, "aggressive efforts to control forest fires in fact made the blazes much more destructive then they might have been." Instead of assuming that "all fire is bad," experts argued for a "natural fire" approach that would prevent "unnatural accumulations of fuel."[22]

What was "natural" and what was "unnatural"? Even if the most "natural" policy could be identified, a second problem overrode the question. Forests were often nice places to live. Many audiences might be convinced of the virtue of fire in nature's restorative cycles. But one would not like to deliver that message—and urge relocation—to bereft property owners sifting "through the burned-out rubble of their homes." Will you rebuild?

Forest in flames.
Photo from Oregon
Journal, *courtesy Oregon
Historical Society*

a reporter asked a burned-out Montanan. "You bet," he answered. "We've got to. That's where we live." If forest fires represented nature beyond management, the loyalty to private property is its corollary in human nature.[23]

III

Pinchot lamented the proliferation of government agencies and the consequent divided responsibility for public lands. He wished for a sensible centralization of authority. By the mid-twentieth century, it was clear that a smooth and happy centralization of federal power was another part of the management utopia not to be realized. There were even more categories now: national parks, national monuments, wilderness areas, Bureau of Land Management lands, all representing separate domains of federal power, beyond the national forests. Even with most of the corresponding agencies concentrated in the Department of the Interior, centralization disclosed a hidden flaw. If a number of supervisory responsibilities were combined in one department, conflict of interest was a more likely outcome than efficiency. For decades, in repeated disputes, Congress handed responsibility for the management of natural resources over to the secretary of the interior, often with touching faith that these matters would then be safe from the pressures of politics and interest groups. By 1980, Interior's jurisdiction was a crazy mosaic. Overseeing the Fish and Wildlife Service, the National Park Service, the Bureau of Mines, the Geological Survey, the Bureau of Indian Affairs, the Bureau of Land Management, and the Bureau of Reclamation, the secretary of the interior wore more hats than a head could support. The interests of mining, for instance, were often in conflict with the interests of wildlife, of Indian people, and of national parks. Beyond the likelihood of conflicting interests among bureaus, the range of each bureau could make the head spin. "Resources managed" by the Bureau of Land Management, for instance, "include timber, minerals, oil and gas, geothermal energy, wildlife habitat, endangered plant and animal species, rangeland vegetation, recreation and cultural values, wild and scenic rivers, designated conservation and wilderness areas, and open space." If one still believes in the higher powers of management and in centralized authority, these sweeping mandates are reassuring. If that faith has yielded to doubt, one does not sleep more soundly because Interior rules such a varied kingdom.[24]

Fully effective management of the national parks alone would require more understanding—of both nature and human nature—than we have available. When Yellowstone became the first national park in 1872, the existence of a park preceded the existence of a rationale or definition for parks. Yellowstone's exotic geothermal features inspired its preservation; the landscape surrounding the geysers and hot springs carried an attached, but only peripheral, value. The early national parks, the historian Alfred Runte has argued, had one distinguishing feature: commercial uselessness. Their remoteness, the absence of visible and abundant minerals, and their unsuitability for farming—rather than their overpowering pristine beauty—made their preservation appealing to congressmen. For over forty years after Yellowstone, the parks remained an administrative stepchild, with no bureau or service clearly designated as their custodian.[25]

In 1916, Congress finally created the National Parks Service, with the mandate to provide for "the enjoyment" of the parks "in such manner and by such means as will leave them unimpaired for the enjoyment of future generations." Over the decades, this phrasing would be studied like a sacred text. Its possible meanings—especially of the word "enjoyment"—provided a variety of apparent mandates. Most confusing was the matter of timing: what limits had to be placed on present-day "enjoyment" in order to leave the parks "unimpaired" for future enjoyment?[26]

Historical contingency put its own twists on this question. Initially, national park administrators and supporters had to recruit visitors. Americans were persuaded to use the parks in order to prove that the parks really served the people, a necessary defense against the criticism that they only "locked up" land. An increase in park visitors would mean more supporters of the system, and such supporters were politically essential. The more visitors, the better.

Success in recruiting visitors earned the usual paradoxical

results of Western history. Park supporters got what they wanted, then had to cope with the consequences. As crowds flooded the parks, Americans demonstrated their substantial fondness for nature—and their ability, in Roderick Nash's phrase, to "love it to death."[27] If the parks were to be showcases of nature, an uncontrolled stream of automotive tourists wore away at the very basis of the parks. Some Americans lobbied for more roads, more campgrounds, more tourist facilities, as necessary developments to meet a healthy public demand. Others saw those developments as desecrations, fundamental violations of what national parks are supposed to be.

The plot was further thickened by the addition in 1964 of the category "wilderness area." Like the parks, wilderness areas had an elegant—and cryptic—definition: areas where "the earth and its community of life are untrammeled by man, where man himself is a visitor who does not remain."[28] Did the existence of a rudimentary road disqualify an area as wilderness? Did a cabin violate its integrity? Could second-growth forests, reverted to nature, fit the category? After centuries of human occupation, what area of North America remained purely "untrammeled by man"?

The hope of enlightened wilderness management, in the "nature preserve" business, was to let nature run itself. The ideal procedure would be to study how a particular place would work naturally, maneuver things around until natural balances return, and then get out of the way.

It was an attractive idea, but it had a few weaknesses. In North America, by the time of the national parks, so much had happened through Indian activity, the fur trade, overland travel, mining, logging, and water projects that a pristine ecology was very hard to come by. Moreover, ecological systems proved to be maddening in their complexity. What was intended to be one quick intervention to restore a lost balance often became a long-range involvement. Nature could resist desired changes and be endlessly responsive to undesired ones. In ecosystems with many variables, a small human act could lead to a multitude of unforeseen consequences. Finally, the idea of nature restored still came with strings attached. Nature running itself should be attractive, interesting, and instructive; it should, in other words, meet certain standards of which humans were fond. The very idea of natural "balance" or "harmony" indicated a model in the mind, by which natural processes would be measured and judged.

With arbitrary borders determined by political and economic expedience more than by science, no national park makes ecological sense. No park extends far enough to include its whole ecosystem; both wildlife species and river systems cross park borders. Park managers who want to let nature run itself thus meet an immediate obstacle. Yellowstone may seem huge at 2.2 million acres, but ecologists now say that an additional 4.0 million acres would have to be managed coherently if Yellowstone were going to make ecological sense. As "showcases of nature," parks were of necessity mere fragments of the original display.[29]

When it came to the mockery of management, wildlife did its part. Wild animals will pursue their own course, despite the best plans of experts—even plans framed with the animals' best interests in mind.

IV

In 1842, on the Fourth of July, on the Great Plains, the explorer John C. Frémont saw wolves chase a buffalo calf, cut off from his herd. The wolves "ran him down before he could reach his friends." To Frémont's regret, he and his men were dismounted. He "watched the chase with the interest always felt for the weak, and had there been saddled horses at hand," the calf "would have fared better." The calf had "friends" outside his herd.[30]

Indians took animals seriously, recognizing them as significant beings with messages to convey and powers to award. By contrast, the theory goes, white people of the nineteenth and twentieth centuries had moved beyond such curious sentiments. Indians might respond to nature with emotional immediacy; science, however, had given white people an objective distance from animals.

Theoretical differences aside, with white people as with other humans, emotion came first. John C. Frémont thought of himself as a scientific observer, conducting an inventory of the West and its contents. Nonetheless, he distinguished good animals from bad ones, victims from villains. A pack of wolves chasing a buffalo calf may look to present-day ecologists like a protein exchange in the making; to Frémont, it was a pack of bullies ganging up on an innocent trying to reach his "friends."

Feelings about animals remain strong and widespread to this day. Young furry animals with big brown eyes, fierce animals with teeth and claws and the readiness to use them, ugly useless animals with scales or stings or too many legs—the varieties of animal experience still provoke emotion in humans. With those instinctual judgments comes the conviction that it would be a nicer world if the proportions were properly adjusted, if the good animals could be increased and the unattractive ones kept to a minimum. Scientific objectivity aside, Frémont was eager to reduce wolves in order to promote buffalo calves. The paradoxes of wildlife management had already, in 1842, taken root on the Great Plains.

Frémont, moreover, was a great hunter of buffalo himself. It may have been unsporting for wolves to gang up on a calf, but Frémont reveled in joining his men to chase and kill buffalo. That paradoxical sentiment emerged in a powerful and articulate interest group—the sport hunters, who wanted to keep game animals alive so that they could kill them. Hunters were among the first Americans to notice that wildlife might disappear. Men of leisure and influence, they were the best-equipped people in America to argue that wildlife was a resource to be protected. While they might themselves be called exploiters of nature, they were at least aware that the continued opportunity to exploit required restraint and planning. Game animals thus had a peculiar set of initial human allies.[31]

In the intervening century, the appeal of wild animals moved beyond hunters. A new and growing group of nature enthusiasts wanted just to look—and not to aim and fire. Some were even willing to give up looking; they wanted to know, for instance, that Alaskan bears existed, whether or not they ever exchanged a glance with those bears. Even with those new groups in the picture, the hunters remained significant. State wildlife bureaus often carried the designation "Fish and Game," making it clear that the animal kingdom had been sorted out and classified according to merit. The good animals—the fishable, huntable trophy animals—had a bureau devoted to their protection; the bad ones did not. In fact, the bad animals were attacked by the government. If the goal was the preservation of game animals, the predators—wolves, coyotes, mountain lions—were enemies and competitors. Not only that, predators had also adapted to the new opportunities for getting protein in the form of domestic livestock, especially sheep. Ranchers joined hunters in condemning the nonhuman carnivores, and government rallied to the cause—trapping, poisoning, and shooting.

The campaign produced ambiguous results. Wolves and cougars diminished, but coyotes rose to the challenge. Their enemies searched for more effective poisons, while the coyotes flaunted their survival, appearing even in the alien territory of suburbs and subdivisions.

Soon, the assumptions of predator eradication began to look doubtful. Eliminate predators, and you eliminate a process of weeding out the weak and vulnerable, and the natural methods of keeping a population in line with food supply. On the Kaibab Plateau north of the Grand Canyon, after a campaign successfully removed predators, the deer multiplied to the point of starvation. Success in eliminating predators did not drive suffering and cruelty from the world. The hungry carnivores of the West, wolf, coyote or human, were all in their own way indispensable.

Even desirable game animals put the benign rules of management to the test. Living tranquilly among inhospitable cliffs and precipices, mountain goats are handsome, vigorous animals. Nearly everyone wants them to prosper. Game managers set out to protect them, using the technique that seemed to work with their kind. But mountain goats did not follow the rules.

In conventional game management, an official sets a limit to the annual permissible hunt. He bases that limit on the species population. How does he know just how many mountain goats dwell in the wilderness? The game manager estimates their numbers on the basis of the preceding year's hunt. If the hunters met the quota easily, the species' population must be abundant and thriving; if the hunters' annual kill drops, the population must be falling and the bag limit must be reduced until the population recovers.

The method works with deer and elk; it does not work with mountain goats. Ordinary game animals run to cover when pursued; mountain goats run to the rocky cliffs, where they can maneuver and other animals cannot. They try to defend themselves with distance and inaccessibility, and that strategy leaves them clearly silhouetted against open rocks or sky, a prime target for a hunter's bullet. The mountain goat kill was not in proportion to their numbers. They were drastically overhunted.[32]

Even the more predictable elk could make a management muddle. The lines that Americans drew on the map to mark national parks and wildlife refuges reflected no more wisdom than did those marking international or state borders. The border of a national park is meaningless to a wild animal, and there management of the elk population foundered. Protected within national parks, elk herds left the park seasonally to travel to their traditional winter range—a range now occupied by ranches and towns. Their official protectors were stymied.

Wildlife remains inclined to seasonal migration, especially the winter retreat to lower altitudes and protected valleys. Those altitudes and valleys have proven attractive to other species, and humans have pitched their towns and cities in those grazing reserves. The results are peculiar encounters: in Boulder, Colorado, the deer are urban, brazen, sophisticated; they will stare down the headlights of a car if it intrudes on their lawn grazing. They linger into the spring and summer, eating the tulips. Residents beg the city council for permission to use electric fences to persuade the deer to respect private property.[33]

More troubling results of interspecies conflict come in harsh winters. In the winter of 1983–84, wildlife came near starvation; driven into the lowlands by deep snow higher up, the deer blundered into human settlements. Sad stories of wild animals starving in city streets inspired relief programs. Easterners sent contributions, and local governments began feeding wildlife. Wyoming, however, stayed hardhearted, insisting that harsh winters were part of natural cycles and that interfering in the reduction of population was "unnatural." But did such a concept apply? The invasion of the lowlands by ranches, towns, and cities was ultimately unnatural, the relief providers argued; human population growth had overturned the old balances, and humans were under a moral obligation to compensate for the harmony they had disturbed. To do nothing while animals starved—the very terms in which the press discussed the issue made it clear that, as always, humans viewed animals with more emotion that detachment.[34]

The sentiment of the nineteenth century had fixed on buffalo and bears as the representatives of Western animals. The vast numbers of the buffalo and the strength of the grizzly were both emblems of Western distinctiveness—of the power and magnetism of Western nature. Into the twentieth century, those two animals remained symbols of the "real West"; their survival was a central statement that intervention came in time, before the real West was entirely lost; and past and present remained linked in the continued life of the West's classic animals.

Neither buffalo nor bear nor human made the preservation of this link easy. Besieged by hide hunters in the 1870s and 1880s, the buffalo came close to disappearing. Preserved in a few isolated herds, they began a gradual, limited return. Yellowstone holds the only continuously wild herd, augmented by animals raised domestically and then released. Preserved, the Yellowstone buffalo still contend with the anomalies of lines and borders. They carry a germ (brucellosis) that does not affect them but that devastates domestic cattle. Therefore, ranchers across the park border see the straying buffalo as a danger, infection on the hoof. If the buffalo stay in Yellowstone Park, they are fine; if they cross the border, they are literally fair game, in a controversial bison hunt licensed in 1985. Stay on one side of the line, and it's the Old West, nature as usual, and buffalo roam wild and free; cross the lines, and buffalo are a public health hazard and a commercial threat. Why not treat the buffalo for the brucellosis and reduce the hostility of ranchers? That goes against national park policy. After years of active management, the Park Service adopted the sentimentally more "pure" policy of letting nature take its course. When Yellowstone mountain sheep contracted pinkeye, for instance, their impaired vision caused them to fall from cliffs. The disease would not have killed them, but the falls often did. Why not treat the pinkeye? Park policy said no. As the chief ranger Thomas J. Hobbs put it, "There's no question nature is harsh. But a National Park is not a ranch or a zoo. A weak animal is nature's way of doing business." On the same principle, a buffalo trapped in an ice-choked river could not be rescued despite the pleas of tourists; the buffalo, federal policy decreed, simply had to stay in the river until natural policy decreed its death.[35]

Noninterventionist park policy has a magnificent naïveté. It is a faith comparable to that of a man who could drive a car into a restaurant, park it at the bar, and enjoin the patrons to ignore it. Buffalo can, in fact, make a considerable adaptation to human presence; they can be domesticated to life on a ranch, to confinement with fences and corrals, even to the status of property.

Yellowstone bear and tourist in an unlikely meeting. *Photo by Ellen Todd, courtesy Denver Public Library, Western History Department*

But while buffalo will cooperate with their preservation in a number of ways, grizzly bears deal only in defiance.

Nearly everyone who supports the idea of national parks supports the idea of bears in the parks. From the nineteenth century on, bears symbolized the power, strangeness, extravagance, and wildness of the West. If the parks are preserved enclaves of the original West, they must have bears—the stars, the protagonists, the leading citizens of the wilderness. For much of the twentieth century, it was possible to go to Yellowstone and see the bears—and to do this predictably and easily. When you located the garbage dumps, you had located the bears. But if bears were a symbol of wilderness, the antithesis of civilization, then a bear in a dump, straining to lick the inside of a tin can, was a symbol denying his significance.[36]

The problem of the garbage bear did a great deal to inspire the policy shift toward nonintervention. Garbage feeding was certainly unnatural; whatever role nature had decreed for bears, tin cans did not figure in it. Embarrassingly opportunistic in their appetites, bears had to be forced back to more fitting, self-reliant behavior. The dumps were closed; tourists lost their regular and reliable entertainment, and bears lost a regular and reliable food source.

What happened to the Yellowstone bear population? No one knows for sure. Like all wild animals, bears will not cooperate in a census; using sightings as evidence, one can count the same bear repeatedly. Moreover, protecting itself, the Park Service has been actively hostile to outside researchers who question the wisdom of current policy. The most knowledgeable of those outside researchers have suggested that an abrupt end to garbage feeding devastated the bear population. The wild food sources of the park were simply inadequate to make up for the lost feedings, bears were forced out of the park boundaries, and there they came into conflict with humans. Moreover, the temperament of bears within the park appeared to change. In the last few years, attacks on humans have increased dramatically; possible causes include the depletion of food, human encroachment on bear territory, and the effect of animal tranquilizers. "Trouble bears," which seem alarmingly cocky among humans and comfortable around campgrounds, are removed three times to less traveled areas; allowed three offenses, they are "controlled"—that is, killed—on the fourth. One scientist is experimenting with bear conditioning; he gives them an aversion training by which they should learn to avoid the company of humans. The scientist insists that he can produce hostility to humans that results in evasion and not in attack. As on all occasions when humans claim to have figured out bears, one wonders.[37]

The grizzly bears of Yellowstone may well be disappearing, reduced to a population with only twenty or thirty sows of breeding age. Since female bears produce cubs infrequently, the numbers begin to sound small and precarious. If more of those bears become trouble bears, and if repeated relocation is followed by the death penalty, how long until bears are purely symbolic—represented in the contiguous forty-eight states only by the Forest Service's Smoky, who has never threatened humans by direct attack, but only by warning them of the consequences of their own actions?

V

Resource management programs might proliferate, but the earth itself sometimes misbehaved, having an effect well beyond any "environmental impact statement." On May 18, 1980, Mount St. Helens, in the Pacific Northwest, exploded, reducing a forest to ruins and turning green hillsides into a gray desert. The transformation went beyond the capacity of even the most ruthless logging company. Mount St. Helens was free to fill the air with ash and to uproot and defoliate square miles of valuable Douglas fir. Neither the Environmental Protection Agency nor the National Forest Service could regulate a volcano. Scientific management of nature retreated to predicting new eruptions and evacuating residents. The eruption of Mount St. Helens made it clear that, the fragileness of ecosystems aside, the planet still held the balance of power. The 1906 San Francisco earthquake made the same point, as have all the threatened and actual tremors of the earth since then.[38]

In earthquakes and volcanic explosions, the role for human folly is at least a limited one. Humans did not provoke the explosions and the quakes; the only way they could add to the disaster was by failing to respond to warnings. In another variety of natural disaster, humans were too often unhappy collaborators. When it came to producing a mess, Western aridity gave humans and nature their prime opportunity to work as a team. In the 1930s Dust Bowl, through overgrazing and careless plowing, humans helped nature fill the air with dust. Large parts of the Western earth turned mobile, and the dust-filled sky over Washington, D.C., carried a message to Congress that the accidents of Western development affected the nation as a whole.[39]

Whether in drought or in flood, the irregular distribution of water in the West appeared to be nature's principal challenge to mastery and management. At the turn of the century, as Gifford Pinchot took up the management of forests, men like him in spirit turned to the management of Western water. Pinchot saw the causes allied; forests were watersheds; clear-cutting forests could have serious consequences downstream. Experts and engineers would tackle the problem of water, one of the bastions of

Conquest and mastery in the wide open spaces: dry farming in Colorado.
Photo by L. C. McClure, courtesy Denver Public Library, Western History Department

Unforeseen results of conquest: "Dust clouds rolling over the prairies."
Courtesy Denver Public Library, Western History Department

irrationality in nature. Caught off guard by the novel use of planning and forethought, nature would be forced to the bargaining table, ready to concede whatever the engineers demanded.[40]

The problem was an old one. While water in the West usually posed a problem of scarcity, deprivation was punctuated by abundance; storms or melting snow could suddenly create floods where a dry channel had been. Here was a clear challenge for management: dams and reservoirs would store the waters, at once preventing flood damage and reserving supplies of water for agricultural and municipal use. Dams, stored water, and gravity presented the further benefit of hydroelectric power; once the generators were in place, power came without effort, skimmed from the happy arrangement of water and earth. No longer a whim of nature, the flow of Western water would become a matter of intelligent decision making.

Building a storage dam certainly required forethought; just how much was open to debate. Rivers like the Colorado carry an enormous amount of silt; dam the river, and you accumulate silt along with water; continue this long enough, and you have a silt-

Improbably located man and town, Kremmling, Colorado. *Photo by L. C. McClure, courtesy Denver Public Library, Western History Department*

filled reservoir. Pitted against the inevitable conflicting demands for water—cities versus farms, upper basin versus lower basin, Indians versus whites—foresight met its match. The schedule for releasing water to meet peak urban demands for electricity may not coincide with the optimal schedule for recreational river travel or for irrigation. Most ironic was the ongoing risk of floods. Extremely heavy snowfall in the winter of 1982–83 led to heavy run-off in the spring. The Bureau of Reclamation failed to release enough water in the early spring to provide room in the reservoirs for the extra runoff. The Colorado River flooded parts of the lower basin; resort businesses and trailer parks went under several feet of water. The thaw had hit hard, and the river, let loose from the canyons, overflowed its channel as the dams were forced to release the floods from their reservoirs. Of course, flooding had been a fairly regular occurrence for several millennia; what put an edge on the story was the role of the federal dams. In the crusade for the Colorado dams, especially for the Boulder Canyon Act of 1928, the selling point of the dam's advocates had to be flood control, since federal responsibility to provide municipal water and power was not clearly established. Once the dams were in place and human rationality ran them, carefully calibrating runoff, Americans could live along the river in peace and prosperity. The people wading hip-deep near their homes in 1983, recognizing the role of the dams, blamed the federal government more than they blamed nature.[41]

In *Alice in Wonderland*, poor Alice was plagued by the problem of regulating her own size. One side of the caterpillar's mushroom made her grow, and the other made her shrink, and Alice was hard put to consume the right stimulus at the right rate to achieve the right size. If she erred on one side, she would swoop into hugeness; if on the other, she would instantly dwindle. Twentieth-century efforts at the management of nature bring Alice's dilemma to mind. The goal is to get humanity's role in nature back to the right size, neither too big nor too small, neither too powerful nor too powerless. Like Alice, the manager finds it difficult to regulate the rate of change; a seemingly subtle move will have enormous repercussions, causing humans abruptly to become huge again; and a seemingly forceful and direct move will meet implacable resistance from nature, causing them to appear as creatures of great self-importance and little actual stature. Swinging from huge to tiny, dominant to dominated, humanity's place in nature changes from day to day, hour to hour.

Ten

The Burdens of Western American History

EVERY HUMAN GROUP has a creation myth—a tale explaining where its members came from and why they are special, chosen by providence for a special destiny. White Americans are no exception. Their most popular origin myth concerns the frontier:

Europe was crowded; North America was not. Land in Europe was claimed, owned and utilized; land in North America was available for the taking. In a migration as elemental as a law of physics, Europeans moved from crowded space to open space, where free land restored opportunity and offered a route to independence. Generation by generation, hardy pioneers, bringing civilization to displace savagery, took on a zone of wilderness, struggled until nature was mastered, and then moved on to the next zone. This process repeated itself sequentially from the Atlantic to the Pacific, and the result was a new nation and a new national character: the European transmuted into the American. Thrown on their own resources, pioneers recreated the social contract from scratch, forming simple democratic communities whose political health vitalized all of America. Indians, symbolic residents of the wilderness, resisted—in a struggle sometimes noble, but always futile. At the completion of the con-

quest, that chapter of history was closed. The frontier ended, but the hardiness and independence of the pioneer survived in American character.

One persistent fact of modern times is this: when professional scholars investigate the past, friction with popular beliefs is almost inevitable. Scientists advance the propositions of evolution and collide with faith in the Bible's version of creation. Archaeologists and anthropologists reconstruct an ancient Indian arrival in North America via the Bering Straits and collide with tribal creation myths. The Western historian runs into similar trouble with the creation myth centered on the frontier. This tale has unquestionable power and influence but bears little resemblance to the events of the Western past. The myth has the undeniable charm of simplicity. Simplicity, alas, is the one quality that cannot be found in the actual story of the American West.

This creation myth—like most others—assumes that times have changed radically. The age of origin was special, dramatic, even magic. Gods walked the earth, which they stopped doing long before our own, more humanly pedestrian times. The old days had a transcendent quality that will not come again.

The United States was a rare case among nations, the Western historian Frederick Paxson wrote in 1930, in a book with the conceptually curious title *When the West Is Gone*. The nation's history was broken in the middle; the present and future were "torn loose from the moorings of a continuous past."[1] This was a professional variation on the creation myth, viewing the Western past with a nostalgia that fractured time. At some point, this faith holds, the "Real West" succumbed to alien forces and was replaced by a tame region of no particular character or significance. The belief that the past was discontinuous, cut in two by a supposed end to the frontier, still keeps us from seeing where we are and how we got here.

When John F. Kennedy accepted the Democratic nomination for president in 1960, "frontier" was his metaphor of preference. "The pioneers of old," he said in Los Angeles, built "a new world here in the West." Their example should inspire Americans in 1960 to conquer their own frontiers. Just like the real pioneers, twentieth-century Americans should be "determined to make that new world strong and free, to overcome its hardships, to conquer the enemies that threatened from without and within." The analogy would become Kennedy's slogan. "I am asking each of you," he said, "to be pioneers on that New Frontier." Soon after Kennedy celebrated this positive image of the frontier, the history of the environment and of minorities ("the enemies that threatened from without") began to present a more complicated picture of the costs and conflicts of expansion. But in 1960 it was to be expected that both Kennedy and the American public would find in "frontier" a simple and attractive metaphor for challenge, struggle, and mastery.[2]

Twenty-five years later, the diligent work of historians had not rippled out to presidents or the public. In his second inaugural address, in 1985, President Ronald Reagan was much taken up with American history. When the president invoked the "echoes of our past," the impact of the new Western history was not much in evidence:

. . . the men of the Alamo call out encouragement to each other; a settler pushes west and sings his song, and the song echoes out forever and fills the unknowing air.

   It is the American sound: It is hopeful, bighearted, idealistic—daring, decent and fair. That's our heritage, that's our song. We sing it still. For all our problems, our differences, we are together as of old.

The image of Western history was still ethnocentric and tied to a simple notion of progress. Other parts of the speech applied the workings of frontier progress directly to the present: "In this blessed land, there is always a better tomorrow"; "We believed then and now there are no limits to growth and human progress when men and women are free to follow their dreams."[3] Much of the address in fact paraphrased mid-nineteenth-century articles of faith. Professional Western historians explored conflict, unintended consequences, and complexities in Western history. Presidents continued to see only freedom, opportunity, abundance, and success in the same story.

Probably no case better represents the problem of history in conflict with faith than does Mormonism. A new church formed in 1830 naturally crystallized many of the values and attitudes of the nineteenth century. One such attitude was the white American belief in Negro inferiority. Blacks were accordingly excluded from the priesthood, to which every other Mormon male in good standing was admitted. This aspect of Mormon origins left the church particularly unprepared for the civil rights movements of the 1950s and 1960s. Southern segregation might have had the support of some churches, but it was primarily a civil and secular order. But here was segregation built right into the theological framework of a religion.

In Mormon theology, blacks bore "the Mark of Cain," burdened with sin from a primal past. In a former struggle between God and Lucifer, they had failed to take sides and were thus still penalized for their neutrality. The inferior status of blacks, Mormons argued, was "not something which originated with man, but goes back to the beginning with God." They were born black "because they sinned in a pre-existent state." The church's position had the unfortunate effect of contradicting a major tenet of Mormonism, as Lowry Nelson pointed in 1974. "Men should be punished for their own sins," Mormonism held; with this one notable exception, "sin is not inheritable." White Mormons, Nelson felt, had "found a comfortable religious sanction for their 'natural' prejudices." Would the church change? Possibly, said President Spencer Kimball in 1977, "if the Lord is willing."[4]

As Mormonism became more and more involved in international missions in the Third World, the exclusion of blacks became increasingly awkward. In South America, Jan Shipps has noted, "determining who has African ancestry and who has not" was a perplexing matter; a change in policy would release Mormons from that trying obligation. The possibility of a reversal brought the 1890 renunciation of polygamy to mind; approaching its 150th anniversary, the church might still be able to use the faith in revelation to adapt theology to changing social conditions.[5]

On June 9, 1978, ending decades of exclusion, President Kimball announced that the priesthood was now open "without regard for race or color." "My faith," said one of the two black members of the famous Mormon Tabernacle Choir, "is strengthened." But the legacy of nineteenth-century attitudes was not to be erased in one stroke. In the debate on black exclusion and in the revelation itself, *Newsweek* noted, "the question of female ordination [was] not even an issue." By announcing the 1978 revelation, Kimball earned the label "progressive." But on the question of women's role, he fully escaped that unsettling label. "Man and woman," Kimball explained in 1977, "are two different kinds of being: He's hard and tough. He's supposed to furnish the family's livelihood. She's more tender, and unless a husband dies or the children are grown, we feel she ought to remain at home and teach the children the things they should know."[6]

This issue plunged the church into another round of publicity in 1979, when Sonia Johnson, a fifth-generation member who claimed to be "Mormon down to [her] toenails," emerged as a feminist leader and supporter of the Equal Rights Amendment. Examined in a bishop's trial, she stood accused of "knowingly teaching false doctrines." Evidently, said *Newsweek*, Johnson must "decide what she believes in most: her church or her politics."[7] Beyond the Johnson case, a larger question lingered: In continuing to advocate a traditional role for women and in fighting the ERA, was the church pursuing a sacred mandate—or simply enshrining the values that happened to be in practice in early-nineteenth-century America, at the time of its founding?

In 1985, the problem of Mormon origins came dramatically into the news. Dealers in historical documents came forth with two letters from the church's founding period, one ostensibly from the Mormon prophet Joseph Smith and one from his early follower Martin Harris. The letter from Smith, "the oldest ever found in his handwriting," dated 1825, told of the techniques of hunting treasure under the guard of "some clever spirit." The 1830 letter from the convert Harris told of Smith's encounter with a white salamander. Harris reported Smith's story:

The old spirt come to me 3 times in the same dream & says dig up the gold. But when I take it up the next morning the spirt transfigured himself from a white salamander in the bottom of the hole and struck me 3 times & held the treasure & would not let me have it because I lay it down to cover over the hole when the spirit says do not lay it down. Joseph says when can I have it. The spirit says one year from today if you obay me.

If authentic, the letters established a central role for magic and superstition in the founding of Mormonism. But were they authentic? Early in 1985, the emerging answer seemed to be yes. On October 15, though, bombs exploded in Salt Lake City, killing two people and the consensus on the letters exploded as well. By February 1986, police had concluded that a Salt Lake documents dealer, Mark Hofmann (who had been injured himself in an explosion the next day, October 16), had been plotting to sell the Mormon church fraudulent documents that seemed to cast suspicion on the sanctity of the church's origins. When his scheme began to go awry, he allegedly turned to violence. Some experts were now prepared to testify that the "white salamander" letter was a forgery, just as other experts were still prepared to vouch for its authenticity. Once more, the past was disrupting the present. History had produced in our own times a real-life murder mystery, worthy of the imagination of Raymond Chandler or Ross MacDonald.[8]

A few facts were settled: Hofmann and the intended victims of the October 15 bombs had been "involved with controversial documents," including the "white salamander" letter; the Mormon church was "Hofmann's most avid customer"; Hofmann had met privately with a senior church adviser after the first bombs exploded, to ask advice on how to conduct himself during the police investigations. Beyond that, the only fact beyond dispute was, as the Salt Lake City police chief put it on the day of the first bombings, that "somebody [was] very, very upset."[9]

Mormonism, noted the *New York Times*, "is a faith whose very history is sacred, since faith in the church depends on faith in the authenticity of the visions and revelations of its founder, Joseph Smith, who said God had asked him to restore the church of Jesus Christ in North America." In this solemn, official version of history, "white salamanders" and "clever spirits" made unsettling presences. "A sense of the past has been central to the Mormon faith," and thus the church was deeply vulnerable to new discoveries and interpretations of the past. This vulnerability was clear before the Hofmann affair gained national publicity. Just a few days before the October 15 bombings, at the 1985 annual church conference, a Mormon authority had warned the faithful against questioning the past. There might well be "spir-

itual peril," said Elder James Faust, "when publicly disparaging
the prophetic calling of Joseph Smith or his successors, or any
of the fundamental, settled doctrines of the church." Even before
the publication of the "white salamander" and "clever spirit" letters, several church leaders had "been harshly critical of the
methods and motives of [Mormon] scholars who attempt 'objective' histories of the Church." Particularly troubling, they felt,
are efforts "to place what are supposed to be divinely inspired
church doctrines in a relevant social and historical context."
Mormon history, said Elder Boyd Packer in 1982, should be a
sacred narrative, in which readers can "see the hand of the Lord
in every hour and every moment of the Church from its beginning till now." If that meant writing history "selectively," so be
it, said Packer, criticizing historians who "write history as they
were taught in graduate school, rather than as Mormons." With
this background, it hardly came as a surprise when the police
investigation of the Hofmann case "revealed the church's hierarchy to be obsessed with stopping any tampering of the church's
official accounting of the past."[10]

Historians were not, however, the only "problem population" who refused to let the more awkward aspects of the church's
past disappear. Splinter groups of Mormons had continued to
insist that plural marriage was a sanctified element of true Mormonism; even if the rest of the church abandoned it, a few would
stay faithful. After church leaders under considerable pressure
renounced polygamy in 1890, "plural marriage," the historian
Jan Shipps noted in 1978, "persisted on the underground never-
theless. In the past decade it has reappeared as the major tenet
of an undetermined number of LDS fundamentalist sects with a
total membership estimated between 3,000 and 20,000." One
fervent believer was Royston Potter, who was fired from the
Murray City, Utah, police force in 1982. Although an exemplary
policeman, Potter at the time of his firing had two wives; he later
married a third. Plural marriage, he and his attorney argued,
was an essential part of his religious belief. Asking that Utah's
antipolygamy laws be declared unconstitutional, Potter sued. "The
practice of polygamy," ruled U.S. District Judge Sherman Christensen in April 1984, in a decision upheld by the appeals court

in May 1985, "is not a fundamental right constitutionally protected by . . . the First Amendment or any right of privacy or liberty under the 14th Amendment." Christensen drew the same distinction between belief and action that had been used in nineteenth-century rulings against polygamy. "Freedom to believe or not to believe is absolute," he said. "Freedom to act, however, is not absolute but limited or qualified by the power of the state. . . ." Potter was demonstrating continuity in one track of Western history; Judge Christensen was demonstrating it in another. Was the prohibition against polygamy a continuation of social prejudices of the nineteenth century? Was the nation, in the matter of Royston Potter and his three wives, allowing anachronistic, vestigial attitudes to set policy in a more tolerant age?[11]

Polygamy and persecution, the historian Sterling McMurrin has explained, gave Mormons a great thirst for respectability. "Then and now," he said in 1983, "the leadership wants the people of America to see Mormons as utterly respectable people." But other groups remained equally determined to deny Mormons the respectability of the mainstream. A story about Mormons in a Western newspaper was almost sure to elicit a certain brand of letter to the editor. "I feel the main point that needs to be cleared up and understood is that Mormons are not Christians!" said a typical specimen in February 1986. "Clearly, if words are to have any meaning," said another, "Mormons are not Christians." An incident in Vail, Colorado, in 1985, brought the issue to a focus. With a shortage of church buildings, Lutherans, Episcopalians, Baptists, Roman Catholics, Presbyterians, Christian Scientists, and Jews shared an "interfaith chapel." When this ecumenical group was asked to allow the eighty-two Mormons in Vail to use the chapel, a firm majority said no. The chapel, said the Baptist minister, was "interfaith," not "intercult." The Mormon tenet that believers could move toward godhood meant, the minister explained, that they were polytheists, not monotheists like the other users of the chapel.[12]

In a similar incident in March of 1986, the Church of Latter-day Saints invited Protestant and Catholic clergy in Denver to an open house at their soon-to-be-completed temple. A group of clergymen rejected the invitation and even circulated a letter urging others to refuse it. The Mormons, explained a Lutheran minister, are "a threat" to other congregations "in terms of proselytizing their members." If it is the ministers' responsibility to take care of their flocks, then, "if there's a wolf loose in the area, we feel we should let them know."[13]

"Falsehoods are swirling everywhere about the true saints of God," said Elder George Lee at the 1985 conference. In many ways, the most unsettling threats came from the unsubdued past, from the prospect that historical "research into the church's past could undermine members' faith." "Religions have an almost infinite capacity to explain things away," said Jan Shipps.[14] Still, it was no pleasure to official Mormondom to have the past come back and ask for explanation. The Mormon problem stood for the larger one of Western history. Celebrating one's past, one's tradition, one's heritage, is a bit like hosting a party: one wants to control the guest list tightly and, as the Mormon elder Boyd Packer put it, "selectively." To celebrate the Western past with an open invitation is a considerable risk: the brutal massacres come back along with the cheerful barn raisings, the shysters come back with the saints, contracts broken come back with contracts fulfilled.

II

On a sandbar along the Arkansas River, not far from downtown Tulsa, Oklahoma, contracts made in the past brought forth an unusual modern fulfillment. The sandbar was one remnant of tribal land assigned to the Creeks, or Muscogees, after their removal from the Southeast in the 1830s. For decades, the sandbar seemed to be of no use at all. Then, beginning in 1979, a new use of Indian territory appeared, starting with the Seminoles in Florida. By the early 1980s, high-stakes bingo had become one of "the hottest issues on Indian reservations across the country"; over one hundred reservations were involved. Bingo was "an economic godsend for tribes that have limited resources, minimal capital and high unemployment." This godsend was made possible by the distinctive legal condition of a reservation. State prohibitions and regulations on gambling, the lower courts held, did not apply to reservations. In Indian country, a special tribal sovereignty still prevailed, held separate from state regulation by "a unique status as sovereign nations within the nation." Non-Indian state and county law enforcement agents brooded about this turn of events: Indian reservation bingo games stole opportunity from the tightly regulated church and charity bingo, argued the critics; they were liable to be infiltrated by organized crime; they made a mockery of state laws. Perhaps most frustrating, reservation income from bingo could not be taxed; already strapped for revenue because of the downturn in oil, the state of Oklahoma found the tax angle a particular mortification. On their formerly useless sandbar, the Creeks had erected a $2 million bingo parlor, seating 1,350 and bringing the tribe a reported $100,000 a month in profits. With their bingo bonanza, the tribe had joined what the *New York Times* called "the largest legal but unregulated and unaudited cash business in the country." The sandbar was still "Indian country," a term that had changed—but not lost—meaning since the nineteenth century.[15]

It is a common exercise in guilt to berate white America for its record of broken Indian treaties. The exercise has lost considerable potency since the 1960s. Certainly, many treaties were ignored, but there is a world of difference between a treaty ignored and a treaty erased. The treaties stayed on the books, where Indian activists and lawyers of a new era could find them. The process of reviving claims got a major push with the Indian Claims Act of 1946, setting up a procedure for tribes to file claims for past losses. The process got an even greater push in the 1960s, with the training of a significant number of Indian lawyers. The *New York Times* noted the result in 1986: "American Indians are fighting today much the same battles over tribal sovereignty and the ownership of land and natural resources that they waged in the 19th century. The difference is that this time . . . they are winning."[16]

Consider, for instance, the fateful words included in the principal nineteenth-century treaties made in the 1850s in the Pacific Northwest: "The right of taking fish at all usual and accustomed grounds and stations is further secured to said Indians in common with all citizens of the Territory." The reasons for including the provisions were hardly a mystery; fish were as

central a resource to the Northwestern Indians as buffalo were
to the Plains Indians. Retaining the right to fish was in some
ways more crucial than retaining the land. Over the next century, first commerce and then sport drew more and more whites
into competition with Indian fishing. By the twentieth century,
if Northwestern whites knew anything about the guarantees in

**Ute Indians with their attorney in 1910, foreshadowing the twentieth-century
shift from conflict on battlefields to conflict in courtrooms.** *Courtesy Colorado
Historical Society*

the Indian treaties, they thought of them as outdated promises, broken to serve the interest of the new majority.[17]

In the resurgence of Indian activism in the 1960s, the Pacific Northwest was a key region. When state fish-and-game wardens attempted to impose state laws on Indian fishermen, they set the stage for a prolonged, determined movement of resistance, as Indian people held to their rights, both in "fish-in" protests and in a long series of courtroom battles. The contest went beyond legal arguments; there were raids, shootings, and incidents of boat ramming. In one case, in October 1965, Washington state game wardens in a powerboat intentionally rammed a dugout "carrying two Indian fishermen, two little boys, their dog, and a newspaper cameraman." The "free-swinging battle" that followed, between Indian protesters and game wardens, provided newsmen with "dramatic stories to write and pictures to show of the wardens' brutality."[18]

In a 1974 landmark decision, Federal Judge George A. Boldt ruled unambiguously in favor of the Indians. A close examination of the treaties, especially of the phrase "in common with all citizens of the Territory," persuaded him that the treaty required the catch to be divided between the two groups. "Accordingly," in the words of Alvin Josephy, Judge Boldt "upheld the right of the treaty tribes to fish and manage the fisheries in their traditional fishing places and ordered that they be given the opportunity to take 50 percent of the harvestable fish." Neither the state of Washington nor many of its white citizens took the Boldt decision peacefully. Some discontented white fishermen threatened Judge Boldt personally; some of them attacked Indians. The state of Washington resisted compliance, with an intransigence that reminded many observers of the white South's resistance to desegregation.[19]

When the Supreme Court affirmed Judge Boldt's ruling in 1979, much of official state resistance dissipated. But individual white people—whether commercial fishermen, sportfishermen, or simply local people made angry by what they saw as archaic special privilege—kept the issue alive. An organization called the Interstate Congress for Equal Rights and Responsibilities, opposed to Indian rights and active in several Western states, found special support in the Pacific Northwest. "We would like to terminate all Indian treaties; we would like to terminate all Indian reservations; we would like to terminate the BIA (Bureau of Indian Affairs)," explained one disgruntled sportfisherman. Groups in the region, as a public television documentary reported in 1982, remained "locked in bitter conflict over who has the moral and legal right to catch the fish." Like the Indian wars of the nineteenth century, the twentieth-century "Indian wars" of the courtroom were not going to come to a clear and final resolution. "There are people out there," said John Echohawk, director of the Native American Rights Fund, "who can't believe that we have these rights, and they won't stop fighting."[20]

By the nature of limited resources, the restoration of an Indian right frequently meant the loss of white people's rights. When the loss involved property, especially property long in the use of non-Indians, the best compromise could seem to be this: let the non-Indians keep their property and give the Indians cash. When the Sioux pressed their claim to South Dakota's Black Hills, this struck the courts as the best resolution. The facts of the case were beyond dispute: by the treaty of 1868, the Black Hills were "set apart for the absolute and undisturbed use and occupation of the Indians." Following the Black Hills gold rush, officials bullied some Sioux leaders into renouncing the land, and Congress abrogated the 1868 treaty in 1877. It was a transaction that provoked one court to remark, "A more ripe and rank case of dishonorable dealings will never, in all probability, be found in our history." The government had done wrong; the Sioux were injured, and the courts, estimating the value of the property in 1877 at $17.5 million, agreed to compensate the Sioux. In 1980, the Supreme Court affirmed the decision and stood by the awarding of interest as well, bringing the total to $122.5 million. By this point, many of the Sioux had reached a conclusion that differed from the Supreme Court's: money was not land, and they wanted the land. Taking the cash would open a Pandora's box of questions. Should the money be held communally for tribal development projects, or should it be distributed on a per capita basis to individuals? If the former, what kind of tribal enterprises—and for which of the eight Sioux reservations? If

Northwest Indians fishing at Celilo, around 1900; fishing rights would become a major arena of Indian self-assertion. *Courtesy Oregon Historical Society*

the latter, how were the Sioux to determine just who was a certifiable descendant of the Sioux who had been defrauded in 1877? Most important, if the tribes took the money, it might well be gone in a generation. The land, by contrast, would be an enduring resource.[21]

In the 1980s, Indian tribes had a special reason to weigh carefully all questions involving their resources and their economic future. The Reagan austerity program deeply affected the group with the longest record of dependence on the federal government. Indians were also, of course, the only group that had secured federal help with treaties, solemn promises, and essential property transactions. President Reagan's staff seemed to have a weak grasp of Indian history. In 1983, James Watt, Reagan's first secretary of the interior and overseer of the Bureau of Indian Affairs, said, "If you want an example of the failure of socialism, don't go to Russia. Come to America and go to the Indian reservations." Bewildering as it was, Watt's remark was also a dazzling demonstration of the power of ideology to over-rule an understanding of history.[22]

Far more serious than the gaffes of the secretary of the inte-rior were the budget cuts brought by the Reagan administration. "Economic development" of the reservations, "without subsidy," requires "a radical break with the past dependency on the Fed-eral Government," the Reagan planners explained. "There has been too much of a dependency on the Federal dollar" in Indian affairs, said a BIA spokesman, "and we're saying that can never happen again." The goal, instead, was Indian self-sufficiency. There was nothing new about this goal; it had been the declared intention of Indian policy through most of the nation's history. But in the Reagan years, the policy cliché intersected with the fervor to cut domestic programs. Programs benefiting Indians entered an era of austerity. As had often happened in Indian policy, the Reagan administration presented the retreat on funding as if it were a service provided with the Indians' inter-ests in mind, a change made for their own good. The Indians would be induced to stand on their own feet "by reducing Fed-eral outlays and encouraging closer ties with the 'private sec-tor' "—a private sector theoretically on good behavior, weaned from its historical habits of exploiting Indians and their resources.[23]

The timing for this "new" approach seemed either inept or cruel. Reservation unemployment in the mid-1980s was a stag-gering 50 percent on average and as high as 70 percent and beyond on particular reservations, including the Pine Ridge and Rosebud Sioux reservations. Most reservations also suffered a chronic shortage of capital. Because reservation land is held in trust by the federal government, it cannot be used as collateral for loans. Conventional credit is therefore difficult to secure. Reservations are usually remote and, therefore, unlikely sites for industrial relocation. Often dependent on natural resources—minerals or timber—they are tied to the unstable boom/bust cycles of the Western economy. With those cycles in a downturn, the 1980s seemed a dangerous time to force through a break with federal dependence.[24]

Determined to cut the budget, Reagan officials sliced not only at job-training and small-business support programs but also at the Indian Health Service. Their timing, here as well, was ignorant or calloused. An Office of Technology Assessment report in 1986 confirmed much of the bad news about Indian health. Indians were "three times more likely to die young" than were other Americans. They were twice as likely to die from pneumonia or influenza, and they were afflicted with cirrhosis at a rate 4.2 times higher than the country's general rate. Perhaps the most disturbing news in Indian health involved adult-onset diabetes. Fully half of the Pimas and Papagos over the age of twenty-five developed diabetes, the *New York Times* reported, as did a fourth of the Zunis over the age of thirty-five. Members of some Indian tribes in the West had become "7 to 10 times as likely as non-Indians" to contract diabetes. Some researchers posited a "thrifty gene" theory to explain this rising epidemic. In the centuries before white contact, Indians "evolved so that they could store fat efficiently, enabling them to survive long periods of famine between harvests or successful hunts. Now that they live in a cash economy, where work is less strenuous than hunting or running great distances, the genetic asset that allowed their ancestors to survive has been turned into a disability," bringing on the devastating incidence of diabetes.[25]

With many of the old problems still unsolved and several new ones on the rise, it was an unfortunate time for cutbacks in medical services. Beyond cutting funding for particular programs (including a successful one that sent paramedics for regular visits to Indians in remote locations), the Reagan administration's strategy was one of cutting eligibility. In a proposal in 1986, the Indian Health Service announced a plan to change the definition of Indian. If the new definition went through, an Indian would be "a person who is a member of a federally recognized tribe, or eligible to be a member, lives on or near a reservation, and has at least one-quarter Indian blood." It was this matter of the blood quantum that aroused the most controversy. An essential element of a tribe's sovereignty, Indian leaders argued, was the power to determine its own membership. From that angle, the revised definitions of the Indian Health Service threatened to crack the bedrock of tribal self-determination. Moreover, the change carried the added threat of making Indianness a racial definition rather than a category of political nationality. Set the blood quantum at one-quarter, hold to it as a rigid definition of Indianness, let intermarriage proceed as it had for centuries, and eventually Indians will be defined out of existence. When that happens, the federal government will be free of its persistent "Indian problem."[26]

If one could not always tell who was an Indian, it was at least possible to tell who was not. The non-Indians could be most easily identified in regions affected by Indian lawsuits; they were the ones fearful that they would lose their land, their water, their chances to fish or to hunt, or their profitable opportunities to lease reservation timber, oil, mineral, or grazing resources. Among non-Indians at a distance from these matters, late-twentieth-century attitudes toward Indians were often vaguely favorable. Americans held a generalized fondness for the Indian as a symbol of ecological restraint and primal wisdom, a ritualized regret for "what we did to them," and sympathy for past sufferings. Closer to the epicenters of the claims disputes, however, the sense of injury turned in the opposite direction.

Non-Indians who found their profit or property threatened by Indian assertiveness cast themselves in a familiar Western role, that of the innocent victim. "We all feel that we're getting a real raw deal out of it," said a non-Indian who had, for twenty-five years, leased resort land on the Fort Apache Reservation at an absurdly low rate. Now the lessee was shocked to learn that the tribe was determined not to renew the leases. "Granted, what the Government did to the Indians a 100 years ago was not right," said a non-Indian woman whose farm in Minnesota was involved in a Chippewa land claim, "but why make the people who own the land now pay? We had nothing to do with what happened back then."[27] Selective amnesia had its uses, even in a nation devoted to the memory of its frontier origins.

III

In the 1980s, a place called the Soccer Field became a routine stop on the itineraries of journalists writing about the problems of the American West. The Soccer Field was an open flat area near Tijuana, where hundreds of people gathered every night. After dark, Mexicans would begin their walk from the Soccer Field into the United States, while the Border Patrol deployed men, vehicles, and heat-seeking surveillance devices to intercept them. The odds of the game were heavily weighted against the home team. Along the nearly 2,000-mile border, for every illegal entrant the Border Patrol caught, two or three (or more) got through. Returned to the Mexican side of the border, the apprehended ones could simply try again. "It doesn't really matter what percent we catch because eventually 100 percent get through," explained one Border Patrol officer. All along the border, American officials and Mexican job seekers played this "nightly game of hide-and-seek," an exercise that carried a repeated, morale-eroding lesson for the Border Patrol, stuck playing doorkeeper to "a revolving door": "There's just too many of them, and not enough of us."[28]

The regulation of the Mexican-American border was not a case study in progress. In the 1980s, Mexico's economic troubles caused the numbers of border crossers to escalate. "We are seeing the greatest surge of people in history across our southern border," Alan Nelson, the commissioner of the Immigration and Naturalization Service, said in 1986. Border apprehensions in 1986 were up nearly 40 percent over the preceding year; officials expected to intercept at least one and a half million illegal entrants in 1986, meaning that two or three times that number would elude them. Even more distressing, there had been a comparable upsurge in the smuggling of drugs. As legitimate forms of income dried up in Mexico's recession, the drug business gathered appeal. A backpacker carrying sixty to one hundred pounds of marijuana across a remote section of the border could earn $250 for his trip, certainly an attractive option for men who planned to take the trip anyway. This increase in the Southwestern drug business was the ironic outcome of success in enforcement elsewhere. A "prolonged crackdown on drug smuggling in the Southeast," especially in Florida, had pushed the problem westward.[29]

With drugs in the picture, and with the increased numbers and desperation of immigrants, crime and violence also seemed to be rising. "Law-enforcement officials," the *New York Times* reported in June 1986, "say that almost every day they find the bodies of shooting victims in the bushes or floating in the Rio Grande, some of them immigrants robbed while trying to cross the border, some of them victims of smuggling deals that went wrong. The officers say, furthermore, that they are frequently caught in battles with drug and weapon traffickers using machine guns."[30]

The border was violent and out of control; drugs and job seekers met no major obstacles in entering the country; then why, Americans started to wonder, could terrorists and spies not take advantage of the same opportunities? Questions of national security began to arise; the open border seemed to make the nation deeply vulnerable to its enemies. Many Americans began to feel like householders who feared intruders and yet lived in a house without doors.

A compelling logic drove the "intruders" to defy the border. A day's labor in the United States was dramatically more rewarding than a day's labor in Mexico. In Mexico in 1984, "the minimum wage" was "the equivalent of 55¢ an hour for those lucky enough to find work." In the United States, their rate of pay would be nearer to the $3.35-an-hour minimum wage. In villages in the interior of Mexico, the news that one could make "$200 a week" took "the breath away." "You're talking about one of the world's highest-wage countries in juxtaposition with a middle-developed country that nonetheless has one of the lowest wage scales," said the border expert Wayne A. Cornelius. "There's simply no legal or police remedy to that." The lure was vastly stronger than the deterrent. In defying the border, Mexico's immigrants had "little to lose and everything to gain."[31]

A variety of Hispanics and Anglos found other ways to gain from this search for opportunity. Smugglers, or "coyotes," charged $250 or more to pilot an immigrant into the United States. There was "big money" in this international escort service. There was also freedom. Operating beyond any government's regulation, the "coyotes" sometimes robbed, beat, or raped their clients. Bandits lay in ambush to attack and rob the immigrants, especially in the desert canyons south of San Diego. In a more sophisticated version of banditry, "lawyers and pseudo-lawyers" in New Mexico in 1984 played on rumors that the U.S. government might soon pass a law providing amnesty to some illegals. For cash up front, these shysters promised, they would make sure that the illegal alien qualified for amnesty. In less crafty schemes, many employers simply cheated illegal aliens, reducing promised wages or refusing to pay them at all. Most of these forms of criminality stayed beyond the reach of penalty and punishment. Fearing deportation, illegal aliens were very reluctant to testify against their tormentors.[32]

In the immigration debates of the 1980s, a number of experts argued that the whole nation gained from the presence of the aliens. The foreign workers supplied essential labor, filling jobs few American citizens would want. Even if the border could be controlled, these experts did "not expect American citizens to replace illegal workers in the low-paying jobs most of them would vacate."[33]

Illegal aliens enrich the American economy and add to its productivity, said one study. Illegal aliens weaken the economy, sap taxpayers' money, and steal jobs from needy American citizens, said another. In 1986, the state of knowledge about aliens was abysmal. One could not unearth so basic a fact as the number of illegal aliens in the country; estimates ranged from two to twelve million. One could certainly not look to the Immigration and Naturalization Service for "the facts"; funding, morale, and record keeping at the INS were, at best, in a state of low-level crisis.[34]

By 1984, Agent Alan Eliason, head of the Border Patrol division that included the famed Soccer Field, was at the end of his rope. "We are overwhelmed," he said. "Congress has to come to grips with the problem." Agent Eliason was one among many Americans who felt that the federal government and its policies had to be held responsible for the immigrant crisis. Many school systems, under pressure from a 1982 Supreme Court decision declaring that America's schools had to educate the children of illegal aliens, thought that the federal government should pay for this extra expense. A city like El Paso, Texas, with a massively overburdened public hospital, held that the federal government should pay the bill for treatment of illegal aliens. The regulation of immigration was a federal responsibility; if the feds were not doing their job, they should pay for the consequences.[35]

But what were the feds to do? Beginning in 1982, Senator Alan Simpson of Wyoming tried to answer the question with an immigration reform bill. Over the next years, Senator Simpson became Congress's Sisyphus, annually rolling the rock up the hill, and annually watching it roll back down. To Senator Simpson, the problem was clear: "The United States cannot perform the most basic function of a sovereign nation, which is to control the entry of aliens across its borders. Immigration to the United States is out of control." The solution, he felt, was nearly as simple. The United States must not only strengthen its Border Patrol but also attack the problem at its root. The jobs lured the immigrants. To immigrate illegally was a federal crime, but to employ an illegal alien was not. The solution was thus to design sanctions against employers of illegal aliens. By disciplining the employers, you would remove temptation from the immigrants, and thus, in the happy ending of the Simpson Immigration Bill, the illegal aliens would stay home and the border would return to American control.[36]

Immigration, the *New York Times* noted in an observation that Senator Simpson's experience would certainly confirm, "has always aroused strong passions." The most persistent and vocal opponents of the Simpson bill were Hispanic leaders who felt that sanctions would cause employers to "reject all foreign-looking applicants, particularly those with Spanish accents." Even more persistent were Western growers of fruits and vegetables, who insisted that low-cost foreign labor was essential to the smooth and affordable harvesting of their crops. With this opposition, the bill seemed, in September 1986, to be dead—"a corpse going to the morgue," one congressman said. Then, abruptly, it returned to life, approved by Congress late in October—and, not coincidentally, just before midterm national elections. The American people wanted their borders controlled, said the representatives and senators, who answered the demand with the Immigration Reform and Control Act of 1986, providing employer sanctions (with, however, special concessions for Western growers) and amnesty (permanent-resident status and possible citizenship) for aliens who could prove continuous, unlawful residence in the United States since before January 1, 1982.[37]

Was this the solution? The law began its life in a forest of doubts. The amnesty provision seemed far too generous to many conservatives; in their eyes, it gave a direct reward to persistent lawbreaking. Even for those who supported it, amnesty had a significant structural irony. Before the passage of this law, illegal aliens had done their best to be invisible and leave as little record of their presence as possible. Now the rules of the game were reversed, and they were faced with a demand for evidence they had done their best to avoid accumulating. What, after all, would constitute definite proof of prolonged residence? Most of the appropriate documents—pay stubs, rent receipts, tax forms— could easily be forged. Perhaps most ironic was the situation confronting *legal* aliens, people who had followed the proce- dures, filled out the forms, and joined in the long waiting line for citizenship. These people gained no advantage at all and watched in frustration as the new law moved long-term illegal aliens to a special place at the head of the line.[38]

Much of the same confusion attended the implementing of the employer sanctions. With the new law, critics charged, the federal government was admitting that it could not control ille- gal immigration. It was, instead, transfering the responsibility to private sector employers, who had no training for this kind of police work. How, after all, were employers to distinguish an illegal alien from a U.S. citizen or a legal alien? They were to ask to see a variety of identification papers. The employer was not expected to authenticate those papers; his legal obligation was to make sure the applicant could produce them. The one certain outcome of the 1986 law, nearly everyone agreed, was a fine new opportunity for creators of fake documents. "Forgers [were] expected to do a land-office business"; even before the act was in effect, "fake rent receipts, utility bills, income tax forms, driver's licenses, birth certificates and the like [were] being tailored to the requirements in the legislation."[39]

Even if federal officials could come up with a foolproof way of identifying forgeries, the Immigration Act was going against the grain of a basic pattern in the Southwest, where "the presence of illegal aliens has been institutionalized in many ways and is accepted, indeed welcomed as essential to the economy." To many people living near the border, wrote a perceptive *New York Times* reporter, "the bill reflects a world that is far more black and white than the crazy quilt of Mexico and America that exists at the border." The law had been designed, written, and approved at a considerable distance from people like Ismael Medina, a forty-two-year-old father of seven, who could not feed his family on his $5-a-day wage in Mexico. Interviewed in Tijuana, near the border, as the new law awaited the president's signature, Medina told a reporter, "It doesn't matter what the law says; we will cross."[40]

Would the law work? Perhaps more important, *should* it work? Was *this* the time to close the border? Senator Paul Simon of Illinois raised the question in debate. If we, by eliminating jobs, "aggravate the economic situation that Mexico faces," he said, "we could have some very serious problems south of the border." A look at the Mexican economy made the dilemma clear: Senator Simpson and his bill were instruments of terrible timing. In 1982, financial troubles caused Mexican officials to devalue the peso and worry about whether they could keep up interest payments on their immense foreign debt. In that same year, oil prices began their decline, plummeting in late 1985. Like American oil operators, Mexico had been banking on higher prices, expecting them to rise to $60 per barrel or beyond. Like American farmers, Mexico had borrowed optimistically in the late 1970s. In 1986, Mexico faced shrinking oil revenue, enormous poverty in both countryside and city, and nearly $100 billion in foreign debt. Its interest payments in 1986 were expected to be near $9 billion. In that hard-pressed economy, the estimated $1 billion or more in income sent home by illegal aliens in the United States was a crucial form of underground foreign aid. In late-twentieth-century Mexico, Frederick Jackson Turner's old concept of the frontier as safety valve had a direct and vital meaning. In the midst of Mexico's increasing hardship, jobs in the United States provided an essential safety valve for desperate men and women.[41]

In the crisis of the 1980s, some American experts began to worry about Mexico's stability. By 1986, Mexico was in its "fourth year of imposed economic sacrifices." Would "the patience" of the Mexican people finally break into "large-scale civil disorder and violence"? "Sooner or later," noted a former Latin American correspondent, "turbulence in Mexico would certainly spill across the common frontier." The United States, the political scientist Alfred Stepan has written, "is not insulated" from Mexico's problems, "but we have been lucky—and Mexico's long-term stability has been an extremely important part of this." If Mexico's economy failed to recover, that stability might be threatened. "Imagine, then," Stepan has said, "what it would mean if Mexico erupted in turmoil of the kind we have seen in El Salvador, Guatemala and Nicaragua. Imagine that chaos and violence, magnified a dozen times, on our very border."[42] The time, in other words, did not seem propitious for closing down an essential safety valve.

In 1986, American commentary about Mexico came from two main groups: those who feared for Mexico's political and economic stability and pled for U.S. aid; and those politicians who deplored the porous border, the Mexican failure to prohibit drug smuggling, and the "deadly disunity" sure to follow if the "illegal invasion" were not stopped. The domestic alarmists, many internationalists argued, were worrying "about symptoms—drugs and migration—but not about the underlying disease." The only way to control immigration and drugs was to "help Mexico build an economy that offers jobs and an improved standard of living to its citizens."[43]

"The economic, political and social perils facing the Mexicans," Alfred Stepan has said, "are grave for them and grave for us." The two countries had deep geographical and historical links. When Mexico's economic troubles set in, American border towns—dependent on retail trade with Mexicans—went into a parallel decline; towns like Laredo, Texas, had "little other eco-

nomic reason for being than commerce with Mexico." If Mexico
had to default on its loans and interest payments, American banks
with Mexican loans would be much shaken. Mexico was a key
Western Hemisphere ally and the third-largest American trading partner. Even the most irritating problems stemmed from
reciprocal, interdependent causes. Was it, after all, Mexico's fault
if the United States had an insatiable appetite for cheap labor
and for drugs, and if Mexicans responded to that market demand?
Immigration, drug production, pollution from copper smelters
on both sides of the border, salinity in the Colorado River, sewage flowing from Tijuana toward San Diego—all of the border
problems called for cultural and historical understanding. The
conquest of the Southwest might be only "a historical footnote"
to Americans, but Mexicans, a reporter in Mexico City noted,
"will never forget that their country was defeated by the United
States in the Mexican-American War of 1848 and forced to cede
half its territory"; the memory of foreign intervention also stayed
fresh. Complicating all of the border issues was a sensitive and
emotional sovereignty on both sides; the old Western problem
of friction between empires and nations still awaited full resolution. History had left the two nations locked into what the former American ambassador John Gavin has aptly called "a
marriage without possibility of divorce."[44]

Mexican people were not, after all, "aliens" in the West. Hispanics had been there first and, according to population projec-
tions, were going to be there in greater numbers in the future.
The Hispanic population of the United States, statisticians
reported in 1986, was growing "nearly five times faster" than the
general population. A group growing that fast might eventually,
some statisticians thought, outdistance blacks and become the
nation's largest minority. Hispanics were clearly going to be a
political influence to reckon with, and Republicans began a campaign to win their traditional loyalty from the Democrats.[45]

The most volatile domestic issue raised by the growing Hispanic presence involved bilingual education. In 1974, in *Lau* v.
Nichols (a case originating in San Francisco), the Supreme Court
ruled that schools had to offer special help to non-English-
speaking students. *Lau* v. *Nichols,* the *Washington Post* noted, was

"as significant for non-English-speaking students as *Brown* v. *Board of Education* was for black students." Many languages were "represented among the four million students with limited proficiency in English," the *New York Times* said in 1985, "but those of Hispanic origin made up three-quarters of the total and constitute an even higher portion of the students who spend four or more years in bilingual education." The funding, method, strategy, and purpose of bilingual education became matters of heated controversy; at the base of the issue was "the question of what role Spanish is to have in the future of this country." "In the modern history of this nation's public schools, nothing except racial desegregation," the *Washington Post* noted ten years after *Lau* v. *Nichols*, "has so thoroughly entangled the classroom with intense feelings about ethnicity, politics and the meaning of becoming an American."[46]

Bilingual education provided one focus in a key question of Western pluralism: How would Hispanics adapt to the political, economic, and social order of the West, and how would that order adapt to them? Electoral politics in Los Angeles also sharpened the question. Founded in 1781 by Spanish colonists, Los Angeles two hundred years later had a population 27 percent Hispanic, and not a single Hispanic on the city council since 1962 (when Ed Roybal had left for Congress). A federal lawsuit filed in 1985 alleged that the drawing of districts in Los Angeles had broken up the Hispanic population and thus weakened their vote. In 1985, in a special election following a council member's resignation, Richard Alatorre became the second Hispanic in the twentieth century to sit on the council. But the question of redistricting still waited for an answer.[47]

As the council and the court set out to find that answer, their search led them to an odd echo of one of the earliest problems in the nation's history. When the new lines were drawn, should "the city's large population of illegal Hispanic immigrants . . . be included in the population figures on which the redistricting" would be based?[48] They were not citizens and could not vote, and yet they were residents of the city and affected by its policies. This problem brings to mind the famous three-fifths compromise of the U.S. Constitution. In allocating proportional representation, the framers of the Constitution wrestled with a comparable question: Should black slaves be included in the population count? Numbers, said the Constitution, "shall be determined by adding to the whole Number of free Persons . . . three fifths of all other Persons." Was the three-fifths compromise the solution for Los Angeles and other cities where the question would be raised? Illegal immigration had revived an old issue that emancipation and Reconstruction had supposedly put to rest. If a group of people lived and labored in this nation and yet were not citizens, what was the nation's obligation to them, and vice versa?

This time, the question was quite distinctively Western. It dealt with Mexicans in a region once Mexican, with people who came voluntarily and not with slaves forcibly imported, and with the West's chronically unsettled contest for legitimacy. In a region shaped by conquest, each arriving group or individual posed the question anew: Who was a legitimate Westerner, and who had a right to share in the benefits of the region? How were people to sort themselves out, and stay sorted, when the cast of characters never stabilized? Consider a description of assimilation in Los Angeles, offered by the urban historian David Clark: "Newcomers could not be absorbed into the majority, for they were the majority." The state of Arizona in 1986 presented a similar picture; "nearly two-thirds of its eligible voters today," the *Christian Science Monitor* reported, "are out-of-staters who moved to Arizona within the last 20 years."[49]

The Bering Straits migration, Spanish colonization, the fur trade, the gold rush, the Plains farming boom, Mexican emigration, the westward push of the middle class in the 1920s, the World War Two employment boom, the Sun Belt migration, the pursuit of jobs, and the pursuit of variant lifestyles: mobility and the transformation of populations never ceased in Western America. Mobility, of course, worked both ways. Some settlements grew, and some declined. In the 1980s the towns that depended on farms, ranches, oil, copper, uranium, and timber all slid down the steep side of the Western boom/bust cycle. Those industries might revive; otherwise the towns would travel the well-established Western path toward the status of ghost town.

Going up or going down, growing or declining, Western areas often left their residents nervously eyeing each other, struggling for turf and legitimacy.

The cast of characters who inherit the West's complex past is as diverse as ever. As Western dilemmas recur, we wish we knew more not only about the place but also about each other. It is a disturbing element of continuity in Western history that we have not ceased to be strangers. The problem of mistaken identity runs from past to present. In incident after incident, whites on punitive expeditions set out to kill Indians—possibly the Indians who had committed the theft or attack about to be avenged, and possibly not. In times of tension, individuals appeared as categories—hostile until proven friendly and, even if friendly, still alien.

One would be happy to consign this pattern of thought to the old frontier West, but the quarantine would not hold. When Anglo-Americans look across the Mexican border or into an Indian reservation, they are more likely to see stereotypes than recognizable individuals or particular groups; the same distortion of vision no doubt works the other way too. The unitary character known as "the white man" has never existed, nor has "the Indian." Yet the phrases receive constant use, as if they carried necessary meaning. Indians, Hispanics, Asians, blacks, Anglos, businesspeople, workers, politicians, bureaucrats, natives, and newcomers, we share the same region and its history, but we wait to be introduced. The serious exploration of the historical process that made us neighbors provides that introduction.

Notes

Sᴇᴇ ᴀʟꜱᴏ Further Readings, for background material drawn on in each chapter.

Abbreviations

AP	Associated Press	*NYTNE*	*New York Times,* national edition
BC	*Boulder Daily Camera*	*RMN*	*Rocky Mountain News*
BG	*Boston Globe*	*RP-E*	*Riverside Press-Enterprise*
CSM	*Christian Science Monitor*	UPI	United Press International
DP	*Denver Post*	*WP*	*Washington Post*
LAT	*Los Angeles Times*	*USNWR*	*U.S. News and World Report*
NYT	*New York Times*		

Introduction

1. Frederick Jackson Turner, "The Signifi-cance of History," in *The Early Writings of Frederick Jackson Turner,* ed. Everett E. Edwards (Madison: Univ. of Wisconsin Press, 1938), 52–53.
2. Nannie Alderson and Helena Huntington Smith, *A Bride Goes West* (1942; Lincoln: Univ. of Nebraska Press, 1969), 40.
3. James Henretta, "The Impact of the 'New Indian History' on the Teaching of United States History," in "The Impact of Indian History on the Teaching of United States History" (Occasional Papers in Curriculum Series, D'Arcy McNickle Center for the History of the American Indian, no. 2, Chi-cago Conference 1984), 97.
4. Frederick Jackson Turner, *The Significance of the Frontier in American History,* ed. Harold P. Simonson (New York: Frederick Ungar, 1963), 28, 29, 27, 58.

5. Howard R. Lamar, "Historical Relevance and the American West," *Venture* (Fall 1968): 62–70, quotations from 63–64.
6. Harold P. Simonson, introd. to Turner, *Significance of the Frontier*, 8.
7. Earl Pomeroy, "Toward a Reorientation of Western History: Continuity and Environment," *Mississippi Valley Historical Review* (March 1955): 579–600; John Walton

Caughey, "The American West: Frontier and Region," *Arizona and the West* (1959): 7–12; Howard R. Lamar, *The Far Southwest, 1846–1912: A Territorial History* (New Haven: Yale Univ. Press, 1966).
8. Louis L'Amour in "Forum: Does America Still Exist?" *Harper's*, March 1984, 53, 54.
9. Bill Walker, "Louis L'Amour's Real-Life Showdown," *DP*, Oct. 6, 1985.

One · Empire of Innocence

1. John Wesley Hardin, *The Life of John Wesley Hardin*, ed. Robert G. McCubbin (Norman: Univ. of Oklahoma Press, 1961), xvii, 6–7.
2. Ibid., 13, 14.
3. Clifford Drury, ed., *First White Women over the Rockies*, vol. 1 (Glendale, Calif.: Arthur H. Clark, 1963), 29.
4. Ibid., 152.
5. Christopher L. Miller, *Prophetic Worlds: Indians and Whites on the Columbia Plateau* (New Brunswick: Rutgers Univ. Press, 1985), 23, 25, 33, Spokan Prophet quoted on 45.
6. Ibid., 60.
7. Ibid., 1; Marcus Whitman quoted in Robert V. Hine and Edwin R. Bingham, eds., *The American Frontier: Readings and Documents* (Boston: Little, Brown, 1972), 162.
8. Miller, *Prophetic Worlds*, 105, 117.
9. Richard White, *Land Use, Environment, and Social Change: The Shaping of Island County, Washington* (Seattle: Univ. of Washington Press, 1980), 46, 68, Walter Crockett quoted on 35.
10. Richard N. Mack, "Invaders at Home on the Range," *Natural History*, Feb. 1984, 43.
11. Dorothy O. Johansen and C. M. Gates, *Empire of the Columbia: A History of the Pacific Northwest*, 2d ed. (New York: Harper & Row, 1967), 250, 252.
12. Robert Utley, *Frontiersmen in Blue: The United States Army and the Indian, 1848–1865* (1967; Lincoln: Univ. of Nebraska Press, 1981), 178–200.
13. "The Angry West vs. the Rest," *News-*

week, Sept. 17, 1979, 31–40; "West Senses Victory in Sagebrush Rebellion," *USNWR*, Dec. 1, 1980, 29, 30.
14. Richard D. Lamm and Michael McCarthy, *The Angry West: A Vulnerable Land and Its Future* (Boston: Houghton Mifflin, 1982), 4.
15. Carole Shammas, "English-Born and Creole Elites in Turn-of-the-Century Virginia," in Thad Tate and David Ammerman, eds., *The Chesapeake in the Seventeenth Century: Essays on Anglo-American Society and Politics* (New York: W. W. Norton, 1979), 274.
16. Anne M. Butler, *Daughters of Joy, Sisters of Mercy: Prostitutes in the American West, 1865–1890* (Urbana: Univ. of Illinois Press, 1985), 68.
17. Marion S. Goldman, *Gold Diggers and Silver Miners: Prostitution and Social Life on the Comstock Lode* (Ann Arbor: Univ. of Michigan Press, 1981), 144, John Milleain quoted on 144.
18. Ibid., 137.
19. Ibid., 158.
20. Ibid., 108.
21. Amelia Stuart Knight, "Diary, 1853," in Lillian Schlissel, ed., *Women's Diaries of the Westward Journey* (New York: Schocken Books, 1982), 206.
22. Ibid., 203, 208, 209, 210.
23. Ibid., 215.
24. Katherine Llewellyn Hill Harris, "Women and Families on Northeastern Colorado Homesteads, 1873–1920" (Ph.D. diss., Univ. of Colorado, 1983).

Two · Property Values

1. Mark Twain (Samuel Clemens), *Roughing It* (New York: New American Library, 1962), 184–89.
2. Thomas Jefferson, *Notes on the State of Vir-*

ginia, ed. Thomas Perkins Abernethy (New York: Harper & Row, 1964), 157; Drew McCoy, *The Elusive Republic: Political Economy in Jeffersonian America* (New York:

W. W. Norton, 1982), 9–10, John Adams quoted on 67.

3. Malcolm J. Rohrbough, *The Land Office Business: The Settlement and Administration of American Public Lands, 1789–1837* (New York: Oxford Univ. Press, 1968), 250–64.

4. Ibid., 257–58, 260.

5. Ibid., 264.

6. Ibid., 270.

7. Ibid., 197, 290.

8. Ibid., 295. For an overview of land policy, see Everett Dick, *The Lure of the Land: A Social History of the Public Lands from the Articles of Confederation to the New Deal* (Lincoln: Univ. of Nebraska Press, 1970).

9. Rohrbough, *Land Office*, 299, 298.

10. Paul Wallace Gates, "The Homestead Law in an Incongruous Land System," *American Historical Review* (July 1936): 652–81, quotations from 654–55.

11. Charles Howard Shinn, *Mining Camps: A Study in American Frontier Government*, ed. Rodman Paul (New York: Harper & Row, 1970).

12. William M. Stewart, *The Reminiscences of William M. Stewart of Nevada*, ed. George Rothwell Brown (New York: Neale, 1908), 21, 23–24.

13. Collis P. Huntington quoted in Russell R. Elliott, *Servant of Power: A Political Biography of Senator William R. Stewart* (Reno: Univ. of Nevada Press, 1983), 65.

14. William Stewart quoted in Elliott, *Servant of Power*, 271.

15. 1866 Mining Law quoted in Joseph Ellison, "The Mineral Land Question in California,

1848–1866," in Vernon Carstensen, ed., *The Public Lands: Studies in the History of the Public Domain* (Madison: Univ. of Wisconsin Press, 1963), 86.

16. Charlie Siringo, *A Texas Cowboy; or, Fifteen Years on the Hurricane Deck of a Spanish Pony* (1885; Lincoln: Univ. of Nebraska Press, 1979), 4.

17. Joyce Appleby, "Commercial Farming and the 'Agrarian Myth' in the Early Republic," *Journal of American History* (March 1982): 833–49, and *Capitalism and a New Social Order: The Republican Vision of the 1790s* (New York: New York Univ Press, 1984).

18. Charles S. Grant, *Democracy in the Connecticut Frontier Town of Kent* (New York: Columbia Univ. Press, 1961), 14, 29, 49, Joshua Lassell quoted on 49; Bernard Bailyn, *The Peopling of British North America: An Introduction* (New York: Alfred A. Knopf, 1986), 65.

19. Frederick Jackson Turner, *The Significance of the Frontier in American History*, ed. Harold P. Simonson (New York: Frederick Ungar, 1963), 52, 27.

20. Robert L. Kelley, *Gold vs. Grain: The Hydraulic Mining Controversy in California's Sacramento Valley* (Glendale, Calif.: Arthur H. Clark, 1959).

21. Reclamation Personnel Committee quoted in William L. Kahrl, *Water and Power* (Berkeley: Univ. of California Press, 1982), 109.

22. J. B. Lippincott quoted ibid., 192.

23. Howard R. Lamar, *Dakota Territory, 1861–1889: A Study of Frontier Politics* (New Haven: Yale Univ. Press, 1956), 83.

Three · Denial and Dependence

1. Martin McGinnis quoted in Earl Pomeroy, *The Territories and the United States, 1861–1890: Studies in Colonial Administration* (1947; Seattle: Univ. of Washington Press, 1969), 104.

2. Howard R. Lamar, *The Far Southwest, 1846–1912: A Territorial History* (1966; New York: W. W. Norton, 1970), 9.

3. Pomeroy, *Territories*, 106.

4. *Vermillion Republican* quoted ibid., 104.

5. Ibid., 36, 101, *Santa Fe Gazette* quoted on 101.

6. Ibid., 106.

7. Howard R. Lamar, *Dakota Territory, 1861–1889: A Study of Frontier Politics* (New Haven: Yale Univ. Press, 1956), 40, 94, 98, 276.

8. Ibid., 225, *Press and Dakotan* quoted on 205.

9. Ibid., 46.

10. Ibid., 88, 130.

11. Michael Malone and Richard B. Roeder, *Montana: A History of Two Centuries* (Seattle: Univ. of Washington Press, 1976), 176.

12. Pomeroy, *Territories*, 30; Lamar, *Dakota*, 79.

13. Gilman M. Ostrander, *Nevada: The Great Rotten Borough, 1859–1964* (New York: Alfred A. Knopf, 1966), xii.

14. Lewis Gould, *Wyoming: A Political History, 1866–1896* (New Haven: Yale Univ. Press, 1968), 80, ix.

15. Ostrander, *Nevada*, 162; Gould, *Wyoming*, 268.

16. T. A. Larson, "The New Deal in Wyo-

ming," 254, 257; James V. Wickens, "The
New Deal in Colorado," 284; Leonard
Arrington, "The New Deal in the West: A
Preliminary Statistical Inquiry," 311, 312,
all in "The New Deal in the West," *Pacific
Historical Review* (Aug. 1969).

17. John T. Schlebecker, *Cattle Raising on the
Plains, 1900–1961* (Lincoln: Univ. of
Nebraska Press, 1963), 133, 141.

18. Larson, "New Deal in Wyoming," 249.

19. Calvin Trillin, "U.S. Journal: Tucson, Ariz.:
Under the Fruitless Mulberry," *New Yorker*,
July 19, 1982, 62–65.

20. Robert W. Johannsen, *Stephen A. Douglas*
(New York: Oxford Univ. Press, 1973).

21. Stephen Douglas quoted ibid., 303.

22. Robert W. Johannsen, ed., *The Lincoln–
Douglas Debates* (New York: Oxford Univ.
Press, 1965), 92.

23. Stephen Douglas quoted in Johannsen,
Douglas, 399.

24. Stephen Douglas quoted ibid., 451.

25. Ibid., 871.

26. Drew McCoy, *The Elusive Republic: Political Economy in Jeffersonian America* (New
York: W. W. Norton, 1982), 252.

27. Ernest Callenbach, *Ecotopia* (1975; New
York: Bantam Books, 1977).

Four · Uncertain Enterprises

1. Wilbur Zelinsky, *The Cultural Geography of
the United States* (Englewood Cliffs, N.J.:
Prentice-Hall, 1973), 13.

2. Mary McDougall Gordon, ed., *Overland to
California with the Pioneer Line: The Gold
Rush Diary of Bernard J. Reid* (Stanford:
Stanford Univ. Press, 1983), 13–14.

3. Ibid., 55, 142–44.

4. Ibid., 148, 145, 147, 164, 166.

5. Ibid., 167, 168.

6. J. D. B. Stillman, quoted in J. S. Holliday,
*The World Rushed In: The California Gold
Rush Experience* (New York: Simon and
Schuster, 1981), 373.

7. Ibid., 67, 336–37.

8. Ibid., 361–62.

9. Ibid., 83, 138–39.

10. Ibid., 310, 320, 338.

11. Ibid., 172, 334, 371, 85, 142, 344, 384, 387.

12. Colonel Richard B. Mason quoted ibid., 40.
On the technological transition in California
and its effect on local society, see Ralph
Mann's *After the Gold Rush: Society in Grass
Valley and Nevada City, California, 1849–
1870* (Stanford: Stanford Univ. Press, 1982).

13. *Gold Hill News* quoted in Mark Wyman, *Hard
Rock Epic: Western Miners and the Industrial Revolution, 1860–1910* (Berkeley: Univ.
of California Press, 1979), 10.

14. Ibid., 120–24. See also Ronald C. Brown,
Hard Rock Miners: The Intermountain West
(College Station: Texas A&M Univ. Press,
1979).

15. Wyman, *Hard Rock Epic*, 98.

16. Ibid., 118–19.

17. Montana Supreme Court quoted ibid., 121.

18. Crystal Eastman quoted ibid., 125.

19. Michael Malone, *The Battle for Butte: Mining and Politics on the Northern Frontier*

(Seattle: Univ. of Washington Press, 1981),
9, 11.

20. Ibid., 14, Warren G. Davenport quoted on
12–13.

21. Ibid., 50.

22. Ibid., 134.

23. Ibid., 113.

24. Ibid., 142, 148.

25. Ibid., 154, 153, 151, Augustus Heinze quoted
on 155, 156.

26. Ibid., 159, 187, Augustus Heinze quoted on
176.

27. William Clark quoted ibid., 196.

28. Ibid., 173–74.

29. Richard E. Lingenfelter, *The Hardrock Miners: A History of the Mining Labor Movement in the American West, 1863–1893*
(Berkeley: Univ. of California Press, 1974),
182, 193.

30. Ibid., 196.

31. Governor James Peabody quoted in James
Edward Wright, *The Politics of Populism:
Dissent in Colorado* (New Haven: Yale Univ.
Press, 1974), 240.

32. Joseph Robert Conlin, *Bread and Roses Too:
Studies of the Wobblies* (Westport, Conn.:
Greenwood, 1969), 71.

33. Ibid., 73.

34. Ibid., 111.

35. The story of the Bisbee deportation comes
from James W. Byrkit, *Forging the Copper
Collar: Arizona's Labor-Management War*
(Tucson: Univ. of Arizona Press, 1982).

36. Ibid., 301; Robert Littell quoted in Malone,
Battle for Butte, 198–99.

37. Byrkit, *Copper Collar*, 326.

38. Richard Peterson, *The Bonanza Kings: The
Social Origins and Business Behavior of
Western Mining Entrepreneurs, 1870–1900*

(Lincoln: Univ. of Nebraska Press, 1977), 74, 77.

39. Song quoted in Joseph King, *A Mine to Make a Mine: Financing the Colorado Mining Industry, 1859–1902* (College Station: Texas A&M Univ. Press, 1977), 55.

40. Gilbert Fite, *The Farmers' Frontier* (New York: Holt, Rinehart and Winston, 1966), 55.

41. Ibid., 17; Everett Dick, *The Sod-House Frontier, 1845–1890* (1937; Lincoln: Univ. of Nebraska Press, 1979), 131.

42. *Wichita City Eagle* quoted in Fite, *Farmers' Frontier*, 61.

43. William Shadwell quoted ibid., 56.

44. Annette Adkins, *Harvest of Grief: Grasshopper Plagues and Public Assistance in Minnesota, 1873–1878* (St. Paul: Minnesota Historical Society Press, 1984), 72, 80.

45. Governor John Pillsbury quoted ibid., 84, E. W. Chase quoted on 90, *Pioneer Press* quoted on 100.

46. Ibid., 78, 4, 47, 76.

47. Ibid., 42, Mary Jones quoted on 41, 35.

48. Fite, *Farmers' Frontier*, 218.

49. Ibid., 84; Gilbert Fite, *American Farmers: The New Minority* (Bloomington: Univ. of Indiana Press, 1981), 236, 238.

50. Raymond Williams, *The Country and the City* (1973; New York: Oxford Univ. Press, 1975), 9–12.

51. Howard Ruede, *Letters from a Kansas Homesteader, 1877–1878*, ed. John Ise (1937; Lawrence: Univ. Press of Kansas, 1983), 3.

52. Ibid., 125, 163, 30–31, 187, 22, 51.

53. Ibid., 123, 194, 218, 136.

Five · **The Meeting Ground of Past and Present**

1. "Horse, Rabbit Collide in Aspen," *BC*, July 20, 1986.

2. Patricia Nelson Limerick, *Desert Passages* (Albuquerque: Univ. of New Mexico Press, 1985), chap. 4.

3. Donald Worster, *Rivers of Empire: Water, Aridity, and the Growth of the American West* (New York: Pantheon Books, 1986), 326.

4. Gay Cook, "Thirsty High Plains States Draining Aquifer" and "West's Water Future Seen as Grim," *DP*, Dec. 16, 1979, "Lifestyle Is Draining Away," *DP*, Dec. 17, 1979, "High Energy Costs Threaten Agricultural Economy," *DP*, Dec. 18, 1979, "For Ecology, a Domino Principle," *DP*, Dec. 19, 1979, "States Tardy in Dealing with Ever-Dropping Water Table," *DP*, Dec. 20, 1979, and "'Solutions' to Plains Water Crisis Explored," *DP*, Dec. 21, 1979; Paul Taylor, "Scientists Mustered to Save Aquifer: Texas Economy Tied to Subterranean Lake," *WP*, Dec. 31, 1984.

5. "Tougher Line Coming on Water Projects," *USNWR*, May 2, 1977, 67; Worster, *Rivers of Empire*, 326; "The Great Western Drought of 1977," *Time*, Mar. 7, 1977, 80; "Carter Changes Course on Tough Water Policy," *USNWR*, May 8, 1978, 27; "Water Projects Dispute: Carter and Congress Near a Showdown," *Science*, June 17, 1977, 1303; "The Browning of America," *Newsweek*, Feb. 23, 1981, 36.

6. William Robbins, "Farmers' Problems Shared by Lenders," *NYT*, Sept. 16, 1985; Andrew Malcolm, "Abundant Cornfields Beckon as Prospect of Deeper Debt Looms," *NYT*, Sept. 30, 1984; Steven V. Roberts, "The Squeeze on Agriculture Makes 'Crisis' Sound Too Mild," *NYT*, Nov. 10, 1985; Laurent Belsie and Howard LaFranchi, "Farmers Produce More, But Get Less," *CSM*, April 25, 1986; Robert Lindsey, "California's Agriculture, Like the Midwest's, Is Encountering Hard Times," *NYT*, Dec. 28, 1985; Malcolm, "Abundant Cornfields," *NYT*, Sept. 30, 1984; James Worsham and Charles Madigan (*Chicago Tribune*), "How the American Farmer Got Into Trouble," *BG*, May 23, 1982; Ben Bradlee, Jr., *BG*, Feb. 10, 1983; William Robbins, *NYT*, Jan. 10, 1985; Mark Drabenstott and Marvin Duncan, *NYT*, Aug. 14, 1985.

7. Seth S. King, "Reagan's Farm Bill Seeks Market Basis for Aid, Block Says," *NYT*, Jan. 23, 1985; William Robbins, "Farm Measure's Ambitious Goals Match Its High Costs, Experts Say," *NYT*, Dec. 23, 1985; Seth S. King, "Should Subsidies for Farm Interests Be Removed from the U.S. Budget?" *NYT*, Feb. 13, 1985.

8. Murray N. Rothbard, "Will the Farmer Ever Stop Wailing?" *NYT*, May 17, 1985.

9. "The Hands of Anger, Frustration, Humiliation," editorial from the *Iowa City Press-Citizen*, reprinted in *NYT*, Dec. 15, 1985; Robbins, "Farmers' Problems Shared," *NYT*, Sept. 16, 1985; King, "Subsidies," *NYT*, Feb. 13, 1985; Neal Pierce, "Rural America: The Greatest Federal Aid Junkie of Them All?" *DP*, April 1, 1985.

10. Duane Vandenbusche and Duane A. Smith, *A Land Alone: Colorado's Western Slope* (Boulder, Colo.: Pruett, 1981), 52, 118.
11. Kit Miniclier, "Craig Mayor Pushes Statehood for Western Slope," *DP*, May 3, 1985; "U.S. Synthetic Fuel Corporation Shuts Down," *NYT*, April 19, 1986; Robert D. Hershey, Jr., "Shale Oil Is Coming of Age," *NYT*, Nov. 6, 1981.
12. Douglas Martin, "Exxon Abandons Shale Oil Project," *NYT*, May 3, 1982; "Setback for Synfuel: Exxon Shuts Down Its Shale Project," *Time*, May 17, 1982, 58, 59; Gary Schmitz, "Synfuels Corp. Dies; Union Fights for Loan Guarantees," *DP*, Dec. 20, 1985; "U.S. Synthetic Fuel," *NYT*, April 19, 1986; Iver Peterson, "Energy Price Drop Mars Mountain States' Hopes," *NYT*, Feb. 4, 1986; Cindy Parmenter, "4,100 Jobs May Be Lost in Oil Shale Shutdown," and "Dreams Dashed for Shale Workers," *DP*, May 4, 1982.
13. Robert O. Anderson, *Fundamentals of the American Petroleum Industry* (Norman: Univ. of Oklahoma Press, 1984), ix, 35.
14. Michael Rounds, "Crash Deals Staggering Blow to Denver," *RMN*, June 9, 1986; Stacey Burling, "Wyoming Takes Hardest Hit in Memory," *RMN*, June 13, 1986.
15. Robert Reinhold, "Texans Shudder As Price of Petroleum Falls," *NYT*, Jan. 26, 1986; Peter Applebome, "Oil Bust Bursts Fragile Texas Bubble of Prosperity," *NYT*, March 31, 1986, and "Texans Take Big Slide on Bad Half of Oil Boom," *NYT*, April 17, 1986.
16. Peter Applebome, "Texas Finds Sympathy in Short Supply," *NYT*, April 20, 1986; Stacey Burling, "Period of 'Price Volatility' Looms," *RMN*, June 14, 1986; Robert Reinhold, "Cheap Oil Stirring Clamor for Relief in Southwest," *NYT*, April 15, 1986; Stacey Burling, "Texas Native Gives Up on Crude," *RMN*, June 11, 1986; Michael Rounds, " 'Price Plunge' Rough on the Energy States," *RMN*, June 8, 1986.
17. Stacey Burling, "Weld Farmers Hit by Double Whammy," *RMN*, June 10, 1986.
18. "Copper Smelter Closes on Coast As Market Shrinks for Metal," *NYT*, March 26, 1985; Paul Taylor, "Copper Industry Languishes in the Economic Pits: Mining Hurt by Competition, Air Standards," *WP*, March 30, 1985; Nicholas D. Kristof, "Copper's Plunge Is Pushing Mining Towns to the Brink," *NYT*, March 23, 1986.
19. William Tucker, *Progress and Privilege: America in the Age of Environmentalism* (Garden City, N.Y.: Doubleday, 1982), xv, 6, 36, 15, 34 (emphasis in original).

20. Cheryl Sullivan, "The Greening of Oregon's Economy," *CSM*, Feb. 24, 1986; "Oregon Coalition Wary on Ecology," *NYT*, Dec. 26, 1971; David Bird, "Gov. McCall Seeks to Curb Oregon's Growth," *NYT*, May 7, 1973, and "Mr. McCall Did Well for the State around Him," *NYT*, Jan. 5, 1975; "Oregon Growth," *NYT*, July 25, 1976.
21. Nicholas D. Kristof, "An Economic Game Plan Short Circuits in Oregon," *NYT*, Jan. 5, 1986; Herbert M. Denton, "Canada Spat Could Backfire on Both Sides," *WP*, June 8, 1986; David R. Francis, "Canada Wants to Avoid Trade War with US: Retaliates with Tariffs, But Seeks Talks with Washington," *CSM*, June 4, 1986.
22. Kathleen Sharp, "A Regional Report: The Pacific Northwest: An Exodus from the Timberlands," *NYT*, June 16, 1985; Kristof, "Game Plan Backfires," *NYT*, Jan. 5, 1986; "Governor Says Oregon Is in Economic Crisis," *NYT*, Jan. 19, 1982; Sullivan, "Greening," *CSM*, Feb. 24, 1986.
23. Robert Lindsey, "Utah Finds No Security in High-Tech Industry," *NYT*, Dec. 19, 1985; Michael Schrage, "Hard Times Descend on Silicon Valley," *WP*, April 28, 1985.
24. Everett M. Rogers and Judith K. Larsen, *Silicon Valley Fever: Growth of High-Technology Culture* (New York: Basic Books, 1984), 70; *Business Week* quoted in ibid., 122.
25. Robert Reinhold, "Shortages Spur Illicit Traffic in Silicon Chips," *NYT*, March 11, 1984; Jodi Schneider, "High Tech and the Law: Complex Technological-Legal Issues Keep Business Booming for Attorneys," *BC*, Oct. 22, 1985; Philip Bulman, "Computer Crimes Going Unpunished," *DP*, March 24, 1986; Rogers and Larsen, *Silicon Valley Fever*, 202, 184, 185, 138; Sandy Graham, "High-Tech Industry Brings New Wave of Environmental Problems to State," *RMN*, April 15, 1985; Daniel A. Beucke, "Regional Report: Colorado High Tech: Cracks in Silicon Mountain," *NYT*, June 30, 1985.
26. Robert Webster, "Silicon Valley's 'Poor,' " *NYT*, Jan. 30, 1985; Ronald Rosenberg, "The Pace Is Faster in the Silicon Valley," *BG*, Nov. 14, 1982; Robert Lindsey, "High-Technology Layoffs Spur Fear in California," *NYT*, Nov. 10, 1985; Ted Delaney, "High-Tech's High Toll," *DP*, Dec. 8, 1985; Rogers and Larsen, *Silicon Valley Fever*, 154; Beucke, "Silicon Mountain," *NYT*, June 30, 1985.
27. Rachel Carson, *Silent Spring* (1962; Greenwich, Conn.: Fawcett Books, n.d.); Philip Shabecoff, " 'Silent Spring' Led to Safer Pesticides, But Use Is Up," *NYT*, April 21,

1986, and "Pesticides Finally Top the Problem List of E.P.A," *NYT,* March 6, 1986.

28. (AP), "Grasshoppers Devastate Idaho, Ravaging Last of Farmers' Hopes," *BC,* June 23, 1985; Iver Peterson, "Western Farmers Fight Plague of Grasshoppers," *NYT,* June 23, 1985.

29. William deBuys, *Enchantment and Exploitation: The Life and Hard Times of a New Mexican Mountain Range* (Albuquerque: Univ. of New Mexico Press, 1985), 232–33, 297.

30. John Schlebecker, *Cattle Raising on the Plains, 1900–1961* (Lincoln: Univ. of Nebraska Press, 1963), chap. 10; Phillip O. Foss, *Politics and Grass: The Administration of Grazing on the Public Domain* (1960; New York: Greenwood, 1969).

31. T. R. Reid, "Western Grazing Fees Slip Out of Budget Noose," *WP,* Feb. 2, 1986; Noel Rosetta, "Herds, Herds on the Range," *Sierra,* March–April 1985, 43–47; William Schmidt, "U.S. Easing Control over Western Rangeland," *NYT,* Feb. 14, 1983; "Debate Heats Up on Plans to Raise Grazing Land Fees," *DP,* April 7, 1985.

32. Edward Abbey, "Even the Bad Guys Wear White Hats: Cowboys, Ranchers, and the Ruin of the West," *Harper's,* Jan. 1986, 51–55.

33. Iver Peterson, "A Dispiriting Spring for Cattle Ranchers," *NYT,* May 1, 1985; Stephen Singular, "Nosing In on Cattle Rustlers," *DP Empire,* Jan. 6, 1985.

34. Jim Robbins, "Range War in Rosebud Valley," *NYT Magazine,* May 6, 1984, 82–89; Stan Steiner, *The Vanishing White Man* (New York: Harper & Row, 1976), 252–53.

35. Peterson, "Dispiriting Spring," *NYT,* May 1, 1985; Iver Peterson, "OK, Pardner, Now's the Time: Ready, Aim . . . Rhyme!" *NYT,* Feb. 3, 1985; Reid, "Western Grazing Fees," *WP,* Feb. 2, 1986.

36. Philip Shabecoff, "President Extends Grazing Fees; Conservationists Assail Decision," *NYT,* Feb. 17, 1986.

37. Molly Ivins, "Desert Is Creeping Up on the Rangelands of the West," *NYT,* July 29, 1979.

38. Leonard A. Paris, "How the H-Blast Will Serve Mankind," *Coronet,* Jan. 1959, 68–72.

39. Karen Odom, "Retrial Sought in '53 Sheep Deaths," *DP,* March 15, 1985; (AP), "Utah Ranchers Lose Bid to Reopen Fallout Suits," *DP,* Jan. 22, 1986; John G. Fuller, *The Day We Bombed Utah: America's Most Lethal Secret* (New York: New American Library, 1985).

40. Howard Ball, *Justice Downwind: America's Atomic Testing Program in the 1950s* (New York: Oxford Univ. Press, 1986), 161; Jay Mathews *(Washington Post),* "Court Backs Fallout Victims," *BG,* May 11, 1984; Iver Peterson, "U.S. Ruled Negligent in A-Tests Followed by Nine Cancer Deaths," *NYT,* May 11, 1984; Daniel Schorr quoted in Ball, *Justice Downwind,* 169.

41. "Three Prime Sites Chosen for First N-Waste Pit," *DP,* Dec. 20, 1984.

42. Robert D. Hershey, Jr., "U.S. Suspends Plan for Nuclear Dump in East or Midwest," *NYT,* May 29, 1986.

43. Robert Reinhold, "Panhandle Worried about Waste Plan," *NYT,* June 1, 1986; Donald L. Rheem, "Choice of Finalists for A-Waste Site Stirs Up Controversy," *CSM,* May 30, 1986.

44. Reinhold, "Panhandle Worried," *NYT,* June 1, 1986; Iver Peterson, "Issue of National Nuclear Waste Dump Polarizes Three States," *NYT,* Jan. 25, 1985; "Three Prime Sites," *DP,* Dec. 20, 1984; Thomas Graf, "Nuclear Winter and Frosty Mugs: Burritos the Real Peril When at J.D.'s Rocky Flats Lounge," *DP,* March 16, 1986.

45. Robert Fogelson, *The Fragmented Metropolis: Los Angeles, 1850–1930* (Cambridge: Harvard Univ. Press, 1967), 144, 145, 185, 274.

46. Robert Lindsey, "The Cloud on the Phoenix Horizon Is Made Up of Smog," *NYT,* Jan. 26, 1986; Iver Peterson, "In Colorado, the Breathtaking Vistas Now Include Traffic Jams," *NYT,* Dec. 30, 1985; Daniel P. Jones and Neil Westergard, "Adrift in a Sea of Bad Air," *DP,* Feb. 9, 1986; Gary Delsohn, "L.A. of the Rockies: Sprawl Creating Metroplex along I-25," *DP,* March 17, 1985.

47. Gary Delsohn, "War Declared on City Image as Cowtown," *DP,* May 9, 1985; Neil Westergard, "State's Image in Trouble?" *DP,* Nov. 29, 1985; Lou Chapman, "Chamber Fervently Wooing Firms," *DP,* March 15, 1986; Gary Delsohn, "Is America's Love Affair with Denver Ending? Queen City, State Spruce Up Image," *DP,* March 2, 1986.

48. Iver Peterson, "Past and Future Collide in Plan for Albuquerque," *NYT,* Feb. 5, 1985, and "Growth Is Issue in Albuquerque Race," *NYT,* Nov. 12, 1985.

49. Iver Peterson, "Increasing the Speed Limit to 65 on Interstates in Rural Areas," *NYT,* Feb. 6, 1985, and "Rebellion Gains in West and the Plains over U.S. Speed Limit," *NYT,* June 13, 1986; T. R. Reid, "Westerners Drive Around the Limit," *WP,* June 22, 1986.

50. Dave Foreman, ed., *Ecodefense: A Field Guide to Monkeywrenching* (Tucson: Earth First! Books, 1985), 3; Robert Ebisch, "Earth

First! Fights for a Colorado Foothold," *BC Sunday Magazine*, July 21, 1985; Richard Homer, "Radical Nature Lovers Fight for Wilderness," *DP*, July 8, 1985; Nicholas D. Kristof, "Forest Sabotage Is Urged by Some," *NYT*, Jan. 22, 1986.

51. Foreman, *Ecodefense*, v, 24, 29, 33, 67.

52. "Oil Boys and Indians," transcript of "60 Minutes," CBS Television Network, April 12, 1981; Debra Whitefield, "Indians Lost Royalties on Unreported Wyoming Oil Sales, Records Show," *LAT*, Jan. 12, 1981; Eleanor Randolph, "Oil Fee Losses Put at $1 Million a Day," *LAT*, Aug. 28, 1981.

53. John Aloysius Farrell, "The New Indian Wars," 8-pt. series in *DP*, Nov. 20–Nov. 27, 1983, reprinted by newspaper as pamphlet.

54. Mark Singer, *Funny Money* (New York: Alfred A. Knopf, 1985).

55. Jeanie Kasindorf, *The Nye County Brothel Wars: A Tale of the New West* (New York: Simon and Schuster, 1985).

56. Robert Lindsey, "Investment Fraud Abounds on Coast," *NYT*, March 24, 1985; David Clark Scott, "Turning Up the Heat on the 'Boiler Rooms': Big Task Force Cracking Down on Investment Con Games in US," *CSM*, March 31, 1986.

57. Paul Hutchinson, "Bank Robberies Popular Out West, But Success Rate Relatively Low," *DP*, Sept. 1, 1985.

58. Robert Lindsey, "Marijuana Crops Blooming in State's Backyards," *NYT*, Oct. 28, 1984, and "Raids Reduce Marijuana Planting 40%," *NYT*, July 25, 1985; James Conaway, "The Golden Harvest of Humboldt County," *WP*, Nov. 26, 1984; Carole Rafferty, "Marijuana Raids Angering Retirees:

Spy Planes Infringe on Rights and Shatter Their Peace, Californians' Suit Says," *NYT*, July 10, 1984.

59. Lindsey, "Marijuana Crops," *NYT*, Oct. 28, 1984; Bob Wiedrich *(Chicago Tribune)*, "Pot Growers' Traps Injure Park Visitors," *DP*, Jan. 20, 1985.

60. Lindsey, "Raids," *NYT*, July 25, 1985; Conaway, "Golden Harvest," *WP*, Nov. 26, 1984; Neal Pierce, "Main Street Learns to Love Pot," July 14, 1985; Robert Grabbe (UPI), "Uprooting Calif.'s Illicit Crop," *BG*, Sept. 11, 1983.

61. (UPI), "Escaped Mountain Man Killer Sought," *DP*, April 1, 1986; Jeff Long, *Outlaw: The True Story of Claude Dallas* (New York: William Morrow, 1985), 165.

62. Jim Robbins, "Olympian Feared for Her Life," *DP*, May 8, 1985; *(Chicago Tribune)*, " 'Mountain Men' Story Is Hot Property," *BC*, May 12, 1985; Bill Walker, "Old West Trappings: Virginia City Stage for Trial of 'Mountain Men,' " *DP*, May 5, 1985; "Slayings Admitted by Mountain Man: He Testifies He Shot Searcher for an Abducted Woman," *NYT*, May 10, 1985.

63. Gary Schmitz, "Trail of Racist Violence Leads to Resort," *DP*, Dec. 23, 1984; Tobby Hatley, "Inside the Aryan Nations," *BC Sunday Magazine*, Jan. 6, 1985, 6–11, 14–16; Wallace Turner, "5 Neo-Nazis Get Stiff Sentences for Crime Spree," *NYT*, Feb. 7, 1986; Wayne King, "Coast Trial Begins for Neo-Nazis Who Sought Racial War in U.S.," *NYT*, Sept. 13, 1985, and "Neo-Nazis' Dream of Racist Territory in Pacific Northwest Refuses to Die," *NYT*, July 5, 1986; Butler quoted in *BC Sunday Magazine*, Jan. 6, 1985, 7.

Six · **The Persistence of Natives**

1. Keith H. Basso, *Portraits of "The Whiteman": Linguistic Play and Cultural Symbols among the Western Apache* (New York: Cambridge Univ. Press, 1979), 90.

2. George Catlin, *Letters and Notes on the Manners, Customs, and Conditions of North American Indians*, vol. 1 (1844; rpt. New York: Dover, 1973), 16. I wrote this section before I read Lee Clark Mitchell's *Witnesses to a Vanishing America: The Nineteenth-Century Response* (Princeton: Princeton Univ. Press, 1981) and discovered I was in some ways replicating Mitchell's argument; in addition, Brian Dippie's *The Vanishing American: White Attitudes and U.S. Indian

Policy* (Middletown, Conn.: Wesleyan Univ. Press, 1982) covers similar ground.

3. Catlin, *Letters*, 259–61.

4. Ibid., 21.

5. Ibid., 10, 60.

6. Ibid., 210, 85, 102.

7. Ibid., 85, 84.

8. Ibid., 155–57, 176, 183.

9. Ibid., 183, 60.

10. Ibid., 183–84.

11. Ibid., 184.

12. Ibid., 23, 22.

13. Ibid., 4, 5.

14. Ibid., 59, 85, 61.

15. Mark Twain (Samuel Clemens), *Roughing It*

(New York: New American Library, 1962), 289.

16. Catlin, *Letters*, 61.

17. Paul Kane, *Wanderings of an Artist among the Indians of North America* (1859; Rutland, Vt.: Charles S. Tuttle, 1968), 125.

18. Paul Radin, ed., *The Autobiography of a Winnebago Indian* (1920; New York: Dover, 1963), 36.

19. I am drawing primarily on Bernard Sheehan, *Seeds of Extinction: Jeffersonian Philanthropy and the American Indian* (New York: W. W. Norton, 1974).

20. George Washington quoted ibid., 269.

21. Thomas McKenney quoted ibid., 253; see also Herman J. Viola, *Thomas L. McKenney: Architect of America's Early Indian Policy, 1816–1830* (Chicago: Swallow Press, 1974).

22. Andrew Jackson quoted in Michael Paul Rogin, *Fathers and Children: Andrew Jackson and the Subjugation of the American Indian* (New York: Alfred A. Knopf, 1975), 215.

23. Russell Thornton, "Cherokee Population Losses during the Trail of Tears: A New Perspective and a New Estimate," *Ethnohistory* (1984), 289, 294, 298.

24. Joel R. Poinsett and President Martin Van Buren quoted in Rogin, *Fathers*, 247.

25. Henry R. Schoolcraft quoted in Dippie, *Vanishing American*, 48.

26. Francis Paul Prucha, ed., *Americanizing the American Indian: Writings by the "Friends of the Indian," 1880–1900* (1973; Lincoln: Univ. of Nebraska Press, 1978), Carl Schurz quoted on 14, 21, Henry L. Dawes quoted on 28–29, Ezra Hayt quoted on 80.

27. Lyman Abbott quoted ibid., 32–34, Hiram Price quoted on 95, Merrill E. Gates quoted on 334.

28. Hiram Price quoted ibid., 89, Henry L. Dawes quoted on 30, Philip C. Garrett quoted on 65.

29. Wilcomb Washburn, *The Indian in America* (New York: Harper & Row, 1975), 243.

30. Clyde Milner II, *With Good Intentions: Quaker Work among the Pawnees, Otos, and Omahas in the 1870s* (Lincoln: Univ. of Nebraska Press, 1982), 7, 46, 25.

31. Fred Hoxie, *A Final Promise: The Campaign to Assimilate the Indians, 1880–1920* (Lincoln: Univ. of Nebraska Press, 1984), 33–34, 39, 113, 173, 187, *Journal of Education* quoted on 67.

32. John Collier, *Indians of the Americas: The Long Hope* (1947; New York: New American Library, n.d.), 10. On the early Collier, see Lawrence C. Kelly, *The Assault on Assimilation: John Collier and the Origins of Indian Policy Reform* (Albuquerque: Univ. of New Mexico Press, 1983).

33. Collier, *Indians*, 7; John Collier, *From Every Zenith: A Memoir* (Denver: Sage Books, 1963), 119; Collier, *Indians*, 14.

34. Collier, *Zenith*, 123.

35. Kenneth Philp, *John Collier's Crusade for Indian Reform, 1920–1954* (Tucson: Univ. of Arizona Press, 1977), 57–60, Collier quoted on 58.

36. Collier, *Indians*, 168.

37. Collier, *Zenith*, 174; O. H. Lipps quoted in Francis Paul Prucha, *The Great Father: The United States Government and the American Indians*, 2 vols. (Lincoln: Univ. of Nebraska Press, 1984), 2:956.

38. Joseph Bruner and "Bulletin of American Indian Federation" quoted ibid., 2:996–97.

39. Ibid., 964–65.

40. Collier, *Zenith*, 177.

41. Graham D. Taylor, *The New Deal and American Tribalism: The Administration of the Indian Reorganization Act, 1934–45* (Lincoln: Univ. of Nebraska Press, 1980), 102.

42. Ruth Underhill quoted ibid., 51.

43. Collier, *Indians*, 7; Collier, *Zenith*, 246.

44. Richard White, *The Roots of Dependency: Subsistence, Environment, and Social Change among the Choctaws, Pawnees, and Navajos* (Lincoln: Univ. of Nebraska Press, 1983), 251, Soil Conservation Service quoted on 251. See also Donald Parman, *The Navajos and the New Deal* (New Haven: Yale Univ. Press, 1976).

45. Collier, *Indians*, 156, 155.

46. Ibid., 159.

47. John Echohawk, conversation with the author, Aug. 5, 1986.

48. Larry W. Burt, *Tribalism in Crisis: Federal Indian Policy, 1953–1961* (Albuquerque: Univ. of New Mexico Press, 1982), 4–5.

49. Ibid., 5; House Concurrent Resolution 108 quoted in Nicholas Peroff, *Menominee Drums: Tribal Termination and Restoration, 1954–1974* (Norman: Univ. of Oklahoma Press, 1982), 16. Peroff is also the best source on Menominee termination.

50. Dippie's *Vanishing American* is a hypnotizing study of this idea.

51. Anna Dooling, "Painted Portraits of Indians," *BC*, Aug. 12, 1984.

52. Margarite Del Giudice, "High Court Nominee Queried, Praised by Senators," *BG*, Sept. 10, 1981.

53. Juan Nentuig quoted in Edward Spicer, *Cycles of Conquest: The Impact of Spain, Mexico, and the United States on the Indians of the Southwest, 1533–1960* (1962: Tucson: Univ. of Arizona Press, 1976), 322.

54. Frederick Merk, *History of the Westward Movement* (New York: Alfred A. Knopf, 1978), 9.

55. Roger Williams quoted in Robert Berkhofer, Jr., *The White Man's Indian: Images of the American Indian from Columbus to the Present* (New York: Random House, 1979), 15.

56. José del Carmen Lugo quoted in George Phillips, *Chiefs and Challengers: Indian Resistance and Cooperation in Southern California* (Berkeley: Univ. of California Press, 1975), 50.

57. Peter Nabokov, ed., *Two Leggings: The Making of a Crow Warrior* (Lincoln: Univ. of Nebraska Press, 1982), 36.

58. Thomas Dunlay, *Wolves for the Blue Soldiers: Indian Scouts and Auxiliaries with the United States Army, 1860–90* (Lincoln: Univ. of Nebraska Press, 1982), 2.

59. Phillips, *Chiefs and Challengers*, 174, 175.

60. David Beaulieu, ed., "Breaking Barriers: Perspectives on the Writing of Indian History" (Newberry Library Occasional Papers Series, no. 1, Chicago, 1978), 17, 18, 11.

61. Francis Jennings, "The Discovery of Americans," *William and Mary Quarterly* (July 1984), 441. See also Jennings, "The Newberry Library Center for the History of the American Indian: Its Impact on School and Community Constituencies," *AHA Perspectives*, April 1983, 20–21.

62. Thomas H. Leflorge, as told by Thomas B. Marquis, *Memoirs of a White Crow Indian* (1928; Lincoln: Univ. of Nebraska Press, 1974), 171.

63. Richard Erdoes and Alfonso Ortiz, eds., *American Indian Myths and Legends* (New York: Pantheon Books, 1984), 46–47.

Seven • **America the Borderland**

1. Cyclone Covey, ed. and trans., *Cabeza de Vaca's Adventures in the Unknown Interior of America* (New York: Collier Books, 1961), 123, 125, 127.

2. Herbert Bolton, *Coronado: Knight of Pueblos and Plains* (Albuquerque: Univ. of New Mexico Press, 1949).

3. John Francis Bannon, *The Spanish Borderlands Frontier, 1513–1821* (New York: Holt, Rinehart and Winston, 1970), chaps. 3, 5; Oakah L. Jones, Jr., *Los Paisanos: Spanish Settlers on the Northern Frontier of New Spain* (Norman: University of Oklahoma Press, 1979), xi, 3, 82, 109, 133–34. See also David Weber, ed., *New Spain's Far Northern Frontier: Essays on Spain in the American West, 1540–1821* (Albuquerque: Univ. of New Mexico Press, 1979).

4. Jones, *Paisanos*, 118; Alistair Hennessy, *The Frontier in Latin American History* (Albuquerque: Univ. of New Mexico Press, 1978), 19; Bannon, *Frontier*, chaps. 5, 8.

5. Bannon, *Frontier*, chaps. 6, 7, 8, 9.

6. Herbert I. Priestly, *José de Gálvez: Visitor General of New Spain* (Berkeley: Univ. of California Press, 1916).

7. Bannon, *Frontier*, 110–21.

8. Ibid., chap. 11; Arthur Preston Whitaker, *The Spanish-American Frontier, 1783–1795* (1927; Lincoln: Univ. of Nebraska Press, 1969).

9. Zebulon Pike, *The Expeditions of Zebulon Pike*, ed. Elliot Coues, 3 vols. (New York: F. P. Harper, 1895); Whitaker, *Frontier*, 96–152; Dan Flores, *Jefferson and Southwestern Exploration* (Norman: Univ. of Oklahoma Press, 1984), 77–83.

10. David J. Weber, *The Mexican Frontier, 1821–1846: The American Southwest under Mexico* (Albuquerque: Univ. of New Mexico Press, 1982).

11. Weber, *Frontier*, chap. 9; T. R. Fehrenbach, *Lone Star: A History of Texas and the Texans* (New York: Macmillan, 1968), 61–278.

12. Weber, *Frontier*, chap. 10, Alta California Legislature quoted on 255; Richard Griswold del Castillo, *The Los Angeles Barrio, 1850–1890: A Social History* (Berkeley: Univ. of California Press, 1979), 74–123.

13. Gene M. Brack, *Mexico Views Manifest Destiny, 1821–1846: An Essay on the Origins of the Mexican War* (Albuquerque: Univ. of New Mexico Press, 1975); Albert K. Weinberg, *Manifest Destiny: A Study of National Expansionism in American History* (Baltimore: Johns Hopkins Press, 1935); Frederick Merk, *Manifest Destiny and Mission in American History* (1963; New York: Alfred A. Knopf, 1966); Reginald Horsman, *Race and Manifest Destiny: The Origins of American Racial Anglo–Saxonism* (Cambridge: Harvard Univ. Press, 1981), chaps. 11–12.

14. K. Jack Bauer, *The Mexican War* (New York: Macmillan, 1974); Otis Singletary, *The Mexican War* (Chicago: Univ. of Chicago Press, 1960); Seymour V. Connor and Odie B. Faulk, *North America Divided: The Mexican War, 1846–1848* (New York: Oxford Univ. Press, 1971), 134.

15. See, for instance, William Stockton, "Mexico's Bad Image in the U.S., and Vice Versa," *NYT*, June 1, 1986.
16. John D. P. Fuller, *The Movement for the Acquisition of All Mexico* (New York: Da Capo Press, 1969).
17. John Russell Bartlett, *Personal Narrative of Explorations and Incidents Connected with the United States and Mexican Boundary Commission* (New York: D. Appleton, 1854); Odie B. Faulk, *Too Far North . . . Too Far South* (Los Angeles: Westernlore Press, 1967); Robert V. Hine, *Bartlett's West: Drawing the Mexican Boundary* (New Haven: Yale Univ. Press, 1968.)
18. Holman Hamilton, *Prologue to Conflict: The Crisis and Compromise of 1850* (New York: W. W. Norton, 1966); David Potter, *The Impending Crisis, 1848–1861* (New York: Harper & Row, 1976), chaps. 4–5.
19. Ralph A. Smith, "The Scalp Hunter in the Borderlands, 1835–1850," *Arizona and the West* (Spring 1964): 5–22, and "The Scalp Hunt in Chihuahua—1849," *New Mexico Historical Review* (April 1965): 117–140.
20. Frank McNitt, *Navajo Wars: Military Campaigns, Slave Raids, and Reprisals* (Albuquerque: Univ. of New Mexico Press, 1972), 97, 118–19; Donald Worcester, *The Apaches: Eagles of the Southwest* (Norman: Univ. of Oklahoma Press, 1979), 36–50, 56, 59.
21. Treaty reprinted in David Weber, ed., *Foreigners in Their Native Land: Historical Roots of the Mexican Americans* (Albuquerque: Univ. of New Mexico Press, 1973), 162–68; Victor Westphall, *Mercedes Reales: Hispanic Land Grants of the Upper Rio Grande Region* (Albuquerque: Univ. of New Mexico Press, 1983), chap. 4.
22. Deena Gonzáles, "The Spanish–Mexican Women of Santa Fé: Patterns of Their Resistance and Accommodation, 1820–1880" (Ph.D. diss., Univ. of California at Berkeley, 1985), 2, 121, 129, 50.
23. Howard R. Lamar, *The Far Southwest, 1846–1912: A Territorial History* (1966; New York: W. W. Norton, 1970), 135, 149.
24. Westphall, *Mercedes*, 234, 235; Victor Westphall, *Thomas Benton Catron and His Era* (Tucson: Univ. of Arizona Press, 1973), 34, 73, Catron quoted on 149.
25. Mario Barrera, *Race and Class in the Southwest: A Theory of Racial Inequality* (Notre Dame: Univ. of Notre Dame Press, 1979), 22, 20.
26. Leonard Pitt, *The Decline of the Californios: A Social History of the Spanish-Speaking Californians, 1846–1890* (Berkeley: Univ. of California Press, 1971), 60–61.

27. Pitt, *Decline,* 43, 45, 202.
28. Del Castillo, *Los Angeles Barrio,* 115–16; Lamar, *Far Southwest,* 27–28, 105, 108, 115, 131; Rodolfo Acuña, *Occupied America: A History of Chicanos,* 2d ed. (New York: Harper & Row, 1981), 1, 48–49, 54, 69, 78–79, 103–5.
29. Albert Camarillo, *Chicanos in a Changing Society: From Mexican Pueblos to American Barrios in Santa Barbara and Southern California, 1848–1930* (Cambridge: Harvard Univ. Press, 1979); del Castillo, *Los Angeles Barrio;* Mario T. García, *Desert Immigrants: The Mexicans of El Paso, 1880–1920* (New Haven: Yale Univ. Press, 1981); Arnoldo de León, *The Tejano Community, 1836–1900* (Albuquerque: Univ. of New Mexico Press, 1982), Ricardo Romo, *East Los Angeles: A History of a Barrio* (Austin: Univ. of Texas Press, 1983).
30. Richard Henry Dana, *Two Years before the Mast* (1840; New York: New American Library, 1964), 163.
31. Francis Parkman, *The Oregon Trail* (1849; New York: New American Library, 1978), 14, 230; Pitt, *Decline,* 45–82.
32. Clarence King, *Mountaineering in the Sierra Nevada* (1872; Lincoln: Univ. of Nebraska Press, 1970), 113; see also Arnoldo De León, *They Called Them Greasers: Anglo Attitudes toward Mexicans in Texas, 1821–1900* (Austin: Univ. of Texas Press, 1983).
33. Pitt, *Decline,* 148–66; De León, *Greasers,* chaps. 7–8; Julian Samora, Joe Bernal, and Albert Peña, *Gunpowder Justice: A Reassessment of the Texas Rangers* (Notre Dame: Univ. of Notre Dame Press, 1979).
34. Charles H. Brown, *Agents of Manifest Destiny: The Lives and Times of the Filibusters* (Chapel Hill: Univ. of North Carolina Press, 1980), chaps. 8–9, esp. 174, Walker quoted on 195, 200.
35. Thomas Foster quoted ibid., 207–8.
36. Ibid., chaps. 11–17, esp. 281.
37. Acuña, *Occupied America,* chaps. 6–8; García, *Desert Immigrants,* chaps. 2–3; Mark Reisler, *By the Sweat of Their Brow: Mexican Immigrant Labor in the United States, 1900–1940* (Westport, Conn.: Greenwood, 1976); George C. Kiser and Martha Kiser Woody, eds., *Mexican Workers in the United States: Historical and Political Perspectives* (Albuquerque: Univ. of New Mexico Press, 1979); Lawrence A. Cardoso, *Mexican Emigration to United States, 1897–1931* (Tucson: Univ. of Arizona Press, 1980).
38. Manuel Gamio, comp. and ed., *The Life Story of the Mexican Immigrant* (1931; New York: Dover, 1971), 65.
39. Ibid., 49, 91, 139, 269.

40. Ibid., 44, 172; del Castillo, *Los Angeles Barrio*, 11, 25.
41. Reisler, *Sweat of Their Brow*, James J. Davis quoted on 69, Frederick Simpich quoted on 127, Harry Laughlin quoted on 155, Glen E. Hoover quoted on 133.
42. Ibid., 266, James J. Davis quoted on 137.
43. Texas farmer quoted ibid., 140.
44. Albert Johnson and Albert Bushnell Hart quoted ibid., 154, unnamed superintendent of schools in Colorado, quoted on 164.
45. Ibid., 174–83.
46. Ibid., 128.
47. Ibid., 213.
48. See, for instance, Julian Samora, *Los Mojados: The Wetback Story* (Notre Dame: Univ. of Notre Dame Press, 1971).
49. Abraham Hoffman, *Unwanted Mexican Americans in the Great Depression: Repatriation Pressures, 1929–1939* (Tucson: Univ. of Arizona Press, 1974); Juan Ramon García, *Operation Wetback: The Mass Deportation of Undocumented Workers in 1954* (Westport, Conn.: Greenwood, 1980), 23, 44, 198, Joseph Swing quoted on 225.
50. W. Dirk Raat, *Revoltosos: Mexico's Rebels in the United States* (College Station: Texas A&M Press, 1981); Oscar Martínez, *Fragments of the Mexican Revolution: Personal Accounts from the Border* (Albuquerque: Univ. of New Mexico Press, 1983).
51. Clarence Clendenon, *Pancho Villa and the United States: A Study in Unconventional Diplomacy* (Ithaca: Cornell Univ. Press, 1961); Clarence Clendenon, *Blood on the Border: The United States Army and the Mexican Irregulars* (London: Collier-Macmillan, 1969).
52. Romo, *East Los Angeles*, 101, *Los Angeles Times* quoted on 96, 106.

53. Gamio, *Immigrant*, 173; Westphall, *Mercedes*, 273; Armando B. Rendon, *Chicano Manifesto* (New York: Macmillan, 1971), chap. 6.
54. *Gaceta Diaria de Mexico* quoted in Weber, *Frontier*, 207.
55. Earl Pomeroy, "Toward a Reorientation of Western History: Continuity and Environment," *Mississippi Valley Historical Review* (March 1955): 590.
56. Romo, *East Los Angeles*, 12.
57. Carey McWilliams, *North from Mexico: The Spanish-Speaking People of the United States* (1949; New York: Greenwood, 1968), 35–47, 19.
58. Sherburne F. Cook, *The Conflict between the California Indian and White Civilization* (1943; Berkeley: Univ. of California Press, 1976), pt. 1, pp. 62, 30, 33.
59. Ibid., pt. 3, pp. 56–60.
60. Samora, Bernal, and Peña, *Gunpowder Justice*, 1, 2; Walter Prescott Webb, *The Texas Rangers: A Century of Frontier Defense* (1935; Austin: Univ. of Texas Press, 1965), v.
61. Nixon quoted in Samora, Bernal, and Peña, *Gunpowder Justice*, 5.
62. Américo Paredes, *With His Pistol in His Hand: A Border Ballad and Its Hero* (1958; Austin: Univ. of Texas Press, 1982), 24; Samora, Bernal, and Peña, *Gunpowder Justice*, 91, 131.
63. Samora, Bernal, and Peña, *Gunpowder Justice*, 42; George Sanchez, personal correspondence with author, April 2, 1986. See also John R. Chávez, *The Lost Land: The Chicano Image of the Southwest* (Albuquerque: Univ. of New Mexico Press, 1984).

Eight · **Racialism on the Run**

1. Don Schellie, *Vast Domain of Blood: The Story of the Camp Grant Massacre* (Los Angeles: Westernlore Press, 1968).
2. Murray's opinion reprinted in Cheng-Tsu Wu, *Chink! A Documentary History of Anti-Chinese Prejudice in America* (New York: World, 1972), 37, 38.
3. Ibid., 40, 41.
4. Ibid., 42.
5. Isaac Kalloch quoted in Alexander Saxton, *The Indispensable Enemy: Labor and the Anti-Chinese Movement in California* (1971; Berkeley: Univ. of California Press, 1975), 139–40.
6. Ibid., 258.

7. Ibid., 139, California constitution of 1879 quoted on 128; Mary Roberts Coolidge, *Chinese Immigration* (New York: H. Holt, 1909), 120.
8. *Manifesto* of Workingmen's Party, quoted in Coolidge, *Immigration*, 109; Mrs. Ana Smith quoted in Victor and Brett de Bary Nee, *Longtime Californ': A Documentary Study of an American Chinatown* (1973; Boston: Houghton Mifflin, 1974), 53.
9. Stuart Creighton Miller, *The Unwelcome Immigrant: The American Image of the Chinese* (1969; Berkeley: Univ. of California Press, 1974), 191.
10. Leland Stanford quoted in Saxton, *En-*

emy, 62, James Strobridge quoted on 65; Charles Crocker quoted in Nee, *Californ';* 50, San Jose Woolen Mills president quoted on 45.

11. H. Brett Melendy, *The Oriental Americans* (New York: Twayne, 1972), 40–41.

12. Gunther Barth, *Bitter Strength: A History of the Chinese in the United States, 1850–1870* (Cambridge: Harvard Univ. Press, 1964), 157, 158.

13. Ibid., 158.

14. Ibid., 161, *Alta California* quoted on 161–62.

15. Report to the State Senate of the Special Committee on Chinese Immigration quoted in Coolidge, *Immigration*, 87.

16. Governor Henry Haight quoted in Wu, *Chink!*, 112.

17. Frank M. Pixley quoted in Coolidge, *Immigration*, 96.

18. James Duvall Phelan quoted in Roger Daniels, *The Politics of Prejudice: The Anti-Japanese Movement in California and the Struggle for Japanese Exclusion* (1962; Berkeley: Univ. of California Press, 1977), 21.

19. Speech from Chinese Exclusion Convention, quoted ibid., 23, Richard Pearson Hobson quoted on 71.

20. Western congressmen quoted in Roger Daniels, *Concentration Camps: North America: Japanese in the United States and Canada during World War II* (Malabar, Fla.: Robert E. Krieger, 1981), 19.

21. *San Francisco Chronicle* quoted ibid., 11, *San Francisco Examiner* quoted on 30; Asiatic Exclusion League quoted in Robert F. Heizer and Alan F. Almquist, *The Other Californians: Prejudice and Discrimination under Spain, Mexico, and the United States to 1920* (Berkeley: Univ. of California Press, 1971), 189–90; Daniels, *Politics*, 77; Daniels, *Camps*, 32.

22. C. O. Young quoted in Daniels, *Politics*, 16, *Grizzly Bear* quoted on 85.

23. *Grizzly Bear* quoted ibid., 85; Asiatic Exclusion League quoted in Heizer and Almquist, *Other Californians*, 191; Asiatic Exclusion League speaker quoted in Daniels, *Politics*, 28, Ralph Newman quoted on 59.

24. Daniels, *Camps*, 7.

25. Melendy, *Oriental Americans*, 112; *Campanile Review* quoted in Daniels, *Camps*, 26.

26. Headlines from *LAT* quoted in Daniels, *Camps*, 33–34, Earl Warren quoted on 76.

27. Mike Masaoka, JACL creed, quoted ibid., 24–25.

28. John DeWitt quoted ibid., 54; DeWitt quoted in Jacobus ten Broek, Edward N. Barnhart, and Floyd W. Matson, *Prejudice, War and the Constitution: Causes and Consequences of the Evacuation of the Japanese-Americans in World War Two* (1954; Berkeley: Univ. of California Press, 1975), 110; DeWitt quoted in Daniels, *Camps*, 51.

29. Ed Ainsworth quoted in Daniels, *Camps*, 33.

30. Milton S. Eisenhower quoted in ten Broek, Barnhart, and Matson, *Prejudice*, 123; Governor Nels Smith of Wyoming quoted in Daniels, *Camps*, 94.

31. Governor Herbert B. Maw of Utah quoted in Daniels, *Camps*, 94.

32. Ten Broek, Barnhart, and Matson, *Prejudice*, 220; Justice William O. Douglas quoted in Daniels, *Camps*, 134, Justice Hugo Black quoted on 137–39.

33. Justice Frank Murphy, quoted in Daniels, *Camps*, 140.

34. Elizabeth McLagan, *A Peculiar Paradise: A History of Blacks in Oregon, 1788–1940* (Portland: Gregorian Press, 1980), 57, Peter Burnett quoted on 29.

35. Samuel Thurston quoted ibid., 30–31.

36. *Oregon Statesman* quoted ibid., 69; Eugene H. Berwanger, *The West and Reconstruction* (Urbana: Univ. of Illinois Press, 1981), 180.

37. McLagan, *Paradise*, 79; Elmer R. Rusco, *"Good Time Coming?" Black Nevadans in the Nineteenth Century* (Westport, Conn.: Greenwood, 1975), 208, Police Chief R. C. Leeper quoted on 208.

38. Leonard Arrington and Davis Bitton, *The Mormon Experience: A History of the Latter-Day Saints* (New York: Vintage Books, 1980), 45.

39. Joseph Smith in William Mulder and A. Russell Mortensen, eds., *Among the Mormons: Historical Accounts by Contemporary Observers* (1958; Lincoln: Univ. of Nebraska Press, 1973), 11.

40. Ibid., 15.

41. Brigham Young, Heber C. Kimball, and William Richards, quoted ibid., 232.

42. Perry Brocchus quoted ibid., 250, 251, W. W. Drummond quoted on 293–95.

43. Howard Stansbury quoted ibid., 249, Brigham Young quoted on 297.

44. John M. Coyner quoted ibid., 406.

45. Elizabeth Cumming quoted ibid., 314, Mrs. Benjamin Ferris quoted on 265, Samuel Bowles quoted on 361–64.

46. John M. Coyner quoted ibid., 407–8.

47. Wilford Woodruff quoted ibid., 417.

48. Horace Greeley and Brigham Young quoted ibid., 325.

49. Ibid., 418, Charles S. Varian quoted on 419.

50. Horace Greeley quoted ibid., 327, Brigham Young on 325, Charles S. Varian on 419.

51. Laurence Veysey, ed., *Law and Resistance: American Attitudes toward Authority* (New

York: Harper & Row, 1970), 208, *San Diego Sun* quoted on 214–15.

52. Graham Adams, *The Age of Industrial Violence, 1910–1915: The Activities and Findings of the United States Commission on Industrial Relations* (New York: Columbia Univ. Press, 1966), 146.

53. Patrick Renshaw, *The Wobblies: The Story of Syndicalism in the United States* (Garden City, N.Y.: Doubleday, 1968), 94.

54. Ray Allen Billington, *The Far Western Frontier, 1830–1860* (1956; New York: Harper & Row, 1962), 238.

Nine · Mankind the Manager

1. Gifford Pinchot, *Breaking New Ground* (New York: Harcourt, Brace, 1947), 42.
2. Ibid., 103.
3. Ibid., 2, 1.
4. Ibid., 1, 23, 24.
5. Ibid., 29, 30, 31.
6. Ibid., 163.
7. Ibid., 145, 318.
8. Theodore Roosevelt, *An Autobiography* (New York: Scribner, 1929), 394.
9. Pinchot, *Breaking New Ground*, 31, 32, 29.
10. Ibid., 259, 152.
11. Gifford Pinchot, *The Fight for Conservation* (1910; Seattle: Univ. of Washington Press, 1973), 49.
12. Ibid., 88. On the elitism of conservation management, see Samuel P. Hays, *Conservation and the Gospel of Efficiency: The Progressive Conservation Movement, 1890–1920* (1959; New York; Atheneum, 1974).
13. Pinchot, *Breaking New Ground*, 132, 177–81.
14. Philip Shabecoff, "Dispute Flares over Harvest of Pristine Natural Forests," *NYT*, Jan. 12, 1985.
15. The National Forest Multiple Purpose and Sustained Yield Act quoted in William K. Wyant, *Westward in Eden: The Public Lands Conservation Movement* (Berkeley: Univ. of California Press, 1982), 280.
16. T. R. Reid, "Guerrilla War for the Wilderness," *WP*, Nov. 25, 1984; John Aloysius Farrell, "Timber Harvest Plans May Hurt State's Tourism," *DP*, Dec. 23, 1984, and "Logging Plan Fuels Western Rebellion," *DP*, Dec. 24, 1984; Gary Blonston (Knight-Ridder News Service), "Ecology Activists, Conservatives Join to Challenge Forest Policies," *DP*, Jan. 13, 1985; T. R. Reid, "Forest Service to Revise Timber Sales: Agriculture Wants Money-Losing Practices Reexamined," *WP*, Aug. 8, 1985.
17. Daniel P. Jones, "Critics Claim Logging Roads Spoiling Forests," *DP*, Oct. 21, 1984; Iver Peterson, "50-Year Plan for Forests Renews Debate on Use," *NYT*, April 16, 1986.

18. Shabecoff, "Dispute Flares," *NYT*, Jan. 12, 1985.
19. Nancy Lofholm, "Aspens in Preservation Tug of War," *DP*, July 22, 1984; Gary Schmitz, "Aspen Clear-Cutting Plan Raises Hopes, Stirs Fears," *DP*, Oct. 1, 1984; "Beetles Overrun Forests," *DP*, Aug. 22, 1984; "Pest Issue 'Politics' Worrying Foresters," *DP*, Aug. 26, 1984, and "Politics of Pine Beetle Eradication Worrying Foresters," *DP*, Aug. 27, 1984; Daniel P. Jones, "Forest Chief Fulfills Reagan Pledge," *DP*, Oct. 21, 1984.
20. Pinchot, *Fight for Conservation*, 44–45.
21. Gary Schmitz, "5,000 Fail to Subdue Major Montana Blazes," *DP*, Aug. 30, 1984; Jim Robbins, "Rains Give Firefighters an Edge," *DP*, Sept. 1, 1984; Andrew Malcolm, "Contained Montana Fire Leaves an Eerie World," *NYT*, Sept. 2, 1984.
22. Schmitz, "5,000 Fail," *DP*, Aug. 30, 1984.
23. T. R. Reid, "Smokey Bear Up in Smoke?" *WP*, Sept. 5, 1984; (AP), "Burned-Out Residents Try to Save Belongings," *DP*, Aug. 30, 1984.
24. Gerald P. Carinen, Robert M. Warner, and John E. Byrne, *United States Government Manual, 1983–4* (Washington, D.C.: Office of the Federal Register, 1983), 321.
25. Alfred Runte, *National Parks: The American Experience* (Lincoln: Univ. of Nebraska Press, 1979), chap. 3.
26. National Park Service Act quoted ibid., 104.
27. Roderick Nash, *Wilderness and the American Mind*, 3d ed. (New Haven: Yale Univ. Press, 1982), 316.
28. Wilderness Act quoted in Wyant, *Westward in Eden*, 283.
29. Jim Robbins, "Coalition Says Yellowstone Needs Elbow Room," *NYT*, Oct. 21, 1984, and "Six-Million-Acre Buffer Zone Pushed for Yellowstone," *DP*, June 9, 1985; T. R. Reid, "Yellowstone Has to Be Bigger: America's Only Whole Ecosystem Can't Survive without Growing," *WP*, June 23, 1985; Gary Schmitz, "Yellowstone's Boundaries, Nature's Needs at Odds?" *DP*, Dec. 1, 1985.

30. John C. Frémont, *The Expeditions of John Charles Frémont*, ed. Donald Jackson and Mary Lee Spence, vol. I (Urbana: Univ. of Illinois Press, 1970), 191.

31. James B. Trefethen, *An American Crusade for Wildlife* (New York: Winchester Press, 1975), chap. 6.

32. Douglas H. Chadwick, *A Beast the Color of Winter: The Mountain Goat Observed* (San Francisco: Sierra Club Books, 1983), 164–73.

33. Joanne Ditmer, "Crowding Out the Deer and the Elk: Wildlife Losing More Ground to Developers," *DP*, Feb. 3, 1985; Linda Cornett, "Boulder Eyes 'Defenses' against Deer," *BC*, Feb. 6, 1985; William Schmidt, "Deer Making a Meal of Boulder, Colorado," *NYT*, April 7, 1985; Jack Kisling, "Home on the Urban Range," *DP*, July 8, 1985.

32. Jim Robbins, "Donations Feed Starving Wildlife," *BG*, Feb. 20, 1984.

35. Jim Robbins, "Yellowstone Buffalo Said to Threaten Cattle," *BG*, March 19, 1984, "After a 100-Year Hiatus, Bison-Hunting Season Is Set to Begin," *NYT*, Nov. 11, 1985, "Mood Uneasy As Bison at Yellowstone Hunted," *DP*, Dec. 31, 1985, and "Buffalo Slayings Outside of Park Stir 3-Way Fight," *DP*, Feb. 24, 1986.

36. Frank C. Craighead, Jr., *The Track of the Grizzly* (San Francisco: Sierra Club Books, 1979); Thomas McNamee, *The Grizzly Bear* (New York: Alfred A. Knopf, 1984); Jim Robbins, "Do Not Feed the Bears?" *Natural History*, Jan. 1984, 12–21; Alston Chase, "The Last Bears of Yellowstone," *Atlantic*, Feb. 1983, 63–73, "The Grizzly and the Juggernaut," *Outside*, Jan. 1986, 29–34, 55–63, and *Playing God in Yellowstone* (Boston: Atlantic Monthly Press, 1986).

37. (UPI), "Problem Grizzlies Can Be Taught to Behave, Expert Says," *DP*, Jan. 20, 1985; Iver Peterson, "Rocky Mountain Journal: Three Quarrels: TV, Peace and Bears," *NYT*, July 1, 1985; Jim Robbins, "Bugging a Bear: Montana Scientists Seek to Restore Fear of Man to Reduce Park Attacks," *DP*, July 7, 1985; David McQuay, "No One Seems to Know What We Should Do about the Grizzlies," *DP*, April 9, 1986.

38. Charles Rosenfield and Robert Cooke, *Earthfire: The Eruption of Mount St. Helens* (Cambridge: MIT Press, 1982); Stephen L. Harris, "Volcanic Hazards in the West: Vulcan Stokes His Fires for Future Spectaculars," *American West*, Nov. / Dec. 1983, 30–39; (AP), "Mount St. Helens Remains Dynamite Keg with Unpredictable Fuse," *DP*, March 24, 1985; Rick Sylvain (Knight-Ridder News Service), "Mount St. Helens Left Slow-Healing Scars," *DP*, June 9, 1985; Lee Siegel (AP), "California Preparing for Great Los Angeles Quake," *DP*, Aug. 24, 1984; Robert Lindsey, "Little by Little, California Prepares for the Big One," *NYT*, Sept. 2, 1984; (UPI), "San Francisco on Shaky Ground for Inevitable Big Quake," *DP*, April 13, 1986; Robert Lindsey, "San Francisco Battles Torpor on Quake Planning," *NYT*, April 16, 1986.

39. Paul Bonnifield, *The Dust Bowl: Men, Dirt, and Depression* (Albuquerque: Univ. of New Mexico Press, 1979); Donald Worster, *Dust Bowl* (New York: Oxford Univ. Press, 1979).

40. Hays, *Conservation and the Gospel of Efficiency;* Lawrence B. Lee, *Reclaiming the American West: An Historiography and a Guide* (Santa Barbara: ABC Clio, 1980); Donald Worster, *Rivers of Empire: Water, Aridity, and the Growth of the American West* (New York: Pantheon Books, 1986).

41. David Boyles, "Businesses on River Sharply Critical of Flood Management," *RP-E*, Sept. 8, 1983; William Schmidt, "Floods along Colorado River Set Off a Debate over Blame," *NYT*, July 17, 1983.

Ten · **The Burdens of Western American History**

1. Frederick Paxson, *When the West Is Gone* (New York: Henry Holt, 1930), 5.

2. John F. Kennedy in Maxwell Meyerson, ed., *Memorable Quotations of John F. Kennedy,* (New York: Thomas Y. Crowell, 1965), 275, 276.

3. "Transcript of Second Inaugural Address by Reagan," *NYT*, Jan. 22, 1985.

4. "Mormons and the Mark of Cain," *Time*, Jan. 19, 1970, 46; "Second-Class Mormons," *Newsweek*, Jan. 19, 1970, 84; James T. Tinney and Edward Plowman, "Message to Mormons: Open the Gates," *Christianity Today*, Nov. 22, 1974; Lowry Nelson, "Mormons and Blacks," *Christian Century*, Oct. 16, 1974, 949–50; "Mormon Utah: Where a Church Shapes the Life of a State," *USNWR*, Dec. 19, 1977.

5. "Race Revelations," *Newsweek*, June 19, 1978, 67; Jan Shipps, "The Mormons:

Looking Forward and Outward," *Christian Century*, Aug. 16–23, 1978; Robert Lindsey, "The Mormons: Growth, Prosperity and Controversy," *NYT Magazine*, Jan. 12, 1986, 19.

6. "Race Revelations," *Newsweek*, June 19, 1978, 67; "Mormon Utah," *USNWR*, Dec. 19, 1977, 61.

7. "Can a Mormon Support the ERA?" *Newsweek*, Dec. 3, 1979, 88.

8. *(LAT)*, "Founder's Letter Suggests Mormon Origins Tied to Magical Lore," *DP*, May 11, 1985; Marjorie Hyer, "Mormon Church Stirred by Founder's Letter," *WP*, May 11, 1985; "Text of an 1830 Letter on the Origins of the Mormon Church," *NYT*, Oct. 18, 1985; (AP), "Dealer in Rare Mormon Documents Charged in 2 Utah Killings," *NYT*, Feb. 5, 1986.

9. "Mormon Writings Traced to Texas: Investigators Seeking Clues to Fatal Bombings in Utah," *NYT*, Dec. 3, 1985; (AP), "Mormon Papers, Dealer Face First Test at Murder Hearing," *DP*, April 13, 1986; "Utah Bombings Kill Executive, Associate's Wife," *DP*, Oct. 16, 1985.

10. Iver Peterson, "Mormon Puzzle: Bombs and Documents," *NYT*, Nov. 6, 1985, and "Police Name 2nd Suspect in Salt Lake Bombings," *NYT*, Oct. 20, 1985; (Religious News Service), "Mormons Told Not to Criticize," *DP*, Oct. 11, 1985; "Apostles vs. Historians," *Newsweek*, Feb. 15, 1982, 77; Lindsey, "Mormons," *NYT Magazine*, Jan. 12, 1986, 21.

11. Shipps, "The Mormons," *Christian Century*, Aug. 16–23, 1978, 764; "Validity of Utah's Ban on Polygamy Affirmed," *NYT*, April 29, 1984; (AP), "Polygamist Argues Religious Freedom Violated," *DP*, March 11, 1985, and "Polygamist Cop to Fight Firing in Supreme Court," *DP*, May 3, 1985.

12. "Mormon Church Faces a Fresh Challenge," *USNWR*, Nov. 21, 1983, 61–62; William N. Oleson, "Not the Same as Christianity," *BC*, Feb. 6, 1986; R. P. Woolley, "Mormons Not Christians," *BC*, Jan. 31, 1986; (AP), "Group Denies Vail Mormons Access to Interfaith Chapel," *BC*, Aug. 31, 1985.

13. Dana Parsons, "Protestant, Catholic Clergy Wary of Mormon Invitation," *DP*, March 18, 1986.

14. "Mormons Told," *DP*, Oct. 11, 1985; Lindsey, "Mormons," *NYT Magazine*, Jan. 12, 1986, 40, 42.

15. Howard LaFranchi, "States vs. Indian Bingo: Tribes Set Up Gambling Operations to Replace Federal Funding; States Want to Tax Proceeds," *CSM*, Feb. 24, 1986; *(Dallas Morning News)*, "Creek Indians in Oklahoma Strike Gold, Controversy with Bingo," *DP*, April 20, 1986; Stephen Magagnini, "Indian Bingo: New Hot Spot in the Desert," *BG*, Dec. 6, 1983; T. R. Reid, "Indians Play a New Card," *WP*, Oct. 27, 1984; Iver Peterson, "Bingo That Doesn't Get Any Bigger," *NYT*, Nov. 3, 1985.

16. Iver Peterson, "Rights Reserved for the Reservation," *NYT*, Feb. 2, 1986; Robert Emmitt and Vicki Groninger, " 'The Indians Are Winning': An Interview with John Echohawk," *BC Sunday Magazine*, July 22, 1984, 6–11, 14–15; Charles Wilkinson, "The Quest to Enforce Old Promises: Indian Law in the Modern Era," *Native American Rights Fund Legal Review*, Special 15th Anniversary Edition, Summer 1985, 5–22; Imre Sutton, ed., *Irredeemable America: The Indians' Estate and Land Claims* (Albuquerque: Univ. of New Mexico Press, 1985).

17. Alvin Josephy, Jr., *Now That the Buffalo's Gone: A Study of Today's Indians* (New York: Alfred A. Knopf, 1982), chap. 6, quotation from treaties on 182.

18. Ibid., 197.

19. Ibid., 206, 209.

20. Transcript of "Salmon on the Run," Jan. 10, 1982, "Nova," Public Broadcasting System, pp. 8, 1; Echohawk, quoted in Peterson, "Rights," *NYT*, Feb. 2, 1986.

21. "$105 Million Award to Sioux Is Upheld: Court Holds U.S. Liable for Interest on $17.5 Million for Lost Land," *NYT*, July 1, 1980; Vine Deloria, Jr., "Like the Victory over Custer, the Sioux's Legal Win Can Mean Defeat," *LAT*, July 6, 1980; Molly Ivins, "Sioux Face Complex Decisions in Accepting $122 Million Award," *NYT*, July 14, 1980; Marc Goldstein, "Sioux Agonize over Taking Money or Regaining Black Hills," *NYT*, July 16, 1984.

22. "Watt Sees Reservations as Failures of Socialilsm," *NYT*, Jan. 19, 1983.

23. Iver Peterson, "Indians Resist Shift in Economic Goals Urged by U.S. Panel," *NYT*, Jan. 13, 1985, and "Bringing Decentralization to the Reservation," *NYT*, Oct. 30, 1983.

24. Hazel W. Hertzberg, "Reaganomics on the Reservation," *New Republic*, Nov. 22, 1982, 15–18; William Schmidt, "Economy Carves Trail of Tears for Tribe," *NYT*, Jan. 31, 1983; John Aloysius Farrell, "The New Indian Wars," series in *DP*, Nov. 20–27, 1983; Benjamin Weiser, "Inside a Sioux Reservation: Villages of Despair," *WP*, Sept. 9, 1984.

25. Lee May, "American Indians Found Three Times More Likely to Die Young," *LAT*, May 1, 1986; (AP), "U.S. Indians' Health Lags Despite Advances," *NYT*, May 4, 1986;

Iver Peterson, "Surge in Indians' Diabetes Linked to Their History," *NYT*, Feb. 18, 1986.

26. Spencer Rich, "HHS Proposes to Curb Indian Health Benefits," *WP*, June 29, 1986.

27. (AP), "Apaches End Leases and a Resort is Fading," *NYT*, June 12, 1984; William E. Schmidt, "Many Victims, No Villains in Indian Land Dispute," *NYT*, July 15, 1985.

28. " 'We Are Overwhelmed': With Illegal Immigration Rising, Congress Belatedly Tries to Act," *Time*, June 25, 1984, 16–17; Philip Shenon, " 'Startling' Surge Is Reported in Illegal Aliens from Mexico," *NYT*, Feb. 21, 1986; Joel Brinkley, "U.S. Set to Act on Mexico Border Drug Flow," *NYT*, June 26, 1986; Richard J. Meislin, "To Mexicans, Law on Aliens Is Cruel Joke," *NYT*, June 24, 1984; Mary Ann Sieghart, "Border Game: Illegals Get Sent Back to 'Go,' " *WP*, Sept. 4, 1984.

29. Shenon, " 'Startling' Surge," *NYT*, Feb. 21, 1986; Mary Thornton, "Rio Grande: Refuge Line for Drug-Moving Army," *WP*, April 21, 1986; Scott Armstrong, "Drug Smugglers Shift to Southwestern Border: Surge in Heroin Traffic Linked to Flagging Mexican Economy," *CSM*, Jan. 23, 1986.

30. Brinkley, "U.S. Set to Act," *NYT*, June 26, 1986.

31. " 'Overwhelmed,' " *Time*, June 25, 1984; William Stockton, "Rural Mexico Sees the U.S. as a Magnet," *NYT*, May 18, 1986; Richard J. Meislin, "Fear and Skepticism across the Border," *NYT*, July 1, 1984; Jim Robbins, "Fighting Flow of Illegal Aliens," *BG*, April 15, 1984.

32. Robbins, "Fighting Flow," *BG*, April 15, 1984; Robert Lindsey, "Illegal Entry by Non-Mexicans on Rise at Border," *NYT*, Oct. 7, 1985; Jules Loh, "Many Nations Fuel Surge of Illegal Entrants to U.S.," *DP*, Dec. 8, 1985; Scott Armstrong, "Violence Surges with Alien Influx," *CSM*, March 12, 1986; Jack Kisling and Judith Gaines, "Immigration Bill Ruse Bilks Aliens," *DP*, Aug. 12, 1984.

33. Meislin, "Fear and Skepticism," *NYT*, July 1, 1984.

34. (AP), " 'Tenement Trail' Mires Hispanics: California Benefits from Cheap Labor," *DP*, Dec. 10, 1985; Judith Cummings, "Study Hails Effect of Mexicans on California," *NYT*, Dec. 10, 1985; John Dillin, "Leaked White House Report Adds Fuel to New Immigration Debate," *CSM*, Jan. 24, 1986; *(WP)*, "Illegal Aliens Sap U.S., Study Says: Americans Lose Jobs, Taxpayers' Costs Put at $7 Billion a Year," *DP*, April 20, 1985; John Crewdson, *The Tarnished Door: The New Immigrants and the Transformation of America* (New York: Times Books, 1983); James Fallows, "Immigration: How It's Affecting Us," *Atlantic*, Nov. 1985, 45–106. To sample the vast split in opinion on this matter, compare Richard D. Lamm and Gary Imhoff, *The Immigration Time Bomb: The Fragmenting of America* (New York: E. P. Dutton, 1985), and James D. Cockcroft, *Outlaws in the Promised Land: Mexican Immigrant Workers and America's Future* (New York: Grove Press, 1986).

35. Eliason quoted in " 'Overwhelmed,' " *Time*, June 25, 1984, 16; Alan E. Eliason, "One Illegal Alien Every 35 Seconds" (letter to editor), *NYT*, April 29, 1986; Peter Applebome, "Aliens and Poverty Lay Heavy Burden on Hospital in El Paso," *NYT*, March 22, 1986.

36. Robert Pear, "Sweet Land of Multiple Visions," *NYT*, Sept. 28, 1985, and "Senate Will Get Immigration Bill," *NYT*, April 18, 1985.

37. Robert Pear, "Immigration Bill Is Hardly Home Free," *NYT*, April 8, 1984; Steven V. Roberts, "Roybal Digs in His Heels on Immigration," *NYT*, June 10, 1984; Robert Pear, "Immigration Bill: How 'Corpse' Came Back to Life," *NYTNE*, Oct. 13, 1986, and "President Signs Landmark Bill on Immigration," *NYTNE*, Nov. 7, 1986.

38. Robert Pear, "Immigration Bill Approved: Bars Hiring Illegal Aliens, But Gives Millions Amnesty," *NYTNE*, Oct. 18, 1986; Robert Reinhold, "Legal Aliens Criticize Status under New Law," *NYTNE*, Nov. 8, 1986.

39. Jeffrey Leib, "Employers Bear Brunt of Immigration Bill: Act an Admission of Defeat by Government, Experts Say," *DP*, Oct. 27, 1986; John Dillin, "Immigration Bill on Move: But Neither Friend Nor Foe Likes the Compromise," *CSM*, Oct. 16, 1986; Robert Reinhold, "Surge in Bogus Papers Predicted in Wake of Change in Alien Law," *NYTNE*, Oct. 20, 1986.

40. Robert Reinhold, "Woven in Illegally, They're Part of America's Fabric," *NYTNE*, Oct. 12, 1986; Peter Applebome, "Border People Doubt Bill Will Slow Alien Flow," *NYTNE*, Oct. 29, 1986; William Stockton, "Mexicans Expecting No Good of Immigration Law," *NYTNE*, Nov. 6, 1986.

41. Robert Pear, "Immigration Bill Weighed in Senate," *NYT*, Sept. 12, 1985; James L. Rowe, Jr., "Mexico Again on the Brink in Debt Crisis," *WP*, June 8, 1986; Peter G. Chronis, "Trouble South of the Border: Mexico's Plan for $60 Oil Led to Economic Disaster," *DP*, June 29, 1986.

42. Carl J. Migdail, "Mexico and the US: A Case for Interdependence" (editorial), *CSM*, March 5, 1986; Alfred Stepan, "Mexico Deserves Full U.S. Attention" (editorial), *NYT*, June 17, 1986.

43. Ann Schmidt, "Learn English, Lamm Tells Aliens," *DP*, May 30, 1986; Stepan, "Mexico," *NYT*, June 17, 1986; Henry Cisneros, "Helping Mexico to Help Itself," *DP*, March 23, 1986.

44. Stepan, "Mexico," *NYT*, June 17, 1986; Robert Reinhold, "Pinning Hopes on the Peso," *NYT*, July 14, 1985; John Yemma, "Among Losers in Oil-Price Drop, Mexico Worries Bankers Most," *CSM*, Feb. 21, 1986; "U.S. and Mexico Plan to Curb Pollution by Copper Smelters," *NYT*, July 23, 1985; Alan Weisman, "A Matter of Jurisdiction: Border Politics May Assure a Continued Flow of Raw Sewage from Tijuana to San Diego," *Atlantic*, July 1984, 16–24; William Stockton, "Mexico's Bad Image in the U.S., and Vice Versa," *NYT*, June 1, 1986; and Gavin, quoted in Roger Morris, "Mexico: The U.S. Press Takes a Siesta," *Columbia Journalism Review*, Jan.–Feb. 1985, 36.

45. (AP), "U.S. Hispanic Population Fastest Growing Sector," *NYT*, Jan. 31, 1986; "Study Sees Hispanic Growth," *NYT*, July 17, 1983; Robert Lindsey, "Hispanic Voters Are at the Right Time and Place," *NYT*, June 3, 1984; Henry Cisneros, "Whither the Loyalty of Hispanics?" *DP*, March 11, 1986.

46. Edward B. Fiske, "One Language or Two: The Controversy over Bilingual Education in America's Schools," *NYT*, Nov. 10, 1985; Cynthia Garney, "Bilingual Education's Dilemmas Persist," *WP*, July 7, 1985; Gene I. Maeroff, "Debate on U.S. Bilingual Education: Blending Methodology and Sociology," *NYT*, Sept. 22, 1985.

47. Judith Cummings, "Bias Is Charged in Redistricting of Los Angeles," *NYT*, Nov. 27, 1985, and "Hispanic Surge Is Seen in Los Angeles Election," *NYT*, Dec. 8, 1985; (UPI), "Hispanic Assemblyman Wins Los Angeles Post," *NYT*, Dec. 12, 1985.

48. Judith Cummings, "Los Angeles Districting May Not Settle Discrimination Suit," *NYT*, March 9, 1986, and "Los Angeles Minorities Split over Council Plan," *NYT*, July 6, 1986.

49. David Clark, "Improbable Los Angeles," in Richard M. Bernard and Bradley R. Rice, eds., *Sunbelt Cities: Politics and Growth since World War II* (Austin: Univ. of Texas Press, 1983), 269; Bill Grover, "With Gov. Babbitt Retiring, Democrats Face Tough Test in Republican Arizona," *CSM*, May 13, 1986.

Further Reading

Introduction

Interpretations and Overviews of Western American History

Athearn, Robert G. *The Mythic West in Twentieth-Century America*. Lawrence: Univ. Press of Kansas, 1986.

Billington, Ray Allen. *America's Frontier Heritage*. New York: Holt, Rinehart and Winston, 1966.

————. *Frederick Jackson Turner: Historian, Scholar, Teacher*. New York: Oxford Univ. Press, 1973.

————. *Land of Savagery, Land of Promise: The European Image of the American Frontier*. New York: W. W. Norton, 1981.

———— and Martin Ridge. *Westward Expansion*. 5th ed. New York: Macmillan, 1982.

Drinnon, Richard. *Facing West: The Metaphysics of Indian-Hating and Empire-Building*. Minneapolis: Univ. of Minnesota Press, 1980.

Fussell, Edwin. *Frontier: American Literature and the American West*. Princeton: Princeton Univ. Press, 1965.

Garreau, Joel. *The Nine Nations of North America*. Boston: Houghton Mifflin, 1981.

Goetzmann, William H. *Exploration and Empire: The Explorer and Scientist in the Winning of the American West*. New York: Alfred A. Knopf, 1966.

Hine, Robert V. *The American West: An Interpretive History*. 2d ed. Boston: Little, Brown, 1984.

Hollon, W. Eugene. *The Great American Desert Then and Now*. New York: Oxford Univ. Press, 1966.

Lamar, Howard, ed. *The Reader's Encyclopedia of the American West*. New York: Crowell, 1977.

———— and Leonard Thompson, eds. *The Frontier in History: North America and Southern Africa Compared*. New Haven: Yale Univ. Press, 1981.

Lowitt, Richard. *The New Deal and the West*. Bloomington: Indiana Univ. Press, 1984.

Malin, James C. *The Grassland of North America: Prolegomena to Its History*. Lawrence, Kan.: n.p., 1947.

Malone, Michael, ed. *Historians and the American West*. Lincoln: Univ. of Nebraska Press, 1983.

Nash, Gerald D. *The American West in the Twentieth Century: A Short History of an Urban Oasis*. Englewood Cliffs, N.J.: Prentice-Hall, 1973.

————. *The American West Transformed: The Impact of the Second World War*. Bloomington: Indiana Univ. Press, 1985.

Slotkin, Richard. *Regeneration through Violence: The Mythology of the American Frontier, 1600–1860.* Middletown, Conn.: Wesleyan Univ. Press, 1973.

———. *The Fatal Environment: The Myth of the Frontier in the Age of Industrialization, 1800–1890.* New York: Atheneum, 1985.

Smith, Henry Nash. *Virgin Land: The American West as Symbol and Myth.* Cambridge: Harvard Univ. Press, 1950.

Starr, Kevin. *Americans and the California Dream, 1850–1915.* New York: Oxford Univ. Press, 1973.

———. *Inventing the Dream: California through the Progressive Era.* New York: Oxford Univ. Press, 1985.

Steffen, Jerome O., ed. *The American West: New Perspectives, New Dimensions.* Norman: Univ. of Oklahoma Press, 1979.

———. *Comparative Frontiers: Proposals for Studying the American West.* Norman: Univ. of Oklahoma Press, 1980.

Turner, Frederick Jackson. *The Early Writings of Frederick Jackson Turner.* Edited by Everett E. Edwards. Madison: Univ. of Wisconsin Press, 1938.

———. *The Significance of Sections in American History.* New York: H. Holt, 1932.

Turner, Frederick. *Beyond Geography: The Western Spirit against the Wilderness.* New York: Viking, 1980.

Webb, Walter Prescott. *The Great Frontier.* Austin: Univ. of Texas Press, 1964.

———. *The Great P. ns.* 1931; New York: Grosset & Dunlap, 1971.

Wiley, Peter, and Robert Gottlieb. *Empires in the Sun: The Rise of the New American West.* New York: G. P. Putnam's Sons, 1982.

One · **Empire of Innocence**

Pacific Northwest

Bowen, William A. *The Willamette Valley: Migration and Settlement on the Oregon Frontier.* Seattle: Univ. of Washington Press, 1978.

Burns, Robert Ignatius. *The Jesuits and the Indian Wars of the Northwest.* New Haven: Yale Univ. Press, 1966.

Drury, Clifford. *Marcus and Narcissa Whitman and the Opening of Old Oregon.* Glendale, Calif.: Arthur H. Clark, 1973.

———, ed. *First White Women over the Rockies.* 2 vols. Glendale, Calif.: Arthur H. Clark, 1963.

Edwards, G. Thomas, and Carlos A. Schwantes, eds. *Experiences in a Promised Land: Essays in Pacific Northwest History.* Seattle: Univ. of Washington Press, 1986.

Fahey, John. *The Inland Empire: Unfolding Years, 1879–1929.* Seattle: Univ. of Washington Press, 1986.

Johansen, Dorothy O., and Charles M. Gates. *Empire of the Columbia: A History of the Pacific Northwest.* New York: Harper & Row, 1967.

Josephy, Alvin M., Jr., *The Nez Perce Indians and the Opening of the Northwest.* New Haven: Yale Univ. Press, 1971.

Miller, Christopher L. *Prophetic Worlds: Indians and Whites on the Columbian Plateau.* New Brunswick, N.J.: Rutgers Univ. Press, 1985.

White, Richard. *Land Use, Environment, and Social Change: The Shaping of Island County, Washington.* Seattle: Univ. of Washington Press, 1980.

Western Women's History

Barnhart, Jacqueline Baker. *The Fair but Frail: Prostitution in San Francisco, 1849–1900.* Reno: Univ. of Nevada Press, 1986.

Blackwelder, Julia Kirk. *Women of the Depression: Caste and Culture in San Antonio, 1929–1939.* College Station: Texas A&M Univ. Press, 1984.

Butler, Anne M. *Daughters of Joy, Sisters of Misery: Prostitutes in the American West, 1865–90.* Urbana: Univ. of Illinois Press, 1985.

Faragher, John Mack. *Women and Men on the Overland Trail.* New Haven: Yale Univ. Press, 1979.

Fischer, Christiane, ed. *Let Them Speak for Themselves: Women in the American West, 1849–1900.* New York: E. P. Dutton, 1978.

Goldman, Marion S. *Gold Diggers and Silver Miners: Prostitution and Social Life on the Comstock Lode*. Ann Arbor: Univ. of Michigan Press, 1981.

Jeffrey, Julie Roy. *Frontier Women: The Trans-Mississippi West, 1840–1880*. New York: Hill and Wang, 1979.

Jordan, Teresa. *Cowgirls: Women of the American West*. Garden City, N.Y.: Doubleday, 1982.

Kolodny, Annette. *The Land before Her: Fantasy and Experience of the American Frontiers, 1630–1860*. Chapel Hill: Univ. of North Carolina Press, 1984.

Luchetti, Cathy, with Carol Olwell. *Women of the West*. St. George, Utah: Antelope Island Press, 1982.

Myres, Sandra L. *Westering Women and the Frontier Experience, 1800–1915*. Albuquerque: Univ. of New Mexico Press, 1982.

Riley, Glenda. *Women and Indians on the Frontier, 1825–1915*. Albuquerque: Univ. of New Mexico Press, 1984.

Schlissel, Lillian. *Women's Diaries of the Westward Journey*. New York: Schocken, 1982.

Stratton, Joanna L. *Pioneer Women: Voices from the Kansas Frontier*. New York: Simon and Schuster, 1981.

Van Kirk, Sylvia. *Many Tender Ties: Women in Fur Trade Society, 1670–1870*. Norman: Univ. of Oklahoma Press, 1983.

Two · **Property Values**

Land and Property

Carstensen, Vernon, ed. *The Public Lands: Studies in the History of the Publilc Domain*. Madison: Univ. of Wisconsin Press, 1963.

DeConde, Alexander. *This Affair of Louisiana*. New York: Scribner, 1976.

Dick, Everett. *The Lure of the Land: A Social History of the Public Lands from the Articles of Confederation to the New Deal*. Lincoln: Univ. of Nebraska Press, 1970.

Elliott, Russell R. *Servant of Power: A Political Biography of Senator William R. Stewart*. Reno: Univ. of Nevada Press, 1983.

Gates, Paul Wallace. *History of Public Land Law Development*. Washington: U.S. Government Printing Office, 1968.

McCoy, Drew. *The Elusive Republic: Political Economy in Jeffersonian America*. Chapel Hill: Univ. of North Carolina Press, 1980.

Peffer, E. Louise. *The Closing of the Public Domain: Disposal and Reservation Policies, 1900–1950*. Stanford: Stanford Univ. Press, 1951.

Reid, John Phillip. *Law for the Elephant: Property and Social Behavior on the Overland Trail*. San Marino, Calif.: Huntington Library, 1980.

Robbins, Roy M. *Our Landed Heritage: The Public Domain, 1776–1970*. 2d ed. Lincoln: Univ. of Nebraska Press, 1976.

Rohrbough, Malcolm J. *The Land Office Business: The Settlement and Administration of American Public Lands, 1789–1837*. New York: Oxford Univ. Press, 1968.

Sosin, Jack. *Whitehall and the Wilderness: The Middle West in British Colonial Policy, 1760–1775*. Lincoln: Univ. of Nebraska Press, 1961.

Wyant, William K. *Westward in Eden: The Public Lands and the Conservation Movement*. Berkeley: Univ. of California Press, 1982.

Three · **Denial and Dependence**

Territories

Eblen, Jack. *The First and Second United States Empires: Governors and Territorial Government, 1784–1912*. Pittsburgh: Univ. of Pittsburgh Press, 1968.

Gould, Lewis. *Wyoming: A Political History, 1868–1896*. New Haven: Yale Univ. Press, 1968.

Lamar, Howard R. *The Far Southwest, 1846–1912: A Territorial History*. New Haven: Yale Univ. Press, 1966.

————. *Dakota Territory, 1861–1889: A Study of Frontier Politics*. New Haven: Yale Univ. Press, 1956.
Ostrander, Gilman. *Nevada: The Great Rotten Borough, 1859–1964*. New York: Alfred A. Knopf, 1966.
Pomeroy, Earl. *The Territories and the United States, 1861–1890: Studies in Colonial Administration*. 1947; Seattle: Univ. of Washington Press, 1969.
Spence, Clark C. *Territorial Politics and Government in Montana, 1864–89*. Urbana: Univ. of Illinois Press, 1976.

Sectionalism, Slavery and Expansion

Berwanger, Eugene H. *The Frontier against Slavery: Western Anti-Negro Prejudice and the Slavery Extension Controversy*. Urbana: Univ. of Illinois Press, 1967.
Hamilton, Holman. *Prologue to Conflict: The Crisis and Compromise of 1850*. Lexington: Univ. of Kentucky Press, 1964.
Johannsen, Robert W. *Frontier Politics on the Eve of the Civil War*. Seattle: Univ. of Washington Press, 1955.
————. *Stephen A. Douglas*. New York: Oxford Univ. Press, 1973.
Potter, David M. *The Impending Crisis, 1848–1861*. New York: Harper & Row, 1976.
Rawley, James A. *Race and Politics: "Bleeding Kansas" and the Coming of the Civil War*. Philadelphia: Lippincott, 1969.

Four · Uncertain Enterprises

Overland Travel

Gordon, Mary McDougall, ed. *Overland to California with the Pioneer Line: The Gold Rush Diary of Bernard J. Reid*. Stanford: Stanford Univ. Press, 1983.
Holliday, J. S. *The World Rushed In: The California Gold Rush Experience*. New York: Simon and Schuster, 1981.
Potter, David M. *Trail to California: The Overland Journal of Vincent Geiger and Wakeman Bryarly*. New Haven: Yale Univ. Press, 1945.
Unruh, John David. *The Plains Across: The Overland Emigrants and the Trans-Mississippi West, 1840–60*. Urbana: Univ. of Illinois Press, 1974.

Mining

Elliott, Russell R. *Nevada's Twentieth-Century Mining Boom: Tonopah, Goldfield, Ely*. Reno: Univ. of Nevada Press, 1966.
Greever, William S. *The Bonanza West: The Story of the Western Mining Rushes, 1848–1900*. Norman: Univ. of Oklahoma Press, 1963.
Kelley, Robert L. *Gold vs. Grain: The Hydraulic Mining Controversy in California's Sacramento Valley*. Glendale, Calif.: Arthur H. Clark, 1959.
King, Joseph E. *A Mine to Make a Mine: Financing the Colorado Mining Industry, 1859–1902*. College Station: Texas A&M Univ. Press, 1977.
Malone, Michael P. *The Battle for Butte: Mining and Politics on the Northern Frontier, 1864–1906*. Seattle: Univ. of Washington Press, 1981.
Mann, Ralph. *After the Gold Rush: Society in Grass Valley and Nevada City, California, 1849–1870*. Stanford: Stanford Univ. Press, 1982.
Paul, Rodman Wilson. *Mining Frontiers of the Far West, 1848–1880*. New York: Holt, Rinehart and Winston, 1963.
Peterson, Richard H. *The Bonanza Kings: The Social Origins and Business Behavior of Western Mining Entrepreneurs, 1870–1900*. Lincoln: Univ. of Nebraska Press, 1977.
Smith, Duane A. *Rocky Mountain Mining Camps: The Urban Frontier*. Bloomington: Indiana Univ. Press, 1967.
Spence, Clark C. *Mining Engineers and the American West: The Lace Boot Brigade, 1849–1933*. New Haven: Yale Univ. Press, 1970.

Labor

Byrkit, James W. *Forging the Copper Collar: Arizona's Labor Management War of 1901–1921.* Tucson: Univ. of Arizona Press, 1982.

Brown, Ronald C. *Hard-Rock Miners: The Intermountain West, 1860–1920.* College Station: Texas A&M Univ. Press, 1979.

Conlin, Joseph Robert. *Bread and Roses Too: Studies of the Wobblies.* Westport, Conn.: Greenwood, 1969.

Daniel, Cletus E. *Bitter Harvest: A History of California Farmworkers, 1870–1941.* Ithaca, N.Y.: Cornell Univ. Press, 1981.

Dubofsky, Melvyn. *We Shall Be All: A History of the Industrial Workers of the World.* Chicago: Quadrangle, 1969.

Ducker, James H. *Men of the Steel Rails: Workers on the Atchison, Topeka and Santa Fe Railroad, 1869–1900.* Lincoln: Univ. of Nebraska Press, 1983.

Jensen, Vernon H. *Lumber and Labor.* New York: Farrar and Rinehart, 1945.

Kern, Patrick, ed. *Labor in New Mexico: Unions, Strikes, and Social History since 1881.* Albuquerque: Univ. of New Mexico Press, 1983.

Lingenfelter, Richard E. *The Hardrock Miners: A History of the Mining Labor Movement in the American West, 1863–1893.* Berkeley: Univ. of California Press, 1974.

McGovern, George and Leonard F. Guttridge. *The Great Coalfield War.* Boston: Houghton Mifflin, 1972.

Papanikolas, Zeese. *Buried Unsung: Louis Tikas and the Ludlow Massacre.* Salt Lake City: Univ. of Utah Press, 1982.

Renshaw, Patrick. *The Wobblies: The Story of Syndicalism in the United States.* Garden City, N.Y.: Doubleday, 1967.

Schwantes, Carlos A. *Coxey's Army: An American Odyssey.* Lincoln: Univ. of Nebraska Press, 1985.

———. *Radical Heritage: Labor, Socialism, and Reform in Washington and British Columbia.* Seattle: Univ. of Washington Press, 1979.

Tyler, Robert L. *Rebels of the Woods: The IWW in the Pacific Northwest.* Eugene: Univ. of Oregon Press, 1967.

Wyman, Mark. *Hard Rock Epic: Western Miners and the Industrial Revolution, 1860–1910.* Berkeley: Univ. of California Press, 1979.

Farming, Populism, Dust Bowl

Atkins, Annette. *Harvest of Grief: Grasshopper Plagues and Public Assistance in Minnesota, 1873–78.* St. Paul: Minnesota Historical Society Press, 1984.

Baldwin, Sidney. *Poverty and Politics: The Rise and Decline of the Farm Security Administration.* Chapel Hill: Univ. of North Carolina Press, 1968.

Bogue, Allan G. *From Prairie to Corn Belt: Farming on the Illinois and Iowa Prairies in the Nineteenth Century.* Chicago: Univ. of Chicago Press, 1963.

Bonnifield, Matthew Paul. *The Dust Bowl: Men, Dirt, and Depression.* Albuquerque: Univ. of New Mexico Press, 1979.

Burbank, Garin. *When Farmers Voted Red: The Gospel of Socialism in the Oklahoma Countryside, 1910–1924.* Westport, Conn.: Greenwood, 1976.

Clanton, O. Gene. *Kansas Populism: Ideas and Men.* Lawrence: Univ. Press of Kansas, 1969.

Curti, Merle. *The Making of an American Community: A Case Study of Democracy in a Frontier County.* Stanford: Stanford Univ. Press, 1959.

Dick, Everett. *The Sod-House Frontier, 1854–1890.* New York: D. Appleton-Century, 1937.

Emmons, David M. *Garden in the Grasslands: Boomer Literature of the Central Great Plains.* Lincoln: Univ. of Nebraska Press, 1971.

Fite, Gilbert C. *American Farmers: The New Minority.* Bloomington: Indiana Univ. Press, 1981.

———. *The Farmers' Frontier, 1865–1900.* New York: Holt, Rinehart and Winston, 1966.

Gates, Paul Wallace. *The Farmer's Age: Agriculture, 1815–1860.* New York: Holt, Rinehart and Winston, 1960.

Goodwyn, Lawrence. *The Populist Movement: A Short History of the Agrarian Revolt in America.* New York: Oxford Univ. Press, 1978.

Hewes, Leslie. *The Suitcase Farming Frontier: A Study in the Historical Geography of the Central Great Plains.* Lincoln: Univ. of Nebraska Press, 1973.

Larson, Robert W. *New Mexico Populism: A Study of Radical Protest in a Western Territory.* Boulder: Colorado Associated Univ. Press, 1970.

Morlan, Robert L. *Political Prairie Fire: The Nonpartisan League, 1915–1922.* St. Paul: Minnesota Historical Society Press, 1985.

Pollack, Norman. *The Populist Response to Industrial America: Midwestern Populist Thought.* Cambridge: Harvard Univ. Press, 1962.

Saloutos, Theodore. *The American Farmer and the New Deal.* Ames: Iowa State Univ. Press, 1982.

Shannon, Fred A. *The Farmers' Last Frontier: Agriculture, 1860–1897.* New York: Farrar and Rinehart, 1945.

Stein, Walter S. *California and the Dust Bowl Migration.* Westport, Conn.: Greenwood, 1973.

Swierenga, Robert P. *Pioneers and Profits: Land Speculation on the Iowa Frontier.* Ames: Iowa State Univ. Press, 1968.

Worster, Donald. *Dust Bowl: The Southern Plains in the 1930s.* New York: Oxford Univ. Press, 1979.

Wright, James Edward. *The Politics of Populism: Dissent in Colorado.* New Haven: Yale Univ. Press, 1974.

Railroads

Athearn, Robert G. *Rebel of the Rockies: A History of the Denver and Rio Grande Western Railroad.* New Haven: Yale Univ. Press, 1962.

Chandler, Alfred. *The Railroads: The Nation's First Big Business.* New York: Harcourt, Brace and World, 1965.

Hofsommer, Don. *The Southern Pacific, 1901–1985.* College Station: Texas A&M Univ. Press, 1986.

Lewis, Oscar. *The Big Four: The Story of Huntington, Stanford, Hopkins, and Crocker, and of the Building of the Central Pacific.* New York: Alfred A. Knopf, 1938.

Martin, Albro. *James J. Hill and the Opening of the Northwest.* New York: Oxford Univ. Press, 1976.

Riegel, Robert Edgar. *The Story of the Western Railroads.* New York: Macmillan, 1926.

Five · **The Meeting Ground of Past and Present**

Water

Dunbar, Robert G. *Forging New Rights in Western Waters.* Lincoln: Univ. of Nebraska Press, 1983.

Fradkin, Philip L. *A River No More: The Colorado River and the West.* New York: Alfred A. Knopf, 1981.

Hoffman, Abraham. *Vision or Villainy: Origins of the Owens Valley–Los Angeles Water Controversy.* College Station: Texas A&M Univ. Press, 1981.

Hundley, Norris. *Dividing the Waters: A Century of Controversy between the United States and Mexico.* Berkeley: Univ. of California Press, 1966.

———. *Water and the West: The Colorado River Compact and the Politics of Water in the American West.* Berkeley: Univ. of California Press, 1975.

Kahrl, William. *Water and Power: The Conflict over Los Angeles' Water Supply in the Owens Valley.* Berkeley: Univ. of California Press, 1982.

Lee, Lawrence B. *Reclaiming the American West: An Historiography and Guide.* Santa Barbara, Calif.: ABC-Clio, 1980.

Pisani, Donald J. *From the Family Farm to Agribusiness: The Irrigation Crusade in California, 1850–1931.* Berkeley: Univ. of California Press, 1984.

Reisner, Marc. *Cadillac Desert: The American West and Its Disappearing Water.* New York: Viking, 1986.

Richardson, Elmo R. *Dams, Parks, and Politics: Resource Development and Preservation in the Truman-Eisenhower Era.* Lexington: Univ. Press of Kentucky, 1973.

Stegner, Wallace. *Beyond the Hundredth Meridian: John Wesley Powell and the Second Opening of the West.* Boston: Houghton Mifflin, 1954.

Weatherford, Gary D., and F. Lee Brown, eds. *New Courses for the Colorado River: Major Issues for the Next Century.* Albuquerque: Univ. of New Mexico Press, 1986.

Livestock

Dale, Edward Everett. *The Range Cattle Industry: Ranching on the Great Plains from 1865–1925*. Norman: Univ. of Oklahoma Press, 1960.

Dary, David. *Cowboy Culture: A Saga of Five Centuries*. New York: Alfred A. Knopf, 1981.

Foss, Phillip O. *Politics and Grass: The Administration of Grazing on the Public Domain*. Seattle: Univ. of Washington Press, 1960.

Gressley, Gene M. *Bankers and Cattlemen*. New York: Alfred A. Knopf, 1966.

Kramer, Jane. *The Last Cowboy*. New York: Harper & Row, 1977.

McGregor, Alexander Campbell. *Counting Sheep: From Open Range to Agribusiness on the Columbia Plateau*. Seattle: Univ. of Washington Press, 1982.

Osgood, Ernest. *The Day of the Cattleman*. Minneapolis: Univ. of Minnesota Press, 1929.

Schlebecker, John T. *Cattle Raising on the Plains, 1900–1961*. Lincoln: Univ. of Nebraska Press, 1963.

Skaggs, Jimmy M. *Prime Cut: Livestock Raising and Meatpacking in the United States, 1607–1983*. College Station: Texas A&M Univ. Press, 1986.

Nuclear Affairs

Ball, Howard. *Justice Downwind: America's Atomic Testing Program in the 1950s*. New York: Oxford Univ. Press, 1986.

Fuller, John G. *The Day We Bombed Utah: America's Most Lethal Secret*. New York: New American Library, 1985.

Loeb, Paul. *Nuclear Culture: Living and Working in the World's Largest Atomic Complex*. New York: Coward, McCann and Geoghegan, 1982.

Mojtabai, A. G. *Blesséd Assurance: At Home with the Bomb in Amarillo, Texas*. Boston: Houghton Mifflin, 1986.

Safer, Thomas H., and Orville E. Kelly. *Countdown Zero: GI Victims of U.S. Atomic Testing*. New York: G. P. Putnam's Sons, 1982.

Energy

Boatwright, Mody, and William A. Owens. *Tales from the Derrick Floor: A People's History of the Oil Industry*. Garden City, N.Y.: Doubleday, 1970.

Franks, Kenny Arthur. *The Oklahoma Petroleum Industry*. Norman: Univ. of Oklahoma Press, 1980.

Ise, John. *United States Oil Policy*. New Haven: Yale Univ. Press, 1926.

Lambert, Paul F., and Kenny A. Franks, eds. *Voices from the Oil Fields*. Norman: Univ. of Oklahoma Press, 1984.

Nash, Gerald D. *United States Oil Policy, 1890–1964: Business and Government in Twentieth Century America*. Pittsburgh: Univ. of Pittsburgh Press, 1968.

Noggle, Burl. *Teapot Dome: Oil and Politics in the 1920s*. Baton Rouge: Louisiana State Univ. Press, 1962.

Righter, Robert W. *The Making of a Town: Wright, Wyoming*. Boulder, Colo.: Roberts Rinehart, 1985.

Singer, Mark. *Funny Money*. New York: Alfred A. Knopf, 1985.

Vandenbusche, Duane, and Duane A. Smith. *A Land Alone: Colorado's Western Slope*. Boulder, Colo.: Pruett, 1981.

Williamson, Chilton, Jr., *Roughnecking It*. New York: Simon and Schuster, 1982.

Williamson, Harold Francis. *The American Petroleum Industry*. 2 vols. Evanston: Northwestern Univ. Press, 1959–63.

Western Cities and Towns

Abbott, Carl. *Portland: Planning, Politics, and Growth in a Twentieth-Century City*. Lincoln: Univ. of Nebraska Press, 1983.

Barth, Gunther P. *Instant Cities: Urbanization and the Rise of San Francisco and Denver*. New York: Oxford Univ. Press, 1975.

Bernard, Richard M., and Bradley R. Rice, eds. *Sunbelt Cities: Politics and Growth since World War II*. Austin: Univ. of Texas Press, 1983.

Brown, Andrew. *Frontier Community: Kansas City*. Columbia: Univ. of Missouri Press, 1963.

Clark, Norman H. *Mill Town: A Social History of Everett, Washington*. Seattle: Univ. of Washington Press, 1970.
Decker, Peter. *Fortunes and Failures: White-Collar Mobility in Nineteenth-Century San Francisco*. Cambridge: Harvard Univ. Press, 1978.
Doyle, Don Harrison. *The Social Order of a Frontier Community: Jacksonville, Illinois, 1825–70*. Urbana: Univ. of Illinois Press, 1978.
Dykstra, Robert R. *The Cattle Towns*. New York: Alfred A. Knopf, 1968.
Fogelson, Robert. *The Fragmented Metropolis: Los Angeles, 1850–1930*. Cambridge: Harvard Univ. Press, 1967.
Hudson, John C. *Plains Country Towns*. Minneapolis: Univ. of Minnesota Press, 1985.
Jackson, William Turrentine. *Treasure Hill: Portrait of a Silver Mining Camp*. Tucson: Univ. of Arizona Press, 1963.
Larsen, Lawrence. *The Urban West at the End of the Frontier*. Lawrence: Regents Press of Kansas, 1978.
Lotchin, Roger W. *San Francisco, 1846–1856: From Hamlet to City*. New York: Oxford Univ. Press, 1974.
McComb, David G. *Houston: The Bayou City*. Austin: Univ. of Texas Press, 1969.
Reps, John W. *Cities of the American West: A History of Frontier Urban Planning*. Princeton: Princeton Univ. Press, 1979.
Rohrbough, Malcolm J. *Aspen: The History of a Silver-Mining Town, 1879–1893*. New York: Oxford Univ. Press, 1986.
Sale, Roger. *Seattle, Past and Present*. Seattle: Univ. of Washington Press, 1976.
Wade, Richard C. *The Urban Frontier: The Rise of Western Cities, 1790–1830*. Cambridge: Harvard Univ. Press, 1959.
Wheeler, Kenneth. *To Wear a City's Crown: The Beginnings of Urban Growth in Texas, 1836–1865*. Cambridge: Harvard Univ. Press, 1968.

Violence

Ball, Larry D. *The United States Marshals of New Mexico and Arizona Territories, 1846–1912*. Albuquerque: Univ. of New Mexico Press, 1978.
Brown, Richard Maxwell. *Strain of Violence: Historical Studies of American Violence and Vigilantism*. New York: Oxford Univ. Press, 1975.
France, Johnny, and Malcolm McConnell. *Incident at Big Sky*. New York: W. W. Norton, 1986.
Hollon, W. Eugene. *Frontier Violence: Another Look*. New York: Oxford Univ. Press, 1974.
McGrath, Roger D. *Gunfighters, Highwaymen, and Vigilantes: Violence on the Frontier*. Berkeley: Univ. of California Press, 1984.
Malcolm, Andrew. *Final Harvest: An American Tragedy*. New York: Times Books, 1986.
Prassel, Frank Richard. *The Western Peace Officer: A Legacy of Law and Order*. Norman: Univ. of Oklahoma Press, 1972.
Thompson, Hunter. *Hell's Angels: A Strange and Terrible Saga*. New York: Random House, 1967.

Six · **The Persistence of Natives**

English Colonial Background—Initial Contacts

Axtell, James. *The Invasion Within: The Contest of Cultures in Colonial North America*. New York: Oxford Univ. Press, 1985.
Cronon, William. *Changes in the Land: Indians, Colonists, and the Ecology of New England*. New York: Hill and Wang, 1983.
Jennings, Francis. *The Invasion of America: Indians, Colonialism, and the Cant of Conquest*. Chapel Hill: Univ. of North Carolina Press, 1975.
Kupperman, Karen Ordahl. *Settling with the Indians: The Meeting of English and Indian Cultures in America, 1580–1640*. Totowa, N.J.: Rowman and Littlefield, 1980.
Salisbury, Neal. *Manitou and Providence: Indians, Europeans, and the Making of New England, 1500–1643*. New York: Oxford Univ. Press, 1982.
Sheehan, Bernard W. *Savagism and Civility: Indians and Englishmen in Colonial Virginia*. New York: Cambridge Univ. Press, 1980.

Vaughan, Alden T. *New England Frontier: Puritans and Indians, 1620–1675*. Boston: Little, Brown, 1965.

Indian History

Athearn, Robert G. *William Tecumseh Sherman and the Settlement of the West*. Norman: Univ. of Oklahoma Press, 1956.

Berkhofer, Robert F. *Salvation and the Savage: An Analysis of Protestant Missions and American Indian Response, 1787–1862*. Lexington: Univ. of Kentucky Press, 1965.

————. *The White Man's Indian: Images of the American Indian from Columbus to the Present*. New York: Alfred A. Knopf, 1978.

Bowden, Henry Warner. *American Indians and Christian Missions: Studies in Cultural Conflict*. Chicago: Univ. of Chicago Press, 1981.

Burt, Larry W. *Tribalism in Crisis: Federal Indian Policy, 1953–1961*. Albuquerque: Univ. of New Mexico Press, 1982.

Crosby, Alfred. *The Columbian Exchange: Biological and Cultural Consequences of 1492*. Westport, Conn.: Greenwood, 1972.

Danziger, Edmund. *Indians and Bureaucrats: Administering the Reservation Policy during the Civil War*. Urbana: Univ. of Illinois Press, 1974.

Dippie, Brian W. *The Vanishing American: White Attitudes and U.S. Indian Policy*. Middletown, Conn.: Wesleyan Univ. Press, 1982.

Dunlay, Thomas W. *Wolves for the Blue Soldiers: Indian Scouts and Auxiliaries with the United States Army, 1860–1890*. Lincoln: Univ. of Nebraska Press, 1982.

Edmunds, R. David, ed. *American Indian Leaders: Studies in Diversity*. Lincoln: Univ. of Nebraska Press, 1980.

Erdoes, Richard, and Alfonso Ortiz, eds. *American Indian Myths and Legends*. New York: Pantheon Books, 1984.

Fixico, Donald. *Termination and Relocation: Federal Indian Policy, 1945–1960*. Albuquerque: Univ. of New Mexico Press, 1986.

Hoxie, Frederick E. *A Final Promise: The Campaign to Assimilate the Indians, 1880–1920*. Lincoln: Univ. of Nebraska Press, 1984.

Iverson, Peter. *Carlos Montezuma and the Changing World of American Indians*. Albuquerque: Univ. of New Mexico Press, 1982.

————, ed. *The Plains Indians of the Twentieth Century*. Norman: Univ. of Oklahoma Press, 1985.

Keller, Robert H. *American Protestantism and United States Indian Policy, 1869–92*. Lincoln: Univ. of Nebraska Press, 1983.

Kelly, Lawrence C. *The Assault on Assimilation: John Collier and the Origins of Indian Policy Reform*. Albuquerque: Univ. of New Mexico Press, 1983.

Leacock, Eleanor Burke, and Nancy Oestreich Lurie, eds. *North American Indians in Historical Perspective*. New York: Random House, 1971.

Martin, Calvin. *Keepers of the Game: Indian-Animal Relationships and the Fur Trade*. Berkeley: Univ. of California Press, 1978.

Milner, Clyde A. *With Good Intentions: Quaker Work among the Pawnees, Otos and Omahas in the 1870s*. Lincoln: Univ. of Nebraska Press, 1982.

Mitchell, Lee Clark. *Witnesses to a Vanishing America: The Nineteenth-Century Response*. Princeton: Princeton Univ. Press, 1981.

Moses, L. G., and Raymond Wilson, eds. *Indian Lives: Essays on Nineteenth- and Twentieth-Century Native American Leaders*. Albuquerque: Univ. of New Mexico Press, 1985.

Nichols, Roger L., ed. *The American Indian: Past and Present*. 3d ed. New York: Alfred A. Knopf, 1986.

Olson, James C. *Red Cloud and the Sioux Problem*. Lincoln: Univ. of Nebraska Press, 1965.

Parman, Donald L. *The Navajos and the New Deal*. New Haven: Yale Univ. Press, 1976.

Peroff, Nicholas. *Menominee Drums: Tribal Termination and Restoration, 1954–1974*. Norman: Univ. of Oklahoma Press, 1982.

Peterson, Jacqueline, and Jennifer S. H. Brown. *The New Peoples: Being and Becoming Metis in North America*. Lincoln: Univ. of Nebraska Press, 1985.

Phillips, George Harwood. *Chiefs and Challengers: Indian Resistance and Cooperation in Southern California*. Berkeley: Univ. of California Press, 1975.

Philp, Kenneth R. *John Collier's Crusade for Indian Reform, 1920–1954*. Tucson: Univ. of Arizona Press, 1977.

Prucha, Francis Paul. *The Great Father: The United States Government and the American Indian.* 2 vols. Lincoln: Univ. of Nebraska Press, 1984.

Ray, Arthur J. *"Give Us Good Measure": An Economic Analysis of Relations between the Indians and the Hudson's Bay Company before 1763.* Toronto: Univ. of Toronto Press, 1978.

———. *Indians in the Fur Trade: Their Role as Trappers, Hunters, and Middlemen in the Lands Southwest of Hudson Bay, 1660–1870.* Toronto: Univ. of Toronto Press, 1974.

Rogin, Michael Paul. *Fathers and Children: Andrew Jackson and the Subjugation of the American Indian.* New York: Alfred A. Knopf, 1975.

Satz, Ronald N. *American Indian Policy in the Jacksonian Era.* Lincoln: Univ. of Nebraska Press, 1975.

Saum, Lewis O. *The Fur Trader and the Indian.* Seattle: Univ. of Washington Press, 1965.

Sheehan, Bernard W. *Seeds of Extinction: Jeffersonian Philanthropy and the American Indian.* New York: W. W. Norton, 1973.

Swagerty, W. R., ed. *Scholars and the Indian Experience: Critical Reviews of Recent Writings in the Social Sciences.* Bloomington: Indiana Univ. Press, 1984.

Taylor, Graham D. *The New Deal and American Indian Tribalism: The Administration of the Indian Reorganization Act, 1934–45.* Lincoln: Univ. of Nebraska Press, 1980.

Trennert, Robert A. *Alternative to Extinction: Federal Indian Policy and the Beginnings of the Reservation System, 1846–1951.* Philadelphia: Temple Univ. Press, 1975.

Utley, Robert M. *The Indian Frontier of the American West, 1846–1890.* Albuquerque: Univ. of New Mexico Press, 1984.

Viola, Herman. *Thomas L. McKenney: Architect of America's Early Indian Policy, 1816–1830.* Chicago: Swallow Press, 1974.

Wallace, Anthony F. C. *The Death and Rebirth of the Seneca.* New York: Alfred A. Knopf, 1970.

Washburn, Wilcomb. *The Indian in America.* New York: Harper & Row, 1975.

White, Richard. *The Roots of Dependency: Subsistence, Environment, and Social Change among the Choctaws, Pawnees, and Navajos.* Lincoln: Univ. of Nebraska Press, 1983.

Seven · **America the Borderland**

Borderlands History

Acuña, Rudolfo. *Occupied America: A History of Chicanos.* 2d ed. New York: Harper & Row, 1981.

Bannon, John Francis. *The Spanish Borderlands Frontier, 1513–1821.* New York: Holt, Rinehart and Winston, 1970.

Barker, Eugene Campbell. *The Life of Stephen F. Austin, Founder of Texas, 1793–1836.* 1926; Austin: Univ. of Texas Press, 1980.

Barrera, Mario. *Race and Class in the Southwest: A Theory of Racial Inequality.* Notre Dame: Univ. of Notre Dame Press, 1979.

Bauer, K. Jack. *The Mexican War, 1846–1848.* New York: Macmillan, 1974.

Camarillo, Albert. *Chicanos in a Changing Society: From Mexican Pueblos to American Barrios in Santa Barbara and Southern California, 1848–1930.* Cambridge: Harvard Univ. Press, 1979.

Cardoso, Lawrence A. *Mexican Emigration to the United States, 1897–1931.* Tucson: Univ. of Arizona Press, 1980.

Chávez, John R. *The Lost Land: The Chicano Image of the Southwest.* Albuquerque: Univ. of New Mexico Press, 1984.

Cockcroft, James D. *Outlaws in the Promised Land: Mexican Immigrant Workers and America's Future.* New York: Grove Press, 1986.

Connor, Seymour V., and Odie B. Faulk. *North America Divided: The Mexican War, 1846–1848.* New York: Oxford Univ. Press, 1971.

Cook, Sherburne F. *The Conflict between the California Indian and White Civilization.* Berkeley: Univ. of California Press, 1976.

DeBuys, William. *Enchantment and Exploitation: The Life and Hard Times of a New Mexico Mountain Range.* Albuquerque: Univ. of New Mexico Press, 1985.

De León, Arnoldo. *The Tejano Community, 1836–1900.* Albuquerque: Univ. of New Mexico Press, 1982.

———. *They Called Them Greasers: Anglo Attitudes toward Mexicans in Texas, 1821–1900.* Austin: Univ. of Texas Press, 1983.

Fehrenbach, T. R. *Lone Star: A History of Texas and the Texans*. New York: Macmillan, 1968.

Friend, Llerena. *Sam Houston: The Great Designer*. Austin: Univ. of Texas Press, 1954.

García, Juan Ramon. *Operation Wetback: The Mass Deportation of Mexican Undocumented Workers in 1954*. Westport, Conn.: Greenwood, 1980.

García, Mario. *Desert Immigrants: The Mexicans of El Paso, 1880–1920*. New Haven: Yale Univ. Press, 1981.

Gibson, Charles. *Spain in America*. New York: Harper & Row, 1966.

Griswold del Castillo, Richard. *The Los Angeles Barrio, 1850–1890: A Social History*. Berkeley: Univ. of California Press, 1979.

Hennessy, Alistair. *The Frontier in Latin American History*. Albuquerque: Univ. of New Mexico Press, 1978.

Hinojosa, Gilberto Miguel. *A Borderlands Town in Transition: Laredo, 1755–1870*. College Station: Texas A&M Univ. Press, 1983.

Hoffman, Abraham. *Unwanted Mexican Americans in the Great Depression: Repatriation Pressures, 1929–1939*. Tucson: Univ. of Arizona Press, 1974.

Horsman, Reginald. *Race and Manifest Destiny: The Origins of American Racial Anglo-Saxonism*. Cambridge: Harvard Univ. Press, 1981.

Johannsen, Robert W. *To the Halls of the Montezumas: The Mexican War in the American Imagination*. New York: Oxford Univ. Press, 1985.

John, Elizabeth. *Storms Brewed in Other Men's Worlds: The Confrontation of Indians, Spanish, and French in the Southwest, 1540–1795*. College Station: Texas A&M Univ. Press, 1975.

Jones, Oakah. *Los Paisanos: Spanish Settlers on the Northern Frontier of New Spain*. Norman: Univ. of Oklahoma Press, 1979.

Kessell, John L. *Friars, Soldiers, and Reformers: Hispanic Arizona and the Sonora Mission Frontier, 1767–1856*. Tucson: Univ. of Arizona Press, 1976.

McWilliams, Carey. *North From Mexico: The Spanish-Speaking People of the United States*. 1948; New York: Greenwood, 1968.

Martínez, Oscar J. *Border Boom Town: Ciudad Juarez since 1848*. Austin: Univ. of Texas Press, 1978.

―――, ed. *Fragments of the Mexican Revolution: Personal Accounts from the Border*. Albuquerque: Univ. of New Mexico Press, 1983.

Mazón, Mauricio. *The Zoot-Suit Riots: The Psychology of Symbolic Annihilation*. Austin: Univ. of Texas Press, 1984.

Meier, Matt S., and Feliciano Rivera. *The Chicanos: A History of Mexican Americans*. New York: Hill and Wang, 1972.

Meinig, Donald. *Imperial Texas: An Interpretive Essay on Cultural Geography*. Austin: Univ. of Texas Press, 1969.

―――. *Southwest: Three Peoples in Geographical Change, 1600–1970*. New York: Oxford Univ. Press, 1971.

Merk, Frederick. *Manifest Destiny and Mission in American History: A Reinterpretation*. New York: Alfred A. Knopf, 1963.

Paredes, Américo. *With His Pistol in His Hand: A Border Ballad and Its Hero*. 1958; Austin: Univ. of Texas Press, 1982.

Perrigo, Lynn. *The American Southwest: Its People and Cultures*. New York: Holt, Rinehart and Winston, 1971.

Pitt, Leonard. *The Decline of the Californios: A Social History of the Spanish-Speaking Californians, 1846–1890*. Berkeley: Univ. of California Press, 1966.

Reisler, Mark. *By the Sweat of Their Brow: Mexican Immigrant Labor in the United States, 1900–1940*. Westport, Conn.: Greenwood, 1976.

Robinson, Cecil. *Mexico and the Hispanic Southwest in American Literature*. Tucson: Univ. of Arizona Press, 1977.

Romo, Ricardo. *East Los Angeles: History of a Barrio*. Austin: Univ. of Texas Press, 1983.

Samora, Julian, Joe Bernal, and Albert Peña. *Gunpowder Justice: A Reassessment of the Texas Rangers*. Notre Dame: Univ. of Notre Dame Press, 1979.

Simmons, Marc. *Spanish Government in New Mexico*. Albuquerque: Univ. of New Mexico Press, 1968.

Singletary, Otis. *The Mexican War*. Chicago: Univ. of Chicago Press, 1960.

Spicer, Edward H. *Cycles of Conquest: The Impact of Spain, Mexico, and the United States on the Indians of the Southwest, 1533–1960*. Tucson: Univ. of Arizona Press, 1962.

Swadesh, Francis Leon. *Los Primeros Pobladores: Hispanic Americans on the Ute Frontier*. Notre Dame: Univ. of Notre Dame Press, 1974.

Webb, Walter Prescott. *The Texas Rangers: A Century of Frontier Defense*. 1935; Austin: Univ. of Texas Press, 1965.
Weber, David J. *The Mexican Frontier, 1821–1846: The American Southwest under Mexico*. Albuquerque: Univ. of New Mexico Press, 1982.
———, ed. *New Spain's Far Northern Frontier: Essays on Spain in the American West, 1540–1821*. Albuquerque: Univ. of New Mexico Press, 1979.
Weinberg, Albert K. *Manifest Destiny: A Study of Nationalist Expansionism in American History*. Baltimore: Johns Hopkins Press, 1935.

Eight · Racialism on the Run

Asian-Americans

Barth, Gunther. *Bitter Strength: A History of the Chinese in the United States, 1850–1870*. Cambridge: Harvard Univ. Press, 1964.
Chen, Jack. *The Chinese of America*. San Francisco: Harper & Row, 1980.
Cheng, Lucie, and Edna Bonacich, eds. *Labor Immigration under Capitalism: Asian Workers in the United States before World War II*. Berkeley: Univ. of California Press, 1984.
Coolidge, Mary Roberts. *Chinese Immigration*. New York: H. Holt, 1909.
Daniels, Roger. *Concentration Camps: North America: Japanese in the United States and Canada during World War II*. Malabar, Fla.: Robert E. Krieger, 1981.
———. *The Politics of Prejudice: The Anti-Japanese Movement in California and the Struggle for Japanese Exclusion*. 1962; Berkeley: Univ. of California Press, 1977.
———, Sandra C. Taylor, and Harry H. L. Kitano. *Japanese Americans: From Relocation to Redress*. Salt Lake City: Univ. of Utah Press, 1986.
Heizer, Robert F., and Alan F. Almquist. *The Other Californians: Prejudice and Discrimination under Spain, Mexico, and the United States to 1920*. Berkeley: Univ. of California Press, 1971.
Irons, Peter H. *Justice at War*. New York: Oxford Univ. Press, 1983.
Melendy, Howard Brett. *The Oriental Americans*. New York: Twayne, 1972.
Miller, Stuart Creighton. *The Unwelcome Immigrant: The American Image of the Chinese, 1785–1882*. Berkeley: Univ. of California Press, 1969.
Modell, John. *The Economics and Politics of Racial Accommodation: The Japanese of Los Angeles*. Urbana: Univ. of Illinois Press, 1977.
Nee, Victor, and Brett de Bary Nee. *Longtime Californ': A Documentary Study of an American Chinatown*. New York: Pantheon Books, 1973.
Saxton, Alexander P. *The Indispensable Enemy: Labor and the Anti-Chinese Movement in California*. Berkeley: Univ. of California Press, 1971.
Thomson, Jr., James C., Peter W. Stanley, and John Curtis Perry. *Sentimental Imperialists: The American Experience in East Asia*. New York: Harper & Row, 1981.
TenBroek, Jacobus, Edward N. Barnhart, and Floyd W. Matson. *Prejudice, War, and the Constitution*. Berkeley: Univ. of California Press, 1954.
Wu, Cheng-Tsu, ed. *"Chink!" Anti-Chinese Prejudice in America*. New York: World, 1972.

Black Americans

Athearn, Robert G. *In Search of Canaan: Black Migration to Kansas, 1879–1880*. Lawrence: Regents Press of Kansas, 1978.
Berwanger, Eugene. *The West and Reconstruction*. Urbana: Univ. of Illinois Press, 1981.
Conot, Robert. *Rivers of Blood, Years of Darkness: The Unforgettable Account of the Watts Riot*. New York: Morrow, 1968.
Daniels, Douglas Henry. *Pioneer Urbanites: A Social and Cultural History of Black San Francisco*. Philadelphia: Temple Univ. Press, 1980.
Durham, Philip, and Everett L. Jones. *The Negro Cowboys*. New York: Dodd, Mead, 1965.
Goode, Kenneth G. *California's Black Pioneers: A Brief Historical Survey*. Santa Barbara, Calif.: McNally and Loftin, 1974.
Katz, William. *The Black West*. Garden City, N.Y.: Anchor Press, 1973.
Lapp, Rudolph. *Blacks in Gold Rush California*. New Haven: Yale Univ. Press, 1977.

Leckie, William. *The Buffalo Soldiers: A Narrative of the Negro Cavalry in the West.* Norman: Univ. of Oklahoma Press, 1967.
McLagan, Elizabeth. *A Peculiar Paradise: A History of Blacks in Oregon, 1778–1940.* Portland, Ore.: Georgian Press, 1980.
Painter, Nell. *Exodusters: Black Migration to Kansas after Reconstruction.* New York: Alfred A. Knopf, 1977.
Porter, Kenneth Wiggins. *The Negro on the American Frontier.* New York: Arno Press, 1971.
Rice, Lawrence D. *The Negro in Texas, 1874–1900.* Baton Rouge: Louisiana State Univ. Press, 1971.
Rusco, Elmer. *"Good Time Coming?" Black Nevadans in the Nineteenth Century.* Westport, Conn.: Greenwood, 1975.
Savage, William Sherman. *Blacks in the West.* Westport, Conn.: Greenwood, 1976.

Mormons

Alexander, Thomas G. *Mormonism in Transition: A History of the Latter-day Saints, 1890–1930.* Urbana: Univ. of Illinois Press, 1986.
Anderson, Nels. *Desert Saints: The Mormon Frontier in Utah.* Chicago: Univ. of Chicago Press, 1942.
Arrington, Leonard J. *Brigham Young: American Moses.* New York: Alfred A. Knopf, 1985.
———. *Great Basin Kingdom: An Economic History of the Latter-day Saints, 1830–1900.* Cambridge: Harvard Univ. Press, 1958.
——— and Davis Bitton. *The Mormon Experience: A History of the Latter-day Saints.* New York: Alfred A. Knopf, 1979.
Bringhurst, Newell G. *Brigham Young and the Expanding American Frontier.* Boston: Little, Brown, 1985.
Brodie, Fawn McKay. *No Man Knows My History: The Life of Joseph Smitih, the Mormon Prophet.* 1945; New York: Alfred A. Knopf, 1971.
Bushman, Richard L. *Joseph Smith and the Beginnings of Mormonism.* Urbana: Univ. of Illinois Press, 1984.
Furniss, Norman. *The Mormon Conflict, 1850–1859.* New Haven: Yale Univ. Press, 1960.
Hansen, Klaus J. *Mormonism and the American Experience.* Chicago: Univ. of Chicago Press, 1981.
Larson, Gustive. *The "Americanization" of Utah for Statehood.* San Marino, Calif.: Huntington Library, 1971.
Leone, Mark P. *Roots of Modern Mormonism.* Cambridge: Harvard Univ. Press, 1979.
Mulder, William, and A. Russell Mortensen, eds. *Among the Mormons: Historic Accounts by Contemporary Observers.* 1958; Lincoln: Univ. of Nebraska Press, 1973.
Nelson, Lowry. *The Mormon Village: A Pattern and Technique of Land Settlement.* Salt Lake City: Univ. of Utah Press, 1952.
O'Dea, Thomas F. *The Mormons.* Chicago: Univ. of Chicago Press, 1957.
Shipps, Jan. *Mormonism: The Story of a New Religious Tradition.* Urbana: Univ. of Illinois Press, 1985.
Simmonds, A. J. *The Gentile Comes to Cache Valley.* Logan: Utah State Univ. Press, 1976.

European Ethnic Groups

Burchell, R. A. *The San Francisco Irish, 1848–1880.* Berkeley: Univ. of California Press, 1980.
Douglass, William A., and Jon Bilbao. *Amerikanuak: Basques in the New World.* Reno: Univ. of Nevada Press, 1975.
Eccles, William J. *The Canadian Frontier, 1534–1760.* 1969; Albuquerque: Univ. of New Mexico Press, 1983.
Jordan, Terry G. *German Seed in Texas Soil: Immigrant Farmers in Nineteenth-Century Texas.* Austin: Univ. of Texas Press, 1966.
Luebke, Frederick C. *Immigrants and Politics: The Germans of Nebraska, 1880–1900.* Lincoln: Univ. of Nebraska Press, 1969.
———, ed. *Ethnicity on the Great Plains.* Lincoln: Univ. of Nebraska Press, 1980.
Rolle, Andrew. *The Immigrant Upraised: Italian Adventurers and Colonists in an Expanding America.* Norman: Univ. of Oklahoma Press, 1968.
Toll, William. *The Making of an Ethnic Middle Class: Portland Jewry over Four Generations.* Albany: State Univ. of New York Press, 1982.

Nine · **Mankind the Manager**

Preservation, Conservation, and Natural Resources

Baden, John, and Richard L. Stroup, eds. *Bureaucracy vs. Environment: The Environmental Costs of Bureaucratic Governance.* Ann Arbor: Univ. of Michigan Press, 1981.

Buchholtz, C. W. *Rocky Mountain National Park: A History.* Boulder: Colorado Associated Univ. Press, 1983.

Burch, William R. *Daydreams and Nightmares: A Sociological Essay on the American Environment.* New York: Harper & Row, 1971.

Chadwick, Douglas. *A Beast the Color of Winter: The Mountain Goat Observed.* San Francisco: Sierra Club Books, 1983.

Chase, Alston. *Playing God in Yellowstone: The Destruction of America's First National Park.* Boston: Atlantic Monthly Press, 1986.

Cohen, Michael. *The Pathless Way: John Muir and American Wilderness.* Madison: Univ. of Wisconsin Press, 1984.

Cox, Thomas. *Mills and Markets: A History of the Pacific Coast Lumber Industry to 1900.* Seattle: Univ. of Washington Press, 1974.

———, Robert S. Maxwell, Phillip Drennon Thomas, and Joseph J. Malone. *This Well-Wooded Land: Americans and Their Forests from Colonial Times to the Present.* Lincoln: Univ. of Nebraska Press, 1985.

Dunlap, Thomas. *DDT: Scientists, Citizens, and Public Policy.* Princeton: Princeton Univ. Press, 1981.

Ekirch, Arthur. *Man and Nature in America.* New York: Columbia Univ. Press, 1963.

Flader, Susan. *Thinking like a Mountain: Aldo Leopold and the Evolution of an Ecological Attitude toward Deer, Wolves, and Forests.* Columbia: Univ. of Missouri Press, 1974.

Fox, Stephen. *John Muir and His Legacy: The American Conservation Movement.* Boston: Little, Brown, 1981.

Hays, Samuel P. *Conservation and the Gospel of Efficiency: The Progressive Conservation Movement, 1890–1920.* Cambridge: Harvard Univ. Press, 1959.

Huth, Hans. *Nature and the American: Three Centuries of Changing Attitudes.* Berkeley: Univ. of California Press, 1957.

Ise, John. *Our National Park Policy: A Critical History.* Baltimore: Johns Hopkins Press, 1961.

———. *The United States Forest Policy.* 1920; New York: Arno Press, 1972.

Limerick, Patricia Nelson. *Desert Passages: Encounters with the American Deserts.* Albuquerque: Univ. of New Mexico Press, 1985.

McCarthy, Michael. *Hour of Trial: The Conservation Conflict in Colorado and the West.* Norman: Univ. of Oklahoma Press, 1977.

McGeary, M. Nelson. *Gifford Pinchot: Forester-Politician.* Princeton: Princeton Univ. Press, 1960.

McNamee, Thomas. *The Grizzly Bear.* New York: Alfred A. Knopf, 1984.

McPhee, John. *Encounters with the Archdruid.* New York: Farrar, Straus and Giroux, 1971.

Marx, Leo. *The Machine in the Garden: Technology and the Pastoral Ideal in America.* New York: Oxford Univ. Press, 1964.

Nash, Roderick. *Wilderness and the American Mind.* 3d ed. New Haven: Yale Univ. Press, 1982.

Palmer, Tim. *Stanislaus: The Struggle for a River.* Berkeley: Univ. of California Press, 1982.

Petulla, Joseph M. *American Environmentalism: Values, Tactics, Priorities.* College Station: Texas A&M Univ. Press, 1980.

Pinkett, Harold T. *Gifford Pinchot: Private and Public Forester.* Urbana: Univ. of Illinois Press, 1970.

Pyne, Stephen J. *Fire in America: A Cultural History of Wildland and Rural Fire.* Princeton: Princeton Univ. Press, 1982.

Richardson, Elmo R. *The Politics of Conservation: Crusades and Controversies, 1897–1913.* Berkeley: Univ. of California Press, 1962.

Righter, Robert. *Crucible for Conservation: The Creation of Grand Teton National Park.* Boulder: Colorado Associated Univ. Press, 1982.

Robbins, William G. *American Forestry: A History of National, State, and Private Cooperation.* Lincoln: Univ. of Nebraska Press, 1985.

———. *Lumberjacks and Legislators: Political Economy of the U.S. Lumber Industry, 1890–1941.* College Station: Texas A&M Univ. Press, 1982.

Rowley, William D. *U.S. Forest Service Grazing and Rangelands: A History*. College Station: Texas A&M Univ. Press, 1985.

Runte, Alfred. *National Parks: The American Experience*. Lincoln: Univ. of Nebraska Press, 1979.

Sax, Joseph L. *Mountains without Handrails: Reflections on National Parks*. Ann Arbor: Univ. of Michigan Press, 1980.

Schrepfer, Susan R. *The Fight to Save the Redwoods: A History of Environmental Reform, 1917–1978*. Madison: Univ. of Wisconsin Press, 1983.

Schullery, Paul. *Mountain Time*. New York: Schocken, 1984.

Shankland, Robert. *Steve Mather of the National Parks*. 1951; New York: Alfred A. Knopf, 1970.

Steen, Harold K. *The U.S. Forest Service: A History*. Seattle: Univ. of Washington Press, 1977.

Strong, Douglas. *Tahoe: An Environmental History*. Lincoln: Univ. of Nebraska Press, 1984.

Swain, Donald C. *Federal Conservation Policy, 1921–1933*. Berkeley: Univ. of California Press, 1963.

———. *Wilderness Defender: Horace M. Albright and Conservation*. Chicago: Univ. of Chicago Press, 1970.

Tucker, William. *Progress and Privilege: American in the Age of Environmentalism*. Garden City, N.Y.: Doubleday, 1982.

Turner, Frederick. *Rediscovering America: John Muir in His Times and Ours*. New York: Viking, 1985.

Twining, Charles E. *Phil Weyerhauser, Lumberman*. Seattle: Univ. of Washington Press, 1985.

Ten · **The Burdens of Western American History**

Indian Persistence and Resurgence

Barsh, Russel Lawrence, and James Youngblood Henderson. *The Road: Indian Tribes and Political Liberty*. Berkeley: Univ. of California Press, 1980.

Bowden, Charles. *Killing the Hidden Waters*. Austin: Univ. of Texas Press, 1977.

Cohen, Fay. *Treaties on Trial: The Continuing Controversy over Northwest Indian Fishing Rights*. Seattle: Univ. of Washington Press, 1986.

Cole, Douglas. *Captured Heritage: The Scramble for Northwest Coast Artifacts*. Seattle: Univ. of Washington Press, 1985.

Deloria, Vine, Jr., and Clifford M. Lytle. *American Indians, American Justice*. Austin: Univ. of Texas Press, 1983.

———. *The Nations Within: The Past and Future of American Indian Sovereignty*. New York: Pantheon Books, 1984.

Josephy, Alvin, Jr., *Now That the Buffalo's Gone: A Study of Today's American Indians*. New York: Alfred A. Knopf, 1982.

———, ed. *Red Power: The American Indians' Fight for Freedom*. New York: McGraw-Hill, 1971.

Knack, Martha C., and Omer C. Stewart. *As Long as the River Shall Run: An Ethnohistory of Pyramid Lake Indian Reservation*. Berkeley: Univ. of California Press, 1984.

Lawson, Michael. *Dammed Indians: The Pick-Sloan Plan and the Missouri River Sioux, 1944–1980*. Norman: Univ. of Oklahoma Press, 1982.

Matthiessen, Peter. *Indian Country*. New York: Viking, 1984.

Sutton, Imre, ed. *Irredeemable America: The Indians' Estate and Land Claims*. Albuquerque: Univ. of New Mexico Press, 1985.

Wilkinson, Charles. *American Indians, Time, and the Law: Native Societies in a Modern Constitutional Democracy*. New Haven: Yale Univ. Press, 1986.

Wilson, Terry P. *The Underground Reservation: Osage Oil*. Lincoln: Univ. of Nebraska Press, 1985.

Immigration and Bilingualism

Crewdson, John. *The Tarnished Door: The New Immigrants and the Transformation of America*. New York: Times Books, 1983.

Hakuta, Kenji. *Mirror of Language*. New York: Basic Books, 1986.

Lamm, Richard D., and Gary Imhoff. *The Immigration Time Bomb: The Fragmenting of America*. New York: E. P. Dutton, 1985.

Miller, Tom. *On the Border; Portraits of America's Southwestern Frontier*. New York: Harper & Row, 1981.

Poggie, John J., Jr., ed. *Between Two Cultures: The Life of an American-Mexican*. Tucson: Univ. of Arizona Press, 1973.

Reimers, David M. *Still the Golden Door: The Third World Comes to America*. New York: Columbia Univ. Press, 1985.

Riding, Alan. *Distant Neighbors: A Portrait of the Mexicans*. New York: Alfred A. Knopf, 1985.

Rodriguez, Richard. *Hunger of Memory: The Education of Richard Rodriguez*. Boston: David R. Godine, 1982.

Ross, Stanley R., ed. *Views across the Border: The United States and Mexico*. Albuquerque: Univ. of New Mexico Press, 1978.

Index